AN ETYMOLOGICAL GLOSSARY OF THE SINHALESE LANGUAGE

WILHELM GEIGER

GYAN

Published by

GYAN

Gyan Publishing House
5, Ansari Road
Daryaganj, New Delhi-110002
Phone: 011-47034999, 9811692060
E-mail: books@gyanbooks.com

Distribution Network
gyanbooks.com
India, USA, Canada, UK, Australia, France

ISBN : 978-81-212-4371-1 (PB)
First Published, Colombo, 1941

2nd Impression 2020

Printed at: Gyan Press, Delhi.

An Etymological Glossary of the Sinhalese Language
Author: Wilhelm Geiger

AN ETYMOLOGICAL GLOSSARY OF THE SINHALESE LANGUAGE

PREFATORY NOTE

Since the appearance in 1897 of Professor WILHELM GEIGER's *Etymologie des Singhalesischen* a large number of Sinhalese lithic records and many important classical texts have been carefully examined and edited by competent scholars. With the new materials thus made available, and in the light of studies in Indo-Aryan linguistics carried on in the meantime by himself and other specialists like Professors R. L. TURNER, J. BLOCH, and S. K. CHATTERJI, the author revised the above glossary and prepared the present enlarged edition. This, as well as his Sinhalese Grammar (1938), he considered as a part of his work on the Sinhalese Dictionary and gifted it, as he had already done the Grammar, to the Dictionary Managing Committee of the Royal Asiatic Society, Ceylon Branch.

The whole Manuscript was set in type in 1937-38 and I was charged with the duty of seeing it through the press. Owing to heavy pressure of other work, and in the circumstances set out below, the printing of the book proceeded rather slowly. Professor GEIGER had corrected and returned proofs covering the first sixty-nine pages, when the war broke out in Europe, rendering it no longer possible to discuss any question with him through correspondence. The Managing Committee then decided, though reluctantly, that the printing of the book should not be suspended for the duration of the war but be proceeded with, as the printer could not hold the matter in type indefinitely. Accordingly, I have seen the rest of the work through the press with the invaluable help and advice given by SIR D. B. JAYATILAKA, who, at the request of the Managing Committee, kindly undertook to pass the final proofs.

In correcting these proof-sheets SIR D. B. JAYATILAKA refrained from making drastic changes and directed his attention mainly to the meanings of words, interfering as little as possible with the etymological section of articles for which the author is responsible. However, a few head-words, the existence of which was extremely doubtful, were replaced by others, the words so inserted being all well known ones with universally accepted etymologies.

Professor GEIGER did not send with his Manuscript an account of his sources and authorities. The list appended below was prepared by me, so far as I was able to ascertain them. I have also added a list of Abbreviations indicating the languages referred to in the book. The other ordinary abbreviations used by the author were considered to be too well known to need a similar list.

The value of this Etymological Glossary is inestimable, especially to those who are interested in Indo-Aryan linguistics. Grateful thanks of all students are therefore due to the learned author for the pains which, in spite of his advancing years, he has taken to produce it, to SIR D.B. JAYATILAKA for the valuable help which he so readily extended to me, and to the Dictionary Managing Committee of the Royal Asiatic Society (Ceylon Branch) for undertaking to publish it.

JULIUS DE LANEROLLE.

Dictionary Office,
Colombo.
November, 1941.

SOURCES AND AUTHORITIES

Abhp = Abhidhānappadīpikā, ed. W. SUBHŪTI, 1900.

AIC = Ancient Inscriptions in Ceylon, see MÜLLER.

AmāV = Amā-Vatura, ed. RICHARD DE SILVA, 1922.

APTE = V. S. APTE, Sanskrit-English Dictionary.

AYRTON = E. R. AYRTON, Ceylon Notes and Queries, 1913.

B, BEAMES = J. BEAMES, Comparative Grammar of the Modern Aryan Languages of India, 1872.

BELL = H. C. P. BELL, Archaeological Survey of Ceylon, Report on the Kégalla District of the Province of Sabaragamuwa, 1904.

BL = Bengali Language, see Ch.

Bl = JULES BLOCH.

Bl, IA = JULES BLOCH, L'indo-aryen du Véda aux temps moderne, 1934.

Bl, LM = JULES BLOCH, La formation de la langue marathe, 1914.

BōvGp = Bōdhi-vaṃsa-Gäṭapadaya, ed. ŚRI DHARMARAMA, 1910.

BR = BÖHTLINGK und ROTH, Sanskrit Wörterbuch, Petersberg.

Bull. School Or. St. = Bulletin of the School of Oriental Studies.

Bull. Soc. de Lingu. = Bulletin de la Société de Linguistique de Paris.

Ca = C. CARTER, A Sinhalese-English Dictionary, 1924.

Ch = S. K. CHATTERJI, The Origin and Development of the Bengali Language, 1926.

CHILDERS = R. C. CHILDERS, Notes on the Siṃhalese Language, No. 2: Proof of the Sanskritic Origin of Siṃhalese (Journal of the Royal Asiatic Society, New Series, Vol. VIII, 1876-77). — A Dictionary of the Pali Language, 1875.

Cl = B. CLOUGH, Siṃhalese-English Dictionary, 2nd ed., 1892.

CopPD = A Critical Pali Dictionary by V. TRENCKNER, DINES ANDERSEN and HELMER SMITH, Copenhagen.

D' ALWIS = JAMES D' ALWIS, On the Origin of the Sinhalese Language II (JRAS, CB, Vol. V, No. 14, 1867-70). — Sidath Sangaráwa, Grammar of the Singhalese Language, translated.... 1852, Introduction.

DBJ = D. B. JAYATILAKA.

DE LANEROLLE = JULIUS DE LANEROLLE, Introduction to DSL (Orthography).— Personal communications and observations.

Dhp-a = Dhammapadaṭṭhakathā, ed. Pali Text Society.

DhpAGp = Dhampiyā-Aṭuvā-Gäṭapadaya, ed. D. B. JAYATILAKA, 1933.

DSL = A Dictionary of the Sinhalese Language, Royal Asiatic Society, Ceylon Branch, 1935 —.

EdM = ED. MÜLLER.

EpZ = Epigraphia Zeylanica.

GEIGER = WILHELM GEIGER.

Ggr = W. GEIGER. — Gr = A Grammar of the Sinhalese Language, 1938.— Etymological Vocabulary of the Maldivian Language (JRAS, 1902). — P. Gr. = Pali Grammar.

GOLDSCHMIDT = PAUL GOLDSCHMIDT, Note on Ancient Siṇhalese Inscriptions (JRAS, CB, Vol. VI, No. 20, 1879, p. 1 ff.). — Cf. Report upon Inscriptions . . . (Indian Antiquary, Vol. VI, 1876).

Gr = G. A. GRIERSON, On the Phonology of the Modern Indo-Aryan Vernaculars (Zeitschrift der deutschen morgenländischen Gesellschaft).— Linguistic Survey of India.

Greater India Society's Journal.

GUṆASEKARA = A. M. GUṆASEKARA, Comprehensive Grammar of the Siṇhalese Language, 1891.

Guttila Kávya, ed. BAṬUVANTUḌAVE, Colombo 1886.

H = A. F. R. HOERNLE, A Comparative Grammar of the Gaudian Languages.

HaṃsSd = Haṃsa-Sandēśaya, ed. ŚRI DHARMARAMA, 1926.

Hem = Hemacandra, ed. R. PISCHEL.

HJ, JAYATILAKA = HENDRIK JAYATILAKA, Eḷu-akārādiya, Colombo 1895.

Hobson-Jobson = H. YULE and A. C. BURNELL, Hobson Jobson, new ed. by W. CROOKE.

HORN = P. HORN, Grundriss der neupersischen Etymologie.

HSm = HELMER SMITH.

HULTZSCH = E. HULTZSCH, Inscriptions of Aśoka.

Ind. Hist. Qu. = Indian Historical Quarterly.

Jā = Jātaka, ed. V. FAUSBÖLL.

JdeL = J. DE LANEROLLE.

JRAS = Journal of the Royal Asiatic Society, Great Britain.

JRAS, CB = Journal of the Royal Asiatic Society, Ceylon Branch.

KIRFEL = W. KIRFEL, Kosmographie der Inder.

KUHN = E. KUHN, Über den ältesten arischen Bestandteil des singhalesischen Wortschatzes (Bavarian Academy of Sciences, Report 1879, II).

Kus = Kusa Játaka, ed. A. M. GUṆASEKARA, Colombo 1897.

LM = Bl, LM, q.v.

LSI = Linguistic Survey of India.

Mahāvastu, ed. É. SENART.

Mhvs = Mahāvaṃsa (GEIGER).

MÜLLER = E. MÜLLER, Ancient Inscriptions in Ceylon, London 1883. — Notes on Ancient Siṇhalese Inscriptions (JRAS, CB, Vol. VIII, No 26, 1883).

PARANAVITANA = S. PARANAVITANA, Epigraphia Zeylanica.

PARKER = H. PARKER, Village Folk Tales of Ceylon.

PISCHEL = R. PISCHEL, Grammatik der Prakrit-sprachen.

PTSPD = Pali Text Society's Pali-English Dictionary, T. W. RHYS DAVIDS and W. STEDE.

Rājaratnākaraya, ed. Saddhananda, Colombo 1887.

Raṇasiṇha = W. Raṇasiṇha, The Connection of Sinhalese with the Modern Aryan Vernaculars of India (JRAS, CB, Vol. VII, No. 25, 1882).

Ruv = Ruvanmal-Nighaṇṭuva, ed. D. P. de Alwis Wijayasekara, 1914.

SälSd = Sälaḷihiṇi-Sandēśaya, ed. Macready; Śri Dharmarama, 1925.

Schmidt = R. Schmidt, Nachträge zum Sanskrit Wörterbuch.

SdhRv = Saddharma-Ratnāvaliya, ed. D. B. Jayatilaka.

Stede = W. Stede (PTSPD).

T, Turner = R. L. Turner, A Comparative and Etymological Dictionary of the Nepali Language.

Ummagga Játaka, ed. Simon de Silva, Colombo 1893.

Whitney = W. D. Whitney, Sanskrit Grammar.

Wickr = D. M. de Z. Wickremasinghe, Epigraphia Zeylanica.

Wilson = H. H. Wilson.

LANGUAGES

AMg. = Ardhamāgadhī
Ap., Apabhr. = Apabhraṃśa
ass. = Assamese
b. = Bihārī
bg. = Bengali
Dhau. = Dhauli (inscription of Aśoka)
Eng. = English
g. = Gujarātī
Germ., germ. = German
Gilgit = Gilgitī (dialect of Shina)
h. = Hindī
Jau. = Jaugada
JM. = Jaina Mahārāṣṭrī
kalasa = Kalāśā
khowar = Khowar
kśm. = Kāśmīrī
l. = Lahndā
M. = Mahārāṣṭrī
m. = Marāṭhī
mald. = Maldivian
MIAVs = Modern Indo-Aryan Vernaculars
MInd. = Middle Indian
nep. = Nepali
OInd., OldInd. = Old Indian
OldIr. = Old Iranian
oṛ. = Oṛiyā
PaiśP. = Paiśācī Prakrit
P. = Pali
pj. = Pañjābī
Pk. = Prakrit
Ś. = Śaurasenī
Shina = Ṣiṇā
si. = Siṇdhī
Sinh. = Sinhalese; Sinh. Pk. = Sinhalese Parakrit
Sk. = Sanskrit
Tam. = Tamil
Väddā = Väddā dialect
Ved., ved. = Vedic

CORRIGENDA

Page 1. No. 3, line 1. For noun read nouns

4. Delete **අටවනවා aṭavanavā** etc.

Delete **අඩාළ aḍāḷa** etc.

5. 61. For **අඹූදෑවා** read **අඹුදෑවා**

62. For **අඹූව** read **අඹුව**

6. 76, 1. For st. f. °*ru* read st. ff. *aturu*, *atara*,

8. 118, 3. For *apphālēï* read *apphālēi*

9. 134, 1. For st. f. °*uru* read st. f. *am̐bara*

13. 198, 2. For *avan-a* read *avana*

16. 249, 2. For *tṭ* read *ṭṭ*

17. 256, 3. For s.v. *kam* read s.v. *kama*^{2}

19. 297, 4. For *maha* read *mā*^{1}-

20. 309, 1. For Pk. read P.

21. 320, 2. For *uddhumāï* read *uddhumāi*

22. 333, 2. For *īn̆du*^{1} read *in̆du*^{1}

25. 374, 3. For *uggāhēï* read *uggāhēi*

28. 418, 3. For *ullan̆ghēï* read *ullan̆ghēi*

30. 451, 2. Delete Cf. *mäta*

31. 463, 2. For *ēï* read *ēi*

469, 1. For **එල්ලිඹු** read **එල්ලිඹු**

33. 489, 3. For *vahasa* read *vahasa*^{2}

34. 509, 3. For *khaṇḍēï* read *khaṇḍēi*

35. For **kaṇa**^{2} read ***kaṇa**^{2}

36. 532, 3. For *khāï* read *khāi*

539, 3. For *kappēï* read *kappēi*

38. 556, 1. For **කරඹූව** read **කරඹුව**

558, 3. For *karēï*, *kāravēï* read °*ēi*, *ēi*

42. 609, 2. For *kampēï* read *kampēi*

43. 636, 3. For *kahēï* read *kahēi*

636, 4. For *kahāvēï* read *kahāvēi*

45. 654, 1. After **kisuṇu**, add **කසිණු kasiṇu**,

Page 48. No. 702, line 2. For *-khīm* read *-khīm*

61. 885, 1. After **täna,** add **තෙන tena,**

65. 941, 2. After *tiras*, add TURNER s.v.

72. For ***dalanavā** read ***dalanavā**$^{1, 2}$

74. 1071, 2. For *daḷa*^{2} read *daḷa*^{3}

76. 1118, 1. After °*kus*, add °*kusu*,

77. 1125, 2. For *dalanavā* read **dalanavā*^{1}

1139, 1. For *dasaya* read *dasaya*^{2}

86. 1266, 1. For st.f. *nǣ* read st.ff. *nǣ*, *nähä*,

89.-90. 1319-1322. Rearrange order of words

91. s.v. **ne-penenavā**. For **na**^{2} read **na** 2

92. 1367, 3. For *päṭi* read *päṭiya*

1369, 2. For *päṭi* read *päṭiya*

109. 1620, 1. For **piḷi** read **piḷi**^{1}

1621, 1. For **piḷi-** read **piḷi**^{2}**-**

120. 1792, 1. For **ba**^{1} read **bā**^{1}

s.v. **bära.** For **bara** read **bara**^{2}

125. 1863, 2. For *mat*^{1} read *mat*

1869, 4. After 24. Add Cf. *vakanavā*.

129. s.v. **mas**$^{1, 2}$. For **maha**$^{1, 2}$ read **maha**$^{2, 3}$

s.v. **maha**^{1}**-**. For **mā-** read **mā**^{1}**-**

135. 2007, 2. For *mut* read *mut*^{2}

136. 2030, 2. For **mudrañguli* read **muddañguli*

146. s.v. **rika.** For **ruka** read **ruka**^{2}

156. Between numbers 2326 and 2327. Add — **වන්**^{2}**, van**^{2}, see s.v. **vana.**

162. 2418, 1. For *vähi-lihiṇīyā* read *vähi-lihiṇiyā*

2418, 4. After *vässa* add =

167. 2514, 1. After **veta**^{1}, add s.,

168. 2515, 2. For *veya* read *veya*^{2}

171. 2571, 3. For *kaṇa*^{2} read **kaṇa*^{2}

185. 2811, 1. For *pata* read *pata*^{1}

187. 2828, 1. After w h o delete comma.

In Pk. and P. words. For *e* and *o* not followed by a consonant-group read *ē* and *ō*.

In all Sk. words. For *e* and *o* read *ē* and *ō*.

AN ETYMOLOGICAL GLOSSARY
OF THE
SINHALESE LANGUAGE

අ A

1. **අ a-**, before vowels **අන් an-**, prefix with negative or privative sense: u n-, i n-, -l e s s, n o t. a) *a-nisa* not everlasting, *a-sak* innumerable, *an-iṭu* undesired &c.; b) *a-dama* unrighteousness, *a-väḍa* harm, injury (v. *väḍa*) &c.; c) *a-rū* having no form, formless, *an-aturu* having no interstice, unintermitting &c.— In *nē* many, *nat* endless (q.v.), the initial *a* has dropped by the influence of the accent in the following syllable. — Pk. *a-*, *aṇ-*, P., Sk. *a-*, *an-* [W. 3]. In Modern Sinhalese such compounds are made with *no-*, *nu-* (v. *n-*): *no-tira* not firm, *no-dämi* unsubdued, *no-y-ek* not one, many, *nu-duru* not far &c.

2. **අ a-**, prefix = Pk., P., Sk. *ā-*, a) in nouns: *a-keva* objection, *a-raka* protection, *a-riyana* entreating &c.; b) in verbs: *a-turanavā* to spread, *a-matanavā* to invite &c.

3. **අ a-, හ ha-, ස sa-** (*an̆-*, *han̆-*, *san̆-*), prefix = Pk., P., Sk. *sam-*, a) in noun: *an̆-guḷa* double canoe, *(h)a-vurudda* year &c.; b) in verbs: *a-kuḷanavā* (*ha-*, *sa-*) to fold, *(h)a-madinavā* to sweep &c.

— **අං aṃ** (spelt for *an̆*), s., see **an̆ga.**

— **අක් ak,** see **aga**[3].

4. **අක aka**[1], s., st. f. *ak*, e y e. — P. *akkha*, Sk. *akṣa*. Cf. *äsa* [DSL p. xxi. 18].

5. **අක aka**[2], s., st. f. *ak*, a) name of a t r e e, Terminalia belerica, and its seed; b) a small w e i g h t (cf. *akak* a little); c) a d i e used in gambling. — P. *akkha*, Sk. *akṣa*.

6. **අක aka**[3], s., st. f. *ak*, a x l e. — P. *akkha*, Sk. *akṣa*; si. *akh*, g. m. h. *āṃkh*, pj. *akkh*.

7. **අක aka**[4], s., st. f. *ak*, m a r k, j o t. — Pk., P., Sk. *aṅka*; kśm. *oṃkh*, si. *aṅgu*, m. *aṃk*, *āṃk*, *aṃkh*, g. h. *aṃk*, *āṃk*. Cf. *äkaya*.

8. **අක aka**[5], s., st. f. *ak*, name of a t r e e, Asclepias gigantea. — Pk., P. *akka*, Sk. *arka*. Cf. T s. v. *āk*, *āṃk*.

9. **අකුණ akuṇa**, s., st. f. °*ṇu*, l i g h t n i n g. — P. *akkhaṇa* in *a°-vēdhin* an archer who shoots by the flash of lightning = *vijju-vēdhin*, Sk. *a-kṣaṇa* not lasting a moment.

10. අකුර **akura**[1], s., st. f. °*ru*, letter. — Pk., P. *akkhara*, Sk. *akṣara*; (kśm. *achur*), si. *akharu*, ass. bg. h. nep. *ākhar*, pj. l. *akkhar*.

11. අකුර **akura**[2], s., st. f. °*ru*, germ, sprout. — Pk., P., Sk. *aṅkura*.

— අකුර **akura**[3], s., see **hakuru.**

12. අකුව **akuva**[1], s., st. f. *aku*, clavicle, collar-bone. — P. *akkhaka*, Sk. *akṣaka*.

13. අකුව **akuva**[2], s., st. f. *aku*, stake. — P. *saṅku(-ka)*, Sk. *śaṅkuka*.

14. අකුස්ස **akussa,** s., st. f. °*su*, hook used by an elephant-keeper. — Pk., P. *aṅkusa*, Sk. *aṅkuśa* (+ *-ka*); m. *aṃkuśī*, ass. *āṃkuhī*, h. *āṃkus*, nep. *āṃkus, aṅkus*.

15. අකුළනවා **akuḷaṇavā,** හ° **ha°**, ස° **sa°**, v., prt. *(h)äkuḷuvā*, to contract, fold, roll up. Caus. *(h)akuḷavanavā*, prt. *(h)äkiḷevuvā*, to cause to roll up; intr. *(h)äkiḷenavā*, prt. °*ḷuṇā*, to curl up, shrink. — Sk. *sam-* + $\sqrt{}$*kuṭ*, *saṃkuṭati*. Cf. P. *(paṭi)kuṭati*.

16. අකෙව **akeva,** s., t. t. rhet., objection, opposition. — Pk. *akkhēva* P. *akkhēpa*, Sk. *ākṣēpa*, Daṇḍin, Kāvyâdarśa II. 120 [HSm].

17. අකොස **akosa,** s., st. f. *akos*, insult, abuse.—Pk., P. *akkōsa*, Sk. *ākrōśa*. Cf. *äksuma*.

18. අක්දිවියා **ak-diviyā,** s., st. f. °*vi*, dice-player, gambler.—P. *akkha-dēvin*, Sk. *akṣa-dēvin*; v. *aka*[2].

19. අක්පතළ **ak-pataḷa,** a., large or wide at the top or end. —*ak* (*aga*) + *pataḷa*. The s. *akpatala* a kind of earthen vessel (coll. *akpallē, appallē*) is probably the same word inaccurately spelt with *l* instead of *ḷ*.

20. අක්පල්ල **ak-palla** (*-patula, -patla*), s., the tip of the sole of the foot, tip-toe. —*ak* (*agga*) + *palla*. Cf. *at-tala, alla*.

21. අක්මන **akmana,** s., st. f. °*man*, treading upon, stepping upon. — Pk., P. *akkamaṇa*, Sk. *ākramaṇa*. Cf. *äkmenavā*.

22. අක්මල **ak-mala,** s., st. f. *-mal*, rosary. —*aka*[2] + *mala* (P., Sk. *mālā*) necklace. The seeds of the *aka*-tree are used as rosary; *aka-paṭa* string of *aka*-seeds has the same meaning.

23. අක්මාව **ak-māva,** s., st. f. *-mā*, liver. — Sk. *agra-māṃsa* heart, lit. the best flesh.

24. අක්මුල් **ak-mul,** sg. අගමුල **aga-mula,** s., end and beginning, root and top. *ak-mul-näti* (the Sansāra) having no beginning or end. —*ak* (*aga*) + *mul*.

— අක්වටා **ak-'vaṭā,** see **ag'-uvaṭā.**

25. අග **aga**[1], s., house. — P. *agga* (only e. cpds).

26. අග **aga**[2], s., fire. — Pk., P. *aggi*, Sk. *agni*; si. *āgi*, g. m. ass. bg. h. *āg*, nep. *āgo*, pj. l. *agg*. Cf. *gini*.

27. අග **aga**[3], අග් **ag**, අක් **ak**, a., first, foremost, best, chief, principal. *aga-tän-pat* who has reached the highest place; *ak-yāḷa* the first load (of paddy set apart for the gods) —s., *aga*, st. f. *ak*, top, end; *ak-mul* q.v., *ak-sun* broken at the end. — Pk., P. *agga*, Sk. *agra*. Cf. g. *āgō*, m. *agyā*, oṛ. *āgu*, ass. bg. h. *āgē* = Sk. *agrē*. Gr. 50. 25.

28. අගන **agana**, °නා °**nā**, a., valuable, worth (so much). — P. *agghanaka*.

29. අගය **agaya**, අගේ **agē**, s., value, price. — Pk., P. *aggha*, Sk. *argha* (+ *-ka*). See s.v. *mahagu*. Cf. *ägi*.

30. අගස් **agas**, අගහස් **aga-has**, අගසස් **aga-sas**, s., first-fruits, the first corn of a crop. —*aga*[3] + *as*[3] q.v.

31. අගිනවා **aginavā**, v., to be worth. — P. *agghati*, Sk. *arghati*.

32. අගුළ **aguḷa**, s., st. f. *aguḷu*, mod. *agul*, bolt (of a door), bar, lock. *agul-damanavā* to bolt. — Pk. *aggala*, P. *aggala* or °*ḷa*, Sk. *argala*; g. *āgḷo*, m. *agaḷ*, *āgaḷ*, bg. *āgaṛ*, *āgal*, h. *āgal*, nep. *āglo*.

33. අගුවටා **ag'-uvaṭā**, s., st. f. id. chief servitor or attendant (Ānanda). —*aga*[3] + *uvaṭā*. P. *aggupaṭṭhāka*. — Also *ak-'vaṭā*.

34. අඟ **aṅga**[1], s., limb. *aṅga-pasaṅga* the greater and smaller members, the whole body. — Pk., P., Sk. *aṅga* (P. *aṅga-paccaṅga*, Sk. **aṅga-pratyaṅga*); si. *aṅu*, g. m. h. *āṃg*, bg. *āṅg*, nep. *āṅ*, pj. *aṅg*. Cf. *äṅga*.

35. අඟ **aṅga**[2], s., st. f. *aṃ*, *aṅga*, horn. *aṃ-keḷiya* horn-game; *aṅga-rāṇa* horn cord, head-rope to restrain buffaloes. — Pk., P. *siṅga*, Sk. *śṛṅga*; kśm. *heṅg*, si. *siṅu*, g. *śiṃg*, m. *śīṃg*, oṛ. *siṅga*, bg. *siṅ*, *siṃg*, pj. l. *siṃgg*. Also Sinh. *sigu*, *siṅgu*, *suṅgu*, *suṃ*, probably Slww. P.

36. අඟන **aṅgana**, s., woman. — P., Sk. *aṅganā*.

37 අඟනිය **aṅganiya**, s., st. f. °*ni*, assembly, congregation. — P. *saṅgaṇikā*. If this etymology is correct, the Sinh. word should be spelt with *ṇ*.

38. අඟරය **aṅgaraya**, s., st. f. *aṅgara*, gesture, the particular gesture of the Malabar dancing girls. — <**aṅgāraya*=Sk. *aṅgahāra* [HSm].

39. අඟරා **aṅgarā** or °ර °**ra**, s., unguent for anointing. — P., Sk. *aṅgarāga*.

40. අඟවනවා **aṅgavanavā**, හ° **ha**°, v., prt. *(h)äṅgevuvā*, to intimate (by signs), make known, inform. Intr. *(h)äṅgenavā*, prt. °*ṅguṇā*, to be informed, to know, perceive. — The v. is the traditional trsl. of P. *saññāpeti*. Cf. *haṅgavay* DhpAGp. 247[26], trsl. of *saññāpetvā*; *haṅgavannaṭa* ib. 282[38], trsl. of *saññāpetuṃ*. It is, however, difficult to explain the relation of the P. and Sinh. verbs.

41. අඟාරනවා **aṅgāranavā**, v., to gesticulate (in dancing). — Haplology of **aṅgarāranavā* < *aṅgara(-ya)* q.v. + *karanavā*.

42. අඟුට **aňguṭa,** °ටුව **°ṭuva,** s., st. f. *°ṭu*, thumb, big toe. *aňguṭu-miṭiyā* dwarf (Germ. Däumling). — Pk., P. *aṅguṭṭha*, Sk. *aṅguṣṭha* (+ *-ka*); si. *ãṅūṭho*, g. *aṃguṭho*, m. *aṃgṭho*, oṛ. *ãṅuṭhi*, h. pj. *aṃgūṭhā*, nep. *auṃṭho*, l. *aṅgūṭh*, Gr. 50. 27.

43. අඟුණුව **aňguṇuva,** s., st. f. *°ṇu*, courtyard, compound. — Pk., P. *aṅgaṇa*, Sk. *aṅgana* + *-ka*; kśm. *āmgun*, si. *aṅaṇu*, g. *āṃgaṇ*, m. *āṃgṇeṃ*, oṛ. *agaṇā*, bg. *āṅginā*, h. *āṃgan*, nep. *āṅan*, *āṃgan*, l. *aṅgaṇī*.

44. අඟුර **aňgura,** s., st. f. *°ru*, charcoal. — P., Sk. *aṅgāra*; si. *aṅaru*, g. *aṃgāro*, m. *aṃgārā*, oṛ. *aṅgāra*, bg. *āṅgār*, h. pj. *aṃgār*, nep. *aṅār*, *aṃgār*.

45. අඟුව **aňguva,** s., st. f. *aňgu*, bracelet, armlet. — P., Sk. *aṅgada*.

46. අඟුළ **aňguḷa** (Cl *haňguḷuva*), s., st. f. *aňgul*, double canoe. *aňgul-polla* pole that fastens the two canoes together. — P. *saṅghāṭa*, Sk. *saṃghāṭa*. Cf. *saňgaḷa*.

47. අට **aṭa¹,** s., quarrel. — P. *aṭṭa* lawsuit, CopPD s.v.

48. අට **aṭa²,** num., eight. *aṭa-veni* eighth; *daha-aṭa* eighteen. — Pk., P. *aṭṭha*, Sk. *aṣṭa*; kśm. *öṭh*, si. *aṭha*, g. m. *āṭh*, oṛ. *āṭha*, h. nep. *āṭh*, pj. l. *aṭṭh*.

— අට **-aṭa**, Dat. affix, v. **-ṭa.**

49. අටකොන **aṭa-kona,** s., octagon; the eight points of the compass. — Sk. *aṣṭa-kōṇa*.

50. අටඟ **aṭ'-aňga,** a., eightfold, octuple. — *aṭa²* + *aňga¹*; P. *aṭṭhaṅga*, Sk. *aṣṭâṅga*.

51. අටපාවා **aṭa-pāvā,** s., octoped. — *aṭa²* + *pā* (*paya*); Sk. *aṣṭa-pād*, *-pāda* spider.

52. අටර **aṭara,** num., eighteen. — Archaic word corresponding to the MIAVs g. *arāḍ*, m. *aṭharā*, oṛ. *aṭhara*, bg. *āṭhāra*, h. *aṭhārah*, nep. *aṭhāra*, pj. *aṭhārāṃ*.

53. අටරස **aṭarasa,** අටළොස **aṭaḷosa,** °හ **°ha,** num., eighteen. — Pk. *aṭṭhārasa*, P. *aṭṭhādasa*, *°rasa*, Sk. *aṣṭādaśa*. Cf. *aṭara*.

54. අටල්ල **aṭalla,** s., st. f. *°lu*, high stand, scaffold. — Pk. *aṭṭālaya*, P., Sk. *aṭṭālaka*; g. *aṭārī*, m. *aṭāḷī*, *°ḷā*, h. *aṭāl*, nep. *aṭāli*, pj. *aṭāḷā*.

— අටවනවා **aṭavanavā,** v. Add.

55. අටුව **aṭuva,** s., st. f. *aṭu*, bin, garner. *aṭu-mässa* garner-platform, stand for bins. — P., Sk. *aṭṭaka*. Cf. *doraṭuva*.

56. අටුවාව **aṭuvāva,** s., st. f. *aṭuvā*, commentary. — P. *aṭṭha-kathā*.

57. අඩ **aḍa,** a., half. *aḍa-telesa* thirteen minus a half = 12½. — Pk. *aḍḍha*, P. *aḍḍha*, *addha*, Sk. *ardha*; kśm. *oḍu*, si. *adhu*, *ādho*, g. *ādhe*, *adh-*, m. *ādhā*, *aḍ-*, oṛ. *adhe*, ass. bg. h. nep. *ādhā*, pj. l. *addhā*.

58. අඩය **aḍaya,** s., stopper, prop. — TURNER compares nep. *aṛinu* intr. to stop = kśm. *aḍun* to persevere, si. *aṛaṇu* tr., g. *aḍvuṃ* intr., m. *aḍṇeṃ* h. *āṛnā* tr.

— අඩාළ **aḍāḷa,** v. Add.

59. අඩු **aḍu**, a., l e s s, d e f i c i e n t, l o w e r. *aḍu-pāḍu* deficiencies and losses; *aḍu-luhuňḍu* lack and defect. —Perhaps from MInd. **aḍḍhaka* <**ardhaka*. As to the meaning cf. *aḍa* in *aḍa-teḷesa* (57).

60. අඬ **aňḍa,** s. e g g ; t e s t i c l e. *aňḍa-sun* castrated (v. *sun*). — Pk., P. *aṇḍa* (cf. P. *aṇḍacchēda* gelder); Sk. *aṇḍa*, *āṇḍa*.

61. අඬුදාවා **aňḍu-dāvā,** s., st. f. *-dā*, b i r d. — < MInd. **aṇḍa-jāta*. Cf. P. *aṇḍa-ja*. Sk. *aṇḍa-ja*, *āṇḍa-ja*.

62. අඬුව **aňḍuva,** s., st. f. *aňḍu*, p i n c e r s, f o r c e p s. — Pk. *saṃḍāsa*, P. *saṇḍāsa*, Sk. *saṃdaṃśa(-ka)* [EdM, AIC, p. 142]; kśm. *sanasi*, si. *sanju*, g. *sā̃ṃḍso*, m. *sā̃ṃḍas*, oṛ. *sanḍuāsi*, ass. *xaṃrāh*, bg. *sā̃ṃrāsi*, b. *saṃrsi*, h. *saṃḍāsā*, *saṃṛsī*, nep. *sanāso*, *saṃṛāso*, *saṛā̃ṃso*, pj. *saṇḍāsī*, *sannhī*.

63. අණ **aṇa,** s., o r d e r, c o m m a n d. *aṇa-sak* wheel of command, EpZ II 225 A^{22}, 12th c. — Pk., P. *āṇā*, Sk. *ājñā*; kśm. *ān*, si. *āṇa*, g. m. *āṇ*, h. *ān* (v. T Add. s.v. *jānnu*). Cf. *äṇavanavā*.

64. අණව **aṇava,** s., o c e a n. — P. *aṇṇava*, Sk. *arṇava*. The form *aṇa* occurs in SälSd 97 : *sat-aṇa* ocean of arts, Sn : *śāstra namäti samudraya*.

65. අත **ata^1,** s., st. f. *at*, e n d. — Pk., P., Sk. *anta*. Frequently *-ata* (*-at*) occurs at the end of cpds. (v. *ekat*), but it is often difficult to decide whether *-ata* is derived from *anta* or from *hattha* (v. *ata^5*). I assume *anta* in *uḍat* higher, upper, *yaṭat* humble, below (but also *yaṭahat*).

66. අත **ata^2,** s., st. f. *at*, w e a l t h ; m e a n i n g. — Pk., P. *attha*, *aṭṭha*, Sk. *artha*.

67. අත **ata^3,** s., st. f. *at*, w e s t, s u n s e t. — Pk., P. *attha*, Sk. *asta*.

68. අත **ata^4,** s., st., f. *at*, s e l f, i n d i v i d u a l i t y. *at-pema* self-love; *at-duṭu* experienced; *at-väḍa* self-interest, personal gain. — Pk. nom. *attā*, acc. *attāṇaṃ*, P. *attā*, °*ānaṃ*, Sk. *ātmā*, °*ānam*; but g. m. bg. h. *āp*, oṛ. *āpe*, nep. *āphu* < Pk. M. AMg. *appā*. Cf. Sinh. *api*.

69. අත **ata^5,** හත **hata,** s., st. f. *(h)at*, h a n d, e l e p h a n t ' s t r u n k ; s i d e, d i r e c t i o n. In numerous cpds., cf. *ata-miṭa* hand and fist, means of living; *at-akura* handwriting, written letter; *at-atura* lit. interval between the hands, breast; *at-gala* hand-stone (for grinding curry-stuffs &c.); *at-piṭa* adv. upon the hands; *at-pota* handbook; *at-väḍa* handiwork. At the end of cpds. (v. *ata^1*) probably in *mäta* on this side, *piṭat* outward; *muvat*, *muvahat*, *muvāt* cutting edge of an instrument &c. With verbs: cf. *ata-arinavā* to withdraw the hands, abandon; *ata-gahanavā* to apply the hand; *ata-naňganavā* to raise the hand; *ata-lanavā* to put the hand on; *at-hiṭinavā* to stop, cease. — Pk., P. *hattha*, Sk. *hasta*; kśm. *atha*, si. *hathu*, g. *hāth*, m. *hāt*, oṛ. *hāta*, ass. bg. *hāt*, b. h. *hāth*, nep. *hāt*, pj. l. *hatth*.

70. අතඋරුව **atauruva,** අතවුරුව **atavuruva,** ඈතොවුර **ätovura,** ඈතොර **ätora,** s., st. f. °*ru*, h a r e m. — Pk. *antēura*, P. *antēpura*, Sk. *antaḥpura*.

— අතර **atara,** a., see **atura**.

71. **අතරණය ataraṇaya,** s., st. f. °*ṇa,* cloth (to be spread over a seat), sheet. — P. *attharaṇa,* Sk. *āstaraṇa* (+ *-ka*).

72. **අතරතුර ataratura,** s., st. f. °*ru,* interval. — P. *antarantarā,* °*rē,* °*rēna.*

73. **අතවැසියා atavāsiyā, °වැස්සා °vässā,** s., st. f. °*väsi,* servitor, follower, disciple. — P. *antēvāsin,* °*vāsika,* Sk. *antēvāsin.*

74. **අතිර atira,** a., unstable, inconstant. — *a-*[1] + *tira,* Sk. *a-sthira.*

75. **අතුණ atuṇa,** s., st. f. °*ṇu,* bowel. pl. °*ṇu* bowels, entrails. — P. *antāni,* Sk. *antrāṇi.*

76. **අතුර atura**[1], **අතර atara,** s., st. f. °*ru,* intervening space, interval. *atara,* °*rehi, aturehi,* postp., among, amidst ; *ataren* from amongst. — Pk., P., Sk. *antara* ; kśm. *andar,* si. *andaru* inside, °*ri,* °*roṃ* in, out of, g. *āṃtro,* m. *āṃtar,* pj. cf. *anḍaroṃ,* l. *andir.* T Add. s.v. *bhitra.* Cf. *ätuḷu.*

77. **අතුර atura**[2], s., st. f. °*ru,* connecting rope between coconut trees. — Hardly = *atura*[1] ; more probably < P. *atthāra,* Sk. *āstāra.*

78. **අතුරනවා aturanavā,** v., prt. *atuḷā* or *äturuvā,* to spread (out or over). Caus. *aturavanavā,* prt. *ätirevuvā,* to cause to spread ; intr. *ätirenavā,* prt. *ätiruṇā,* to spread out. — Pk. ger. *atthariūṇa,* P. *attharati,* Sk. *ā* + √*stṛ.*

79. **අතුළ atuḷa, අතළ ataḷa,** a. pprt., out-spread, strewn. — P. *atthaṭa* (or *atthata*), Sk. *āstṛta.*

80. **අත්ගිර at-gira,** s., the western mountain behind which the sun is supposed to set. — P. *attha-giri,* Sk. *asta-giri.*

81. **අත්ත atta,** s., st. f. *atu,* branch (of a tree). — P. **hattha-ka,* Sk. **hasta-ka.*

82. **අත්තම attama, අත්කම at-kama,** s., st. f. °*am,* hand-work, handicraft. — P. *hattha-kamma.*

— **අත්තල at-tala, අත්ල atla,** s., see **alla.**

83. **අත්පත් at-pat,** a., in hand or possession, obtained. *at-pat-venavā* to come into one's possession. — P. *hattha-ppatta,* Sk. *hasta-prāpta.*

84. **අත්පා at-pā,** s., pl. = st. f. (sg. *ata*[5]*-paya*), hand and foot. — P. *hattha-pāda,* Sk. *hasta-pāda.*

85. **අත්පස at-pasa,** s., st. f. *-pas,* arm-space, the space enclosed by the arms placed horizontally with the elbows kept by the side. *at-pas-gē* lit. arm-space-house, i.e. privy. — P. *hattha-pāsa.*

86. **අත්බව at-bava,** s., st. f. *-bäv,* one's ownself. — P. *atta-bhāva,* Sk. *ātma-bhāva.*

— **අත්ල atla,** s., see **alla.**

— **අත්ලස atlasa,** s., see **allasa.**

87. **අද ada**[1], adv., today. — Pk., P. *ajja,* Sk. *adya* ; kśm. *az,* si. *aju,* g. m. *āj,* oṛ. *āja, āji,* ass. *āzi,* bg. h. *āj, āju,* nep. *āja, āju,* pj. *ajj, ajjo,* l. *ajj.* Gr. 50. 26.

88. **අද ada**[2], a., moist, wet. — Pk., P. *adda,* Sk. *ārdra* ; g. *āduṃ,* oṛ. *adā,* ass. bg. h. *ādā.* Cf. m. *aleṃ, āleṃ,* nep. *aduvā* ginger.

89. **අදන්මග adan-mañga,** s., lengthy way, long road. — *adan* = Pk. *addhan, addhāṇa*, P. *addhan, addhāna*, Sk. *adhvan* + *mañga* q.v.

90. **අදම adama,** s., unrighteousness. — P. *adhamma*, Sk. *a-dharma*.

91. **අදවේ ada-vē,** s., lit. 'goat's road,' path of the constellation Aries. — P. *aja-vīthi*, Sk. *aja-vīthī*.

92. **අදහනවා adahanavā,** v., prt. *ädahuvā*, to believe in, trust in, worship. *adahā-gannavā* id. — Pk. *saddahaï*, P. *saddahati*, Sk. *śraddadhāti*. Cf. Sinh. *ädahilla*, st. f. °*ili* creed.

93. **අදහස adahasa,** s., st. f. °*has*, intention, purpose, wish. — Slw. P. *ajjhāsaya*.

94. **අදාරනවා adāranavā, හදා° hadā°,** v., prt. *(h)adāḷā*, *(h)ädäruvā*, to recite, commit to memory. — <**(h)adā* = P. *sajjhāya*, Sk. *svādhyāya* + *karanavā* ; cf. P. *sajjhāyaṃ karoti* [HSm].

95. **අදිනවා adinavā,** v., prt. *äddā*, to pull, drag, draw. — P., Sk. *ajati*. Cf. *padinavā*.

96. **අඳ añda,** a., blind ; ignorant. — Pk., P., Sk. *andha* ; kśm. *onu*, si. *andho*, h. *andhā*, nep. *andho*, pj. *andhā*, *annhā*, l. *andhā* ; cf. g. *āṃdhḷuṃ*, m. *aṃdhḷā*, oṛ. ass. *andhaḷā*.

97. **අඳනය añdanaya,** s., st. f. *añdana*, the lower robe or skirt of a Buddhist monk. —? P. *sandāna*, Sk. *saṃdāna* bond, fetter + *-ka*. Cf. *añdinavā*^{2}.

98. **අඳබල añda-bala,** a., very childish. — P., Sk. *andha-bāla*.

99. **අඳිනවා añdinavā**^{1}, v., prt. *ändā*, to anoint, paint. — P., Sk. *añjati*. Cf. *äñdi*.

100. **අඳිනවා añdinavā**^{2}, **හ° ha°,** v., prt. *(h)ändā*, to don, attire, wear. Double caus. *(h)andavanavā* <*(*h)añdd°* <**(h)añdv°*, prt. *(h)ändevuvā*, to dress, clothe. — Sk. *sam-* + $\sqrt{}$*dā* to bind.

101. **අඳුන añduna,** s., st. f. °*un*, eyesalve, collyrium, lampblack. *añdun-van* dark blue. — Pk. *añjaṇa*, P., Sk. *añjana* ; g. *āṃjṇī*, m. *āṃjaṇī*, *āṃjiṇī*, bg. h. *āṃjan*. T s.v. *ānu*.

102. **අඳුනනවා añdunanavā, හ° ha°,** v., prt. *(h)äñdinnā*, to be acquainted with, know, recognise. Caus. *añdunvanavā*, prt. *äñdinnevuvā*, to make known ; intr. *äñdinenavā*, prt. *äñdinuṇā*, to become acquainted with. — P. *sañjānāti*, Sk. *sam-* + $\sqrt{}$*jñā*, *saṃjānāti*. Cf. *dannavā*.

103 **අඳුර añdura, ඇඳිරිය äñdiriya,** s., st. ff. °*ru*, °*ri*, darkness, dimness. *añduru-kama* duskiness ; *äñdiri-geya* dungeon, prison ; *añduru-karanavā* to darken, obscure ; *añduru-* (*äñdiri-*) *venavā* to become dusky. — Pk. *andhaāra*, P., Sk. *andhakāra* ; si. *andhāru*, g. *aṃdhāruṃ*, *aṃdheruṃ*, m. *aṃdhār*, oṛ. *andhār*, bg. *āṃdhār*, b. *ānhar*, h. *aṃdhyārā*, *aṃdherā*, nep. *aṃdhyāro*, *aṃdhero*, *anyāro*, pj. *anhārā*, *anherā*.

104. **අන් an,** pron. a., other, foreign; *anikā*, f. °*kī* the other; *anikek* another. *an-satu* belonging to another. — Pk. *aṇṇa*, P. *añña*, Sk. *anya*; si. *añā*, g. *ane*, m. *āṇi*, oṛ. *āna*, ass. *ān*, h. (*ān*), *ani*, nep. *ani*. In the MI AVs mostly used for "and".

105. **අනඟ anaga, °ගි °gi,** a., valuable, costly, precious. — P. *anaggha*, °*gghika*, Sk. *anargha*, °*rghya*.

106. **අනතුර anatura,** s., st. f. °*ru*, danger, calamity. — Probably a blending of P. *anattha* (Sk. *anartha*) and P., Sk. *antarāya*.

107. **අනතුරු anaturu,** a., immediately following, next. — P., Sk. *anantara*.

108. **අනිටු an-iṭu,** a., pprt., undesired, ominous. — P. *an-iṭṭha*, Sk. *an-iṣṭa*.

109. **අනිස anisa,** a., transient, passing away. — Pk. *a-ṇicca*, P. *a-nicca*, Sk. *a-nitya*.

110. **අනු anu, නු nu,** prefix = Pk. *aṇu-*, P., Sk. *anu-*. Cf. s. vv. *anu-meveni*; *nu-mut*, *nu-rā*, *nu-vā* &c.

111. **අනුමෙවෙනි anu-meveni,** a., thanks-giving, benedictive. — P. *anu-mōdana*, *°*nika*, Sk. *anu-mōdin*.

112. **අනුසසුන anusasuna,** s., st. f. °*sun*, admonition, exhortation, DhpAGp 22[16]. — Pk. *anu-sāsaṇa*, P. *anu-sāsana*, Sk. *anu-śāsana*.

113. **අනූව anūva,** num., st. f. *anū*, ninety. — Pk. *nauiṃ*, P. *navuti*, Sk. *navati*; kśm. *namath*, si. *nave*, g. *nevuṃ*, m. *navvad*, oṛ. *nabe*, ass. *navai*, bg. *nabbaï*, b. *nabbai*, h. nep. *nabbe*, pj. l. *navve*. The initial *a* of *anūva* seems to be due to the analogy of *asūva* eighty.

114. **අන්දිටු an-diṭu,** a., of other views, heretic. — P. *añña-diṭṭhika*.

115. **අපි api,** pron. 1. pers. pl., we; obl. c. *apa*. — Derived from the pron. refl. = Pk. *appa-* alternating with *atta-* (PISCHEL § 277). In the Dhau. and Jau. inscrs. of Asoka we meet with *aphe* us, *aphākă* of us, *aphesū* in us (Hultzsch InscAs, p. cvi) for **apphe* &c.; cf. Paiś Pk. *ampha* we.

116. **අපිරිසෙ, °සෙය් a-pirise, °sey,** a., without remainder, all-enclosing, side by side with *anat* endless, EpZ I. 25[3]. 46[2]. 10th c.—P. *a-parisēsa*, Sk. *a-pariśēṣa*, Wickr, ib. p. 27, n. 3.

117. **අපිස් apis,** a., of little desire; s. °*sa* contentedness. — Pk., P. *appa*, Sk. *alpa* + Pk., P., Sk. *icchā*; P. a. *appiccha*.

118. **අපුල්ලනවා apullanavā,** prt. *äpulluvā*, to wash (clothes by beating). Pprs. *apullannā* the washerman. — <**apulvanavā*, caus. of **apulanavā*; Pk. *apphālēi*, Sk. *ā* + √*sphal*, caus. *āsphālayati* dashes against; g. *aphālvuṃ*, m. *aphaḷṇeṃ*, nep. *aphālnu*, *āph°*.

119. **අබ aba,** s., cloud. — Pk., P. *abbha*, Sk. *abhra*; kśm. *abur*, si. *abhu*, g. m. *ābh*. Beames II. 21.

120. **අබතුර abatura,** s., st. f. *°ru,* inside. — Pk., P. *abbhantara,* Sk. *abhyantara*; g. m. ass. bg. *bhitar,* oṛ. *bhitara,* h. *bhītar,* nep. *bhitra.*

121. **අබවස abavasa,** s., st. f. *°vas,* open place. — P. *abbhōkāsa,* Sk. *abhyavakāśa.*

122. **අබි abi-, අබ් ab-, බි bi-,** prefix = Pk. *abhi-, ahi-,* P., Sk. *abhi-.* Cf. *abatura, abiduva* &c., *bisev.*

123. **අබි abi,** a., fearless: s. *abiya* fearlessness. — P., Sk. *abhaya.* Cf. nom. propr. *Abā* = *Abhaya,* frequent in inscs.

124. **අබිදුව abiduva,** s., st. f. *°du,* covetousness. — P. *abhijjhā,* Sk. *abhidhyā.*

125. **අබින් abin,** s., opium. — Sk. *aphēna* (*ahiphēṇa*).

126. **අබිබවනවා abi-bavanavā,** v., prt. *abibävuvā,* to subdue. *abi-bävīma, °vuma* subjugation. — Pk. *abhi-bhavaï,* P., Sk. *abhi-bhavati.* Prob. Slw.

127. **අබිමන් abiman,** s., haughtiness, pride. — Pk. *abhimāṇa,* P., Sk. *abhimāna.*

128. **අබිමුව abimuva,** s., presence, the front. *°muvehi* in front (of), in the presence (of). — Pk. *abhimuha,* P., Sk. *abhimukha.*

129. **අබියස abiyasa, °යෙස °yesa,** s., proximity, nearness. — Slw. P. *abhyāsa,* Sk. *abhyāśa, °sa.*

130. **අබිසරය abisaraya,** s., st. f. *°ra,* going to an assignation; *°ruva* a woman who goes to an assignation. — P. **abhisāra, °sāriyā,* Sk. *abhisāra, °sārikā.*

131. **අඹ aṁba[1],** s., st. f. *aṁbu,* wife, mother. — Pk., P., Sk. *ambā.* Sinh. *ammā,* lw. P. *ammā*; si. *amāṃ,* h. *ammā,* nep. *āmā.*

132. **අඹ aṁba[2],** s., st. f. *aṁbu,* water. — Pk., P., Sk. *ambu.*

133. **අඹ aṁba[3],** s., mango, tree and fruit. — Pk., P. *amba,* Sk. *āmra*; kśm. *amb,* si. *āmo,* g. *āṃbo,* m. *āṃbā,* bg. *āṃb,* ass. h. *ām,* nep. *āṃp,* pj. l. *amb.*

134. **අඹර aṁbara,** s., st. f. *°uru,* sky. — Pk., P., Sk. *ambara.*

— **අඹල aṁbala,** s., see **ämbula, siyaṁbalā.**

135. **අමතනවා amatanavā,** v., prt. *ämatuvā,* to address, invite. *ämatīma, °tuma* invitation. — P *āmantēti,* Sk. *āmantrayatē.*

136. **අමදිනවා amadinavā, හ° ha°,** v., prt. *(h)ämäddā,* to sweep. — Pk. *sammajjaï,* P. *sammajjati,* Sk. *sam-* + $\sqrt{}$*mṛj, saṃmārjati.* Cf. *madinavā.*

137. **අමාව amāva,** s., st. f. *amā,* ambrosia. *amā-vatura* a flood of ambrosia, the title of a book. — Pk *amaya,* P. *amata,* Sk. *amṛta.*

138. **අමු amu,** a., fresh, raw, immature. — Pk., P., Sk. *āma*; kśm. *ōmu,* si. *āṃuṃ,* g. *ām,* m. *āṃv,* oṛ. *āma,* ass. bg. *ām* dysentery, h. *āṃv,* nep. *āuṃ* dysentery, pj. *āṃuṃ.*

139. **අමුණ amuṇa,** s., st. f. *°ṇu,* a grain measure, a measure of land. — P. *ammaṇa* (cf. PTSPD s.v.), Sk. *armaṇa.*

140. **අමුණනවා amuṇanavā, අවුණ° avuṇa°**, v., prt. *ämuṇuvā, äv°*, to string; to thread a needle. — P. *āvuṇāti*, Sk. *ā-* + √*vṛ, ā-vṛṇāti*.

141. **අමුව amuva, හ° ha°**, s., presence. *(h)amuvehi*, (°*yehi*) in front (of), in the presence (of). — Pk. *saṃmuha*, P. *sammukha*, Sk. *saṃmukha*.

142. **අය aya[1]**, s., revenue, income. *aya-väya* income and expenditure; *aya-kämiyā* tax collector. — P., Sk. *āya*.

143. **අය aya[2]**, s., person, individual. — Pk. *ajja*, P. *ayya*, Sk. *ārya*. Cf. No. 162 and T s.v. *ājā*.

144. **අයති ayati, අයත් ayat, අයිති ayiti**, a., belonging to. *ayiti-karanavā* to make over to; *ayiti-kārayā* owner, possessor. — P., Sk. *ā-yatta*. Cf. Bl s.v. *aitā*; m. *āytā* ready, g. *āytuṃ*, h. *āyitā*.

145. **අයදිනවා ayadinavā**, v., prt. *ayäddā* (or *ayaduvā*), to pray, invoke, request. — P. *āyācati*, Sk. *ā-* + √*yāc, āyācatē*. Cf. *yadinavā*.

146. **අයම ayama**, s., st. f. *ayam*, length. — P., Pk. *āyāma*. Cf. *vāyama*.

147. **අයල් ayal**, s., st. f. *ayal*, aloe wood. — Pk. *agaru, agaluya*, P. *agaru*, Sk. *aguru*; kśm. *agur*, si. m. ass. bg. *agaru*, oṛ. *aguru*, h. nep. pj. *agar*.

148. **අයස ayasa**, s., evil, scandal, infamy. — P. *a-yasa*, Sk. *a-yaśas*.

149. **අයින් ayin**, a., not given, stolen. — P. *adinna*. Cf. *ayin-ādan*, Slw. P. *adinnâdāna* theft.

150. **අයිරා ayirā-**, adv., above, more than. *ayirā-dahasak* above a thousand. — P., Sk. *atirēka*; cf. Pk. *aïritta*.

151. **අයු ayu**, a. pprt., past, preterite; s. *äya* the past. — Pk. *aïa*, P., Sk. *atîta*.

152. **අයුණ ayuṇa**, s., st. f. °*ṇu*, fault, wrong, badness. — Pk. *a-uṇa*, P., Sk. *a-guṇa*.

153. **අයුතු ayutu**, a., improper, wrong. *a-yutu-kama* wrong act. — P. *a-yutta*, Sk. *a-yukta*. Cf. *yutu*.

154. **අයුර ayura**, s., st. f. °*ru*, form, manner; end of cpds. *-ayuru* like, similar to; *ek-ayuru* of the same kind. — Pk. *āāra*, P., Sk. *ākāra*. Cf. *-yuru*.

155. **අර ara**, pron. dem., that (opp. *mē* this). — I derive the word from st. *āra* far in P., Sk. *ārē* far from, P. *ārā*, Sk. *ārāt* from afar.

156. **අරක araka**, s., st. f. *arak*, protection, preservation. *arak-deviyā* tutelar deity. — Pk., P. *ārakkha*, Sk. *ārakṣa*. Cf. *rakinavā*.

157 **අරබ araba, ඇරබ äraba, °ඹ °m̐ba**, postp., beginning from, on behalf of, for. — Pk., P. *ārabbha*, Sk. *ārabhya*.

158. **අරඹ aram̐ba**, s., grove, garden. — This is, I think, the genuine Sinh. word for Pk., P., Sk. *ārāma*, whilst *arama* is probably Slw.

159. **අරඹය aram̐baya, ඇර° ära°**, s., st. f. °*m̐ba*, beginning. — Pk., P., Sk. *ārambha*.

160. **අරමුණ aramuṇa**, s., st. f. °*ṇu*, sense-object. — P. *ārammaṇa*, Sk. cf. *ālambana*.

161. අරළු **araḷu,** s., st. f., name of a tree and its fruit, yellow myrobalan, Terminalia chebula. — Pk. *haraaī, haraḍaī, harīḍaī,* P., Sk. *harītaka* (tree), °*kī* (fruit) ; si. *harīṛa,* °*ra,* g. *harḍuṃ, harḍī,* m. *harḍā, hirḍā,* oṛ. *hariṛā,* h. *harṛā, harrā, haṛṛaī,* nep. *harro,* pj. *haraṛ,* l. *harīṛ,* °*rīr.*

162. අරි **ari-** in cpds., excellent: *ari-savuvā* an eminent disciple ; *ari-saṅga* the holy Buddhist community. — P. *ariya,* Sk. *ārya.* Cf. *aya*[2].

163. අරිටු **ariṭu,** a., wicked, bad; unfavourable (omen). — P. *ariṭṭha,* Sk. *ariṣṭa* + *-ka.* Cf. *riṭuvā.*

164. අරිනවා **arinavā,** හරි° **hari°,** v., prt. *haḷā,* (*h*)*äriyā,* to send away, dismiss, abandon; to open (a door). Caus. *aravanavā,* prt. *ärevuvā,* to cause to be sent away ; intr. *ärenavā,* prt. *äruṇā,* to become abandoned, to be left out. — Pk. *haraï,* P. *harati, hārēti* or *harāpēti,* Sk. $\sqrt{}$*hṛ, harati, hārayati* ; kśm. *harun,* g. *harvuṃ,* m. *harṇeṃ,* oṛ. *haribā,* ass. *hariba,* bg. *harā,* h. pj. *harnā,* nep. *harnu.*

165. අරියනවා **ariyanavā,** v., pprt. *ariyū* EpZ I. 25[4], 33[2], 10th c., ger. *ariyay* ib. I. 46[10], 10th c., to serve, honour, worship; to win (one's heart) ; *ariyana,* a., entreating. — Archaic ; Pk. *ārāhēi, ārāhaṇa* ; P. *ārādhēti, ārādhana* ; Sk. *ā-* + $\sqrt{}$*rādh, ārādhayati.*

166. අරිසස **arisasa,** s., st. f. °*sas,* piles, hemorrhoids. — Slw. Sk. *arśas, arśasa,* (P. *arisa*).

167. අරූ **a-rū,** a., formless, immaterial. *arū-tala,* the four Brahma worlds where the inhabitants are without form. — P., Sk. *a-rūpa.*

168. අලඟ **alaṅga,** s., embracing, kissing. — P., Sk. *āliṅga, āliṅgana.* T's etymology (s.v. *aṃgālo*) seems to be improbable. T himself adds a ?

169. අලතාව **alatāva,** s., st. f. °*tā,* lac. — P. *alattaka,* Sk. *alaktaka.*

170. අලන **alana,** s., st. f. *alan,* elephant post, post for tying elephants to. — Pk. *ālāṇa,* P., Sk. *ālāna.* Ca has also *alavuna* (? for *alanuva*), st. f. *alanu.* This would be = **ālānaka.*

171. අලප් **alap,** s., speaking to, addressing; in gram. the vocative case. — Pk. *ālappa* <**ālāpya* ; cf. Pk. *ālāva,* P., Sk. *ālāpa.*

172. අලය **alaya**[1], s., st. f. *ala* ; house; fondness, desire. — Pk. *ālaa,* P., Sk. *ālaya* ; cf. g. m. *devaḷ* &c. = *dēvâlaya,* T s.v. *deurāli.*

173. අලය **alaya**[2], s., st. f. *ala,* yam, potato. — Pk. *ālua,* P. *ālu,* Sk. *ālu(ka)* ; kśm. *ālū,* m. *āḷūṃ,* oṛ. *āḷū,* ass. bg. nep. *ālu,* h. pj. l. *ālū.*

174. අලලනවා **alalanavā,** හ° **ha°,** v., prt. (*h*)*älaluvā,* to agitate, shake, stir about. Intr. (*h*)*älalenavā,* prt. °*luṇā,* to be agitated, rage (as the sea). — T, s.v. *hallinu,* compares the word with Pk. *hallaï,* kśm. *halun,* si. *halaṇu* (*halhali*), g. *hālvuṃ,* m. *hālṇeṃ* (for **hallṇeṃ,* Bl, LM § 471), *halhalṇeṃ,* h. *hālnā,* pj. *hallṇā.* Or perhaps < Sk. *sam-* + $\sqrt{}$*luḍ, lul* ? In this case the spelling *alaḷanavā* would be preferable.

175. අලියා **aliyā**, s., st. f. *ali*, scorpion. — P., Sk. *āli* + *ka* (why no umlaut ?) Sinh. *aliyā* wasp, crow, cuckoo is certainly Sk. lw.

176. අලුත් **alut**, a., new, fresh. *alut-karanavā* to make new, renovate.— ? *a-* priv. + **lut* = P. *lutta*, Sk. *lupta* destroyed, lost, disappeared.

177. අලුප **alupa**, s., st. f. *alup*, small piece, bit, fragment. — ? < MInd. **āluppa*, P. *ālōpa*.

178. අලුව **aluva**, s., st. f. *alu*, dawning. *alu-yama* the third watch of the night, daybreak, dawn. — P., Sk. *ālōka*. Ca also *halu* (Cl *haḷu*). It seems that the words *(h)eḷi* open, clear, and *(h)eḷiya* s. light, must be separated from *aluva*. Their traditional spelling is with *ḷ* (thus Ca, but Cl *l*).

179. අලෙවුව **alevuva**[1], s., st. f. *alevu*, painting, picture. — Pk. *ālēha*, P. *ālēkha*, Sk. *ālēkhya*. Cf. T s.v. *lekho*[2], Bl s.v. *lekh*.

180. අලෙවුව **alevuva**[2], s., st. f. *alevu*, anointing. — Pk. *ālēva*, Sk. *ālēpa*. Cf. T s.v. *lipnu*, Bl s.v. *limpṇem*.

181. අල්ල **alla**, අත්ල **atla**, අත්තල **attala**, s., the flat or palm of the hand. — P. *hattha-tala*, Sk. *hasta* + *tala* ; mald. *aitala*.

182. අල්ලනවා **allanavā**, v., prt. *älluvā*, to lay hold of; to catch, seize. Caus. *allavanavā* prt. *ällevuvā*, to cause to seize.—Probably for *at-lanavā* (Ca) to take in hand. But cf. *alvanavā* SdhRv 34[8] &c.

183. අල්ලස **allasa**, අත්ලස **atlasa**, s., st. f. *-las*, bribe. — *ata*[5] + *lasa*, P. *hattha* + *lañca*.

184. අවට **avaṭa**, a., circular, surrounding; adv. around. — Pk. M. *āvaṭṭa*, P. *āvaṭṭatō* in circumference, Sk. *āvarta* turning, whirl. Cf. Bl, LM § 114, T s.v. *oiṭo*.

185. අවදන **avadana**, s., st. f. °*dan*, meditation, excogitation. — P. *āvajjana*, Sk. *āvarjana* Mahāvastu II. 423[18].

186. අවන **avana**[1], s., market-place, see **avuṇa**.

187. අවන **avana**[2], s., st. f. *avan*, danger, risk. — Pk. *āvanna*, P., Sk. *āpanna*.

188. අවන **avana**[3], s., st. f. *avan*, drinking. *avan-hala* dram shop, tavern ; *avan-keḷiya* a carousal. — P., Sk. *āpāna*.

189. අවනවා **avanavā**, හ° **ha**°, v., prt. *(h)ävuvā*, to imprecate, curse. *(h)ävilla*, *(h)ävīma* cursing, imprecation. — Pk. *sāva* curse, P. *sapati*, *sāpa*, Sk. √*śap*, *śapati*, *śāpa*. Cf. T s.vv. *srāp*, *srāpnā*.

190. අවන්සත් **avansat**, අවනසත් **avanasat**, a., pregnant. — P. *āpanna-sattā* pregnant woman.

191. අවර **avara**, a., hinder, posterior; western; s. *avaraya* the after part, stern. *avara-diga* the west, occident. — Pk. *avara*, P., Sk. *apara* ; kśm. *ōr-* step-(brother etc.), si. *amum*, g. *or*, *oṛ*. bg. *āra*, ass. *āru*, h. *aur*, nep. *aru*, pj. *ar*. (all meaning "other, and"). Gr 50. 16.

— අවරණය **avaraṇaya**, s., see s.v. **avura**.

192. අවස **avasa,** s., st. f. *avas, avā,* dwelling place, house. — Pk., P., Sk. *āvāsa* ; g. *avās,* m. *āvsā,* h. *āvās.*

193. අවළ **avaḷa,** a. pprt., overspread. — P. *āvaṭa,* Sk. *āvṛta.* Cl, Ca erroneously spell *avala.*

194. අවා(ය) **avā(ya),** s., st. f. *avā,* hell. — Pk. *avāa,* P., Sk. *apāya.*

195. අවා(ව) **avā(va),** s., st. f. *avā,* marriage. —P., Sk. *āvāha.*

196. අවිය **aviya,** s., st. f. *avi,* weapon; tool, implement. *avi-saram̆ba* brandishing weapons (v. *haram̆ba*), *avi-sip* the art of using weapons. — Pk. *āuha,* P. *āvudha, āyudha,* Sk. *āyudha.*

197. අවියා **aviyā,** s., st. f. *avi,* goat. *avi-paṭa* woollen cloth. — P., Sk. *avi* sheep.

198. අවුණ **avuṇa,** s., st. f. *avuṇu,* market place, bazaar. — Pk. *āvaṇa,* P., Sk. *āpaṇa.* Cl Ca also *avan-a.*

— අවුණනවා **avuṇanavā,** s., see **amuṇanavā.**

199. අවුර **avura,** s., st. f. *°ru,* cover, shelter, rampart. — Sk. *āvāra* in *durāvāra, skandhâvāra* (Sinh. *kam̆davura*). Sinh. *avaraṇaya* is, as the ending *-aya* and the *a-* vowel in the 2nd syll. show, a Slw. Sk. *āvaraṇa.*

200. අවුරනවා **avuranavā,** v., prt. *ävuruvā,* to cover, screen, shelter. —P. *āvārēti,* Sk. *ā* + $\sqrt{}$*vṛ,* Caus. *āvārayati* ; kśm. *āvarun.* T s.v. *bārnu* Add.

201. අවුරුද්ද **avurudda,** හ° **ha°,** s., st. f. *°du,* year. — Metathesis for *havuduru* = Pk., P. *saṃvacchara,* Sk. *saṃvatsara.* Sinh. Pk. HAVAJARA, EpZ III. 251[3], end of 4th c.

202. අවුල් **avul,** a., confused, crowded; s. *°la* confusion. — Pk. *āula,* P., Sk. *ākula.* Sinh. *avul-dätiyā* (v. *dätta*) crocodile, alligator (lit. having thick-set teeth).

203. අවුව **avuva,** s., st. f. *avu,* sunshine. — Pk. *āava,* P., Sk. *ātapa.*

204. අස් **as**[1], අසු **asu,** s., horse. *as-beṭi* horse-dung ; *as-vedā* horse doctor, farrier ; *as-hala* stable. — Pk., P. *assa,* Sk. *aśva* (Sinh. lw. *aśvayā*) ; cf. m. *āsupāṭhī* on horseback. In the MIAVs the derivates of Sk. *ghōṭaka* are substituted for *aśva* ; T s.v. *ghoṛā.*

— අස් **as**[2], s., see **ahā.**

205. අස් **as**[3], හස් **has,** සස් **sas,** s., corn, grain. *has-kara, sas-kara* cultivator ; *as-vaddanavā* to till, cultivate ; *as-van* cultivated. — Pk., P. *sassa,* Sk. *sasya.* Cf. *agas.*

206. අස් **as**[4], හස් **has,** s., seal, signet. *as-mudda* id., *as-obanavā* to seal. — According to DE LANEROLLE the same as *has* swan, q.v. The royal signet was a *haṃsa.* Cf. HaṃsaSd 2 d.

207. අස **asa**[1], s., st. f. *as,* part, portion; a little. — P. *aṃsa,* Sk. *aṃśa.*

208. අස **asa**^{2}, s., st. f. *as*, side, shoulder. — Pk., P., Sk. *aṃsa* ; h. *hāṃs* collarbone, pj. *hass*, l. *hassī* ; T s.v. *hāṃsuli*.

209. අස **asa**^{3}, s., st. f. *as*, edge, corner. — Pk., P. *assa*, Sk. *aśra* ; m. *ās*(*pās*). Bl, LM § 198. Cf. *sivur-ās*.

210. අසක් **asak**^{1}, a., eyeless, blind. — *a*- priv. + *saka*^{2}, Sk. *acakṣus*.

211. අසක් **asak**^{2}, a., innumerable. — *a*- priv. + *sak*, P. *asaṅkhiya*.

212. අසන් **asan**, a., near. *dakuṇ dor asanhi* near the Southern Gate, EpZ I. 46^{7}, 10th c. — Pk., P., Sk. *āsanna*. Cf. *nisan*.

213. අසර **asara**^{1}, s., goddess. — Pk., P. *accharā*, Sk. *apsaras* ; m. *āsre* (pl.), h. *acchar*.

214. අසර **asara**^{2}, හ° **ha°**, s., way, road. — Pk. *saṃcāra*, P. *sañcāra*, Sk. *saṃcāra*.

215. අසරුවා **asaruvā**, s., st. f. *°ru*, horseman. — P. *assârōha*, Sk. *aśvârōha*. Cf. *ätaruvā*.

216. අසල **asala**^{1}, s., st. f. *asal*, mountain, rock. — Pk. *ayala*, P., Sk. *acala*.

217. අසල **asala**^{2}, s., st. f. *asal*, border, margin; nearness. *asal-väsiyā* neighbour. — T s. v. *āṃcal*, refers to Sk. *añcala* border of a garment. Doubtful. Perhaps = *asan* (*l* for *n*, Ggr, Gr. § 60. 1).

218. අසැක **asäka**, අසක **asaka** (for *nisäka*), s., certainty. — *a*- priv. + *säka* doubt. See *häka*.

219. අසිය **asiya**^{1}, s., st. f. *asi*, flame. — Pk., P. *acci*, Sk. *arci*, *arcis* ; g. m. bg. h. nep. *āṃc*.

220. අසිය **asiya**^{2}, s. pprt., st. f. *asi*, female friend. — P. *accitā*, Sk. *arcitā*.

221. අසිරිය **asiriya**, s., st. f. *°ri*, astonishment, surprise. *asiri-rū*, n. of the Cupid, lit. of wonderful beauty. — Pk. *acchēraa*, P. *acchariya*, *acchēra*, Sk. *āścarya*.

— අසුන්, **asun**, °න **°na**, see **asna**$^{1,\ 2}$.

222. අසූව **asūva**, num., st. f. *asū*, eighty. *asūveni* eightieth. — Pk. AMg. *asīiṃ*, P. *asīti*, Sk. *aśīti*; kśm. *śīth*, si. *asī*, g. *eṃśī*, m. *eṃśīṃ*, *aiśīṃ*, oṛ. *aśī*, ass. *āśī*, bg. *āśi*, h. pj. l. *assī*, nep. *assi*.

223. අස්කන් **askan**, n. of a tree (lit. horse-ear). — P. *assakaṇṇa* Vatica robusta, Sk. *aśvakarṇa*.

224. අස්න **asna**^{1}, අසුන **asuna** (*asana*), s., st. f. *asun*, *asan*, seat. *us-asna* high seat, throne. — Pk. *āsaṇa*, P., Sk. *āsana*. Also Sinh. *hasuna* (*hasana*) by false analogy.

225. අස්න **asna**^{2}, හස්න **hasna**, සස්න **sasna** (also *asuna*, *ha°*, *sa°*), s., st. f. *asun*, *ha°*, *sa°*, message, letter, news, intelligence. — Pk. *sāsaṇa*, P. *sāsana*, Sk. *śāsana* (*śāsana-hārin*) ; h. *sāsan*.

226. **අහනවා ahanavā, අස° asa°**, v., prt. *ähuvā, äs°*, to hear. Caus. *asvanavā, ass°*, prt. *äsvevuvā, äss°*, to cause to hear; intr. *ähenavā, äs°*, prt. *ähuṇā, äs°*, to be heard, to be audible. — P. *āsuṇāti, °ṇōti*, Sk. *ā-* + √*śru, ā-śṛṇōti.* We expect as prs. st. **ahuṇa-, *asuṇa-*. The st. *aha-, asa-* is, as T s.v. *sunnu*, has shown, a new formation from the prt. st. *ähu-, äsu-* which is correctly derived from Sk. *āśruta*, according to the proportion (*aha-*): *ähu-* = *gasa-* : *gäsu-*. Cf. *ukanavā, unanavā.*

227. **අහම්බ ahamba,** a., sudden, accidental; s. *°mbaya* chance, accident. *ahamben* suddenly. — T compares nep. *acamba* wonder, surprise = g. *acaṃbo*, m. *acaṃbā*, oṛ. *ācambit*, bg. *ācambā*, h. *acambā, °bhā*, nep. *acamba, °bha*, pj. *acambhā* (? *ahamba* < *°m̆bba* < *m̆biya.*)

228. **අහර ahara,** s., food. — Pk., P., Sk. *āhāra* ; nep. *āhāro.*

229. **අහස ahasa, ආස āsa,** s., st. f. *ahas*, sky. *ahas-diya* celestial water, rain. — Pk. *āāsa*, P. *ākāsa*, Sk. *ākāśa.*

230. **අහස්ගඟ ahas-gaṅga,** s., celestial river; the milky way. — P. *ākāsa-gaṅgā*, Sk. *ākāśa-gaṅgā.*

231. **අහා ahā** in *val-ahā*, s., st., f. *as*, bear. Sinh. Pk. *aca* in *aca-girika* bear-hill, topogr. name, AIC No. 1, of *as-giriya*, n. of a monastery near Kandy. — (Pk. *riccha, rikkha*), P. *accha*, Sk. *ṛkṣa* ; kśm., *ich*, (si. *ricchu*, g. *rīṃch*, m. *rīs, rīṃs*, h. *rīch*, pj. *ricch*). Gr. 50. 26.

232. **අහිවිසයා ahivisayā, අසි° asi°**, s., st. f. *°sa*, venomous snake. — P. *āsīvisa*, Sk. *āśīviṣa.*

233. **අහුර ahura, අසුර asura,** s., st. f. *°ru*, the closed hand, handful. — P. *sañcara*, Sk. *saṃcara* (but see *asara* <*saṃcāra*).

234. **අහුරනවා ahuranavā, අසු° asu°**, v., prt. *ähuruvā, äs°*, to put together, set up, pile up; to enclose, block up, stop (as by a fence). Caus. *asuruvanavā*, prt. *äsirevuvā*, to cause to be piled up; intr. *äsirenavā*, prt. *°ruṇā*, to move about, act, behave. — P. **sañcārēti*, Sk. *sam-* + √*car, saṃcārayati.* Cf. T s.v. *carnu.* It is not easy to connect the various meanings.

235. **අළ aḷa, හළ haḷa,** a. pprt., removed away from, sent away dismissed. — (Pk. *haa*), P. *haṭa*, Sk. *hṛta.* Cf. *arinavā.*

236. **අළුව aḷuva,** s., st. f. *aḷu*, post to which elephants are tied. — P. *āḷhaka* ; cf. Pk. *āḍhaa*, Sk. *āḍhaka* a measure of capacity.

ආ Ā

237. **ආ ā¹**, a. pprt., come, arrived, present. — Pk. *āa*, P., Sk. *āgata* ; kśm. *āv*, m. *ā(lā)*. Cf. *enavā*

237a. **ආ ā²**, s., age, lifetime. *ā-väḍīma-ṭa* for the prolongation of life, Kus 654. — Pk. *āu*, P. *āyu*, Sk. *āyus*. Cf. *digā, digāyu.*

238. **ආරය āraya,** s., st. f. *āra,* m i n e. — Pk. *āgara,* P., Sk. *ākara.*

— **ආස āsa,** s., see **ahasa.**

ඇ Ä

239. **ඇකය äkaya,** s., st. f. *äka,* s i d e, h i p, l a p. — Pk., P., Sk. *aṅka.* Cf. *aka*[4].

240. **ඇකි äki, හැකි häki, සැකි säki,** a., a b l e, p o s s i b l e. — Pk., P. *sakka,* Sk. *śakya* ; cf. Bl s. v. *saknem,* T s.v. *saknu.*

241. **ඇකිල්ල äkilla, ඇකිලිය äkiliya, හැ° hä°, සැ° sä°,** s., st. f. *°ili,* c h a i n, f e t t e r. — Pk. *siṅkhala,* P. *saṅkhala, °lā,* Sk. *śṛṅkhala, °lā* ; kśm. *höṃkal,* si. *saṅghara,* g. *sāṃkaḷ,* m. *sāṃkhaḷ, sāṃkaḷ, sākaḷ,* oṛ. *sāṅkoḷi, sikuḷi,* ass. *xikali,* bg. *sīkal,* b. *siṃkar, sīkar,* h, *sāṃkal, sāṃkar, sīkar,* nep. *sāṅlo, sāṃglo,* pj. *saṅgal,* l. *saṅglī.* Gr. 50. 35.

242. **ඇක්මෙනවා äkmenavā,** v., prt. *äkmuṇā,* t o b e t r a m p l e d, c r u s h e d. —Intr. of **akmanavā* = Pk. *akkamaï,* P. *akkamati,* Sk. *ā-* + √ *kram, ā-kramatē.* Cf. *akmana.*

243. **ඇක්සුම äksuma,** s., st. f. *°sum,* c u r s i n g, i m p r e c a t i o n. — Nom. verb., cf. Pk. *akkōsaï,* P. *akkōsana,* Sk. *ākrōśana* ; see *akosa.*

244. **ඇගෑව ägǟva,** s., st. f. *ägǟ,* f e s t o o n w o r k. — P. *agghika, °kā,* CopPD s.v. Sinh. Pk. *ayika* (EpZ I. 258) cannot be compared with *agghikā.*

245. **ඇගි ägi,** a., p r e c i o u s. — P. *agghiya,* Sk. *arghya.* Cf. *agaya, aginavā.*

246. **ඇඟ äṅga,** s., b o d y. — P., Sk. *aṅgi* (neutr. of a. *aṅgin*), lit. consisting of limbs ; cf. *aṅga*[1].

247. **ඇඟිල්ල äṅgilla,** s., st. f. *°ili,* f i n g e r. — Pk., P. *aṅguli,* Sk. *aṅguli, °ri* ; kśm, *oṅgujü,* si. *aṅuri,* g. *āṃglī,* m. *aṃguḷī, aṃglī, aṃgoḷī,* oṛ. *aṅguḷī,* ass. *āṅguli.* bg. *āṅgul,* h. *uṅglī,* nep. *auṃli,* pj. *uṅgal,* l. *aṅgil.*

248. **ඇටය äṭaya,** s., st. f. *äṭa,* b o n e ; s t o n e (of a fruit), a s e e d. — Pk., P. *aṭṭhi,* Sk. *asthi* + *-ka* ; kśm. *öṃṭü,* oṛ. ass. *āṃṭhu,* bg. *āṃṭi* ; Cf. T s.v. *hāṛ.*

248[a]. **ඇටසැකිල්ල äṭa-säkilla,** s., st. f. *°ili,* s k e l e t o n. — *äṭaya* + (*s*)*äkilla* ; P. *aṭṭhi-saṅkhalikā,* (Sk. *asthi-śṛṅkhala,* name of a plant).

249. **ඇට්ටර äṭṭara,** a., o b s t i n a t e ; s. *°rayā* obstinate man. — T compares the word with nep. *aṭer* obstinacy, *aṭeri, aṭṭeri* obstinate. But in Sinh. *ṭṭ* would be difficult to explain.—? lw.

250. **ඇණය äṇaya, ඇණේ äṇē,** s., st. f. *äṇa,* n a i l, p e g. — P., Sk. *āṇi* + *-ka.*

251. **ඇණවනවා äṇavanavā,** v., prt. *äṇevuvā,* t o c o m m a n d. — P. *āṇāpēti,* Sk. *ā-* + √*jñā,* caus. *ā-jñāpayati.* Cf. *aṇa.*

252. **ඇණිය äṇiya,** s., st. f. *äṇi,* (lit. forepart, front) b o w (of a ship) ; a r m y, m i l i t a r y c a m p. *äṇi-kumbaya* bowsprit. — Pk. AMg. *aṇiya,* P., Sk. *anīka.* Cf. DE LANEROLLE, DSL, p. xlii, II, § 3a.

— **ඇත äta,** v., see s.v. **äti.**

253. **ඇතරුවා ätaruvā,** s., st. f. °*ru*, elephant rider. — P. *hatthārōha*, Sk. *hastyārōha*. Cf. *asaruvā*.

254. **ඇතා ätā,** s., st. f. *ät*, elephant; fem. *ätinī*, °*nnī*, °*nna*, st. f. *ätini*, she-elephant. *ät-daḷa* elephant's tusk; *ät-soṅḍa* elephant's trunk. — Pk. *hatthi*, P. *hatthin* (*hatthinī*), Sk. *hastin* (*hastinī*); kśm. *hostu*, si. g. *hāthī*, m. *hattī*, oṛ. ass. bg. nep. *hāti*, h. pj. *hāthī*. B I. 313, Gr. 50. 8.

255. **ඇතැණිය ät-äṇiya,** s. st. f. °*ṇi*, troop of war elephants. — P. *hatthânīka*.

256. **ඇති äti, ඇත äta,** v., there is, there are; *ää-da* is there, are there, does it suffice? *-äti*, as a. in cpds., having, possessing: *agē-äti* valuable, precious; *nam-äti* having a name; *kam-äti* see s.v. *kam*; as s. *ättā* owner, possessor. Cf. also *ätta*, *ättā*, *näti*. — Pk., P. *atthi*, Sk. *asti*. Cf. Sk. *āstika*, P. *atthika*.

257. **ඇතිරිය ätiriya,** s., st. f. °*ri*, a cloth to spread out, coverlet; also with the *l*-suffix *ätirilla*, st. f. °*ili*. — P. *atthāra*, Sk. *āstāra*. Cf. *atura*².

258. **ඇතුළු ätuḷu, ඇතුල් ätul,** a., inner, inside. *ätuḷu-geya*, *ätul-geya* inner house, room; *ätuḷu-* or *ätul-nuvara* inner city, citadel. — P., Sk. *antara*. Cf. *atura*¹, *atara*.

— **ඇතොර ätora, ඇතොවුර ätovura,** s., see *atauruva*.

259. **ඇත්කන් ät-kan,** s., lit. elephant's ear, name of a tree = *gaskāla*, Butea frondosa. — Sk. *hasti-karṇa*.

260. **ඇත්ගොවුවා ät-govuvā,** s., st. f. °*vu*, elephant-keeper. — P. *hatthi-gōpaka*.

261. **ඇත්ත ätta,** s., fact, reality, truth. — P. *atthitta* (*atthitā*) existence.

— **ඇත්තා ättā,** s., see s.v. **äti**.

262. **ඇත්දත ät-data,** s., st. f. *-dat*, elephant's tusk, ivory. — Sk. *hasti-danta*.

263. **ඇත්හල ät-hala,** s., st. f. *-hal*, elephant-stable. — P. *hatthi-sālā*, Sk. *hasti-śālā*.

264. **ඇද äda, හැද häda,** a., oblique, crooked, s. (*h*)*ädaya*, (*h*)*äda-kama* crookedness; *äda-kuda* deflection(s), fault(s); *äda-näti* without crookedness, straight; *äda-karanavā* to make crooked, distort. — P. *sāci*(*-yōga*), Sk. *sāci*.

265. **ඇදහිල්ල ädahilla,** s., st. f. °*ili*, creed. — Nom. verb. of *adahanavā* q.v.

266. **ඇදිල්ල ädilla,** s., st. f. °*ili*, fingers or palms of the hands when joined. *ädili-baṅdinavā* to join the fingers or palms (for worship). — Pk., P., Sk. *añjali*; kśm. *anzal*, m. *oṃjaḷ*, oṛ. *āñjuḷī*, ass. *āṃzali*, bg. *āṃjlā*, h. *uñjal*, nep. *aṃjulo*, pj. *añjlī*.

267. **ඇදුර ädura,** s., rock. — Slw. Sk. *adri*, (P. *addi*).

268. **ඇදුරා ädurā,** s., st. f. °*ru*, teacher, instructor. *vaḍu-ädurā* master carpenter. — Pk. *āaria*, P. *ācariya*, Sk. *ācārya*.

269. **ඇඳ äňda, හැ° hä°**, s., bed, bedstead. — Pk. *sejjā*, P. *seyyā*, Sk. *śayyā*; si. *seja*, g. *sej*, m. *śej*, oṛ. *sesa*, ass. *xezā*, bg. *seṃj*, h. nep. pj. *sej*.

270. **ඇඳි äňdi**, a. pprt., painted, drawn. — P., Sk. *añjita*. Cf. *aňdinavā*.

— **ඇඳිරිය äňdiriya**, s., see *aňdura*.

271. **ඇප් äp**, a., small. — Pk., P. *appa*, Sk. *alpa*.

272. **ඇඹිල්ල äm̆billa**, s., st. f. °*ili*, generic name antidesma. *bū-äm̆billa* Antidesma ghesaembilla. — Pk. *ambiliyā*, Sk. *amlikā*, *āmlika* tamarind ; si. *āmiṛī*, g., *āmlī*, m. *āṃblī*, b. h. *imlī*, nep. *imli*, pj. *immlī*. The Sinh. name of the tamarind tree is *siyam̆balā*.

273. **ඇඹුල් äm̆bul[1]**, a., acid, sour. *äm̆bul-kesel* sour plantain; *ä°-doḍam* sour orange. *äm̆bula*, s., var. of water lily = *am̆bala* bog-bean. — Pk., P. *ambila*, Sk. *amla*; m. g. *āṃb* sort of vinegar.

274. **ඇඹුල් äm̆bul[2], ඇඹුළු äm̆buḷu**, s., the myrobalan tree, Phylanthus emblica. — Pk. *āmalaya*, P., Sk. *āmalaka* (cf. Sk. *āmla*); kśm. *ōmala*, si. *āṃuro*, g. *āmḷuṃ*, m. *āvḷā*, oṛ. *āṃaḷā*, bg. *āmlā*, h. *āṃvlā*, nep. *amalo*, *āmlo*, pj. *āṃulā*. Commonly called *nelli*. Cf. also Sinh. *buḷu*, n. of the beleric myrobalan.

275. **ඇම äma[1]**, s., bait. *äm-damanavā* to bait fish with bait. — P. *āmisa*, Sk. *āmiṣa*.

276. **ඇම äma[2], හැම häma, සැම säma**, a., all. *äma-kala* always. — Pk., P., Sk. *sama* ; Sk. *sama-kālam* at the same time.

277. **ඇමතියා ämatiyā**, s., st. f. *ämati*, minister of state. — The word is a blending of Sk. *amātya* = Pk., P. *amacca* and Sk. *mantrin* = P. *mantin*.

278. **ඇමියාව ämiyāva**, s., st. f. °*yā*, dyspepsia. — P., Sk. *āma* raw, undigested, *āmaya* sickness; kśm. *ōmu*, si. pj. *āṃuṃ*, g. ass. bg. *ām*, oṛ. *āma*, m. h. *āṃv*, nep. *āuṃ*. Also *amiyāva*.

279. **ඇර ära, හැර hära**, postp., except, besides. — ger. of *arinavā*.

— **ඇරඹ äraba, °ඹ °m̆ba**, postp., see **araba**.

280. **ඇල් äl, හැල් häl**, s., paddy grown on dry land, hill-paddy; *äl-vī* id., *äl-keta* hill-paddy field. — Pk., P. *sāli*, *sālikhetta*, Sk. *śāli* ; g. *sāliyuṃ*, *śāḷ*, m. *sāḷ*, h. *sālī*.

281. **ඇලෙනවා älenavā**, v., prt. *äluṇā*, to stick to, adhere to. — Pk. *allīṇa*, P. *allīyati*, *allīna*, Sk. *ā* + $\sqrt{}$*lī*, *ā-līyatē*, *ā-līna*.

282. **ඇල්ගොවුවා äl-govuvā**, s., st. f. °*vu*, one who looks after a field of hill-paddy; fem. *äl-gevī* woman who guards a hill-paddy field. —Sk. *śāli-gōpaka* (°*pikā*).

283. **ඇවැත ävät a**, s., st. f. *ävät*, offence, fault. — P., Sk. *āpatti*.

284. **ඇවෑම ävǟma**, s., demise, decease. *ävǟmen*, °*mehi*, postp., through the decease of, in succession, after. — P., Sk. *apagama*.

285. **ඇවිටි äviṭi, °ටු °ṭu,** a. pprt., entered, possessed (by a demon), mad. — Sk. *āviṣṭa*.

286. **ඇස äsa**[1], **ඇහැ ähä,** s., st. f. *äs, ähi,* eye. *äs-bäma, ähi-°* eyebrow, *äs-vedā* eye-doctor. — Pk. *acchi,* P. *acchi, akkhi,* Sk. *akṣi.* From *akkhi*: si. *akhi,* g. *āṃkh,* oṛ. ass. *ākhi,* bg. *āṃkhi,* h. *āṃkh,* nep. *āṃkho,* pj. l. *akkh.* From *acchi*: kśm. *achi,* kalāsā *ec, ech,* khowar *ec.* Sinh. agrees with the Dardic languages.

287. **ඇස äsa**[2], s., st. f. *äs,* tear. *äs-dahara, -dāra* tears. — Pk., P. *assu,* Sk. *aśru*; kśm. *ośu,* g. *āṃsu,* m. h. *āṃsū,* nep. *āṃsu.*

288. **ඇස්ගුළිය äs-guḷiya,** s., st. f. *°ḷi,* eyeball. — Sk. cf. *akṣi-gōla.*

289. **ඇස්බැඳුම äs-bäňduma,** s., st. f. *°ňdum,* jugglery, delusion. *äsbäňdum-karanavā* or *äs-baňdinavā,* to juggle, deceive. — Cf. Sk. *akṣi-bandha* (R. SCHMIDT Nachtr. z. Sk.-Wtb. s. v.).

290. **ඇස් රුදාව äs-rudāva,** s., st. f. *°dā,* ophthalmy. — Sk. *akṣi-ruj* (R. SCHMIDT s.v.)

291. **ඇස්වහ äs-vaha,** s., evil eye, envious eye. — Lit. eye-poison: *äsa*[1] + *vaha.*

— **ඇහැ ähä,** s., see s. v. **äsa**[1].

292. **ඇහැටු ähäṭu, ඇසටු äsaṭu, ඇසතු äsatu,** s., name of a tree = *eḷa-nuga* (Ca) Ficus tsiela. — P. *assattha,* Sk. *aśvattha* Ficus religiosa.

293. **ඇහැළ ähäḷa, ඇසළ äsaḷa,** s., name of a month = *ä°-masa.* — Pk. *āsāḍha,* P. *āsāḷha,* Sk. *āṣāḍha*; kśm. *hār,* si. *hāṛu,* ass. *āhār,* bg. *āṣāṛ,* h. *asāṛh,* nep. *asār, asārh,* pj. *hāṛh,* l. *hāhṛ.*

294. **ඇළ äḷa,** s., water-course, channel; canal. — Pk., P., Sk. *āli* line, dike, embankment; m. *āl,* oṛ. *āḷī,* ass. bg. *āli,* h. *ālī,* nep. *āli.* The spelling with *ḷ* of *äḷa* is confirmed by inscs. EpZ I 33[21], 10th c., BELL p. 79, A[8], 14th c.

ඈ Ā̈

295. **ඈ ā̈**[1], a., first, foremost. *-ā̈,* in cpds., such-like, et cetera; *ā̈y* EpZ I 92 A[78], 10th c. — Pk. *āi,* P., Sk. *ādi.*

296. **ඈ ā̈**[2], pron. pers. 3. sg. f., she. — Probably <**eyi*; see s.v. *ē.*

297. **ඈපා ā̈pā,** s., prince of the royal house, frequently in mediaeval inscs. — P. *ādipāda,* Mhvs 53-4 etc. — PARANAVITANA, EpZ III 82, suggests that *ā̈* in *ā̈pā* is = Sinh. Pk. *aya,* Sk. *ārya.* Hardly plausible. Cf. *aya*[2] and *mahayā* s.v. *maha.*

ඉ I

298. **ඉ i-**[1], prefix = Pk. *aï-,* P., Sk. *ati-.* Cf. *ipiṇī* DhpAGp 34[17] = P. *ati-paṇītaṃ.* See below *i-kut, i-kmana, i-vat.*

299. ඉ **i-²**, prefix=Pk. *ahi-*, P., Sk. *adhi-*. See below *i-ṭana, i-vasanavā*.

— ඉක් **ik,** see **uk.**

— ඉකන **ikana,** s., see s.v. **ebikana.**

— ඉකිණි **ikiṇī,** s., see **ukuṇā**.

300. ඉකිලිය **ikiliya,** s., st. f. *°li,* vessel. — Pk. *okkhala* (Hem. 2.90), P. *ukkhali*; kśm. *vökhul*, si. *ukhirī*, g. m. *ukhaḷ*, h. *ūkhal*, *ūkhar*, *ūkhlī*, *okhlī*, nep. *okhli*, *ukhli*, pj. *ukkhal*, l. *ukhlī*.

301. ඉකුත් **ikut,** a. pprt., surpassed, past, transpired. *ikut-däya* former existence. *ikut-venavā* to pass away, die. — Pk. *aïkkanta*, P. *atikkanta*, Sk. *atikrānta*.

302. ඉක්බිති **ikbiti,** adv., thereafter, then. In inscs. also *ekbitten*, EpZ I 197B¹², 10th c., and *ekbittehi*, ib. II 271³³, 12th c. *ikbiti-venavā* to succeed, follow. — Sk. *ēka* + *bhitti* having one (the same) wall, immediate neighbour [HSm]. Cf. DhpAGp 28¹ where *ikbiti* is trsl. of P. *paṭivissaka* neighbour.

303. ඉක්මන **ikmana,** s., st. f. *°man*, celerity, speed. *ikman-karanavā* or *-venavā* to hasten. — P. *atikkamana*, Sk. *atikramaṇa*.

304. ඉක්මෙනවා **ikmenavā,** v., prt. *ikmuṇā*, to pass away, expire (as time). — Pk. *aïkkamaï*, P. *atikkamati*, Sk. *ati-* + $\sqrt{}$*kram*, *ati-krāmati*.

— ඉගු **igu,** ඉඟු **iṅgu,** s., see **uk.**

305. ඉඟිය **iṅgiya,** s., st. f. *iṅgi*, hint, wink. *iṅgi-karanavā* to wink. — Pk. *iṅgia*, P., Sk. *iṅgita*. Also Sinh. *hiṅgiya* with inorganic *h*.

306. ඉඟුරු **iṅguru,** හි° **hi°,** සි° **si°,** s., st. f. *°ru*, ginger. — P. *siṅgivēra*, Sk. *śṛṅgavēra*.

307. ඉඟුල් **iṅgul,** හි° **hi°,** s., st. f. *°gul*, vermillion, red-lead. — P. *hiṅguli*, *°laka*, Sk. *hiṅgula*, *°li*, *°lu*, *°lāka*; si. *hiṃgulū*, g. *hiṃglo*, m. *hiṃgūḷ*, bg. *hiṃgūl*, h. *hiṃgul*.

308. ඉටන **iṭana,** s., st. f. *iṭan*, determination, resolve. — P. *adhiṭṭhāna*, Sk. *adhiṣṭhāna*.

309. ඉටනවා **iṭanavā,** v., prt. *iṭuvā*, to determine, resolve. — Pk. *adhiṭṭhāti*, *°ṭṭhahati*, Sk. *adhi-* + $\sqrt{}$ *sthā*.

310. ඉටි **iṭi,** හිටි **hiṭi,** s., wax. — On account of the spelling with *ṭ* the word cannot be compared with P. *sittha*, Sk. *sikha*. It is = Sk. *śiṣṭa* in *madhu-śiṣṭa* wax. Cf. P. *madhucchiṭṭha*, Sk. *madhûcchiṣṭa*.

311. ඉටු **iṭu,** a. pprt., desired, auspicious. Cf. *an-iṭu*. — Pk., P. *iṭṭha*, Sk. *iṣṭa*.

312. ඉට්ටම **iṭṭama,** s., st. f. *iṭṭam*, emancipation, liberation. — < * *iṭuyama* < * *iṭu-kama*.

313. ඉණි මග **iṇi-maga,** හි° **hi°,** s., st. f. *°maṃ*, ladder. — *iṇi* = Pk., P. *sēṇi*, *°ṇī*, Sk. *śrēṇi*, *°ṇī*; kśm. *hēr*, g. *sīḍī*, m. *śiḍhī*, *śiḍī*, oṛ. *siṛhi*, bg. *siṃṛi*, b. h. pj. *sīṛhī*, nep. *siṃṛi*, *siṃṛhi*, + *maga*.

314. **ඉතිරි itiri**[1], **ඉතුරු ituru,** a., remaining, surplus, residual. *it°-karanavā* to reserve, save; *it°-venavā* to be left over, to remain. — Pk., P., Sk. *uttara*. Cf. *uturanavā*.

315. **ඉතිරි itiri**[2], s., woman, wife. — Slw. Sk. *strī* (Pk., P. *thī*, *itthī*); kśm. *triy*, ass. *tiri*, h. *triyā*, nep. *tiriyā*, pj. *tiryā*.

316. **ඉද ida, හිද hida,** s., st. f. *(h)idi*, needle; *idi-katuva* id. — Pk. *sūī*, P., Sk. *sūci*; kśm. *suva*, g. *soy*, m. *suī*, *sū*, bg. *suṃ*, *sūc*, *chūṃc*, b. h. pj. *sūī*, nep. *siyo*. Sinh. *hiňduva* porcupine quill is perhaps the same word + *-ka* with spontaneous nazalisation. The first syllable of *ittǟvā* porcupine, hedgehog, seems also to contain the stem *idi*.

317. **ඉදි idi**[1], **ඉදු idu**[1], **උදු udu,** a., straight. — Pk. AMg. Ś. *ujju*, P *uju*, *ujuka*, *ujju*, Sk. *ṛju*; m. *ujū*.

318. **ඉදි idi**[2], **ඉදු idu**[2], s., power, superhuman power. — Pk. AMg. JM. *iḍḍhi*, *riddhi* (Pischel, Pk. § 57), P. *iddhi*, Sk. *ṛddhi*.

319. **ඉදි කරනවා idi-karanavā,** v., to make, construct. *behedak idi-k°* to make a medicine (by mixing), SdhRv. 44^{27}. — *idi* = Pk., P., Sk. *siddha*; si. *sido* cooked, m. *śidhā*, bg. *sidhā*, b. h. *sīdhā*; nep. *sidro*, *sīdhro*, + *karanavā*.

320. **ඉදිමෙනවා idimenavā,** v., prt. *idimuṇā*, to swell, become bloated. — Pk. *uddhumāï* (Hem 4-8); P. *uddhumāyati*, Sk. *ud-* + √*dhmā* (*dhmāyatē*, °*ti*).

— **ඉදු idu**[1,2], see **idi**[1,2].

321. **ඉදෙනවා idenavā,** v., prt. *iduṇā*, to ripen, mature. — (Pk. *rijjhaï*) P. *ijjhati*, Sk. √*ṛdh*, *ṛdhyatē*; (pj. *rijjhṇā* to be cooked; cf. T s.v. *rijhinu*).

322. **ඉදොලුව idoluva, හි° hi°,** s., st. f. °*lu*, palanquin, sedan. — Sk. *hin-dōla-ka* swing.

— **ඉඳගොවුවා iňdagovuvā,** s., see **iňdug°**.

323. **ඉඳි iňdi-** in *iňdi-gaha*, n. of a tree, date-tree, Phoenix Zeylanica. — m. *śiṃd*.

324. **ඉඳිනවා iňdinavā, හි° hi°, ඉන්නවා innavā,** v., prt. *(h)unnā*, to sit; to be, exist (of animates). Caus. *(h)iňduvanavā*, prt. *(h)iňdevuvā*, to cause to sit, to plant. — Pk. *sīaï*, P. *sīdati*, Sk. √*sad*, *sīdati*. Cf. *un*.

325. **ඉඳු iňdu**[1], s., moon; camphor. — P., Sk. *indu* (with both meanings).

326. **ඉඳු iňdu**[2], s., the god Indra; *-iňdu* in cpds. eminent, lord, master, chief. — Pk., P. *inda*, Sk. *indra*. Sinh. *iňduru* is a Slw. Sk.

327. **ඉඳුකිලය iňdu-kilaya,** s., st. f. °*la*, threshold. — P. *inda-khīla*, Sk. *indra-kīla* Mahāvastu II 396^3.

328. **ඉඳුගොවුවා iňdu-govuvā, ඉඳ° iňda°,** s., st. f. °*vu*, a red worm that issues out of the ground after rain. — P. *inda-gōpaka*, Sk. *indra-gōpa-ka*.

329. ඉඳුදැල **iňdu-däla,** s., st. f. *°däl,* j u g g l e r y (lit. Indra's net).— Pk. *indajāla,* Sk. *indra-jāla.* The Slw. *iňduru-däliyā* juggler corresponds to P. *indajālika.*

330. ඉඳුදද **iňdu-dada,** s. r a i n b o w (lit. Indra's flag). — Sk. *indra-dhvaja.*

331. ඉඳුදුන්න **iňdu-dunna,** s., st. f. *°nu,* r a i n b o w (lit. Indra's bow). — P. *inda-dhanu,* Sk. *indra-dhanu.*

332. ඉඳුනිල් **iňdu-nil,** s., s a p p h i r e. — P. *inda-nīla,* Sk. *indra-nīla.*

333. ඉඳුපුත් **iňdu-put,** s., t h e p l a n e t M e r c u r y (lit. son of the moon, *iňdu*[1]). — Sk. *indu-putra.*

334. ඉඳුර **iňdura,** s., st. f. *°ru,* v i r i l e p o w e r, p o w e r o f s e n s e s. — Slw. Sk. *indriya.*

335. ඉඳුවර **iňduvara,** s., b l u e l o t u s. — Sk. *indīvara.*

336. ඉඳුසැව් **iňdu-säv,** s., r a i n b o w (lit. Indra's bow). — Sk. *indra-cāpa.*

— ඉපල් **ipal,** ඉපුල් **ipul,** s., see **upul.**

337. ඉපිල්ල **ipilla,** s., f l o a t; o u t r i g g e r of a canoe. — <**ipiluva* = Sk. *up-lavā* canoe. Cf. *upulvanavā.*

338. ඉබ **iba,** s., e l e p h a n t. — P., Sk. *ibha.*

339. ඉඹිනවා **im̆binavā,** සි° **si°,** v., prt. *(s)imbā,* t o s m e l l a t, k i s s. — Pk. *cumbaï,* P., Sk. *cumbati;* kśm. *cumun,* si. *cumaṇu,* g. *cumvuṃ, çumbvuṃ,* m. *cumṇeṃ, cuṃbṇeṃ,* oṛ. *cumbibā,* ass. *sumiba,* h. *cūmnā,* pj. *cummṇā,* l. *cummaṇ.* T s.v. *cummā.*

340. ඉඹුල් **im̆bul,** s., s i l k c o t t o n t r e e, Bombax malabaricum. —Pk. *simbali,* P. *simbalī, °la,* ved. *śimbala* (Pischel, Pk. § 109); g. *simḷo,* m. *śeṃvrī* oṛ. *simiḷi, simuḷi,* ass. *ximalu,* h. *seṃbal, semal,* nep. *simal,* pj. *simbal, simmal.* Gr. 49.403, 50.14.

341. ඉම **ima,** හිම **hima,** සිම **sima,** s., st. ff. *im, him, sim,* b o u n d a r y. *im-kaṇuva, im-ṭäm̆ba* boundary post; *kaḍa-ima* boundary of a district; *im-gahanavā* to mark a boundary. — Pk., P., Sk. *sīmā;* si. *sīaṃ,* g. *sīm,* m. *śīv,* h. *sīṃv,* nep. *simānā, siṃvānā,* pj. *sīṃ, sīvāṃ,* l. *sīṃ.*

342. ඉය **iya,** හිය **hiya,** also *(h)īya,* s., st. f. *(h)ī,* a r r o w. *(h)ī-gaha* id., *(h)ī-tala* arrow-head. — Sk. *śita* sharp (arrow in Wilson and Apte).

343. ඉර **ira**[1]**,** හිර **hira**[1]**,** s., st. f. *(h)iri,* l i n e, s t r e a k. — ? = P., Sk. *cīra,* or (with HSm) from Sk. √*si,* connected with *sīra* plough, *sītā* furrow, *sīmā* boundary.

344. ඉර **ira**[2]**,** හිර **hira**[2]**,** s., st. ff. *(h)iri, (h)iru, (h)ira,* s u n. *iri-dā, iru-dina* Sunday; *iri-udē* (Sk. *sūryôdaya*) sunrise; *hira-baṭu* sunset; *iru-räs* (Sk. *sūrya-raśmi*) sunbeam. — (Pk. *sujja, suyya*), P. *suriya,* Sk. *sūrya.*

345. ඉරියවුව **iriyavuva,** s., a t t i t u d e, p o s i t i o n of the body. — P. *iriyā-patha,* Sk. (Buddh.) *iryāpatha.*

— ඉල් **il,** a., c o l d, see s.v. **hil.**

346. ඉවත් **ivat,** a., distant, remote; *ivata* or *ivata-ṭa* aside, off, out of the way; *ivata-lanavā* to cast away; *ivat-venavā* to depart. — Sk. *ativṛtta, ati-* + √*vṛt,* P. *ati-vattati.*

347. ඉවසනවා **ivasanavā,** v., prt. *ivasuvā,* to endure patiently, tolerate. — P. *adhi-vāsēti,* Sk. *adhi-* + √*vas,* caus. *adhi-vāsayati.*

348. ඉස **isa,** ඉසිය **isiya,** ඉසාව **isāva,** s., st. ff. *isa, isi, isu,* envy, jealousy. *isi-bada* envious, lit. bounded by envy. — Pk. *īsā,* P. *issā,* Sk. *īrṣyā.*

349. ඉසිය **isiya,** s., st. f. *isi,* wish, desire.— Pk. *icchia,* P., Sk. *icchita*; cf. Pk., P., Sk. *icchā.*

350. ඉසුර **isura,** s., st. f. *isuru,* splendour, wealth. — P. *issariya, issēra,* Sk. *aiśvarya.*

351. ඉසුරා **isurā,** s., st. f. *isuru,* lord, ruler, chief. — Pk. *īsara,* P. *issara,* Sk. *īśvara.*

352. ඉස්කබල **is-kabala,** s., st. f. °*bal,* skull, cranium. — *iha* + *k*°; Sk. *śīrṣa-kapāla.*

353. ඉස්බ **isba,** ඉසුබුව **isubuva,** s., st. ff. *isba, isubu,* a measure of length (70 yards). — P. *usabha.*

354. ඉස්වැටිය **is-väṭiya,** s., st. f. °*ṭi,* turban. — *iha* + *paṭa* + *-ka*; Sk. *śīrṣa-paṭṭaka.*

355. ඉස්සා **issā,** ඉසියා **isiyā,** s., st. ff. *isi, ihi,* shrimp, prawn. — Sk. *iñcāka.*

356. ඉහ **iha,** ඉස **isa,** s., st. ff. *isa, is, his, sis,* head; *ihata* (cf. *ata*[1]), a., adv., preceding, above. *isa-kē* hair, *is-muduna* top of the head &c. — Pk. *sīsa, sissa,* P. *sīsa,* Sk. *śīrṣa*; si. *sīsu,* g. *śīś,* m. *śīs,* h. pj. *sīs*; väddā *īca, isi, iya,* mald. *is.*

357. ඉහළ **ihaḷa,** a., adv., upper; above, aloft. *ihaḷa-pahaḷa* upper and lower, above and below. — < MInd. **ati-haṭa* + *pa-haṭa* (thus P.), Sk. *atihṛta, prahṛta.* Doubtful.

— ඉහි **ihi**[1], s., see s.v. **issā.**

358. ඉහි **ihi**[2], ඉසි **isi,** s., a sage. — Pk. *isi* (or *risi*), P. *isi,* Sk. *ṛṣi.*

359. ඉහි **ihi**[3], postp., with, along with. *siyan-ihi* with the relations, SälS 1. — Pk. *sahia,* P., Sk. *sahita.*

360. ඉහිනවා **ihinavā,** ඉසිනවා **isinavā,** v., prt. *issā,* to sprinkle, scatter about. Intr. *ihenavā,* prt. *ihuṇā,* to become sprinkled. — Pk. *siñcaï,* P., Sk. *siñcati*; g. *siṃcvuṃ,* m. *śiṃcṇeṃ,* ass. *xiṃsiba, xisiba,* h. *sīṃcnā,* nep. *siṃcnu,* pj. *siñjṇā.*

361. ඉහිරෙනවා **ihirenavā,** ඉසි° **isi°,** v., prt. *ihiruṇā, isi*°, to be scattered about, spilt. Caus. *ihiravanavā,* prt. *ihirevuvā,* to scatter about. — The base-v. would be **uhuranavā* or **ihi*° = Sk. *ud-* + √*sṛ,* caus. *ut-sārayati,* MInd. **ussārēti.*

362. **ඉහිල් ihil, ලිහිල් lihil, ලීල් līl,** a., soft, loose, slack, simple. *lihil--karanavā* to loosen, relax, simplify. — (Pk. *siḍhila, saḍhila,* PISCHEL, Pk. § 115), P. *sithila,* Sk. *śithila.* Cf. T s.v. *ḍhilo.* The formation of *lihil* seems to be influenced by *luhu.*

ඊ Ī

— **ඊ ī[1],** pron. dem., see **ē.**

— **ඊ ī[2], හී hī,** s., see **iya.**

363. **ඊයේ iyē,** adv., yesterday. — Pk. *hiō, hijjō,* P. *hīyō, hiyyō,* Sk. *hyas*; nep. *hijo, hiju.* Cf. T s.v.

— **ඊරි īri,** s., see s.v. **ūrā.**

උ U

364. **උක් uk, ඉක් ik, උගු ugu, ඉඟු iṅgu,** s., sugar-cane. *uk-gaha, uk--daṇḍa* id.; *uk-päṇi* or *-rasa* sugar-cane juice, molasses; *uk-mōla* sugar-mill. — Pk. *ikkhu* (and *ucchu,* P. *ucchu*), Sk. *ikṣu*; or. *ākhu,* bg. *ukh, ākh,* h. *ūkh, īkh,* nep. *ukhu,* pj. *ikkh* < MInd. **ukkhu, ikkhu*; but g. m. *ūs,* mald. *us* < *ucchu.*

365. **උකට ukaṭa,** s., eminence. — P. *ukkaṭṭha,* Sk. *utkṛṣṭa.*

366. **උකටලි ukaṭali,** a., apathetic, discouraged; s. *ukaṭaliya* apathy, reluctance. — Cf. Pk. *ukkaṇṭhā* (P. *ukkaṇṭhati*), Sk. *utkaṇṭhā* (*utkaṇṭhati*) + suff. *-li.*

367. **උකනවා ukanavā[1],** v., prt. *ikuvā,* to raise. — *ukana-* stands for **ukāna* < **ukahana-*. This is shown by the ger. *ukahā* (alternating with *ukā*). The v. is therefore derived from P. *ukkaṃsēti,* Sk. *ud-* + √*kṛṣ.,* caus. *ut-karṣayati*; g. *ukāṃsvuṃ,* m. *ukasṇeṃ,* h. *uksānā,* nep. *ukāsnu,* pj. *ukāsṇā.*

368. **උකණවා ukaṇavā[2],** v., prt. *ikuvā,* to pick up, scoop out. — This v. is to be separated from the preceding one. It is = Sk. *ud-* + √*khan, ut-khanati,* MInd. **ukkhanati.* We expect the prs. st. **ukani-(navā),* but to explain *uka-navā* we must start from the prt. st. *iku* which is the correct derivate of Sk. *utkhāta* and from which a new prs. st. has been formed after the proportion (*uka-*) : *iku-* = *puda-* : *pidu-*. The process is the same as in v. *ahanavā* q. v. Cf. also *unanavā.*

369. **උකහ ukaha, °ස °sa,** s., st. f. *ukas,* pledge, pawn, security. *ukas--karanavā* or *-tabanavā* to pledge; *ukas-gannavā* to take as a pledge. — Formally = P. *ukkaṃsa,* Sk. *utkarṣa.* Semasiologically difficult.

370. **උකුණා ukuṇā,** s., st. f. °*ṇu,* louse; fem. *ikiṇī.* — Sk. *utkuṇa* (in kōśas). Cf. *makuṇā.*

371. **උකුස්සා ukussā,** s., st. f. °*su,* kite, hawk. — P. *ukkusa,* Sk. *utkrōśa* + *-ka.*

372. උකුල **ukuḷa,** s., st. f. *°ḷu, ukul,* hip, lap. *ukul-äṭaya* hip-bone. — Sk. *utkaṭa* ; cf. *utkaṭuka* or *utkuṭaka* sitting on the hams = P. *ukkuṭika* ; m. *ukaḍ, ukḍā, ukiḍvā, ukuḍvā.*

373. උගත් **ugat,** a. pprt., learned ; s. *ugatā* learned person, scholar. — < **ud-ghṛpta* (see s.v. *gat*). Cf. *ugannavā.*

374. උගන්නවා **ugannavā,** v., prt. *ugattā,* to learn. Caus. *uganvanavā,* prt. *igännuvā,* to teach. — P. *ugganhāti,* Sk. *ud-* + *√gṛh, ud-gṛhṇāti.* Cf. h. *ugāhnā* < Pk. *uggāhēi,* Sk. *ud-grāhayati.*

375. උගුර **ugura,** s., st. f. *uguru,* throat, gorge. *ugurak* a mouthful ; *uguru-äṭaya* throat nut, adam's apple. — P. *uggāra* spitting out, Sk. *udgāra.* Cf. Bl s.v. *ugaḷnem* to vomit, T s.v. *ugelnu* id. Divergent meaning in Sinh.

376. උගුළනවා **uguḷanavā,** v., prt. *igiḷuvā,* to root up. Caus. *uguḷuvanavā, ugullanavā,* prt. *igilluvā,* to cause to root up ; intr. *igiḷenavā,* prt. *igiḷuṇā,* to be uprooted. — P. *ugghāṭēti* (cf. Sinh. *sīmā uguḷan-ṭa* = P. *sīmaṃ ugghāṭētuṃ*), Sk. *ud* + *√ghaṭ,* caus. *ud-ghāṭayati.*

377. උඩඟු **uḍaṅgu,** a., haughty, proud, arrogant. — < MInd. **uḍḍhaṃga* ; cf. Sk. *ūrdhvaga* going upwards, P. *uddhaṃgama* id.

378. උඩනු **uḍanu,** a., long shanked ; s. *uḍanuvā* long shanked person. — <*uḍu* + *dana* + *-ka* ; Sk. *ūrdhva-jānu.*

379. උඩු **uḍu,** a., high, higher, upper. *uḍa, uḍaṭa,* adv. postp., upwards, up, upon ; *uḍin,* adv. postp., higher, over ; *uḍat, uḍu-ataṭa* (cf. *ata*[1]), adv., higher, upper. — Pk. *uḍḍha, uddha,* (*ubbha*), P. *uddha,* (*ubbha*), Sk. *ūrdhva.* The corresponding words in the MIAVs, except perhaps kśm. *vod* upper part of the head, are derived from *ubbha* : si. *ubho,* g. *ūbhuṃ,* m. oṛ. *ubhā,* bg. *ubi,* nep. *umbho,* pj. *ūbh,* l. *ubbhā.*

380. උඩුමුව **uḍu-muva,** a., with face or mouth upward. — P. *uddha-mukha.* Sk. *ūrdhva-mukha.*

381. උණු **uṇu,** a., hot ; s. *uṇa* fever. — Pk., P. *uṇha,* Sk. *uṣṇa* ; g. *ūnuṃ,* m. *ūn.* Sinh. also *huṇu* with inorganic *h.*

— උණුලොම් **uṇu-lom,** s., see **unu-lom.**

382. උණුහුම **uṇuhuma,** උණුසුම **uṇusuma,** s., heat. — Probably *uṇuhuma* for **uṇuyama* < *uṇu* + *kama*[1] (q. v.) ; *uṇusuma* by false analogy.

383. උතුම් **utum,** a., high, excellent ; s. *utumā* excellent person, gentleman. — Pk., P., Sk. *uttama.*

384. උතුරනවා **uturanavā,** v., prt. *itiruvā,* to overflow, run over. Caus. *uturavanavā,* prt. *itirevuvā,* to cause to overflow ; intr. *itirenavā,* prt. *itiruṇā,* to overflow. — Pk. *uttaraï,* P. *uttarati,* Sk. *ud-* + *√tṛ, ut-tarati* ; g. *utarvuṃ,* m. *utarṇem,* oṛ. *uturibā,* bg. *utrā,* h. *utarnā,* nep. *utranu,* pj. *uttarṇā.* Cf. *itiri*[1].

385. උතුරු **uturu,** a., superior, exalted; northern; s. *utura* the north ; *uturu-diga* id. — Pk., P., Sk. *uttara* ; si. *utaru* north, m. *utrān* north wind.

— උතුරු පසතුරු **uturu-pasaturu,** s., see s.v. **pasutura.**

386. උදැල්ල **udälla,** s., st. f. *udalu*, a kind of hoe.— Pk., P., Sk. *kuddāla* ; m. *kudāḷ*, b. *kudār*, h. *kudāl*, pj. *kudāl(ā)*. Pk. also *koddāla* = ass. bg. *kodāl* etc. (T s.v. *kodālo*). The dropping of the initial *k* is perhaps caused by a confusion of the two tree-names *uddāla* Cassia fistula and *kuddāla* Bauhinia variegata.

— උදු **udu,** a., see s.v. **idi**[1].

387. උදුන **uduna,** s., st. f. *udun*, oven, furnace. — P. *uddhana*, Sk. *uddhāna*, *uddhmāna* ; nep. *odhān*, *vadhān*, *odān*.

388. උදුරනවා **uduranavā,** v., prt. *idiruvā*, to pluck up (or out). Intr. *idirenavā*, prt. *idiruṇā*, to become uprooted. — P. *uddharati*, Sk. *ud-* + √*dhṛ*, *ud-dharati* ; nep. *udhranu*. Cf. **T** s.v.

389. උදුල් **udul,** a., bright, brilliant, shining; s. *uduḷa* brightness. Also *dulu*, *dula*. Cf. de Lanerolle, DSL p. xliv, § 15 b. — P. *ujjala*, Sk. *ujjvala* ; si. *ujāro*, m. *ujḷā*, *ujaḷ*, h. pj. *ujālā*, nep. *ujyālo*. Gr. 50. 26.

390. උදෙසා **udesā,** postp., for, on behalf of. — ger. of *udesanavā*. Cf. Pk., P. *uddissa*, Sk. *uddiśya*.

391. උදෙසනවා **udesanavā,** v., prt. *udesuvā*, to enunciate, declare. — Sk. *ud-* + √*diś*, (*ud-diśati*). Caus **uddēśayati*, P. **uddēsēti*.

392. උඳුරා **uñdurā,** උදුරා **udurā,** s., st. f. °*ru*, rat. — P., Sk. *undura* ; g. *undar*, m. *uṃdar*, (h. *indūr*).

393. උන් **un,** හුන් **hun,** a. pprt., seated; who was or were seated. (*h*)*un-asna* the seat one was occupying. — Pk., P., Sk. *sanna*. Cf. *iñdinavā*.

394. උනනවා **unanavā,** v., prt. *inuvā*, to spring, well up. Intr. *inenavā*, prt. *inuṇā* id. — Sk. √*ud*, *unatti*, *undati*. The prt. st. *inu-* is the regular derivate of P., Sk. *unna* ; the prs. st. *una-* is a new formation (cf. s. v. *ahanavā*, *ukanavā*[2]).

395. උනන්දු **unandu,** a. pprt., active, lively. *unandu-karanavā* to rouse to activity. — < **unañddu* < **unañdiya* = Sk. *unnandita*, *ud-* + √*nand*, cheered, enlivened.

396. උනු **unu,** a., imperfect, deficient. Cf. *unu-vissa* nineteen. — Pk. *ūṇa*, *ēg-ūṇa-vīsaṃ*, P. *ūnaka*, *ūna*, *ēk-ūna-vīsaṃ*, Sk. *ūnaka*, *ūna*, *ēkôna-viṃśati* ; cf. si. *ūṇīha* 19, g. *ogṇīs*, m. *ekuṇīs*, oṛ. *ūṇāiśa*, bg. *ūniś*, h. *unīs*, nep. *unais* or *unāis*, pj. l. *unnī*, mald. *ona-vihi*.

397. උනු ලොම් **unu-lom,** s., hair between the eyebrows. — *unu* = P. *uṇṇā*, Sk. *ūrṇā* ; kśm. *vōna*, si. *una*, g. h. *ūn*, nep. *un* + *lom* q.v. — Ca spells *uṇu*°, which, I think, is incorrect.

— උන්නාන්සේ **unnānsē,** honorific, see s.v. **vahansē.**

398. උපත **upata,** s., st. f. *upat*, birth, origin. — Pk., P. *uppatti*, Sk. *utpatti* ; si. nep. *upati*.

399. උපදිනවා **upadinavā,** v., prt. *upannā*, to be born or originated; to arise. Caus. *upadavanavā*, *upaddanavā*, prt. *ipädduvā*, to breed, produce, cause ; intr. *ipadenavā*, prt. *ipaduṇā*, to be born. — Pk. *uppajjaï*, P. *uppajjati*, Sk. *ud-* + √*pad*, *ut-padyatē* ; si. *upajaṇu*, g. *upajvuṃ*, m. *upajṇeṃ*, ass. *opaziba*, bg. *upajā*, h. *upajnā*, nep. *ubjanu*, pj. *upajṇā*.

400. උපන් **upan,** a., pprt., born. — Pk. *uppaṇṇa*, P. *uppanna*, Sk. *utpanna* ; kśm. *vopanun*, si. *upano* (T).

401. උපයනවා **upayanavā,** v., prt. *ipayuvā*, to procure, provide, furnish. — P. *uppādēti*, Sk. *ut-pādayati*. Cf. *sapayanavā*.

402. උපුරනවා **upuranavā,** v., prt. *ipiruvā*, to pluck up, uproot. Caus. *upuravanavā* id. — P. *uppāṭēti*, Sk. *ud-* + √*paṭ*, caus. *ut-pāṭayati* ; si. *upaṭṇu*, g. *upaḍvuṃ*, m. *upaṭṇeṃ*, h. *upaṭnā*. Sinh. has also *upuḷanavā*, which must be derived from MInd- **uppaṭṭēti*. In DhpAGp 22[10] we come across *upuḷanavā* which seems to be more archaic than *upur°*.

403. උපුල **upula,** ඉපුල **ipula,** s., st. f. *°ul*, blue lotus. — Pk., P. *uppala*, Sk. *utpala*.

404. උපුල්වනවා **upulvanavā,** v., prt. *ipilluvā*, to raise, lift up. Caus. *upullavanavā*, prt. *ipillevuvā* id. ; intr. *ipilenavā*, *ipillenavā*, prt. *ipiluṇā*, *ipilluṇā*, to float, rise to the surface, bubble up. — Sk. *ud-* + √*plu*, *plavati*, **utplavati*, caus. **utplāvayati* ; cf. P. *pilavati* swims, floats, *uppilavati*, *uplavati* rises, jumps up ; caus. **uppilāvēti* or **uppilavāpēti*.

405. උඹ **uṁba,** ඔබ **oba,** pron. pers. 2. pl., you. I believe that *uṁba* stands for **yuṁba* < **yumha* = Sk. *yuṣma-*. In Pk. *tubbhē* alternates with *tumhē* ; thus we may suppose that **yubbha* alternates with **yumha*. From this **yubbha* is derived Sinh. *oba* which is used as a more respectful form of address than *uṁba*.

406. උමඟ **umaga,** s., st. f. *umaṃ* (i.e. *umaṅ*), underground canal, tunnel. *umaṃ-kaninavā* to break into (a house). — Pk., P. *ummagga*, Sk. *unmārga*.

407. උමතු **umatu,** a., mad, insane; s. *°tuva* madness. — Pk., P. *ummatta*, Sk. *unmatta*.

408. උමාව **umāva,** s., st. f. *umā*, wave. — Pk. AMg. *ummi*, P. *ūmi*, Sk. *ūrmi*, *ūrmikā*.

409. උමු **umu,** a., having the face upwards, looking up; facing forward; s. *umuva* presence. — Pk. *ummuha*, P. *ummukha*, Sk. *unmukha*,

410. උයන **uyana,** s., st. f. *uyan*, garden. *uyan-govuvā* gardener. — Pk. *ujjāṇa*, P. *uyyāna*, Sk. *udyāna*.

411. **උයනවා uyanavā, හු° hu°**, v., prt. *(h)ivuvā*, to cook. *uyana-geya* kitchen; *uyannā* cook. — Sk. √*sūd*, *sūdatē*. Cf. Pk. *sūya* cook, P., Sk. *sūda*, *sūdana*.

412. **උරදා uradā**, s., son. — *uraya* + *dā* = Sk. *jāta*. Cf. P. *ōrasa*, Sk. *aurasa*.

413. **උරය uraya, ඔරය oraya**, s., st. ff. *ura*, *ora*, breast, bosom, shoulder. *ura-(h)isa* top of shoulders. — Pk., P. *ura*, Sk. *uras*.

414. **උරා urā**, s., snake. In cpds. also *ura*: *ura* (or *urā*)-*rupu* snake-enemy, the Garuḍa bird. — P., Sk. *uraga*.

415. **උරිර urira, හු° hu°**, s., st. f. *(h)uriru*, blood. — Metathesis of **ruhira*. Cf. *rihiri*.

416. **උරුව uruva**, s., st. f. *uru*, thigh. — Pk., P., Sk. *ūru*.

417. **උල ula, හුල hula, සුල sula**, s., st. ff. *ul*, *hul*, *sul*, point of a dart &c., spike, stake. *ul-kaṭuva* stylus for writing; *ul-kota* pointed tower or turret, spire; *ula-tabanavā* to impale. Pk., P. *sūla*, Sk. *śūla*; g. *sūḷ*, *śūḷ*, m. *sūḷ*, h. pj. *sūl*.

418. **උලඞ්ගිය ulaṅgiya, උලාඞ්ගිය ulāṅgiya**, s., st. ff. °*ṅgi*, rising, ascending; going beyond, transgressing. — <MInd. *ullaṅghita*. Cf. Pk. *ullaṅghēï*, P. *ullaṅghēti*, °*ṅghita*; Sk. *ud-* + √*laṅgh*, *ullaṅghayati*, °*ṅghita*; kśm. *volaṅgun*, si. *oraṅgha*, g. *ulaghvuṃ*, h. *ulāṃgnā*, nep. *ulāṃghnu*, pj. *ulanghaṇā*, l. *ulagghan*.

— **උළරු uḷaru**, a., see **oḷaru**.

419. **උලෙල ulela**, s., whirling in the water, wave; commotion. — P., Sk. *ullōla*; cf. Pk. *ullōlaï* rolls.

420. **උව- uva-**, prefix = Pk. *uva-*, P., Sk. *upa-*. See the following words. Cf. also *va-*[3].

421. **උවටන uvaṭana, °ටාන, °ṭāna**, s., st. ff. °*ṭan*, °*ṭän*, ministration, attendance. — Pk. *uvaṭṭhāṇa*, P. *upaṭṭhāna*, Sk. *upasthāna*. Cf. Bl s. v. *vaṭhāṇ*, T s. v. *bathān*.

422. **උවටා uvaṭā, °ටුවා °ṭuvā**, s., st. f. °*ṭu*, servant, attendant. — P. *upaṭṭhāka*, Sk. *upasthāyaka*. Cf. *aguvaṭā*.

423. **උවතම්බය uvatambaya**, s., st. f. °*mba*, aid, support. — P. *upatthambha*, Sk. *upastambha*.

424. **උවදන uvadana**, s., st. f. °*dan*, present, offering. — Sk. *upadāna*.

425. **උවදුර uvadura**, s., st. f. °*ru*, danger, injury. — Slw. Sk. *upadrava*; Pk. *uvaddava*, P. *upaddava*.

426. **උවදෙස uvadesa**, s., st. f. °*des*, instruction, advice, admonition. — Pk. *uvaēsa*, P. *upadēsa*, Sk. *upadēśa*.

427. **උවනිසා uvanisā**, postp., close to, on account of, for. — P. *upanissāya*, Sk. *upa-ni-* + √*śri*.

428. **උවම uvama**, s., figure, comparison. — Pk. *uvamā*, P., Sk. *upamā*.

429. **උවස uvasa,** s., affection, regard. — Sk. *upāsā*; cf. P., Sk. *upāsana*.

430. **උවසරය uvasaraya,** s., st. f. °*ra*, approach; attendance, service. Pk. *uvayāra*, P., Sk. *upacāra*.

431. **උවසුවා uvasuvā,** s., st. f. °*su*, Buddhist lay devotee; fem. *uväsī*. — Pk. *uvāsaya*, °*siyā*, P., Sk. *upāsaka*, °*sikā*.

432. **උවාරණය uvāraṇaya,** s., st. f. °*ṇa*, implement, material, provision. — P., Sk. *upakaraṇa*. Sinh. also *uvăraṇaya* with secondary shortening.

433. **උවිඳා uviňdā,** s., st. f. °*ňdu*, name of god Vishnu. — Sk. *upēndra*.

434. **උස් us,** a., high, elevated, tall; s. *usa*, *uha* height; *us-asna* high seat, throne; *us-karanavā* to highten, elevate; *us-venavā* to become high, rise. — Pk., P., Sk. *ucca*, adv. *uccā*; si. *uco*, g. *ūṃc*, m. *uṃc*, *uṃcā*, bg. *uc*, h. *ūṃcā*, nep. *uṃc*, pj. l. *uccā*.

435. **උසබයා usabayā,** s., st. f. °*ba*, ox, bull. In cpds.: eminent, excellent: *Käta-usab* bull among the kshatriyas, eminent ksh., EpZ I 91 A[1], 10th c. — Pk. *usaha*, *usabha*, P. *usabha*, Sk. *ṛṣabha*.

436. **උසාව usāva,** s., st. f. *usā*, labour, exertion. — Pk. *ucchāha*, P. *ussāha*, Sk. *utsāha*.

437. **උසුන් usun,** a. pprt., cut off. *usun-mul* uprooted. — Pk., P., Sk. *ucchinna*.

438. **උසුරුවනවා usuruvanavā,** v., prt. *isiruvā*, to utter, pronounce. — P. *accārēti*, Sk. *ud-* + √ *car*, *uccāraṇa* pronunciation.

439. **උසුලනවා usulanavā, උහු° uhu°,** v., pprt. *isiluvā*, *ih*°, to carry, support. — P. *uccālēti*, Sk. *ud-* + √*cal*, caus. **uccālayati*; nep. *ucālnu*, pj. *ucālṇā*.

440. **උසොළිය usoḷiya,** s., st. f. *usoḷi*, effort, exertion. — P. *ussoḷhi*, Sk. **utsōḍhi*, *ud.-* + √*sah*.

441. **උස්සනවා ussanavā, ඔසවනවා osavanavā,** v., prt. *issuvā*, *esevuvā*, to lift up, raise. — P. *ussāpēti*, Sk. *ud-* + √*śri*, caus. *ucchrāpayati*.

442. **උළු uḷu[1],** s., star. *uḷu-rada* king of the stars, the moon. — Pk. *uḍu*, P. *uḷu*, Sk. *uḍu*.

443. **උළු uḷu[2],** s. pl., tiles. *uḷu-vaḍuvā* tile-maker, bricklayer. — Can perhaps be connected with P. *sudhā* cement, Sk. *sudhā* brick, if we assume a prakritic **suḍhā* with cerebral, as in *sūḍaṇa* killing (Hem 4-106) = Sk. *sūdana*. — Cf. Tam *ōḷu*.

ඌ Ū

— **ඌ ū,** pron. dem., see **ō**.

444. **ඌරා ūrā, හූරා hūrā,** s., st. f. °*ru*, boar, hog, pig; f. (*h*)*īrī* sow. — Pk. *sūara*, P., Sk. *sūkara*; kśm. *sōr*, g. *suvar*, bg. *suyar*, b. h. *sūar*, nep. *suṃgur*, pj. *sūṃr*, l. *sūr*.

එ E

— **එ e,** pron. dem., see ē.

445. **එක eka,** num., st. f. *ek*, one; *visi-eka* twenty one; *ek-un-vissa* nineteen (v. *un*); *eka-eka* each; *ekaṭ'-eka* tit for tat, lit. one for one; *ek-karanavā* to unite; *ek-venavā* to become united. — < *ekka* (thus Pk.), P., Sk. *ēka*; kśm. *akh*, g. m. ass. bg. h. nep. *ek*, pj. *ikk*. — Sinh. *-ek*, *-k*, as indefinite article: *minihek* a man, *denak* a cow, *kamak* or *kamek* a work.

446. **එකඟ ekaňga,** a., unanimous, acquiescing. — Sk. *ekâṅga* (different meaning).

447. **එකත් ekat[1], එකැති ekäti,** a., positive, certain; adv. on one side, aside. *ekat-pas-va* moving to one side. — P. *ēkanta*, Sk. *ēkânta* (*ekäti* id.) + *-ka*. Cf. *ata*[1].

448. **එකත් ekat[2],** a., of one meaning or purport. — *eka* + *ata*[2], Sk. *ēkârtha*.

449. **එකතු ekatu,** a., united, combined, in *ekatu-karanavā* to unite, collect together; s. *ekatuva* aggregate, total. — P. *ēkatta*, Sk. *ēkatva*.

450. **එකපා eka-pā,** a., uniped. — Sk. *ēka-pāda*.

451. **එකමුතු eka-mutu,** a., unanimous, consentient. — ? Sk. *ēka-mantra*. Cf. *mäta*.

452. **එකලා ekalā,** a., solitary, single. *ekalā-va*, adv., singly. — Seems to be connected with Sk. *ēkala* alone (cf. Pk. *ekkalla* pre-eminent); g. *ekal*, *eklum*, m. *eklā*, oṛ., bg. *ekalā*, h. *ekal*, *akelā*, nep. *eklo* (cf. T s.v.), pj. l. *ikallā*.

453. **එකස් ekas,** a., being on one side. *ekas-karanavā* to put (the robe) on one side (leaving one arm bare). — *eka* + *asa*[2]; P. *ēkaṃsa*.

454. **එකසර eka-sara,** a., walking and acting alone, solitary. — P., Sk. *ēka-cara*.

455. **එකොළහ ekoḷaha, °ළස °ḷasa,** num., st. f. *ekoḷos*, eleven. — Pk. *ekkārasa*, *eggāraha*, *ekkādaha*, P. *ēkādasa*, Sk. *ēkādaśa*; kśm. *kāh*, si. *yāraṃhaṃ*, g. *agyār*, m. *akrā*, oṛ. *egāra*, ass. *eghāra*, bg. *egāra*, h. *egārah*, nep. *eghāra*, pj. *yārāṃ*, l. *yāhrāṃ*.

456. **එක්ක ekka, එක්ව ek-va,** adv. postp., unitedly, together with, along with. — ger. of *ek-venavā*, see s.v. *eka*.

457. **එක්වන් ek-van, °වැනි °väni,** a., like, similar. — Lit. of one colour, *eka* + *vana*, *väni*; Sk. *ēka-varṇin*.

458. **එක්සත් ek-sat,** a., united. — *ek* + *sata*[1]; P. *ēka-cchatta*.

459. **එක්සිත් ek-sit,** a., of one mind, unanimous. — *eka* + *sita* (v. *hita*); P., Sk. *ēka-citta*.

460. **එඬරු eňdaru,** s., castor oil plant. — Metathesis of **eraňḍu*, P. *ēraṇḍa*, *ēlaṇḍa*, Sk. *ēraṇḍa*; si. *herṇī*, g. *eraṃḍo*, m. *eraṃḍ*, ass. *erā*, h. *reṃṛ*, nep. *aṃṛeri*.

461. එත **eta-**[1], adv., in *eta-kal* or *eta-kalaṭa* till then, *eta-koṭa* at that time. — Pk. *ettha*, °*aṃ*, P. *ettha* ; m. *eth*, *ethem̩* (Bl).

462. එත **eta-**[2], a., in *etakin*, *etekin* by that much, by so much. — Pk. *etta*, *ettia*, P. *etta*, *ettaka*. Cf. T s.v. *uti*.

463. එනවා **enavā**, v., prt. *āvā*, to come. Caus. *evanavā*, prt. *evuvā*, to send. — 1) prs. st. *e* = $\sqrt{i}$ + *ā*, Pk. *ēi*, P. *ēti*, Sk. *āiti* ; m. *yeṇem̩*, *eṇem̩* (Bl). 2) prt. st. *ā*, see *ā*[1].

— එන්සාල් **en-sāl**, s., see s.v. **el-biju.**

464. එපා **epā**, particle of prohibition, with the inf. in *-nṭa*, do not, avoid. — = *e-paha* (Ca) that side, aside ; *maranṭa epā* don't kill, means literally : killing, (set it) aside, avoid killing.

465. එබිකන **ebikana**, s., st. f. °*kan*, peeping, peep. — * *eba* = P., Sk. *ābhā* + **ikana* = P. *ikkhaṇa*, Sk. *īkṣaṇa*.

466. එබෙනවා **ebenavā**, v., prt. *ebuṇā*, to peep. — P. *ābhāti*, Sk. *ā* + $\sqrt{bh\bar{a}}$, *ā-bhāti*.

467. එරෙනවා **erenavā**, v., prt. *eruṇā*, to flow down, come down, sink in. Caus. *eravanavā*, prt. *erevuvā*, to cause to sink. — Sk. *ava* + $\sqrt{ri}$, **ava-rīyatē*.

468. එල් **el**, හෙල් **hel**, සෙල් **sel**, a., white. — Probably < Sk. **śvetala*, Cf. T s.v. *seto*.

469. එල්බිජු **el-biju**, s., cardamoms. — *el*=Pk., P., Sk. *elā*, m. *eḷā*, cf. g. *elcī*, oṛ. *alāica*, h. *ilācī*, nep. *alaiṃci*, pj. *ilācī*, *ilāicī* + lw. *biju* = Sk. *bīja* seed. Sinh. has also *en-sāl* Ceylon cardamoms : *en*=*el* (with *n* for *l*) + lw. *sāl* rice (as in *vī-sāl*).

— එළ **eḷa**, හෙළ **heḷa**, එළිය **eḷiya**, a., s., see s. v. **aluva.**

470. එළු **eḷu**, හෙළු **heḷu**, a., pertaining to the language of ancient Ceylon. *(h)eḷubasa* or *(h)eḷuva* the ancient Sinhalese language. — P. *sīhaḷa*, Sk. *siṃhala*.

471. එළුවා **eḷuvā**, s., st. f. *eḷu*, goat. *eḷu-dena* she-goat, ewe. — Pk. AMg. *ēḷaya*, P. *ēḷaka*, Sk. *ēḍaka*.

ඒ Ē

472. ඒ **ē**, එ **e**, pron. st. 3. sg. he. Frequently in cpds : *e-kala* (at) that time ; *e-tana* (in) that place ; *e-lesa* or *e-sē* in that manner, so. Inflected : 1) m. *eyā* he, f. *ā* (? < **eyī*) she, n. *eya* it ; instr. *eyin*, *in*, dat. *eya-ṭa* etc. 2) m. *ēkā*, f. *ēkī*, n. *ēka*. — Pron. st. *e-*, *i-* : Pk. *ēaṃ*, *ēdaṃ*, *ēta-* etc. (PISCHEL § 426), P. *ayaṃ*, *idaṃ*, *ēta-*, Sk. *ayam*, *idam*, *ēta-* etc. ; kśm. *yih*, si. *he*, g. *e*, m. *hā* (?), oṛ. *e*, ass. *ehi*, bg. *e*, b. *ī*, h. *yah* (?), nep. *yo* (?), pj. *eh*, l. *e*.

473. ඒදණ්ඩ **ē-daṇḍa**, s., st. f. *ē-daňḍu*, foot bridge, plank or tree laid across a stream to serve as a bridge. — *ē*=Sk. *sētu*, v.s.v. *heya*, + *daṇḍa* q.v.

ඔ O

474. **ඔ o-,** prefix=Pk., P. *ava-*, *ō-*, Sk. *ava-*. Cf. *o-lam̆banavā*, *ovas(-piyesa)*, *ovā(va)*.

475. **ඔක් ok** in *ok-kāraya* r e t c h i n g. *okkāra-karanavā* to retch. — Cf. g. *okvuṃ*, m. *ok*, *okṇeṃ*, h. *oknā*, nep. *vāk*, *vāknu*.

476. **ඔකඳ okan̆da,** s., Ca : g r e a t s t r e a m, t o r r e n t. — *ō* (v. *oya*) + *kan̆da* mass.

477. **ඔට oṭa,** s., l i p. — Pk. *oṭṭha*, *uṭṭha*, P. *oṭṭha*, Sk. *ōṣṭha* ; kśm. *vuṭh*, g. m. *oṭh*, oṛ. *oṭha*, h. *oṃṭh*, nep. *oṭh*, pj. *hoṃṭh*, l. *hoṭh*.

478. **ඔටුන්න oṭunna, වො° vo°,** s., st. f. *(v)oṭunu*, c r o w n, d i a d e m. — < **veṭ-ṭhana* ; (Pk. *veṭṭhaṇa*, P. *vēṭhana*), Sk. *vēṣṭana* (+ *-ka*) ; kśm. *vuṭhun*, si. *veṭhaṇu*, m. *veṭhaṇ*, b. h. nep. *beṭhan*. Cf. *veḷanavā*.

479. **ඔටුවා oṭuvā, වො° vo°,** s., st. f. *(v)oṭu*, c a m e l. — Pk. *uṭṭa*, P. *oṭṭha*, Sk. *uṣṭra* (+ *-ka*) ; kśm. *vūṃṭh*, si. *uṭhu*, g. m. *ūṃṭ*, oṛ. ass. bg. *uṭ*., h. *ūṃṭ*, nep. *uṃṭ*, pj. l. *uṭṭh*.

— **ඔට්ටුව oṭṭuva,** s., see s.v. **oḍa.**

480. **ඔඩ oḍa,** s., b e t, p l e d g e. — In the MIAVs si. *hoḍa*, g. m. *hoḍ*, bg. h. nep. *hoṛ*. In Sinh. also *oṭṭuva*, s., st. f. *oṭṭu*, w a g e r, b e t, s t a k e. The relation between *oḍa* and *oṭṭuva* is obscure.

481. **ඔත් ot, හොත් hot,** a. pprt., r e c l i n i n g, r e c u m b i n g. — Pk., P. *sutta*, Sk. *supta* (√*svap*) ; si. g. *suto*, b. *sūtal*, h. *sūtā*, pj. *suttā*. Gr. 50. 29.

482. **ඔතප් otap,** s., m o d e s t y, s h a m e, f e a r. — P. *ottappa*, (Sk. *uttāpa* ; cf. P. *uttapatē* Jā V. 219^{20}, Com. *ottapati*, ib. 224^{22}).

483. **ඔද oda,** s., 1) p o w e r, f o r c e, h a u g h t i n e s s, p r i d e, d e l i g h t ; 2) j u i c e ; n e c t a r, a m b r o s i a. — It seems that in MInd. the derivates of Sk. *ōjas* vital power were fused with those of *ūrj*, *ūrjas*, *ūrjā* food, sap, juice. Cf. P. *ōjā*, si. *oju*, m. *oj*, but Pk. *ujja*. Sinh. also lw. *oja*, *ōjāva* delight, juice (from elephant's temples etc.).

— **ඔබ oba,** pron., see **um̆ba.**

484. **ඔබනවා obanavā, හො° ho°,** v., pprt. *(h)ebuvā*, t o p r e s s, p r e s s d o w n, s q u e e z e. Intr. *ebenavā*, prt. *ebuṇā*, to be pressed. — Seems to be connected with si. *cubhaṇu*, g. *copvuṃ* to pierce, *cobvuṃ* to brand, m. *copṇeṃ* to beat a floor, *coṃbṇeṃ* to stuff in, h. *cŭbhnā*, nep. *copnu*, *cobnu* *cobhnu* to dip. Details are obscure.

485. **ඔබින obina, හො ho°, සො so°,** a., f i t, p r o p e r. *obinavā*, *ho°*, *so°*, v., t o b e f i t or p r o p e r. — Pk. *sōhaṇa*, Pk. S. *sōhadi*, P. *sōbhana*, *sōbhati* ; Sk. *śōbhana*, √*śubh*, *śūbhatē* ; si. *sūṃhaṇu*, *suhāiṇu*, g. *sohvuṃ*, *suhāvuṃ*, ass. *xuvāiba*, h. *suhānā*, nep. *suvāunu*, *suhāunu*, pj. *suhāuṇā*.

486. ඔය **oya,** හොය **hoya,** s., st. f. *ō, hō,* s m a l l r i v e r, r i v u l e t. *ō-baḍa* vicinity of a r° ; *ō-kanda* level ground along the banks of a r°. — Pk. *sōa,* P. *sōta,* Sk. *srōtas.*

— ඔරය **oraya,** s., see **uraya.**

487. ඔරුව **oruva,** s., st. f. *oru,* b o a t, c a n o e. *oru-daṇḍa* oar, paddle. — P. *uḷumpa,* Sk. *uḍupa* ; mald. *oruva.*

488. ඔලඹනවා **olam̆banavā,** v., t o w a v e ; pprt. *olam̆bu* hanging, suspended. Intr. *elam̆benavā,* prt. *elam̆buṇā* to come near, to approach. — Pk. *ōlambaï,* P. *ōlambati,* Sk. *ava-* + √*lamb, ava-lambatē.*

489. ඔවස් පියෙස **ovas-piyesa,** s., st. f. °*yes,* o p e n s p a c e, c o u r t y a r d.—*ovasa* = Pk. *ōāsa, ōvāsa, avagāsa,* P. *ōkāsa,* Sk. *avakāśa* + *piyesa* q. v. Cf. also *vahasa.*

490. ඔවා(ව) **ovā(va),** s., st. f. *ovā,* a d v i c e ; *ovā-basa* id. ; *ovā-denavā* to give advice. — P. *ōvāda,* Sk. *avavāda.*

491. ඔවු **ovu,** part., y e s. — Derived by Childers from Sk. *ēvam,* by myself from *sādhu.* Both these etymologies seem to be wrong. We must compare *ovu* with si. *āmim,* g. *āum,* m. *ā, hām,* or. *ā,* bg. *ām,* h. *hām,* nep. *am* (according to T = P. *āma,* Sk. *ām*).

— ඔසවනවා **osavanavā,** v., see **ussanavā.**

492. ඔසුව **osuva,** s., st. f. *osu,* d r u g, m e d i c i n e. — Pk. *ōsaha,* P. *ōsadha,* Sk. *auṣadha.*

493. ඔළරු **oḷaru,** °ර **°ra,** °රි **°ri,** a., l a r g e, g r e a t. — P. *uḷāra* < **uḍāra,* Sk. *udāra.*

ඕ Ō

494. ඕ **ō,** ඔ **o,** ඌ **ū,** pron. st. 3 sg. h e. In cpds.: *o-tana* there (near you) ; *o-homa* such as that ; *o-vitara, o-vicara, occara* so much. Inflected 1) *oyā* he, f *ō* (? <**oyī*) she, n. *oya* it ; sg. obl. c. *ohu, uhu, ū* ; pl. *ovhu, ohu, ū(lā)* tney, obl. c. *ovun, un.* 2) m. *ōkā,* f. *ōkī,* n. *ōka.* — Pron. st. *u, o* ; OldIr. *ava-,* Sk. *avōḥ* ; si. *ū, hū,* bg. *o,* h. *vah,* nep. *ǔ,* pj. *uh,* l. *o.*

495. ඕවිට **ō-viṭa,** s., st. f. °*ṭi,* l o w g r o u n d near a river. — *ō* (v. *oya*) + **viṭa* < *piṭa* (after a vowel).

ක K

496. ක **ka-** (*ki-, ku-, ke-, ko-*) pron. st. interrog. *kav* who ? obl. c. *kā,* pl. *kavru,* obl. c. *kavrun*; *kavara* which ? what ?. To all forms *-da* is added ; *kāṭa-da* to whom? *kavarek-da* who ? — *kim* : *kim-da, kima-da, kimek-da* what ?, *ki-kala* what time ? *kisi* any, some (P. *kiṃci*). — *kumak* what ? *kumaṭa-da* what for, why ? (Cf. P. *kimatthaṃ*).—*ke-sē-da* how ? *ko-tana-da* where ? — Pk. *ka-, ki-* (Pischel § 428), P. *ka-, ki-* (Geiger § 111), Sk. *ka-, ki-, ku-* (Whitney § 504) ; si. *ko, kā,* g. *ko,* or. bg. *ke,* nep. *ko* ; cf. g. m. *koṇ,* ass. bg. *kon,* h. *kaun,* nep. *kun,* pj. *kauṇ.*

497. **කකළ kakaḷa, කකුළු kakuḷu, කැකුළු käkuḷu,** a., rough, severe.— Seems to be a blending of P. *kakkasa*, Sk. *karkaśa* and P., Sk. *kaṭuka*.

498. **කකුල kakula,** s., st. f. *°ul,* foot, leg. *kakul-daḍa* wandering, vagrant (Syn. *pā-daḍa*). — P. *kaṅkala* in *aṭṭhi-kaṅkala* skeleton (cf. germ. *Bein* bone, leg), Sk. *kaṅkāla* ; bg. *kāṃkāl* loin, waist, oṛ. *kaṅkāḷa*.

— **කකුළු kakuḷu,** a., see **kakaḷa.**

499. **කකුළුවා kakuḷuvā,** s., st. f. *kakuḷu,* crab. — Pk. *kakkaḍa,* P. *kakkaṭaka,* Sk. *karkaṭa* ; bg. *kāṃkṛā*.

500. **කග kaga,** s., st. f. *kaga,* sword. *kaga-pata* sword-blade ; *kaga-muva* sword-edge. — Pk., P. *khagga*, Sk. *khaḍga* ; bg. h. *khāg*, nep. *khāg, khāgo* horn of the rhinoceros. — Cf. *kaḍuva*.

501. **කගයා kagayā,** s., st. f. *kaga,* unicorn, rhinoceros. — The words *khagga, khaḍga* also mean rhinoceros. Perhaps *kagayā* is derived from **khāḍga-ka*.

502. **කගවේණා kaga-vēṇā, කඟ° kaṅga°,** s., st. f. *-vēṇu*, pl. *-vēnnu,* unicorn, rhinoceros. — *kaga* + *vēṇa* (q.v.) having a sword as horn. — P. *khagga-visāṇa*.

503. **කට kaṭa^{1},** s., throat, mouth, orifice. — Pk., P., Sk. *kaṇṭha* throat ; g. *kāṃṭho* bank, m. *kāṃṭh, kāṭh* edge, *kāṃṭheṃ* neck, h. *kāṃṭhā* close at hand. cf. T s.v. *kāṃṭh*.

504. **කට kaṭa^{2},** s., dry stick, timber. — Pk., P. *kaṭṭha*, Sk. *kāṣṭha* ; kśm. *kāṭh*, g. *kāṭh*, m. *kāṭhī*, oṛ. *kāṭha*, ass. bg. h. nep. pj. l. *kāṭh*.

505. **කට kaṭa^{3},** s., a short space of time (eight winks). — Sk. *kāṣṭhā*, BR s.v.4.

506. **කටිනවා kaṭinavā,** v., prt. *käṭṭā,* to spin. — <MInd. **kaṭṭati*, Old Ind. **kartati*, Sk. √*kṛt*, *kṛṇatti*, nom. v. *kartana*; kśm. *katun*, si. *kataṇu*, m. *kātṇeṃ*, oṛ. *kaṭaṇā* spinning, ass. *kāṭiba*, bg. *kāṭā*, h. *kātnā*, nep. *kātnu* (cf. T s.v.), pj. *kattṇā*, l. *kattaṇ*.

507. **කටුව kaṭuva,** s., st. f. *kaṭu,* thorn. *äṭ-kaṭuva* elephant hook. — Pk. *kaṇṭaa*, P., Sk. *kaṇṭaka* ; kśm. *konḍu*, si. *kanḍo*, g. *kāṃṭo*, oṛ. *kaṇṭā*, m. bg. h. *kāṃṭā*, nep. *kāṃro*, pj. l. *kanḍā*.

508. **කඩ kaḍa,** s., part, piece, bit of rag or cloth; district. *ya-kaḍa, lō-kaḍa* see s.vv. *ya, lō*; *kaḍa-dat* broken teeth ; *kaḍa-ima* v. *ima*; *kaḍa-kapanavā* to cut into bits ; *kaḍa-karanavā* to break, violate. — Pk., P., Sk. *khaṇḍa*. The corresponding words in the MIAVs generally mean (lumps = *käṭa* of) sugar: kśm. *khanḍ*, g. m. *khāṃḍ*, oṛ. *khaṇḍa*, bg. h. nep. *khāṃṛ*, pj. *khanḍ*.

509 **කඩනවා kaḍanavā,** v., prt. *käḍuvā,* to break. Caus. *kaḍavanavā*, prt. *käḍevuvā*, to cause to break; intr. *käḍenavā*, prt. *käḍuṇā* to be broken. — Pk. *khanḍēi*, P. *khanḍēti*, Sk. √ *khanḍ*, *khanḍayati* ; g. m. h. pj. *khāṃḍ-*.

510. **කඩය kaḍaya,** s., st. f. *kaḍa*, arrow. — Pk., P. *kaṇḍa*, Sk. *kāṇḍa* (+-*ka*); kśm. *kāṃḍ* reed, *kān* arrow, si. *kāno*, g. m. *kāṃḍ*, oṛ. *kāṇḍa*, bg. *kāṃṛā*, h. *kāṃṛī*, nep. *kāṃṛ*, pj. *kānnā*, l. *kānī*, *kāṇī*.

511. **කඩුව kaḍuva,** s., st. f. *kaḍu*, sword, sabre. *kaḍu-miṭa* sword-hilt; *kaḍu-muṇa* sword-point. — Sk. √ *khaṇḍ* (v. *kaḍanavā*); si. *khano*, g. *khāṃḍuṃ*, m. *khāṃḍā*, oṛ. *khaṇḍā*, ass. *khāṇḍā*, bg. h. *khāṃṛā*, nep. *khāṃṛo*, pj. *khaṇḍā*. — Cf. *kaga*.

512 **කඩුවේගං kaḍuvēgaṃ,** s., scorbutic eruption in the feet. — The first part of the word is connected with P., Sk. *kaṇḍūyā* itching; m. *kāṃḍaviṇeṃ*, *kāṃḍuḷṇeṃ* to scratch. Cf. T s.v. *kanyāunu*.

513. **කණ kaṇa**[1], a., one-eyed, blind; s. *kaṇā* blind person; *kaṇa-karanavā* to blind. — Pk., P., Sk. *kāṇa*; kśm. *kōnu*, si. *kāṇo*, g. *kāṇuṃ*, m. *kāṇā*, oṛ. *kaṇā*, bg. *kāṇā*, h. *kānā*, nep. *kānu*, pj. l. *kāṇāṃ*. B II.13.

— **කණ kaṇa**[2], s., see s.v. **keṇehi.**

— **කණනවා kaṇanavā, කණිනවා kaṇinavā,** v., see s.v. **kaninavā.**

514. **කණුව kaṇuva,** s., st. f. *kaṇu*, post, pillar. *im-kaṇuva*, v. *ima*. — P. *khāṇuka*.

515. **කත kata**[1], s., woman. — Pk., P. *kantā*, Sk. *kāntā*.

516. **කත kata**[2], s., lustre. — Pk., P. *kanti*, Sk. *kānti*.

517. **කතර katara,** s., bad or difficult road. — Pk., P. *kantāra*, Sk. *kāntāra*.

518. **කතුර katura,** s., st. f. °*ru*, pair of scissors. — Pk., P. *kattarī*, Sk. *karttarī*; si. *katari*, g. m. *kātar*, oṛ. *katurī*, h. *katarnī*. Cf. T s.v. *katranu*.

519. **කතුරුයටිය katuru-yaṭiya,** s., st. f. °*yaṭi*, walking stick, staff. — P. *kattara-yaṭṭhi*.

520. **කද kada,** s., st. f. *kat*, pingo-load. *kat-līya* yoke for the shoulder, pingo. — Pk. *kāa*, P., Sk. *kāja*, *kāca*.

521. **කදම kadama,** s., st. f. *kadam*, mud. — Pk., P. *kaddama*, Sk. *kardama*.

522. **කදූර kadūra,** s., st. f. id., the wild date-tree, Phoenix sylvestris. — Pk. *khajjūra*, P. *khajjūrī*, Sk. *kharjūra*, °*rī*; kśm. *khazar*, si. *khajūri*, g. *khajur*, m. *khajūr*, oṛ. *khajuri*, ass. *khāzur*, bg. *khājur*, h. pj. l. *khajūr*, nep. *khajur*.

523. **කදෝව kadōva,** s., st. f. *kadō*, light. *kadō-kimiyā* firefly. — P. *khajjōta* firefly; Sk. *khadyōta* firefly, sun, *khajyōtis* firefly.

524. **කඳ kaňda**[1], a., lame in one leg; s. *kaňdayā* lame person. — Pk., P., Sk. *khañja*; cf. nep. *khaṃjāhā* (T).

525. **කඳ kaňda**[2], s., shoulder; trunk (of a tree); mass, multitude. — Pk., P. *khandha*, Sk. *skandha*; si. *khāṃdho*, g. *kāṃdh*, m. *khāṃdh*, oṛ. *kāndha*, ass. *kān*, bg. h. nep. *kāṃdh*, pj. *kannhā*.

526. **කඳකුමරුවා kaňda-kumaruvā,** s., st. f. *°ru,* name of the god Skanda. — P. *khandha* (for *khanda*), Sk. *skanda.*

527. **කඳප kaňdapa,** s., st. f. *°ňdap,* name of the god of Love, Cupid. — Sk. *kandarpa.*

528. **කඳයුර kaňdayura, °වුර °vura,** s., st. f. *°ru,* intrenchment, military encampment. — P. *khandhâvāra,* Sk. *skandhâvāra.*

— **කඳු kaňdu,** s., see **kanda.**

529. **කඳුර kaňdura,** s., st. f. *°ru,* gorge, mountain stream. — P. *kandara* (Jā V. 89[14]), Sk. *kandara.*

530. **කඳුල kaňdula,** s., st. f. *°lu,* tear. — Cf. Pk. *kandaï,* P. *kandati,* Sk. *√krand, krandati* cries, weeps.

531. **කන kana,** s., st. f. *kan,* ear. *kan-vedā* ear-doctor; *kan-denavā* to give ear or heed. — Pk. P. *kaṇṇa,* Sk. *karṇa*; kśm. *kan,* si. *kanu,* g. m. *kān,* oṛ. *kāna,* ass. bg. *kāṇ,* h. nep. *kān,* pj. l. *kann.* Cf. De Lanerolle, DSL p. xii § 3.4.

532. **කනවා kanavā,** v., prt. *kāvā,* to eat. Caus. *kavanavā,* prt. *kävuvā,* to cause to eat, feed. Intr. of caus. *kävenavā,* prt. *kävuṇā* to become eaten; to gnaw (of pain). — Pk. *khāï* (3. pl. *khanti*), P., Sk. *khādati*; si. *khāiṇu,* g. *khāvuṃ,* m. *khāṇeṃ,* oṛ. *khāibā,* ass, *khāiba,* bg. *khāoyā,* h. *khānā,* nep. *khānu,* pj. *khāṇā,* l. *khāvaṇ.* Gr. 50.7.

533. **කනා kanā,** s., gold. — Pk. *kaṇaa,* P., Sk. *kanaka.*

534. **කනිටු kaniṭu,** a., youngest, smallest. — Pk. *kaṇiṭṭha,* P. *kaniṭṭha,* Sk. *kaniṣṭha.* Cf. nep. *kāncho,* T s.v.

535. **කනිනවා kaninavā,** v., prt. *kännā,* to dig, excavate, bore through. — Pk. *khaṇaï,* P., *khanati,* Sk. *√khan, khanati*; si. *khaṇaṇu,* g. *khaṇvuṃ,* m. *khaṇṇeṃ,* ass. caus. *khanāiba,* h. *khannā,* nep. *khannu.* Ca spells *kaṇinavā.*

536. **කන්ද kanda,** s., st. f. *kaňdu,* hill, mountain. *kaňdu-raṭa* mountain region, highland. — Sk. *skandha* (v. *kaňda*[2]) + *-ka.*

537. **කප kapa[1],** s., st., f. *kap,* a kalpa, i.e. a fabulous period of time, a day of Brahma. *kap-keḷavara* end of the world. — Pk., P. *kappa,* Sk. *kalpa.*

538. **කප kapa[2],** s., st. f. *kap,* post, pillar. — Lit. piece cut up (v. *kapanavā*), si. *kapu* edge, g. *kāp* a cut, m. *kāp* slice, ass. *kāp* split cane, h. *kāṃp,* nep. *kāp,* l. *kapp* breach.

539. **කපනවා kapanavā,** v., prt. *käpuvā,* to cut. Caus. *kapavanavā, kappa°* (double caus.: *kappavanavā*), prt. *käpevuvā* (*käppevuvā*) to cause to cut; intr *käpenavā,* prt. *käpuṇā,* to become cut. — Pk. *kappēi,* P. *kappēti,* Sk. *√kḷp,* caus. *kalpayati*; si., *kapaṇu,* g. *kāpvuṃ,* m. *kāpṇeṃ,* nep. *kapnu,* l. *kappaṇ.*

540. කපල්දරයා **kapal-darayā,** s., 1) name of god Siva, lit. skull-bearer; 2) beggar. — Meaning 1) = Slw. **kapal* (v. *kabal*) = Sk. *kapāla*, cf. *kapāla-bhṛt*, + *darayā*=P., Sk.-*dhāraka*. With this term the word for 'beggar' seems to have been confounded, as beggars also carry a skull or shell for collecting alms. But etymologically *kapal* in the second meaning is derived from Sk. *karpaṭa* ragged garments in *karpaṭa-dhārin* beggar. Cf. Pk. *kappaḍa*, P. *kappaṭa* ; kśm. *kapur*, si. *kapaṛu*, g. m. *kāpaḍ*, bg. *kāpaṛ*, nep. *kapaṛā*, pj. *kappaṛ*, l. *kapṛā*.

541. කපු **kapu,** s., cotton. *kapu-gaha* cotton tree. — Pk., P. *kappāsa*, Sk. *karpāsa* cotton, *kārpāsa* the cotton plant ; kśm. *kapas*, si. *kapāha*, g. *kapās*, *kāpus*, m. *kāpūs*, oṛ. *kapā*, ass. *kapāh*, bg. *kāpās*, h. nep. *kapās*, pj. l. *kapāh*. B I. 318.

542. කපුටා **kapuṭā,** °ටුවා **°ṭuvā**., s, st. f. *°ṭu*, crow. — <MInd. **kappuṭṭha* (*-ka*) = Sk. **kat-puṣṭa* badly nourished. Cf. *kavuḍuvā*.

543. කපුරු **kapuru,** s., camphor, Cinnamomum camphora. — Pk., P. *kappūra*, Sk. *karpūra* ; kśm. *kōpuru*, si. *kapūru*, g. *kapūr*, m. *kāpūr*, oṛ. *kapūra*, bg. nep. *kapur*, h. pj. *kapūr*. B I. 318.

544. කපුවා **kapuvā,** s., st. f. *kapu*, barber. — P. *kappaka*, Sk. *kalpaka*. For Sinh. *kapuvā* or *kapurāḷa* demon priest, I refer to Sk. *kalpa* sacred precept, ceremonial rite. Cf. *käpa*.

545. කබර **kabara,** s., white spot or scab; s. *kabarā* or *kabara-goyā* the spotted iguana ; *kabarī* a white spotted or scrofulous female ; *kabar'-aňgayā* lit. one who has a spotted body, the spotted animal, panther. — P. *kabara*, Sk. *kabara*, *kambara*, *karbara* ; si. *kubiro*, g. *kābar*, m. *kabrā*, h. *kābar*, *kabrā*, nep. *kābro*, *kābhro* (?), pj. *kabrā*. Cf. *kaṁburu*.

546. කබල **kabala,** s., st. f. *kabal*, 1) shell (of a tortoise) ; 2) skull, cf. *is-kabala* ; 3) potsherd. *kabal-venavā* to become damaged or broken (as vessels). — Pk. *kavāla*, P., Sk. *kapāla* ; si. *kapāru*, m. *kapāḷ*, oṛ. *kapāḷa*, ass. bg. h. nep. pj. *kapāl*.

547. කඹුරා **kaṁburā,** s., st. f. *°ru*, smith, brazier. *kaṁburu-sama* lit. smith's leather, i.e. smith's bellow (cf. *hama*, *sama*). — P. *kammāra*.

548. කඹුරු **kaṁburu,** a., variegated, dappled. — Pk. *kabbura*, Sk. *karbura*. Cf. *kabara*.

549. කම **kama**[1], s., st. f. *kam*, business, deed, act; need, necessity. *kamak nä* there is no need, never mind ; *kam-näti* useless, needless. In cpds.: frequently used as a suffix (*-kama*,*-kuma*,*-yama*,*-yuma*,*-huma*) to form abstract nouns : *aḍu-kama* deficiency, *udul-kama* brightness ; cf. *uṇu-huma*. — Pk., P. *kamma*, Sk. *karman* ; kśm. *kam*, si. *kamu*, g. m. *kām*, oṛ. *kāma*, ass. bg. h. nep. *kām*, pj. l. *kamm*.

550. කම **kama[2],** s., st. f. *kam*, wish, desire. *kamäti* (or *kämati, kämäti*) wishing, pleased ; s. *kämättā* one who desires, neutr. *kämätta* desired object (cf. s.v. *äti*). — Pk., P., Sk. *kāma*.

551. කමල **kamala,** s., st. f. *kamal*, lotus. *kamal-alaya* lotus bulb, cf. *alaya[2]*. — Pk., P., Sk. *kamala* ; si. *kaṃvalu*, g. *kamaḷ*, bg. *kamal*, h. *kaṃval*, nep. *kamal*, pj. *kaul*.

552. කමාව **kamāva,** සමාව **samāva,** s., st. f. °*mā*, pardon, forgiveness. *kamā-(samā-)karanavā* or *venavā* to forgive. — *kamāva* = P. *khamā* ; g. *khamā*, m. *khamṇeṃ* ; *samāva* = Pk. *chamā*, h. *chimā* B I. 310, Sk. *kṣamā*.

553. කමිස **kamisa,** s., variegated colour (mixture of black and white). — P. *kammāsa*, Sk. *kalmāṣa*.

554. කම්කරුවා **kam-karuvā,** s., st. f. °*ru*, workman, artificer. — Pk. *kammagara*, P. *kammakāraka*, Sk. *karmakāra(-ka)*.

555. කරගෙය **kara-geya,** s., st. f. *-gē*, jail. — *kara*=P., Sk. *kārā*+*geya* q.v.

556. කරඬුව **karaňḍuva,** s., st. f. °*ňḍu*, small box, casket. — Pk. *karaṇḍiā*, P., Sk. *karaṇḍaka* ; kśm. *kronḍu*, g. *karaṃḍo*, m. *karaṃḍā*. Cf. T s.v. *kaṇḍi[2]*.

557. කරඳ **karaňda,** s., name of a plant, Pongamia glabra. — P., Sk. *karañja*.

558. කරනවා **karanavā,** v., prt. *kaḷā*, *käruvā*, *ker*°, pprt. *kaḷa*, ger. *koṭa* q.v., to make, do. Caus. *karavanavā*, prt. *kerevuvā*, to cause to do ; intr. *kerenavā*, *kär*°, prt. *keruṇā*, *kär*°, to be done, to take place. — Pk. *karēi*, *kāravēi* (ger. *kārāviya*), P. *karōti*, *kārēti* or *kārāpēti* ; Sk. √ *kṛ*, *karōti*, *kārayati* ; kśm. *karun*, si. *karaṇu*, g. *karvuṃ*, m. *karṇeṃ*, oṛ. *karibā*, ass. *kariba*, bg. *karā*, h. *karnā*, nep. *garnu*, pj. *karṇā*, l. *karaṇ*. I believe that Sk. √ *kṝ*, *kirati* has been confounded with √ *kṛ* ; the meaning 'to sow' is yet traceable. Cf. *amu kaḷa kenek amu geṇiyat* he who sows amu will reap amu (proverb Atītavākya-dīpaniya, p. 4.).

559. කරඹ **karaṁba,** s., name of a plant, Carissa (two species). — It is difficult to connect the word with the names of the same plant Pk., P. *karamadda*, Sk. *karamardaka* ; h. *karauṃdā*, nep. *karauṃji*.

560. කර(ය) **kara(ya)[1],** s., st. f. *kara*, hand, trunk (of an elephant) ; ray ; tax. Cf. *kärä* tax EpZ I.93 A[38], 10th c. — Probably lw. Pk., P., Sk. *kara* ; g. m. oṛ. bg. h. nep. *kar*.

561. කරය **karaya[2],** s., st. f. *kara*, razor. *kara-katura* id. ; *kara-aga* or *kar'-aga* point of a razor ; *kara-geya* shaving house — P. *khura*, Sk. *kṣura* ; kśm. *khūru*. Cf. *siriya*.

562. කරවත **karavata,** s., st. f. °*vat*, saw. — Pk. *karapatta*, Sk. *karapattra* ; si. *karṭu*, g. m. *karvat*, oṛ. *karata*, ass. *karat*, bg. *karāt*, h. *karāṃt*, *karaut*, *karot*, nep. *karāti*, *karauṃti*, pj. *karvat*, l. *kalvattar*. TURNER.

563. කරවිල **karavila,** කරිවිල **karivila,** s., st. f. id., name of a plant, Momordica charantia. — Sk. *kāravella* ; kśm. *karel,* si. *karelo,* g. *karelī,* oṛ. *kalarā,* bg. *karalā,* h. pj. *karelā,* nep. *karelo.* TURNER.

564. කරිස **karisa,** s., filth, dung.—P. *karīsa,* Sk. *karīṣa* ; b. h. *karsī,* nep. *karsi.*

565. කරුණ **karuṇa,** s., st. f. °*ṇu,* reason, cause; object; matter, thing. — Pk., P., Sk. *kāraṇa* ; kśm. *kāran,* si. *kāraṇu,* g. m. *kāraṇ,* oṛ. *kāraṇa,* ass. bg. h. nep. *kāran,* pj. *kāraṇ.*

566. කරුවා **-karuvā,** s., st. f. *karu,* doer, maker. — Pk. *kāraa,* P., Sk. *kāraka, kāruka.* Only in cpds. : *mehe-karuvā* servant, see s.v. *meheya* ; also *-varayā, -varu.*

567. කල් **kal,** a., beautiful, pleasant, kind. — P. *kalla, kalya,* Sk. *kalya.*

568. කල **kala**[1], s., a measure : digit; a division of time. — Pk., P., Sk. *kalā* ; kśm. *kal,* si. *kala,* g. m. *kaḷ* oṛ. *kaḷa* bg. h. nep. pj. l. *kal.*

569. කල **kala**[2], s., st. f. *kal,* time. *kal-giya* old, ancient ; *ki-kala* when ? *kal-karanavā* or *-yavanavā* to pass the time. — Pk., P., Sk. *kāla* ; kśm. *kāl,* si. *kālu,* g. m. *kāḷ,* oṛ. *kāḷa,* ass. bg. h. nep. pj. *kāl.*

570. කල **kala**[3], s., threshing floor. *kala-viṭa* id. — Pk., P., Sk. *khala* ; kśm. *khal,* si. *kharo,* g. *khaḷuṃ,* m. *khaḷeṃ,* oṛ. *khaḷā,* ass. *khalā,* bg. *khal,* nep. *khalo,* pj. l. *khal(-vāṛā).*

571. කලණ **kalaṇa,** a., salutary, fortunate. — Pk., P. *kallāṇa, kalyāṇa,* Sk. *kalyāṇa.* The river-name *kälaṇi* corresponds to Sk. *kalyāṇī.*

572. කලදයා **kaladayā,** s., st. f. °*da,* squirrel. — P., Sk. *kalandaka.*

573. කලඹ **kalam̆ba,** s., multitude; bundle, bunch. — Pk. *kalāva,* P. Sk. *kalāpa.*

574. කලඹයා **kalam̆bayā,** s., st. f. °*m̆ba,* young elephant.— P. *kalabha,* Sk. *kalabha, karabha* + *-ka.*

575. කලහ **kalaha,** s., st. f. *kalas,* water-jar, water-pot. — Pk., P. *kalasa,* Sk. *kalaśa* ; si. *kalisu,* g. *kaḷsī,* m. *kaḷas,* oṛ. *kaḷasa,* ass. *kalah,* b. *kalsā,* h. *kalas, kalsā,* nep. *kalas.*

576. කළුරිය **kaluriya,** කළු° **kaḷu°,** s., death. — P. *kālakiriyā,* Sk. *kāla-kriyā.*

577. කවඩිය **kavaḍiya,** s., st. f. °*ḍi,* cowry shell. — Pk. *kavaḍḍiā,* Sk. *kapardikā* ; si. g. *koḍī,* m. *kavḍī,* oṛ. *kauṛi,* bg. *kaṛi,* h. *kauṛī,* nep. *kauṛi,* pj. l. *kauḍī.*

578. කවණ **kavaṇa,** a., poor ; s. *kavaṇayā* poor man. — Pk. *kivaṇa, kiviṇa,* P. *kapaṇa,* Sk. *kṛpaṇa* ; m. *kivaṇ.*

579. කවද **kavada,** °ස **°sa,** s. armour, mail. — Pk. *kavaa,* P., Sk. *kavaca.*

580. **කවර kavara,** pron. interr. w h i c h ? w h a t ? *kavara behet* which medicine ? DhpAGp 18^{27}, trsl. of. P. *kiṃ bhesajjaṃ.* — Pk. *kayara,* P., Sk. *katara.* Cf. s.v. *ka-.*

— **කවස kavasa,** s., see s.v. **kavada.**

581. **කවුඩුවා kavuḍuvā,** °**ඩා** °**ḍā,** s., st. f. °*ḍu,* c r o w. — <MInd. **kavuḍḍhaka* = Sk. **kad-vṛddhaka* badly grown up. Cf. *kapuṭā.*

582. **කවුළුව kavuḷuva,** s., st. f. °*ḷu,* w i n d o w. — P. *kavāṭaka,* Sk. *kapāṭa, kavāṭa* ; m. *kavāḍ,* oṛ. bg. *kabāṭ,* h. pj. *kavāḍ.*

583. **කස් kas^1,** s., i t c h, c u t a n e o u s e r u p t i o n. — Pk., P., Sk. *kacchū.* But cf. also *kahanavā.*

584. **කස් kas^2,** s., b e l l - m e t a l, b r o n z e, in *kas-talaya* metal plate, gong. — Pk. *kāsa, kaṃsa,* P., Sk. *kaṃsa* ; kśm. *kenzu,* si. *kañjho,* g. *kāṃsuṃ,* m. *kāṃseṃ,* oṛ. *kaṃsā,* ass. *kāṃh,* bg. h. *kāṃsā,* nep. *kāṃso,* pj. *kāṃsī.*

585. **කස(ය) kasa(ya)^1,** s., st. f. *kasa,* t o u c h s t o n e. — Pk. *kasa,* Sk. *kaṣa* ; kśm. *kah,* g. m. bg. h. pj. *kas,* nep. *kasi.*

586. **කසය kasaya^2,** s., st. f. *kasa,* w h i p, s c o u r g e. — P. *kasā,* Sk. *kaśā, kaṣā, kasā.*

587. **කසයා kasayā,** s., a g r i c u l t u r i s t. — P. *kassaka,* Sk. *karṣaka.* Cf. B, T s.vv. *kisān.*

— **කසළ kasaḷa,** s., see **kahaḷa.**

— **කසා kasā,** s., see **kaha.**

— **කසිණු kasiṇu,** a., see **kisiṇu.**

588. **කසුන් kasun,** s., g o l d. — Pk. *kañcaṇa,* P. *kañcana,* Sk. *kāñcana.*

— **කසුබුවා kasubuvā,** s., see **käsubuvā.**

589. **කහ kaha,** a., y e l l o w, in cpds. such as *kaha-uṇa* sp. of bamboo, Bambusa arundinacea ; *kaha-karavalā, k°-gäraňḍiyā, k°-māpilā,* names of various yellow snakeṣ ; *kaha-ves* the yellow robe. As s. *kaha* or *kasā* means s a f f r o n, t u r m e r i c : *kaha-miris* saffron and chillies, curry-stuff. — Pk. *kasāa,* P. *kāsāya,* °*va,* Sk. *kāṣāya.*

590. **කහනවා kahanavā, කස°** *kasa°,* v., prt. *kähuvā, käs°,* t o i t c h, tr. t o s c r a t c h. — Sk. √ *kaṣ, kaṣati,* °*tē* rubs, scratches. But cf. also *kas^1.*

591. **කහවණුව kahavaṇuva,** s., st. f. °*ṇu,* name of an ancient c o i n. — Pk. *kahāvaṇa,* P. *kahāpaṇa,* Sk. *kārṣāpaṇa.*

592. **කහළ kahaḷa, කසළ kasaḷa,** s., d u n g, d i r t, f a e c e s. *kasaḷa-goḍa* dunghill ; *k°-maga* anus. — Seems to be connected with Pk. *kaccavāra,* P. *kacavara,* Sk. *kaccara* ; si. *kaciro,* °*rī,* g. *kācar, kācrī,* m. h. *kacrā,* nep. *kacar* (TURNER s.v.). Doubtful.

593. **කහිනවා kahinavā, කසි° kasi°,** v., prt. *kässā,* t o c o u g h. — Sk. √*kās, kāsatē* ; m. *khāsṇeṃ, khāṃsṇeṃ,* nep. *khāṃsinu.* Cf. *kässa.*

594. කළ **kaḷa,** a., pprt., done, made. — <MInd. *kaṭa*; Pk. *kaa*, P. *kata, kaṭa*, Sk. *kṛta* ; si. *kerdo*, g. *kīto, kīdho*, m. *kelā*, bg. *karā*, h. *kiyā*, pj. *kītā*. Cf. *karanavā*.

595. කළු **kaḷu,** a., black. In numerous cpds.: *kaḷu-karavalā, k°-poḷaṅgā*, names of black snakes; *k°-muvā* black monkey, etc. — Pk. *kālaa*, P. *kāḷa, kāla*, Sk. *kāla, kālaka* ; kśm. *kōlu*, si. *kāro*, g. *kāḷuṃ*, m. *kāḷā*, oṛ. *kaḷā*, bg. h. pj. *kālā*, nep. *kālo*, l. *kāḷā*.

596. කළුකඳ **kaḷu-kaňda,** s., name of a tree, Diospyros embryopteris (sort of ebony). — Sk. *kāla-skandha*.

— කළුරිය **kaḷuriya,** s., see s.v. **kaluriya.** The spelling with *ḷ* is probably caused by the influence of the word *kaḷu*.

597. කළුලුණු **kaḷu-luṇu,** s., black salt obtained by boiling saline earth. — P. *kāḷa-lōṇa*.

598. කළුවර **kaḷuvara,** s. ebony tree, Diospyros ebenum. — The comparison with P. *kōviḷāra*, Sk. *kōvidāra*, Bauhinia variegata, another sp. of ebony, is doubtful. In this case we must assume a metathesis of *ḷ* and *v* and probably an influence of popular etymology (*kaḷu* black). But cf. *kaḷu* black + *hara* "the hard part of the tree" (Ruv 653).

599. කා **kā[1],** s., crow. — Pk. *kāa*, P., Sk. *kāka* ; kśm. *kāv*, si. *kāṃ, kāṃu*, g. m. *kāū*, h. nep. *kāg*, pj. *kāṃ*.

600. කා **kā[2],** s., body. — Pk. *kāa*, P., Sk. *kāya*.

601. කැක් **käk,** a., sorrowful, doubtful; s., *käk-kuma* (v.s.v. *kama*[1]).— Sk. *kāṅkṣin* (P. *kaṅkhā*, Sk. *kāṅkṣā*).

602. කැකිර **käkira,** s., st. f. *°ri*, cucumber. — Pk. *kakkaḍa.*, *°ḍiā*, P. *kakkārī*, Sk. *karkaṭa*, *°ṭī, karkāru* ; g. *kākaḍ, kākḍī*, m. *kākaḍ, kāṃkḍī*, or. *kākuṛi*, bg. *kāṃkuṛ*, h. *kakṛī*, nep. *kāṃkro, kākhro*, pj. *kakkaṛī*.

— කැකුළු **käkuḷu,** a., see s.v. **kakaḷa.**

603. කැත් **kät,** a., noble (by birth), royal. — Pk. *khattia*, P. *khattiya*, Sk. *kṣatriya*. Cf. B II. 88, 156.

604. කැති **käti,** s, pl., the Pleiades; *käti-näkata* id. — Pk. *kattia*, P. *kattikā*, *°ka*, Sk. *kṛttikā, kārttika* ; nep. *kirkiṭi*, pj. *kirkhaṭī*, l. *kirkaṭāṃ*.

605. කැත්ත **kätta,** s., st. f. *käti*, bill-hook, chopper, hatchet. — Sk. *kartṛkā, kartrikā* ; si. *kātī*, g. *katī*, m. *kattī*, h. *kātī*.

606. කැඳ **käňda,** s., gruel, starch. — P. *kañjika, kañjiya*, Sk. *kāñjika*.

607. කැන **käna,** s., st. f. *kän*, bunch (of fruits), multitude. — Pk. *khāṇī*, Sk. *khānī*; kśm. *khān*, si. *khāṇī*, g. m. *khāṇ, khāṇī*, ass. bg. nep. *khāni*, h. *khānī*. Semasiologically doubtful. In the MIAVs most of the words quoted have the meaning 'mine', but nep. 'abundance', ass. 'quantity'.

608. කැප **käpa,** a., dedicated, consecrated, proper, fit; s., offering (to a deity or demon). *käpa-karuvā* a priest's attendant, servitor. — P. *kappiya*, Sk. *kalpya*. Cf. *kapuvā*.

609. කැපුම **käpuma,** කැපවුම **käpavuma,** s., st. f. °*um*, shaking. — Nom. verb of **kapanavā* (**kapavanavā*) to shake ; Pk. *kampaï*, *kampēi*, P. *kampati*, °*pēti*, Sk. √*kamp*, *kampati*, °*tē*, caus. *kampayati*. Cf. g. m. h. *kāṃp*, nep. *kām* = Sk. *kampa*.

610. කැබැල්ල **käbälla,** °බෙල්ල °**bella,** s., st. f. °*li*, bit, piece, morsel. *käbeli-karanavā* to break into pieces. — Pk. *kavala*, P. *kabala*, Sk. *kavala*+-*ka* ; g. *koḷiyuṃ*, h. *kaul*, *kauliyā*, nep. *kauṃlā*.

611. කැම **käma,** කෙම **kema,** s., order, degree. *kämen*, *kemen* by degrees, gradually. — Pk. *kama*, °*mēṇa*, P. *kama*, °*mēna*, Sk. *krama*, °*mēṇa*.

612. කැමති **kämati,** කැමැත්තා **kämättā,** a. s., see s.v. **kama**[2].

613. කැමියා **kämiyā,** s., st. f. *kämi*, worker, doer; writer. — Pk. *kammia*, P. *kammika*, *kammin*, Sk. *karmika*, *karmin* ; si. *kamī*, m. h. *kāmī*, nep. *kāmi*, l. *kammī*.

614. කැල් **käl,** s., light, morning. — Pk. *kallaṃ*, *kalhiṃ* yesterday, P. *kallaṃ* at dawn, Sk. *kalyē*, *kalyam* id. The corresponding words in the MIAVs mean 'yesterday' or 'to-morrow' : kśm. *kāl*, si, *kalha*, g. m. *kāl*, oṛ. ass. *kāli*, bg. *kāl*, *kāli*, h. *kal*, nep. *kāl*, pj. *kall*, *kallu*, l. *kallh*. B I. 350, 351.

615. කැලිය **käliya,** s., st. f. *käli*, bud of a flower. — Pk. *kaliā*, P., Sk. *kalikā* ; si. *kali*, g. m. *kaḷī*, ass. bg. nep. *kali*, h. pj. l. *kalī*.

616. කැලි **käli,** s., st., f. °*li*, menstrual woman. — I derive the word from P., Sk. *kālikā*, lit. a woman who has her terms. If it is to mean 'black woman' (Ca), it should be spelt *käḷi*.

617. කැස **käsa**[1], s., st. f. *käs*(*a*), armpit. *käs-paṭa* (*käsa-p*°) lower part of the skirt tucked up to the waistband. — Pk. *kaccha* (*kakkha*), P. *kacchā*, Sk. *kakṣā* ; kśm. *kach*, si. *kacha*, °*u*, g. *kāch* (*kākh*), m. *kās* (*kākh*), oṛ. h. nep. *kāch* (*kākh*), bg. *kāch* (*kāṃkh*), pj. l. *kacch*.

618. කැස **käsa**[2], s., st. f. *käs*, thicket. *käs-vaṭuvā* snipe. — P. *kaccha* grass, weeds, Sk. *kakṣa* forest, grass. Cf. kśm. *kach*, g. m. *kās* (Bl).

619. කැසුබුවා **käsubuvā,** s., st. f. *käsubu*, turtle. — The word occurs in Sinh. in various forms : *kasubuvā*, *käsuṁbuvā*, *käsbävā*, st. f. *kasubu*, *käsubu*, *käsuṁbu*, *käsup*, *käsba*. Pk. *kacchava*, P. *kacchapa*, Sk. *kacchapa*, ved. *kaśyapa* ; kśm. *kochuvu*, si. *kachūṃ*, m. *kāsav*, bg. *kāchim*, h. *kachvā*, nep. *kachuvā*, pj. *kacchū*.

620. කැස්ස **kässa,** s., st. f. *käsi*, cough. — <*kāsita* (see *kahinavā*) ; cf. P., Sk. *kāsa*.

621. කිකරුවා **kikaruvā,** s., st. ff. °*ra*, °*ru*, servant. — Pk. *kiṃkara*, P. *kiṃkara*, Sk. *kiṃkara*+-*ka*. — cf. *kīkaru*.

— කිකිළි **kikiḷi,** s., see s.v. **kukuḷā.**

622. කිඩය **kiḍaya,** කිඩිය **kiḍiya,** කිඩුව **kiḍuva,** s., st. ff. *kiḍi, kiḍu,* sport, pleasure; dancing. *kiḍī, kiḍiya* dancing girl; *kiḍi-karanavā* to conjure, juggle; *kiḍu-bima* play-ground. — Pk. *kheḍḍā* (*kīḍā*), P. *khiḍḍā* (*kīḷā*); Sk. *krīḍā*; si. *kheḍa*, pj. l. *kheḍ*. Cf. *keḷiya*.

623. කිඩියරයා **kiḍiyarayā,** s., st. f. °*ra*, player, conjurer. — Sk. *krīḍā-kāra*+-*ka*.

624. කිණසව(යා) **kiṇasava(yā),** s., st. f. °*va*, Buddhist Saint. — P. *khīṇ-âsava*, Sk. *kṣīṇâśrava*.

625. කිණු **kiṇu,** a., black. *kiṇu-maga* fire. — Pk. *kaṇha* (*kasiṇa, kaṇṇa*), P. *kaṇha*, Sk. *kṛṣṇa*; kśm. *krenhonu*. Cf. si. *kānu*, m. *kānhū*, h. pj. *kānh*, names of the God Krishna.

626. කිත් **kit,** s., fame. — Pk., P. *kitti*, Sk. *kīrti*. Cf. nep. *kitan* singing = Sk. *kīrtana*.

627. කිතුල් **kitul,** හිතුල් **hitul,** s., a species of palms, Caryota urens. — P., Sk. *hintāla*.

628. කිඳුරා **kin̆durā,** s., st. f. °*ru*, a fabulous being, half human and half bird-like; fem. *kin̆durī* or *kin̆dur'-an̆gana*. — Pk., P. *kinnara*, °*rī*, Sk. *kiṃnara*, °*rī*.

629. කිපි **kipi,** a. pprt., angry. — <MInd. *kupita*; cf. *kipenavā*.

630. කිපෙනවා **kipenavā,** v., prt. *kipuṇā*, to become irritated, be angry. — Pk. *kuppaï*, P. *kuppati*, Sk. √ *kup, kupyati*; m. *kopṇeṃ*.

631. කිඹිසිනවා **kim̆bisinavā,** °හිනවා °**hinavā,** v., prt. *kim̆bissā*, to sneeze. — <*kim̆bi* +*isinavā*; *kim̆bi* = P. *khipita* sneezing. Cf. Sk. √*kṣiv, kṣīvati, kṣīvyati*.

632. කිඹුලා **kim̆bulā,** s., st. f. °*m̆bul*, crocodile. — Pk., P. *kumbhīla*, Sk. *kumbhīra*; m. *kuṃbhīr*, oṛ. *kumbhira*, ass. *kumbhir*, bg. *kumir*, h. *kumhīr*, nep. *kubir*, *kubhir*.

633. කිඹුල්වන් **kim̆bul-van,** a., fawny. — *kim̆bul* stands for **kim̆bil* = Pk. *kavila*, P., Sk. *kapila*; pj. *kailā*, l. *kêḷā*, nep. *kailo* grey. Cf. *vana*.

— කිම් **kim,** කිමට **kimaṭa,** see s. **ka-.**

634. කිමියා **kimiyā,** s., st. f. *kimi*, worm, insect. *kimi-lom*, lit. worm-hair, silk fibre. — Pk., P. *kimi*, Sk. *kṛmi*.

635. කියත **kiyata,** s., st. f. *kiyat*, saw. *kiyat-kuḍu* sawdust. — P. *kakaca*. Sk. *krakaca* (? *t* < c).

636. කියනවා **kiyanavā,** v., prt. *kiyuvā, kivuvā, kīvā*, to say, tell. *kiyā-denavā* to explain. Caus. *kiyavanavā*, prt. *kiyevuvā*, to cause to say, read: intr. (of caus.) *kiyavenavā*, prt. *kiyavuṇā* to become said or read. — Pk. *kahēi*, caus. *kahāvēi*, P. *katheti*, *kathāpēti*, Sk. *kathayati*; si. *kahaṇu*, g. *kahevuṃ*, oṛ. *kahibā*, hi. *kahnā*, nep. *kahanu*, pj. *kahiṇā*.

637. කියාව **kiyāva,** s., st. f. *kiyā*, hump (of an ox). — P. *kakudha*, Sk. *kakud*, °*da*. Sinh. also *kiyaduva*, *kiyadiya*, st. ff. °*du*, °*di*. Doubtful.

638. කිර **kira**[1] (Cl), කිරවා **kiravā** (Ca), parrot. *kir'-aňgana* female parrot. Also *girā*, *giravā*. — P., Sk. *kīra* (+-*ka*).

639. කිර **kira**[2]**,** s., st. f. *kiri*, milk. *kiri-denavā* to suckle, *kiri-povanavā* id. In numerous cpds. *kiri-daruvā* suckling child ; *kiri-mav* wet-nurse ; *kiri-bat* milk-rice etc. — Pk., P. *khīra*, Sk. *kṣīra* ; kśm. *khir*, si. *khīru*, g. m. *khīr*, bg. nep. *khir*, b. h. pj. l. *khīr*.

640. කිරණව **kiraṇava,** s., sea of milk. — P. *khīraṇṇava*, Sk. **kṣirârṇava*.

641. කිරතා **kiratā,** °තයා °**tayā,** s., a Väddā. — Probably Slw. P., Sk. *kirāta*; nep. *kirāṃt*, *kirāṃti*. Or <**kiratta ?* Cf. Ind. Hist. Qu. xiv, 315.

642. කිරිය **kiriya,** s., st. f. *kiri*, a superficial measure, the extent of ground required to sow eight bushels of paddy. — P. *karīsa* (cf. Stede, PTSPD s.v.).

643. කිරියා **kiriyā,** s., st. f. *kiri*, elephant. — Pk. *kari*, P., Sk. *karin*+-*ka*.

644. කිරිරුක **kiri-ruka,** s., st. f. -*ruk*, name of a tree, Buchanania latifolia, lit. milk-tree. — Formally = Sk. *kṣīravṛkṣa* Ficus glomerata.

— කිරිල්ලි **kirillī,** s., see s.v. **kuruḷuvā.**

645. කිරිවැල **kiri-väla,** s., st. f. -*väl*, name of a creeper, Morinda umbrellata, lit. milk-creeper. — Formally = Sk. *kṣīravallī*, Batatia paniculata. Cf. nep. *khiramlo*, *khiraumlo*.

646. කිරිවුල **kirivula,** කිර° **kira°,** s., st. f. °*vul*, body. — Metathesis of **kilivur* = Pk., P, Sk. *kalēvara*.

647. කිරිසයුර **kiri-sayura,** s., st., f. °*ru*, sea of milk. — P. *khīra-sāgara*, Sk. *kṣīra-sāgara*.

648. කිරුළ **kiruḷa,** s., st. f. °*ḷu*, crown, diadem. *kiruḷu-miṇa* crown-gem. — P., Sk. *kirīṭa*.

— කිලය **kilaya,** s., see **iňdu-kilaya.**

— කිළිටි **kiliṭi,** a., see s.v. **kiluṭu.**

649. කිලිල **kilila** s., st. f. *kilil*, s., coconut cabbage. — P. *kalīra*, Sk. *karīra*.

650. කිළුටු **kiluṭu,** කිළිටි **kiliṭi,** a. pprt., filthy, dirty, impure; s. *kiluṭa* filth, defilement. — Pk., P. *kiliṭṭha*, Sk. *kliṣṭa*, √ *kliś*.

651. කිවි **kivi,** s., poet, name of the planet Venus. *kivi-dina* Friday. — P., Sk. *kavi*.

652. කිවියා **kiviyā,** s., st. f. *kivi*, black monkey. — P. *kapi*, *kavi*, Sk. *kapi*.

— කිස් **kis,** කිසි **kisi.** pron. a. see s. **ka-.**

— කිස **kisa**[1]**,** s., see **kusa.**

653. **කිස kisa²**, s., what should be done, duty.—Pk., P. *kicca*, Sk. *kṛtya* ; MIAVs *kaca* in m. *kacerī* etc., T s.v. *kacahari*.

654. **කිසිණු kisiṇu, කිසුණු kisuṇu**, a., all.—P. *kasiṇa*, Sk. *kṛtsna*.

655. **කිසුම kisuma, කුසුම kusuma**, s., st. f. °*sum*, flower. —Pk., P., Sk. *kusuma*.

656. **කිහිරි kihiri**, s., name of a tree, Acacia sundra (catechu).—Pk. *khaïra*, P. *khadira*, Sk. *khadira* ; kśm. *khaira*, si. *kherī*, g. *kher*, m. *kher*, *khair*, oṛ. *khaïra*, ass. *khair*, bg. *khayer*, b. h. pj. *khair*, nep. *khayar*.

657. **කිහිල්ල kihilla, කිසිල්ල kisilla**, s., st. f. °*li*, armpit.—Pk. *kaccha* etc. (v. *käsa*¹) + *l*-suffix.

658. **කිළිය kiḷiya¹** (or *killa*), s., st. f. *kiḷi*, menses, menstrual flux.—<**kīṭa* = Sk. *kiṭṭa* secretion.

659. **කිළිය kiḷiya²** s., st. f. *kiḷi*, hut, shanty. *gaňda-kiḷiya* q.v.—Pk. *kuḍī*, P., Sk. *kuṭī*, *kuṭikā* ; m. *kuḍī*, oṛ. *kuṛiā*, bg. *kuṛiyā*, nep. *kuri*.

660. **කී kī¹**, pron. interr., how many? In *kī-denek-da* how many persons ? Cf. *kī-pa*, *kī-payak* several.—Pk. *kaï*, P. *kati(-payā)*, Sk. *kati(-payē)* ; si. *kaïṃ*, g. *kaṃi*, bg. *kaek*, h. *kaī*, nep. *kaï*, pj. *kaī* or *kāī*, l. *kāi*.

661. **කී kī²**, a. pprt., said, spoken.—Pk. *kahia*, P., Sk. *kathita*. See *kiyanavā*.

662. **කීකරු kīkaru**, a., obedient, submissive; s. °*ruvā* obedient one; *kīkaru-kama* obedience.—*kī* = Sk. *kathita* + *karu(vā)*. Cf. *kikaruvā*.

663. **කුකුරා kukurā**, s., st. f. °*ru*, dog.—Pk., P. *kukkura*, Sk. *kurkura*, *kukkura* ; g. m. *kukar*, oṛ. *kukura*, ass. bg. *kukur*, h. pj. *kūkar*, nep. *kukur*, *kukkur*.

664. **කුකුස kukusa**, s., st. f. *kukus*, doubt.—P. *kukkucca*.

665. **කුකුළා kukuḷā**, s., st. f. *kukuḷu*, *kukul*, cock ; fem. *kikiḷi* hen. *kukuḷu-mālu* or *kukul-mālu* fowl flesh.—Pk. *kukkuḍa*, °*ḍī*, P., Sk. *kukkuṭa*, °*ṭī* ; kśm. *kokoru*, *kokürü*, si. *kukuṛu*, °*kiṛi*, g. *kukḍo*, °*ḍī*, ass. *kukurā*, oṛ. bg. *kukuṛā*, h. *kukṛā*, °*ṛī*, pj. *kukkaṛ*, °*ṛi*, l. *kukkuṛ*, °*iṛ*, nep. *kukhro*, °*ri*.

666. **කුඩා kuḍā**, a., small, little; s. pl. *kuḍu* little bits, morsels, dust. *kuḍā-kama* smallness, meanness; *kiyut-kuḍu* sawdust ; *kuḍu-karanavā* to powder.—Pk. *khuḍḍa*, Sk. *kṣudra* (+-*ka*). Cf. *kudu*².

667. **කුණු kuṇu**, a., dirty, filthy; s. *kuṇa* dirt, carcase, pl. *kuṇu*. *kuṇu-mas* putrid flesh.—Seems to be connected with P., Sk. *kuṇapa* carcase.

668. **කුදිටු kudiṭu**, a., heretical; s. °*ṭuvā* heretic.—P. *ku-diṭṭhi*, Sk. *ku-dṛṣṭi*, *-dṛṣṭa*. —*ku-* = P., Sk. *ku-* pref. implying badness, contempt + *diṭu* q.v.

669. **කුදු kudu¹**, a., hunch-backed; s. *kudā* (°*dī*) hunch-backed man (woman) —Pk., P. *khujja*, *kujja*, Sk. *kubja* ; m. *khujā*, oṛ. *kujā*, ass. *kuṃzā*, bg. *kuṃjā*, nep. *kujo*.

670. **කුදු kudu[2]**, a., s m a l l, s h o r t, d w a r f i s h. *äda-kuda*, v. *äda*. — Corresponds to P. *khudda*; oṛ. *khūdar*, ass. *khūd*, bg. *khudiyā*, nep. *khudro*.

671. **කුබුදිනවා kubudinavā, පුබු° pubu** °or **කිබිදෙනවා kibidenavā, පිබි° pibi°**, v., prt. *kibiduṇā*, *pibiduṇā*, t o a w a k e. Caus. *kubuddanavā*, *pubuddanavā*, prt. *kibidduvā*, *pibidduvā*, to awaken, arouse. — *kub°* by dissimilation < *pub°*. P. *pabujjhati*, Sk. *pra* + √ *budh*, *pra-budhyatē*; cf. kśm. *bōzun*, si. *bujhaṇu*, g. *bujvuṃ*, m. *buj(h)ṇeṃ*, oṛ. *bujhibā*, ass. *buziba*, bg. *bujhā*, h. *būjhnā*, nep. *bujhnu* to understand, l. *bujhāvaṇ* to beckon. Sinh. also contracted: caus. *kūddanavā*, prt. *kīdduvā*, to awaken, and *pūdinavā* to come into ear, to flower for the first time (cf. *kubudu*).

672. **කුබුදු kubudu, පුබුදු pubudu,** a. pprt., e x p a n d e d, o p e ṇ e d (as a flower). — Sk. *prabuddha*.

673. **කුඹ(ය) kum̆ba(ya)[1]**, **°ඹු(ව)** *°m̆bu(va)*, s., st. f. *kum̆bu*, p o t. — Pk., P., Sk. *kumbha*+-*ka*.

674. **කුඹය kum̆baya[2]**, s., st. f. *kum̆ba*, m a s t (of a ship). *kum̆ba-gaha* id.; *äṇi-kum̆baya*, v. *äṇi*. — Pk. *kūva*, P., Sk. *kūpa*. Cf. also P. *kumbhaka*.

675. **කුඹලා kum̆balā**, s., st. f. *°m̆bal*, p o t t e r. *kum̆bal-saka* potter's wheel. — Cf. *kum̆baya*[1], *kum̆bu-karuvā*; nep. *kumāle*, *kumhāle* (cf. T s.v.). Prob. blending of Sk. *kumbha* and *kulāla* potter.

676. **කුඹුකරුවා kum̆bu-karuvā**, s., st. f. -*karu*, p o t t e r. — Pk. *kumbha-āra*, P., Sk. *kumbha-kāra*; si. *kumbharu* or *°āru*, g. m. *kuṃbhār*, oṛ. *kumbhāra*, ass. *kumār*, bg. *kumar*, h. pj. *kumhār*, l. *kumbhār*.

677. **කුඹුතලය kum̆bu-talaya,** s., st. f. -*tala*, the place of an elephant's f r o n t a l g l o b e, Kus 90, 203. — Sk. *kumbha-sthala*.

678. **කුඹුර kum̆bura,** s., st. f. *°ru*, r i c e - s w a m p, p a d d y f i e l d. — Probably formally = *gäm̆buru* q.v. The initial *k* for *g* shows Tamil influence.

679. **කුමරුවා kumaruvā, °rā,** s., st.f. *°ru*, s o n, c h i l d; p r i n c e; fem. *kumarī* young girl, princess. — Pk. *kumāraa*, P., Sk. *kumāraka*; si. *kuṃāro*, *°rī*, g. *kuṃvar*, *°vāruṃ*, *°varī*, m. *kuṃvar* or *°ār*, oṛ. *kuāṃri* f., ass. bg. *kumāri* f., h. *kuṃvar* or *°ār*, *°ḷirā*, *°vārī*, nep. *kumār*, *kuṃvār*, pj. *kaṃvārā*, *kamārā*, *°rī*, l. *kuārā*, *°rī*.

680. **කුමුක් kumuk,** s., name of a t r e e, Areca palm. — P. *kamuka*, Sk. *kramuka* (?-*uk*). cf. T s.v. *kimbu*.

681. **කුරය kuraya, °රේ °rē,** s., st. f. *kura*, h o o f. *kura-rada* hoof-dust. — Pk., P., Sk. *khura*; si. *khuru*, g. *khur*, m. *khūr*, ass. *khurā*, oṛ. bg. h. nep. pj. *khur*, l. *khurā*.

682. **කුරරයා kurarayā, °ලයා °layā,** s., st. ff. *°ra*, *°la*, s e a - e a g l e, o s p r e y. — P. *kurara*, Sk. *kurara*, *°la*. lw.

683. කුරිරු **kuriru,** a., c r u e l, m e r c i l e s s ; s. *kuriruvā* cruel person. — P. *kurūra,* Sk. *krūra* (cf. Pk. *kūra*).

684. කුරු **kuru,** a., s h o r t, d w a r f i s h ; s. *kurā* dwarf, pigmy. — Cf. Sk. *kharva.*

685. කුරුඟ **kuruṅga,** s., st. f. °*ṅgu, kuruṅgu-muvā,* d e e r, a n t e l o p e. — P., Sk. *kuraṅga.*

686. කුරුඳු **kuruṅdu,** s., c i n n a m o n. *kuruṅdu-gala* cinnamon gem, hyacinth corundum. — P., Sk. *kuruvinda* ; si. *kuriṃdu,* m. *kuruṃd,* h. *kuraṃḍ,* pj. *kuruṃḍ* corundum.

687. කුරුළුවා **kuruḷuvā,** °ල්ලා °**llā,** s., st. f. °*ḷu,* b i r d ; fem. *kirillī.* — Pk. *garuḍa,* °*ḷa,* P. *garuḷa,* Sk. *garuḍa*+-*ka.* The initial *k* for *g* shows Tamil influence. Cf. *guruḷā.*—? Or connected with T. *kuruvi* (De Lanerolle).

688. කුලය **kulaya,** s., st. f. *kula,* f a m i l y, c a s t e, r a n k, t r i b e. *kul'-aṅgana* woman of rank. — Probably lw. Pk., P., Sk. *kula* ; kśm. *kol,* si. *kuru,* g. *kuḷ,* m. *kūḷ,* oṛ. *kuḷa,* ass. bg. h. nep. pj. *kul,* l. *kull.*

689. කුලුණ **kuluṇa,** s., st. f. °*ṇu,* m e r c y, k i n d n e s s. — Pk., P., Sk. *karuṇā.* The spelling *kuḷuṇa* is wrong. Cf. EpZ I. 33^{4}, 10th c. etc.

690. කුස **kusa,** කිස **kisa,** s., st. ff. *kus*(*a*), *kis,* w o m b, i n t e r i o r, h o l l o w. *kusa-ginna* hunger, lit. fire in the interior (of the body). — Pk. *kucchī* (*kukkhī*), P. *kucchi,* Sk. *kukṣi* ; kśm. cf. *kōch* (si. *kukhi,* g. *kukh*), m. *kūs,* (nep. *kokh*), pj. *kucch* (*kukkh*).

691. කුහුල් **kuhul,** a., d o u b t f u l, u n c e r t a i n. *kuhul-kama* doubtfulness. — Pk. *kuūhala,* P., Sk. *kutūha*'*a* curiosity.

692. කුළ **kuḷa^{1},** s., st. f. *kuḷu,* s l e d g e - h a m m e r. *kuḷu-geḍiya* id. — Pk. *kūḍa,* P., Sk. *kūṭa*+-*ka* ; h. *kūṛ,* pj. l. *kuṛ* parts of the plough.

693. කුළ **kuḷa^{2},** s., st. f. *kuḷu,* p e a k of a rock, s u m m i t of a mountain. — P., Sk. *kūṭa*+-*ka.*

694. කුළාර **kuḷāra,** s., b a l c o n y. *kuḷāra-geya* upper room, attic. — P., Sk. *kūṭâgāra.* Cf. *kuḷa*^{2}.

695. කුළාව **kuḷāva,** s., st. f. *kuḷā,* v e s s e l, j u g. — Pk. *kaḍāha,* P., Sk. *kaṭāha*-(*ka*) ; kśm. *krāy,* si. *kaṛāho,* g. *kaḍhā,* m. *kaḍhāī,* oṛ. *kaṛhā,* bg. *kaṛā,* h. *kaṛāhī,* nep. *karāi, karāhī,* pj. *kaṛāhā,* l. *kaṛāh.*

696. කුළු **kuḷu^{1},** a., p u n g e n t, a c r i d. *kuḷu-rasa* pungency ; *k°-tuna*(*-paha*) compound of three (five) pungent spices. — Pk. *kaḍua,* P., Sk. *kaṭu*(*ka*) ; si. *kaṛo,* g. *kaḍvuṃ,* m. *kaḍū,* oṛ. *kaṛuā,* ass. *karuvā,* bg. *kaṛuyā,* b. *karuā,* h. *kaṛvā,* nep. *kaṛuvā,* pj. *kaṛū.*

697. කුළු **kuḷu^{2},** a., d i s o b e d i e n t, w i l d, u n r u l y, f a l s e. *kuḷu-harakā* wild, refractory bullock ; *akuḷu, kuḷu* PPJ 92^{25} (= P. *akūṭa, kūṭa* Jā I. 192^{19}). — P., Sk. *kūṭa.*

— කූද්දනවා **kūddanavā,** v. caus., see s.v. **kubudinavā.**

698. කෙණෙර **keṇera,** s., female elephant. *keṇer'-añgana* id. — Pk. *karēṇu*, P. *kaṇēru*, *karēṇu*, Sk. *karēṇu*.

699. කෙණෙහි **keṇehi,** adv., immediately, forthwith. — Loc. of **kaṇa*[2]; *e-keṇehi* at that very moment. Cf. P. *taṃ khaṇē*, Sk. *tat kṣaṇāt*. Cf. Sinh. *saṇa*, *säṇa*.

700. කෙත **keta,** s., st. f. *ket*, paddy field. — Pk. *khetta* (*chetta*), P. *khetta*, Sk. *kṣētra*; kśm. *khīti*, si. *kheṭru*, g. *khet*, *khetar*, (m. *śet*), ass. *kheti*, bg. b. h. nep. *khet*, pj. *khet*, *khetar*.

701. කෙත්පල්ලා **ket-pallā,** s., st. f. °*lu*, farmer, cultivator, agriculturist. — P. *khetta-pāla*, Sk. *kṣētrapāla*+-*ka*.

— කෙම **kema**[1]**,** s., see **käma.**

702. කෙම **kema**[2]**,** s., st. f. *kem*, happiness, safety, security; a sort of magic. — Pk., P. *khēma*, Sk. *kṣēma*; MIAVs *-khim*, *-khīm*, *-kham* etc. in the derivates of Sk. *yōgakṣēma*. See T s.v. *jokhim*.

703. කෙයුර **keyura,** s., st.f. °*ru*, a bracelet or bangle worn above the elbow. — P., Sk. *kēyūra*.

704. කෙරෙන් **keren,** කෙරෙහි **kerehi,** case-affixes for the abl. and loc. respectively. — Paranavitana, EpZ III 330, n. 3, understands *keren* as instr. (abl.) sg. of *kara* hand, as is *atin* (=P. *hatthena*), used in the same manner, from (the hand of) a p., EpZ III. 329A[12], 12th c.; *kerehi* (<**karahi*=*karē*) would mean, in the hand of a p. The difficulty is, however, that in this case *keren*, *kerehi* would be separated from Sinh. Pk. *keriyahi*, as well as from Pk. *kēra*, and from the corresponding affixes in the MIAVs, B II. 281 sq. According to Pischel, Pk. §176, Pk. *kēra* should be derived from *kārya*.

705. කෙලසනවා **kelasanavā,** කෙලහ° **kelaha°,** v., prt. *kelasuvā*, °*huvā*, to pollute, contaminate. Intr. *kelasenavā*, *kelahe*°, prt. *kelasuṇā*, °*huṇā*, to become polluted. — P. *kilēsēti* (caus. of *kilissati*), Sk. √*kliś*, *kliśyatē*, caus. *klēśayati*.

706. කෙලෙස් **keles** in *keles-kuḷa*, s., name of a sacred mountain. — P. *kēlāsa*, Sk. *kailāsa*.

707. කෙලෙස **kelesa,** s., st. f. *keles*, filth, worldly affection, passion. — Pk., P. *kilēsa*, Sk. *klēśa*.

— කෙවිලි **kevili,** s., see s.v. **kovulā.**

708. කෙවුළා **kevuḷā,** s., st. ff. *kevuḷu*, *kevul*, fisherman; fem. *kevuḷī*. — < MInd. **kēvāṭa*; Pk., P. *kēvaṭṭa*, Sk. *kaivarta*, °*tī*.

709. කෙවෙනවා **kevenavā,** v., prt. *kevuṇā*, to smart, pain, tingle. — *ke* < **kē* = Pk. *khēa*, P., Sk. *khēda*+*venavā*.

710. කෙස **kesa,** s., st. ff. *kes, kehe, kē,* hair of the head. *kes-väṭiya* bunch or knot of hair.—Pk., P. *kēsa,* Sk. *kēśa* ; kśm. *kīh,* si. *kesu,* g. *keś,* m. *kes, keṃs,* oṛ. *keśa,* bg. *keś,* h. nep. pj. l. *kes.*

711. කෙසුරු **kesuru,** s. (pl.), st. f. id., pollen (of flowers), dust.—P., Sk. *kēsara* stamen.

712. කෙස්ස **kessa,** s., st. f. *kesi,* key.—Pk. *kuñcikā, koñcikā,* P., Sk. *kuñcikā* ; kśm. *kunzu,* si. *kuñjī,* g. *kuṃcī,* m. *kuṃjī,* oṛ. *kuñci,* bg. *kuṃjī,* h. pj. l. *kuñjī,* nep. *kuñji.*

713. කෙහෙල් **kehel,** කෙසෙල් **kesel,** s., plantain. *kehel-gaha* the tree, *k.-geḍiya* the fruit.—Perhaps by vowel-levelling from **kadila* ; but Pk. *kaalī, kēlī,* P., Sk. *kadalī* ; si. *kelho, keviro,* g. *keḷ, keḷuṃ,* m. *keḷ, keḷī, keḷeṃ,* ass. bg. *kalā,* b. *kerā,* h. pj. *kelā,* nep. *kero.* *-s-* in *kesel* by false analogy.

714. කෙහෙලිය **keheliya,** කේලිය **kēliya,** s., st.ff. *keheli, kēli,* flag, banner. —< from **kadilikā* ; cf. P., Sk. *kadalī* flag.

715. කෙළ **keḷa[1],** s., end, terminus; a high number (10 millions). *keḷavara* end, extremity.—Pk. *kōḍi,* P., Sk. *kōṭi* ; si. m. pj. *koṭ.* Cf. g. *karoḍ,* h. nep. *karoṛ.*

716. කෙළ **keḷa[2],** s., spittle, saliva. *keḷa-tolu* drivelling, slavering (*tolu* lip), *keḷa-gahanavā* to spit.—Pk. *khēla,* P. *khēḷa,* Sk. *khēṭa.*

717. කෙළපත් **keḷa-pat,** a., that has reached the summit, perfect. —P. *koṭippatta.*

718. කෙළිනවා **keḷinavā,** v., prt. *keḷiyā,* to play, sport.—Pk. *kīḍaï,* P. *kīḷati,* Sk. *krīḍati.* Cf. Sk. √*khēl, khēlati* to move to and fro, swing, Pk. *khēlaï, khellaï* ; kśm. *khēlun,* g. *khelvuṃ,* m. *kheḷṇeṃ,* oṛ. *kheḷibā,* ass. *kheliba,* bg. *khelā,* h. *khelnā,* nep. *khelnu,* pj. *khelṇā.*

719. කෙළිය **keḷiya,** s., st. f. *keḷi,* play, sport.—P. *kēḷi* (Sk. *krīḍā*). Cf. Sk. *khēli* (Pk., P., Sk. *kēli*) ; kśm. *khēla,* si. *khela,* g. *khel,* m. *kheḷ,* oṛ. *kheḷa,* ass. bg. h. nep. pj. *khel.*

720. කෙළිල්ල **keḷilla,** s., st. f. *keḷili,* kneeling, knee. *keḷillen iṅdinavā* to squat.— P. *kōṭilla,* Sk. *kauṭilya* crookedness.

721. කෙළෙඹියා **keḷeṁbiyā,** s., st. f. °*m̆bi,* wealthy person, head of a family.—< **kōṭimbika* ; P. *kuṭumbin,* °*bika, kuṭimbika,* Sk. *kuṭumbin,* °*bika, kauṭumbika.*

722. කේ **kē,** s., name of a tree, Pandanus odoratissimus; *mūdu-keyiyā* id., *dunu-keyiyā* Pandanus foetidus.—Pk. *kēaa,* P., Sk. *kētaka.* Cf. T s.v. *keṃvarā.*

723. කොකුම් **kokum,** s., saffron.—Pk., P., Sk. *kuṅkuma* ; kśm. *kong,* si. *kumgū,* g. *kuṃkuṃ, kaṃkū,* m. *kuṃkūṃ,* h. *kuṃkum,* pj. *kuṃggū.*

724. කොට **koṭa[1],** a., short, abridged; s. *koṭā* short man.—*koṭa-karanavā* to shorten, curtail.—See *koṭanavā* ; cf. P. *koṭṭa,* Sk. *kuṭṭa* breaking.

725. **කොට koṭa**[2], ger. of v. *karanavā*, having done. In mediaev. Sinh. *koṭ*, later *koṭä*, in Sinh. Pk. *kaṭu*, later *koṭu*. — Pk. AMg. *kaṭṭu* (HSm); Cf. P. *katvā*, Sk. *kṛtvā*.

726. **කොටනවා koṭanavā**, v., prt. *keṭuvā*, to cut (as with an axe); to bruise, beat (as paddy when separating the husk from the grain). — Pk. *koṭṭēi*, P. *koṭṭēti*, Sk. *kuṭṭayati*; kśm. *kuṭun*, si. *kuṭaṇu*, g. *kuṭvuṃ*, m. *kuṭṇem*, oṛ. *kuṭibā*, ass. *kuṭiba*, bg. *kuṭā*, h. *kūṭnā*, nep. *kuṭnu*, pj. *kuṭṭṇā*, l. *kuṭṭaṇ*.

727. **කොටස koṭasa**, s., st. f. *koṭas*, part, portion, share. *koṭas-kārayā* shareholder, partner; *koṭas-karanavā* to portion. — P. *koṭṭhāsa*.

728. **කොටාර koṭāra**, s., store-room, store-house. — P. *koṭṭhâgāra*, Sk. *kōṣṭhâgāra*.

729. **කොටියා koṭiyā**, s., st. f. *koṭi*, panther. — P. *koṭṭhuka*, Sk. *krōṣṭu*, *krōṣṭar*.

730. **කොටුව koṭuva**, s., st. f. *koṭu*, enclosure, fortress, castle. *koṭu-pavura* wall of a fortress. — Pk. *koṭṭhaa*, P. *koṭṭha(ka)*, Sk. *kōṣṭha(ka)*; kśm. *kuṭhu*, si. g. *koṭho*, m. oṛ. *koṭhā*, ass. bg. *kuṭhi*, h. *koṭhā*, nep. *koṭho*, pj. *koṭṭhā*, l. *koṭhā*. All these words mean 'inner room, granary' etc. Semasiologically Sinh. *koṭuva* stands nearer to Sk. *kōṭṭa* fort.

731. **කොඬ koňḍa**, s., top of the arm, head of the shoulder (= *ura-isa*, Ca). — Sk. *krōḍa* flank; si. *koṛo*, oṛ. *koḷa*, bg. *kol*, h. *kolā*, nep. *kolṭo*, l. *kolī*.

732. **කොඬයා koňḍayā**, s., st. f. *koňḍa*, pig, huge hog. — Sk. *krōḍa* boar.

733. **කොඬොල koňḍola**, s., st. f. °*ňḍol*, ear ornament, earring. *koňḍolā* snake (Ca). — Pk., P., Sk. *kuṇḍala* (°*lin* snake); kśm. *kondolu*, si. *kuniru*, g. *kuṃḍal*, m. *kuṃḍalī*, oṛ. *kuṇḍaḷa*, bg. h. pj. *kuṇḍal*, nep. *kuṃṛulo*, l. *kundal*.

734. **කොත kota**, s., st. f. *kot*, spear, lance. *ul-kota* see s.v. *ula*. — Pk., P., Sk. *kunta*.

735. **කොතැඹුරු kotaṁburu**, s., coriander seed. — Sk. *kustumburu*, °*barī*; g. *kothmī*, °*mīr*, m. *kothiṃbīr*, h. *kothmīr*, *koṭhmīr*; Sinh. also *kottamalli*.

736. **කොඳ koňda**[1], s., a species of jasmine. — Pk., P., Sk. *kunda*.

737. **කොඳ koňda**[2], s., white esculent water-lily. — < **kunda* < **kum*^{u}*da* = Pk. *kumua*, P., Sk. *kumuda*.

738. **කොඳු koňdu**, a., made of goat's hair. — P. *kōjava*.

739. **කොන kona**, s., st. f. *kon*, corner, angle. *kon-karanavā* to put aside; *k°-venavā* to get to one side. — P., Sk. *kōṇa*; kśm. *kūn*, g. *koṇ*, m. *koṇ*, *kon*, oṛ. *koṇa*, h. *kon*, *konā*, nep. *kunu*, pj. *kūṇ*, *koṇ*, *koṇā*.

740. **කොබෝ kobō-**, s. (st. f.), dove, in *kobō-geḍi-vaḷalla* dove-cote. — P., Sk. *kapōta*. Cf. Sinh. *kobeyiyā* dove, probably from *kapōtaka*.

741. කොමඩු **komaḍu,** s., water-melon. — Sk. *kuṣmāṇḍa(ka)*; but Pk. *kumbhaṇḍa* (AMg. *kohaṇḍa, kūhaṇḍa*); nep. *kubhiṇḍo*, bg. *kumaṛā*, h. *kamṛhā*.

742. කොමු **komu-,** s. (st. f.), goat's hair cloth; also *komu-piḷiya, komu-vata* id. — P. *khōma*, Sk. *kṣauma*.

743. කොර **kora,** a., lame, limping; s. *korā* lame person or animal; *kora-gahanavā* to go limping. — Sk. *khōra, khōḍa*, (P. *koṇḍa*); g. *khoḍuṃ*, m. *khoḍ*, ass. *khorā*, bg. *khoṃṛā*, h. *khorā*, (nep. *khoraṇḍo*).

744. කොවුලා **kovulā,** s., st. f. *kovul*, Indian cuckoo; fem. *kevilī*. — Pk. *kōila*, P., Sk. *kōkila*; si. *koila*, g. *koyal*, m. *koil, koīl, koyāḷ*, oṛ. *koili*, h. *koīl*, nep. *koili*, pj. *koil*.

745. කොස් **kos,** s. (pl.), fruits of the jak-tree. *kos-gaha*, name of the tree, Artocarpus integrifolia. — Sk. *kōśa* the inner part of the jak-fruit, BR s.v. 1, o.

746. කොස්ස **kossa,** s., st. f. *kohu*, brush, broom. — Pk. *kucca*, Sk. *kūrcaka*, °*cikā*; si. *kuco, kūcī*, g. *kūco*, m. *kuṃcā*, °*cī*, bg. *kuci, kuṃci*, h. *kūcā*, °*cī*, nep. *kuco*, pj. *kucc, kūccī*, l. *kuccin*.

747. කොහොන් **kohon,** a., deceptive, hypocritical. — P., Sk. *kuhana*.

748. කොහොල් **kohol,** a., = *kohon*, q. v.

749. කොළනවා **koḷanavā,** v., to press, smooth, flatten. *koḷana-lada*, DhpAGp 25^{24}, trsl. of P. *ākōṭita-paccākōṭitehi*, Dhp-a I 37^{17}. — P. *-kōṭēti*.

750. කෝ **kō,** s., anger. — Either = Pk. *kōva*, P., Sk. *kōpa*, or more probably = Pk. *kōha*, P. *kōdha*, Sk. *krōdha*; g. *koh(paṇ)*, oṛ. *koha*, h. *koh*.

ග GA

751. ගඟ **gaṅga,** s., st. f. *gaṃ*, river, stream. *gaṃ-toṭa* ferry. — Pk., P., Sk. *gaṅgā*.

752. ගටනවා **gaṭanavā,** v., prt. *gäṭuvā*, to dash together. Intr. *gäṭenavā*, prt. *gäṭuṇā*, to strike against, hit, collide. — P. *ghaṭṭēti* touches, joins, Sk. √*ghaṭṭ, ghaṭṭatē, ghaṭṭayati*. Cf. T s.v. *ogaṭnu*.

753. ගඩ **gaḍa,** s., swelling, in *gaḍa-geḍiya* boil, abscess. — Pk., P. *gaṇḍa* swelling, Sk. *gaṇḍa*; kśm. *gonḍu* jaw; si. *gani, ganari*, g. m. *gāṃḍ*, oṛ. *gāṇḍi*, ass. bg. h. nep. *gāṃṛ*, pj. *ganu*, l. *gannh*, all denoting something swollen.

754. ගඩය **gaḍaya,** s., st. f. *gaḍa*, ditch. — Pk. AMg. *gaḍḍa* hole (Pischel § 289 = Sk. *garta*); oṛ. *gāṛa*, b. *gāṛā*; cf. g. *gāḍvuṃ* to bury etc. Turner s.v. *gāṛnu*.

755. ගඩයා **gaḍayā,** s., st. f. *gaḍa*, gilt-head (fish). — Sk. *gaṇḍaka* a kind of fish.

756. ගඩුල **gaḍula,** a., humpbacked; s. °*layā* humpbacked person. — P., Sk. *gaṇḍula*.

757. ගඩුව **gaḍuva,** s., st. f. *gaḍu,* boil, carbuncle. — The same as *gaḍa* (q.v.) + *-ka.*

758. ගණන **gaṇana,** s., st. f. *gaṇan,* counting, reckoning, account. *gaṇan-karanavā* to count, enumerate. — P., Sk. *gaṇana* or °*nā.*

759. ගණය **gaṇaya,** s., st. f. *gaṇa,* company; multitude, assembly. *gaṇa-deṭuvā* president of an assembly. — Pk., P., Sk. *gaṇa.*

760. ගණිනවා **gaṇinavā,** v., prt. *giṇuvā, gännā,* to count, reckon, enumerate. Intr. *gäṇenavā,* prt. *gäṇuṇā,* to become reckoned. — Pk. *gaṇēi,* P. *gaṇēti,* Sk. $\sqrt{}$*gaṇ, gaṇayati* ; si. *gaṇaṇu,* g. *gaṇvuṃ,* m. *gaṇṇeṃ,* oṛ. *gaṇibā,* ass. *gaṇiba,* bg. *gaṇā,* h. *ginnā,* nep. *gannu,* pj. *giṇṇā, guṇṇā,* l. *gaṇaṇ.*

761. ගත් **gat,** a. pprt., taken (v. *gannavā*). — < **ghṛpta.* Cf. Pk. *ghettuṃ, ghettūṇa, ghettavva,* PISCHEL §§ 212, 548.

762. ගත **gata**[1], s., st. f. *gat,* limb, body. *gata-lakuṇu* marks on the body. — Pk., P. *gatta,* Sk. *gātra* ; g. m. *gāt* (ass. bg. *gā* = Pk. *gāa*), h. *gāt,* nep. *gāth.*

763. ගත **gata**[2], s., st. f. *gat,* book, literary composition. *gat-dhura* (a bhikkhu's) duty of studying the sacred texts. — Pk. AMg., P. *gantha,* Sk. *grantha.*

764. ගත්කරුවා **gat-karuvā,** s., st. f. °*ru,* author. — P. *ganthakāra,* Sk. *granthakāra* + *-ka.*

— ගඳඹා **gadam̆bā,** s., see s.v. **gan̆daviyā.**

765. ගදුබුවා **gadubuvā,** s., st. f. °*bu,* ass. — Pk. *gaddaha,* JM. *gaddabbha,* P. *gadrabha,* Sk. *gardabha* ; g. *gadho, gaddho,* oṛ. *gadha,* ass. *gādh,* bg. *gādhā,* b. h. *gadahā,* nep. *gadoho,* pj. *gadhā,* l. *gaddoṃ.* Cf. *gäḍum̆buvā.*

766. ගඳ **gan̆da,** s., smell, perfume, odour, stench. *gan̆da-mal* perfumes and flowers. — Pk., P., Sk. *gandha* ; g. m. h. pj. *gaṃdh,* Cf. g. m. *gāṃdhī* druggist = Sk. *gāndhika.*

767. ගඳකිළිය **gan̆da-kiḷiya,** s., st. f. °*ḷi,* fragrant house, apartment of the Buddha. — P. *gandha-kuṭi.*

768. ගඳවියා **gan̆daviyā,** ගඳඹා **gadam̆bā,** s., st. ff. °*vi,* °*m̆ba, gan̆dev,* musician, chorister. *gan̆dev-kulaya* a family of musicians. — Pk. *gandhavva,* P. *gandhabba,* Sk. *gandharva.* For *gadam̆bā* we must assume a Sk. form **gandharba,* or it is an old P. lw.

769. ගඳැතා **gand'-ätā,** s., st. f. *-ät,* elephant in rut. — Sk. *gandha-hastin.*

770. ගන **gana,** a., thick, dense. *gana-mē-kuḷa* dense cloud ; *gan'-aba* id.; *gana-sā* boughs dense with foliage. — Pk. *ghaṇa,* P., Sk. *ghana* ; kśm. *gonu,* si. *ghaṇo,* g. *ghaṇuṃ,* m. *ghaṇ,* ass. bg. *ghana,* h. *ghanā,* nep. *ghanu,* pj. l. *ghaṇā.*

771. ගනකල **gana-kala,** st. f. *-kal,* rainy season. — Sk. *ghana-kāla.*

772. ගනු **ganu,** ගයනු **gayanu,** s., playing a musical instrument.—P., Sk. *gāna+-ka.* Cf. Pk. *gāaï* sings, P., Sk. *gāyati* : kśm. *gevun,* si. *gāiṇu,* g. *gāvuṃ,* m. *gāṇeṃ,* oṛ. *gāibā,* ass. *gāiba,* bg. *gāoyā,* h. *gānā, gāunā,* nep. *gāunu,* pj. *gāuṇā.*

773. ගන්නවා **gannavā,** v., 3. sg. *ganiyi,* prt. *gattā* (v. *gat*), ger. *gena,* to take, assume. Caus. *ganvanavā,* prt. *gännuvā* (double caus. *gännevuvā*) to cause to take.—Pk. *geṇhaï,* P. *gaṇhāti,* Sk. √*gṛh, gṛhṇāti* ; si. *ginhaṇu,* m. *gheṇeṃ,* oṛ. *ghen,* h. *gahnā.* Sinh. *gena*=P. *gaṇhiya.*

774. ගප්සාව **gapsāva,** ගබ්සාව **gabsāva,** ගස්සාව **gassāva,** s., st. f. °*sā,* abortion. *gapsā-* (*gassā-*) *venavā* to miscarry ; *gassā-heḷanavā* to cause abortion. —Sk. *garbhasrāva* or *garbhâsrava.*

775. ගබ **gaba,** ගැබ **gäba,** s., womb, belly; interior, hollow. *gaba--peḷahara,* s., ceremony for the protection of the child in the womb.—Pk., P. *gabbha,* Sk. *garbha* ; kśm. *gab,* si. *gabhu,* g. *gābh, gābho,* m. *gābh, gābhā,* oṛ. *gābhil* pregnant, bg. *gāb, gābhā,* h. *gābh, gābhā,* nep. *gābho, gubho,* pj. *gabbh, gabbhā.* Gr. 23.1c, 54.2. Cf. *dā-gaba.*

776. ගබ්ගෙය **gab-geya,** s., st. f. *-gē,* inner room, chamber; lying-in chamber.—Sk. *garbha-gṛha.*

— ගබ්සාව **gabsāva,** s., see **gapsāva.**

777. ගම **gama,** s., st. f. *gam,* village, landed property. *gam-deṭuvā* village-chief.—Pk., P. *gāma,* Sk. *grāma* ; kśm. *gām,* si. *gāuṃ,* g. *gām,* m. *gāṃv, gāv,* oṛ. *gāṃ,* ass. *gāuṃ,* bg. *gāṃ,* b. h. *gāṃv,* nep. *gāuṃ.*

778. ගම්වැසියා **gam-väsiyā,** s., st. f. °*si,* villager.—P. *gāma-vāsika,* Sk. *grāma-vāsin.*

779. ගය **gaya,** s., st. f. *gā,* song, singing, verse, stanza.—Pk. *gāhā,* P., Sk. *gāthā.*

780. ගර **gara,** s., house, in the names of the snakes *garan̆ḍiyā, garavilā.*—Pk., P. *ghara* (P. *ghara-sappa* rat-snake); kśm. *gara,* si. *ghara,* oṛ. *ghara,* g. m. ass. bg. b. h. nep. pj. l. *ghar.* Cf. *giriṇi.*

781. ගරහනවා **garahanavā,** v., prt. *gärahuvā,* to reproach, rail at, scoff at. Intr. *gärahenavā,* prt. *gärahuṇā,* to be reviled.—Pk. *garihaï,* P. *garahati,* Sk. *garhati* ; m. *garhāṇeṃ, garāṇeṃ.*

782. ගල **gala**[1]**,** s., st. f. *gal,* stone, rock. *gal-kapannā* stone-cutter ; *gal-kuḷa* rock, peak etc.; frequently in mountain-names : *riṭi-gala, piduru-talā-gala* etc. The connection with Pk., P., Sk. *giri* is very doubtful ; the original meaning is 'stone'. — Cf. Tam. *kal.*

783. ගල **gala**[2]**,** ගෙල **gela,** s., st. ff. *gala, gela,* throat, neck. *gala-rōgaya* bronchitis.—Pk., P., Sk. *gala* lw. ; kśm. *golu* entrance, si. *garo,* g. *gaḷuṃ,* m. oṛ. *gaḷā,* ass. *gal,* bg. h. pj. *galā* nep. *galo,* l. *gaḷ.*

784. ගලනවා **galanavā,** v., prt. *gäluvā,* (intr.) to drip, overflow, flow; (tr.) to dip, submerge. Caus. *galvanavā,* prt. *gälluvā,* to infuse or apply a liquid; to submerge; intr. *gälenavā,* prt. *gäluṇā,* to sink in.—Pk. *galaï,* P. *galati,* Sk. √*gal, galati,* caus. *gālayati*; kśm. *galun,* si. *garaṇu,* g. *gaḷvuṃ,* m, *gāḷneṃ,* oṛ. *gaḷibā,* ass. *galiba,* bg. *galā,* h. *galnā,* nep. *galnu,* pj. *galṇā,* l. *gālaṇ.* See *gilinavā.*

— ගලිනවා **galinavā,** v., see **gilinavā.**

785. ගවයා **gavayā,** s., st. ff. *gava, gō,* ox, bullock; pl. cattle. *gav'-añga, gō-añga* ox-horn; *gav'-añgana* cow; *go-pallā* cowherd.—Pk. *gāvī* cow, P. *gō-, gava,* fem. *gāvī,* Sk. *gō, gava,* °*vī*; si. *gaūṃ,* g. m. *gau,* h. *gau, gaū,* nep. *gau, gauvā,* pj. *gaū,* l. *gaūṃ.*

786. ගවුව **gavuva,** s., st. ff. *gavu, gav,* measure of distance, league (= 5,600 yards).—P. *gāvuta* quarter of a yojana, Sk. *gavyūti* pasture land.

— ගස්සා **gassā,** s., see **gapsāva.**

787. ගහ **gaha,** ගස **gasa,** s., st. f. *gas,* tree. *gas-mīyā* tree-rat. Frequently *-gaha* in tree-names: *nā-gaha* iron-wood tree etc.—P., Sk. *gaccha*; bg. b. h. nep. *gāch.*

— ගහණ **gahaṇa,** a., see s.v. **goṇa.**

788. ගහනවා **gahanavā,** ගසනවා **gasanavā,** v., prt. *gähuvā, gäs*°, to beat, strike, knock; to affix (one thing to another); to drive in (as a nail). Caus. *gasvanavā, gassanavā* (double c. *gassavanavā*), prt. *gässuvā* (*gässevuvā*) to cause to go off (as a trap); intr. *gähenavā, gäs*°, prt. *gähuṇā, gäs*°, to be struck, to crack &c., *gässenavā,* prt. *gässuṇā,* to go off (as a trap).—Pk. *ghasaï,* P. *ghaṃsati,* caus. *ghaṃsāpēti,* Sk. √*ghṛs, gharṣati, gharṣayati*; kśm. *gahun,* si. *gahaṇu, gas*°, g. *ghāsvuṃ,* m. *ghāsṇeṃ,* oṛ. *ghasibā,* bg. *ghasā,* h. *ghasnā, ghisnā,* nep. *ghasnu,* pj. *ghasṇā.* Cf. *gānavā.*

789. ගළපනවා **gaḷapanavā,** v., prt. *gäḷapuvā,* to join, unite, link; compose, construct; intr. *gäḷapenavā,* prt. *gäḷapuṇā,* to become joined, linked together; to cohere. — Blending of Sk. √*ghaṭ,* caus. *ghaṭayati* and √*ar,* caus. *arpayati,* P. *appēti.*

— ගා **gā,** s., see **gaya.**

790. ගානවා **gānavā,** v., prt. *gāvā,* to rub on or over, to smear, plaster — Seems to be a contracted form of *gahanavā* which had preserved the original meaning of Sk. √ *ghṛṣ,* 'to rub' better than the non-contracted form.

791. ගැටය **gäṭaya,** s., st. f. *gäṭa,* knot, tie. *gäṭa-polañgā* knotted viper; *g*°*-huya* knotted thread; *gäṭa-gahanavā* or *-lanavā* to knot.—Pk., P. *ganṭhi,* Sk. *granthi*; kśm. *ganḍ,* si. *ganḍhi,* g. m. *gāṃṭh,* oṛ. *ganṭhi,* ass. *gāṃṭhi,* bg. *gāṃṭi,* h. *gāṃṭh,* pj. l. *ganḍh.* Cf. T s.v. *gānu.*

792. **ගැටයා gäṭayā,** s., st. f. *gäṭa*, lad, boy.—Lit. the unripe one ; cf. *gäṭaya* unripe fruit, *gäṭavarayā* young man.

793. **ගැටිස්සී gäṭissī,** s., st. f. *gäṭisi*, maiden, lass.—*gäṭa* unripe, young (v. *gäṭayā*)+*issī* fem. suffix ; cf. *ḷamissī* id.

794. **ගැඩලුවා gäḍaluvā,** s., st. f. *gäḍalu*, also *gäḍa* in *gäḍa-paṇuvā*, *gäḍa-vilā*, *-vulā* (= *gäḍaluvā*), large earth-worm, slow-worm.—Cf. P. *gaṇḍuppāda*, Sk. *gaṇḍūpāda*, *gaṇḍōlaka*. Cf. T s.v. *gaṛyauṃlo*.

795. **ගැඩඹු gäḍaṁbu, ගැඩුඹ gäḍuṁba, ගැඩුඹු gäḍuṁbu,** s., name of a tree, Trema orientalis.—P. *gaṇḍamba*.

796. **ගැඩවිය gäḍaviya,** s., st. f. *°vi*, Arjuna's bow.—Sk. *gāṇḍīva*.

797. **ගැඩුඹුවා gäḍuṁbuvā,** s., st. f. *°ṁbu*, ass, jackass, mule.—<MInd. **gaḍḍabha* = P. *gaḍḍaha* ; si. *gaḍahu*, m. *gāḍhav*, l. *gaḍḍaṃh*. Cf. *gaḍubuvā*.

798. **ගැඹුරු gäṁburu,** a., deep, profound ; s. *°ra*, depth.—Pk. *gahira*, P., Sk. *ga(m)bhīra* ; si. *gaharo*, g. *gheruṃ*, m. *gahirā*, oṛ. *gahira*, bg. *gairā*, h. *gahrā*, nep. *gairo*, *gahiro*, pj. *gahirā*.

799. **ගැළ gäḷa,** s., st. f. *gäl*, vehicle, cart, carriage. *gäl-akura* axle socket (of a vehicle) ; *gäl-viya* yoke of a cart ; *gäl-padinavā* to drive a vehicle.—Seems to be connected with MIAVs kśm. *goḍi*, si. *gāḍo*, g. m. *gāḍī*, oṛ. *gāṛi*, ass. *gāri*, bg. nep. *gāṛi*, b. h. *gāṛī*, pj. *gaḍḍ*, *gaḍḍī*, *gāḍḍī*, l. *gaḍḍ* (Bl and T s.vv.). In Sinh. we should expect the st. f. as *gäḷa* (not *gäl*).

800. **ගැහැවියා gähäviyā,** s., st. f. *°vi*, householder, husbandman. Also *goviyā* (q.v.) id., Ca.—P. *gahapati*, Sk. *gṛhapati*.

801. **ගැහැනී gähänī, ගෑනී gānī,** s., woman.—Sk. *gehinī*.

802. **ගිගිරිය gigiriya,** s., st. f. *gigiri*, noise, thunder.—<**ghurghurita* ; cf. *guguranavā* ; m. nep. pj. *ghurghur*, h. *gharghar*. Cf. *guguranavā*.

— **ගිතෙල් gitel,** s., see s.v. *giya*[3].

803. **ගිදු gidu, °ජු °ju,** a., greedy, voracious.—Pk., P. *giddha*, Sk. *gṛdhra* greedy, vulture ; g. m. h. *gīdh*, nep. *giddha*, pj. *giddh*. Gr. 34.1. For 'vulture' Sinh. has *giju-lihiṇiyā*. Cf. P. *gijjhati*, Sk. *gṛdhyati* to desire (JdeL).

804. **ගිනිකණ gini-kaṇa,** s., spark of fire.—Cf. Sk. *agni-kaṇa*.

805. **ගිනිකොණ gini-kona,** s., south-east quarter.—Cf. Sk. *agni-koṇa*.

806. **ගිනිදිව gini-diva,** s., tongue or flame of fire.—Cf. Sk. *agni-jihvā*.

807. **ගිනියම gini-yama,** s., st. f. *-yam*, heat, incandescence.—Cf. Sk. *agni-karman* cauterization.

808. **ගිනිරැස gini-räsa,** s., st. f. *-räs*, beam, sun.—Cf. Sk. *agni-rāśi* burning pyre.

809. ගිනිවන් **gini-van,** a., flame-coloured. — Cf. Sk. *agni-varṇa*.

810. ගිනිහල **gini-hala,** s, fire-place, room where fire is kindled. — Cf. Sk. *agni-śālā*.

811. ගින්න **ginna,** s., st. f. *gini*, fire. *gini-uduna* furnace, stove; *gini-gannavā* to catch fire; *g°-lanavā* to set fire to. — <MInd. **àgíni*. Cf. *aga*^{2}.

812. ගිම් **gim,** a., hot, burning; s. *gima*, *guma* heat; *gim-kala* hot season. — Pk., P. *gimha*, Sk. *grīṣma*; m. *gīm*.

813. ගිමන **gimana,** s., st. f. *giman*, heat. *giman-kala* hot season. — P. *gimhāna*.

814. ගිය **giya**^{1}, a. pprt., gone, past. *kal-giya* long-standing, old, ancient. — Pk. *gaa*, P., Sk. *gata*; kśm. *gōv*, g. *gayuṃ*, ass. *gāi*, h. *gayā*, nep. *gayo*, pj. l. *geā* (cf. also Bl s.v. *gelā*). See *yanavā*.

815. ගිය **giya**^{2}, ගීය **gīya,** s., st. f. *gī*, song, chant. *gī-kiyanavā* to sing. — Pk. *gīa*, P. *gīta*, *gītikā*, Sk. *gīta*, *gīti*, *gītikā*.

816. ගිය **giya**^{3}, s., st. f. *gī*, clarified butter. *gi-tel* id. — Pk. *ghaa*, P. *ghata*, Sk. *ghṛta*; kśm. *gev*, si. *gihu*, g. m. *ghī*, oṛ. *ghia*, ass. *ghiu*, bg. *ghi*, b. *ghīv*, *ghyū*, h. *ghī*, nep. *ghiu*, *ghiuṃ*, pj. *gheo*, l. *ghiū*.

817. ගිර **gira,** s., mountain. — Pk., P., Sk. *giri*. Sinh. *giriya*, st. f. *giri*, is lw.

— ගිරා **girā,** ගිරවා **giravā,** s., see s.v. **kira**^{1}.

818. ගිරි **giri,** a., reverend, venerable (Ca). — Pk. *garua*, P. *garuka*, Sk. *guru*; kśm. *goru*, si. *garo*, g. *garvuṃ*, h. *garuā*, nep. *garauṃ*.

819. ගිරිකඳුර **giri-kaňdura,** s., st. f. *°ru*, ravine. — P. *giri-kandara*, Jā V 89^{13}.

820. ගිරිණී **giriṇī, -°ṇiya,** s., st. f. *°ṇi*, wife. — Pk. *ghariṇī*, P. *gharaṇī*. Cf. *gara*.

821. ගිලන් **gilan,** a., invalid, infirm; s. *°nā* invalid person; *gilan-kama* infirmity. — Pk. P. *gilāna*, Sk. *glāna*.

822. ගිලන්පස **gilan-pasa,** s., things proper to be eaten by a sick bhikkhu; liquid food taken by a bh° after mid-day. — P. *gilāna-paccaya*.

823. ගිලි **gili**, a. pprt., fallen off. — Pk. *galia*. P., Sk. *galita*. Cf. *galanavā*.

824. ගිලිනවා **gilinavā,** ගැලිනවා **galinavā** v., prt. *gillā*, *gällā*, to swallow. Caus. *gilvanavā*, *gillanavā* (double c. *gillavanavā*), prt. *gilluvā* (*gillevuvā*), to cause to be swallowed, to immerse, submerge; intr. *gilenavā*, prt. *giluṇā*, to be swallowed, sink in. — P., Sk. *gilati*; cf. Pk. Apabhr. *gilijjaï*, Hem 4. 370. The meanings of *gilinavā* mix with those of *galanavā*.

825. ගිලිහෙනවා **gilihenavā,** v., prt. *gilihuṇā*, to drop or fall off (as flowers from a tree). — *gili*, q.v. + *henavā*, q.v. Ca spells *giḷih°*.

826. ගිව **giva,** s., st. f. *giv*, neck. *giv-baraṇa* neck-ornament. — Pk. P. *gīvā*, Sk. *grīvā*.

827. ගිහිණි **gihiṇi,** a., inherent, possessed of. *kuluṇen g°*, SälS 107.— ? Pk., P. *gahaṇa*, Sk. *grahaṇa*. As to the vocalism see the next word.

828. ගිහිනි **gihini** (Ca), a., thick, dense, close.— ? Pk., *gahaṇa*, P., Sk. *gahana*. See the preceding word.

829. ගිහියා **gihiyā,** s., st. f. *gihi*, layman, householder. *gihi-geya* household or family state.— Pk. *gihi*, P. *gihin*, Sk. *gṛhin+-ka*.

— ගී **gī**[1-2], s., see **giya** [2, 3].

830. ගුගුරනවා *guguranavā*, v., prt. *giguruvā*, to roar, thunder. Caus. *guguruvanavā*, prt. *gigirevuvā*, idem.— P. *ghurughurāyati* snorts, Sk. *ghuraghurāyati*; h. *ghurghurānā* to snarl, nep. *ghurghurāunu*. Cf. *gigiriya*.

831. ගුගුලු **gugulu,** s., fragrant gum, bdellium.— Pk. *guggula*, P. *guggulu*, Sk. *gulgulu*, *guggulu* : si. *guguru*, g. *gugaḷ*, m. *gugūḷ*, or. *guguḷa*, b. *gugul*, h. *gūgal*, nep. *gugul*, pj. *guggal*.

832. ගුටිය **guṭiya,** s., st. f. *guṭi*, blow, stroke; lump, ball.— Sk. *ghṛṣṭi*, *ghṛṣṭa*. Cf. *gahanavā*.

833. ගුම **guma,** s., st. f. *gum*, sound, noise.— <MInd. **ghumha*, OInd. **ghuṣma*; Sk. √*ghuṣ*.

834. ගුමුව **gumuva,** ගොමුව **gomuva,** s., st. ff. °*mu*, thicket.— Pk. *gumma*, P. *gumba(ka)*, Sk. *gulma*.

835. ගුරුළා **guruḷā,** s., st. f. °*ḷu*, a mythical bird, the Garuḍa.— Pk., P., Sk. *garuḍa*. Cf. *kuruḷuvā*.

836. ගුවන **guvana,** s., st. f. *guvan*, sky. *guvan-maga* idem.— Pk. *gaaṇa*, P., Sk. *gagana*.

837. ගුළ **guḷa,** s., st. f. *guḷa*, jaggery, raw or unrefined sugar (SdhRv 28^{23}, 866^{38}). *guḷa-piṇḍaya* lump of raw sugar.— Pk. *guḍa*, *guḷa*, P. *guḷa*, Sk. *guḍa*; kśm. *gōr*, si. *guru*, g. *goḷ*, m. *gūḷ*, or. *guṛa*, ass. *gur*, bg. b. h. nep. pj. l. *guṛ*. Ca spells *gula*, *gul*.

838. ගුළිය **guḷiya,** s., st. f. *guḷi*, ball, pill.— Pk. Mg. *guḍāha*, P. *guḷa*, *guḷikā*, Sk. *guḍaka*, *guḍikā*, *guṭikā*.

839. ගුළු **guḷu,** a. pprt., hidden, profound.— Pk. *gūḍha*, P. *gūḷha*, Sk. *gūḍha*. Cf. g. m. *gūj* = Sk. *guhya* (Bl).

840. ගෙඩිය **geḍiya,** s., st. f. *geḍi*, bulb, boil, fruit.— Probably P. *geṇḍuka*, Sk. *gēṇḍuka*; or. *geṇḍu*, bg. *geṃṛu*, nep. *geṃṛ* ball (to play with). In the other MIAVs *geṃd*=Sk. *genduka*; T, s.v. *geṃd*.

841. ගෙය **geya,** s., st. f. *gē*, pl. *ge-val*, house. *gē-kurullā* house-bird, sparrow.— Pk., P. *gēha*, Sk. *gṛha*. The Sinh. affixes *-gē* of (gen.) and *-gen* from (abl.) correspond to P. *gēhē*, *gēhēna*.

842. ගෙරියා **geriyā,** s., st. f. *geri*, bullock. *geri-mas* beef.— <MInd. **gōra-ka* = Sk. *gaura*.

— ගෙල **gela,** s., see **gala**[2].

843. ගෙවනවා **gevanavā,** v., prt. *gevuvā,* to wear away; to spend, pass (time): to pay. Intr. *gevenavā,* prt. *gevuṇā* to be spent, etc. — For **kevanavā.* Cf. P. *khēpēti,* Sk. *kṣēpayati.* Perhaps influenced by *giya*[1] gone, past.

— ගේ **-gē,** see s.v. **geya.**

844. ගොකටු **gokaṭu,** s., thistle, name of several thorny plants. — P., Sk. *gō-kaṇṭaka.*

845. ගොටලුව **goṭaluva,** s., st. f. *goṭalu,* cottage, hut. — Pk. P. *goṭṭha,* Sk. *gōṣṭha+l-* suffix; kśm. *guṭh,* si. *goṭhu,* g. *goṭho,* m. *goṭhā,* or. *goṭha,* bg. nep. *goṭh.*

846. ගොණ **goṇa,** s., nose (Ruv 287). — Pk., P. *ghāṇa,* Sk. *ghrāṇa.* Sinh. *gahaṇa* nose is a P. lw. with split aspirate.

847. ගොත **gota,** s., st. f. *got,* family, tribe. — Pk., P. *gotta,* Sk. *gōtra*; si. *gotṛu,* g. m. ass. h. nep. pj. l. *got,* bg. *gotā.*

848. ගොතනවා **gotanavā,** v., prt. *getuvā,* to plait, knit. — From √*gut gutth, gunt, gunth*; Pk. M. *guttha*: g. *gūṃth* entanglement, m. *gu(ṃ)tṇeṃ, gu(m)thṇem,* or. *gunthibā,* h. *gū(ṃ)thnā,* nep. *gutnu, guthnu* (see T, s.v.). Cf. P. *ganthati,* Sk. √*granth, granthayati.*

849. ගොදුර **godura,** s., st. f. °*ru,* fodder, pabulum, prey. — Pk. *gōara,* P., Sk. *gōcara.* The intermediate form *gojuru* occurs in DhpAGp 10[33].

850. ගොනා **gonā,** s., st. f. *gon,* bull, bullock, ox. — *gon-kama* bull-like conduct, stupidity. — Pk., P. *gōṇa.*

851. ගොප් **gop,** s., ankle in *gop-äṭaya* ankle-bone; *gop-mas* calf of the leg, lit. ankle flesh. — Pk. AMg. *guppha,* P. *goppha,* Sk. *gulpha*; m. *gophā.*

852. ගොම **goma,** s., cow-dung. — P., Sk. *gōmaya.*

— ගොමුව **gomuva,** s., see **gumuva.**

853. ගොමූ, **gomū.,** °මු °**mu,** s., cattle urine. — Pk. *gōmuttiā,* P. *gōmutta,* Sk. *gōmūtra*; kśm. *gūmith,* si. *gaumṭru,* b. nep. *gaumt.*

854. ගොයම **goyama,** s., st. f. *goyam,* growing corn, standing corn. — Pk. *gōhūma,* P., Sk. *gōdhūma* wheat; si. *gehūṃ,* g. *gahuṃ, ghauṃ,* m. *gahūṃ,* or. *gahama,* bg. *gom,* b. *gahum,* etc., h. *gehūṃ,* nep. *gahuṃ.* Gr. 42.II.4.

855. ගොයා **goyā,** s., large land-lizard, iguana. — Pk. *gōhā,* P., Sk. *gōdhā*; si. *goha,* bg. *go-,* h. pj. l. *goh,* nep. *goho-ro.*

— ගොයියා **goyiyā,** s., see **goviyā.**

856. ගොයුම් **goyum,** s., Gautama in cpds. as *goyum-gota* the Gautama line of descent. — Pk. AMg. *gōyama,* P. *gōtama,* Sk. *gāutama.*

857. ගොර **gora**[1], a., white. — Pk., P. *gōra,* Sk. *gāura*; si. *goro,* g. *goruṃ,* m. or. bg. h. pj. l. *gorā,* nep. *goro.*

858. **ගොර gora^2,** a., dreadful. — Pk., P., Sk. *ghōra.*

859. **ගොවඩ go-vada, ගොවුඩ govuda,** s., cattle pen or stall. — *go* (see *gavayā*) + *vada* ; Sk. *gō-vraja.*

860. **ගොවියා goviyā, ගොයියා goyiyā,** s., st. ff. °*vi*, °*yi*, householder, agriculturist. Also *gähäviyā* (q.v.) id., Ça. *govi-(goyi-)täna* agriculture, husbandry. — Pk. *gōvaa, gōvaga*, P., Sk. *gōpaka;* but cf. Sinh. Pk. GAPATI id. (*gṛhapati*), WICKREMASINGHE, EpZ I p. 20 (Cave No. 9).

861. **ගොවුවා govuvā,** s., st. f. *govu*, caretaker, keeper, cattle-keeper. *ät-govuvā* elephant-keeper; *as-govuvā* horse-keeper. — fem. *geviya* (*gōpikā*), st. f. *gevi*, woman caretaker: *äl-gevi-liya* a woman caretaker of a rice field. — Etymologically = *goviyā*, but semasiologically distinguished from it.

862. **ගොස් gos,** ger. of v. *yanavā*, having gone. — <MInd. **gacca* = Sk. *-gatya.*

863. **ගොස gosa,** s., st. f. *gos*, noise, sound. — Pk. P. *ghōsa*, Sk. *ghōṣa.*

864. **ගෝනා gōnā,** s., pl. *gōnnu*, elk, stag. — P. *gōkaṇṇa*, Sk. *gōkarṇa* + *-ka.*

ට Ṭ

865. **ට -ṭa, අට -aṭa,** affix of the Dative Case. Cf. W. GEIGER, Sinh. Grammar, §112. — Pk. *aṭṭhaṃ, aṭṭhāē*, P. *atthaṃ, atthāya*, Sk. *artham, arthāya.* Cf. Sinh. *ballāṭa* to the dog = MInd. **bhallukass'aṭṭhaṃ*, °*āya*, pl. *ballanṭa* = MInd. **bhallukān'aṭṭhaṃ*, °*āya* ; *ataṭa* to the hand = MInd. **hatth'aṭṭhaṃ*, °*āya*, pl. *atvalaṭa* = MInd. **hattha-vāraṭṭhaṃ*, °*āya.* For the linguistic feeling of a modern Sinhalese *-ṭa* is an affix like *-gē, -gen* : *goviyā-ṭa* etc.

866. **ටැඹ ṭämba,** s., st. f. *ṭäm*, pillar, stone-pillar. — Pk. *ṭhambha* (and *thambha*, PISCHEL § 308), (P. *thambha*), Sk. *stambha* ; (kśm. *tham*, si. *thambhu*, g. *thāṃbhlo.* bg. *thām*, h. *thāṃbh, thāṃb*, nep. *thām*, pj. *thammh*, l. *thamm*).

867. **ටික් ṭik,** s., mark in *talā-ṭik-bandu* like unto a tilaka mark, EpZ I.32^2, 10th c. (WICKREMASINGHE, ib., p. 33 n. 6). Cf. EpZ III. 298 A^2, 300 n. 4. — < MInd. **ṭikka* ; kśm. *ṭikā*, si. *ṭiko*, g. *ṭīko*, m. oṛ. bg. *ṭikā*, h. *ṭīkā*, nep. *ṭiko*, *ṭikā*, pj. l. *ṭikkā.*

868. **ටික ṭika,** a., little, few. *ṭikak* a little, *ṭikakin* in a little while ; *ṭikin-ṭika* little by little, gradually. — Pk. *thokka*, P. *thōka(-ka)*, Sk. *stōka* ; si. *thoku*, oṛ. *thoke*, m. ass. bg. h. nep. pj. l. *thok.* But *-i-* ? Cf. Shina (dial. of Gilgit) *thĭk.*

869. **ටුව -ṭuva,** a. ECpd. standing. Cf. *peraṭuva* (standing) in front. — Pk., P. *-ṭṭha*, Sk. *-stha.*

ඩ Ḍ

870. **ඩහදිය ḍaha-diya, ඩාදිය ḍā-diya,** s., sweat, perspiration.—*ḍaha* = Pk. M. AMg. *ḍāha*, P. *ḍāha* (or *dāha*, Sk. *dāha*) ; m. *ḍāh*, *ḍāho*, kśm. si. h. pj. *ḍāh*, nep. *ḍāh*, *ḍāhā*+*diya*.

871. **ඩහනවා ḍahanavā,** v., prt. *dähuvā*, to bite.—Pk. M. AMg. *ḍasaï*, P. *ḍasati*, Sk. √*daṃś*, *daśati* ; g. *ḍasvuṃ*, m. *ḍasṇeṃ*, h. *ḍasnā*, nep. *ḍasnu*.

ණ Ṇ

872. **ණය ṇaya,** s., debt. *ṇaya-kārayā* debtor ; *-himiyā* creditor ; *ṇaya-gannavā* (*denavā*) to borrow (to lend).—<**iṇaka* = P. *iṇa*, Sk. *ṛṇa* ; but Pk. *riṇa*, kśm. *ren*, m. *rīṇ*, h. nep. pj. *rin*, l. *riṇṇ*.

ත T

— **ත ta-**, pron. 2 pers. sg., see **tō.**

873. **තකතිරු tak'-atiru,** a., stupid, foolish ; s. °*ruvā* stupid person.—*taku* (v. *takka*)+*atiru* (v. *atira*), lit. unstable in logic.

874. **තකනවා takanavā,** v., prt. *täkuvā*, to regard, heed.—Pk. *takkēi*, P. *takkēti*, Sk. *tarkayati* ; si. *takaṇu*, g. *tākvuṃ*, bg. *tākāna*, h. *tāknā*, nep. *tāknu*, l. *takkaṇ*.

875. **තකා takā,** postp., out of regard to, on account of.—ger. of v. *takanavā*.

876. **තකුල් takul,** s. pl., a hairy plant, Hibiscus angulosus (?).—P. *takkōla* (dissimilation), Sk. *kakkōla*, *kaṅkōla* ; m. *kaṃkol*.

877. **තක්ක takka[1],** s., st. f. *taku*, buttermilk, whey.—P. *takka*, Sk. *takra* + *-ka* ; g. m. *tāk*. Also *täk* id.

878. **තක්ක takka[2],** s., st. f. *taku*, reasoning, logic, argumentation, *taku-sata* logic.—Pk., P. *takka*, Sk. *tarka*. Cf. *tak'-atiru*, *takanavā*.

879. **තටුව taṭuva,** s., st. f. *taṭu*, metal vessel, basin or dish.—P. *taṭṭaka* (PTSPD, s.v.).

880. **තණ taṇa[1],** s., grass. *taṇa-giravā* grasshopper, lit. grass-parrot.—Pk. *tiṇa*, *taṇa*, P. *tiṇa*, Sk. *tṛṇa* ; g. *taṇ-*, m. *taṇ*, pj. *tiṇ*.

881. **තණ taṇa[2],** s., desire, avarice.—Pk., P. *taṇhā*, Sk. *tṛṣṇā* ; m. *tahān*, *tānh*, pj. *tāṃgh*. Cf. *muva-taṇa*.

882. **තත tata, තැත täta[1],** s., st. f. *tat*, *tät*, string (of a musical instrument), cord. *tat-äti* stringed ; *tat-damanavā* to string an instr. ; *tat-madinavā* to rub or polish strings.—Pk., P. *tanta*, *tantī*, Sk. *tantra*, *tantrī* ; or. *tanta*, g. m. ass. bg. h. nep. *tāṃt*.

883. **තතු tatu,** s., condition, state, fact in *tatu-lesa* accurately.—Pk. *tatta*, P. *tatta*, Sk. *tattva*.

884. තද **tada,** a., hard, firm; severe, austere; s. *tadayā* hard, obstinate person; *tada-kama* hardness. — Pk. *thaddha* (*thaḍḍha, ṭhaḍḍha*), P. *thaddha*, Sk. *stabdha*; kśm. *thodu*, si. *thadho*, (g. *ṭāḍhuṃ*, m. *ṭhāḍā*, bg. *ṭhāṛa*, h. *ṭhāṛhā*, nep. *ṭhāṛo* pj. *ṭhāḍhā*, l. *ṭhaḍḍhā*).

885. තන **tana,** තැන **tāna,** s., st. ff. *tan, tän*, place. *ko-tana* where? *ko-tanin* from what place? *täna-täna* here and there; *tän-ättā* person; *tan-väsi* suitable for the place or occasion. — Pk. *thāṇa*, (*ṭhāṇa*, P. *ṭhāna*), Sk. *sthāna*; kśm. *thān*, si. *thāṇo*, g. *thāṇuṃ*, (m. *ṭhāṇeṃ*), ass. bg. h. nep. *thān*, pj. *thāṇ*. Cf. *tän-pat*.

886. තනග **tanaga,** s., teat, nipple. — Sk. *stanâgra*.

887. තනතුර **tanatura,** s., st. f. °*ru*, employment, occupation. — Cf. P. *ṭhānantara*.

888. තනනවා **tananavā,** v., prt. *tänuvā*, to make, form, fashion. Caus. *tanavanavā*, prt. *tänevuvā*, to cause to fashion; intr. *tänenavā*, prt. *tänuṇā*, to become formed or disciplined.— <**tānayati*; P. *tanōti*, Sk. $\sqrt{}$*tan, tanōti*; s. *tāṇaṇu*, g. *tāṇvuṃ*, m. *tāṇṇeṃ*, h. *tānnā*, nep. *tānnu*, pj. *tāṇṇā*.

889. තනය **tanaya,** s., st. f. *tana*, female breast. *tana-kiri* woman's milk. — Pk. *thaṇa*, P. *thana*, Sk. *stana*; kśm. *than*, si. *thaṇu*, h. *than*, nep. *thun*. *than*, pj. l. *thaṇ*.

890. තබනවා **tabanavā,** තිබ° **tiba°,** v., prt. *täbuvā*, *tibuvā* or *tibbā*, to put, place, lay. Caus. *tabavanavā* (double c. *tabbav*°), prt. *täbevuvā* (*täbbe*°, *tibbe*°) to cause to put; intr. *tibenavā*, prt. *tibuṇā* to be, exist (coll. *tiyanavā*, *tiyenavā*). — (Pk. *ṭhavēi*, P. *ṭhāpēti*), Sk. $\sqrt{}$*sthā*, caus. *sthāpayati*; kśm. *thāvun*, si. *thāpaṇu*, g. *thāpvuṃ*, m. *thāpṇeṃ*, oṛ. *thāpibā*, h. *thapnā*, nep. *thāpnu*, pj. *thāpṇā*.

891. තබා **tabā,** postp., setting aside, apart from. — Ger. of v. *tabanavā*; P. *ṭhapetvā* is used in the same manner.

892. තඹ **tam̆ba,** a., reddish, s., copper.— Pk., P. *tamba*, Sk. *tāmra*; kśm. *trām*, si. *trāmo*, g. *trāṃbuṃ*, *tāṃbuṃ*, m. *tāṃbeṃ*, oṛ. *tambā*, ass. *tām*, bg. *tāmā*, h. *tāṃbā*, nep. *tāmo*, pj. *tāmbā*, l. *trāmī*.

893. තඹර **tam̆bara,** s., st. f. *tam̆buru*, red waterlily. *bin-tam̆buru*, lit. earth-lotus, name of the plant Ipomoea repens. — Pk., Sk. *tāmarasa*.

894. තඹවන් **tam̆ba-van,** adj., copper-coloured. — P. *tamba-vaṇṇa*, Sk. *tāmra-varṇa*.

895. තඹසිළුවා **tam̆ba-siḷuvā,** s., st. f. °*ḷu*, cock. Lit. the one having a red crest or crown.— P. *tamba-cūḷa*, Sk. *tāmra-cūḍa* + *-ka*.

896. තමලු **tamalu,** s., name of a tree bearing black blossoms, Garcinia xanthochymus. — Pk., P., Sk. *tamāla* Xanthochymus pictorius.

897. **තම්බනවා tambanavā,** v., prt. *tämbuvā,* to seethe, cook by boiling. Intr. *tämbenavā,* prt. *tämbuṇā,* to seethe, become sodden. — *tambanavā* <**taṁbbanavā* <**taṁbvanavā,* caus. of v. **taṁbanavā.* See *tavanavā.*

898. **තර tara, තිර tira,** a., firm, strong; fat, stout; s. *taraya* firmness. — Pk., P. *thira,* Sk. *sthira* ; kśm. *thyoru,* si. *thiri,* g. *thir,* m. *thīr,* oṛ. *thira,* ass. h. pj. *thir,* nep. *thiro.*

899. **තරනවා taranavā,** v., prt. *täruvā,* to cross or go across (a river), DhpAGp 49^{7} ; BōvGp 10^{26}. — Pk. *taraï,* P. *tarati,* Sk. √*tar,* *tarati* ; kśm. *tarun,* si. *taraṇu,* g. *tarvuṃ,* m. *tarṇeṃ,* oṛ. *taribā,* ass. *tariba,* bg. *tarā,* h. pj. *tarnā,* nep. *tarnu,* l. *taraṇ.*

900. **තරස් taras,** s., in *taras-daṇḍa* shuttle. — Metathesis of **tasar* = P. *tasara,* Sk. *tasara, trasara.* Pk. *tasara, ṭasara* means a particular kind of thread ; m. h. nep. *tasar* a kind of silk (T, s.v.).

901. **තරසා tarasā,** s., st. f. *taras,* hyena. — Pk., P. *taraccha,* Sk. *tarakṣa,* °*kṣu* ; g. *taras,* m. *taras, taraṃs,* pj. *tarkh.*

902. **තරහලා tarahalā, °ලුවා °luvā,** s., st. f. °*hal,* goldsmith. — Metathesis of **talaharā* = P., Sk. *tulā-dhāra.* Cf. Pk., P., Sk. *tulā* scales ; kśm. *tul,* si. *turo,* m. *tūḷ,* oṛ. *tuḷa,* ass. bg. *tul,* nep. *tulo.*

— **තරු taru,** s., see **turu.**

903. **තල් tal, තල tala^{1},** s., st. f. *tal,* talipot or palmyra palm, Corypha umbraculifera. *tal-rā* palmyra toddy. — Pk., P., Sk. *tāla* ; kśm. *tāl,* g. m. *tāḍ,* oṛ. *tāḷa,* ass. *tāl,* bg. *tāṛ,* b. nep. *tāṛ, tār,* h. pj. *tāṛ.*

904. **තල tala^{2},** s., the sesamum plant. — Pk., P., Sk. *tila* ; kśm. *tēl,* si. *tiru,* g. *til, tal,* m. *tīḷ,* oṛ. *tiḷa,* ass. bg. h. nep. pj. l. *til.*

905. **තලන් talan,** s., beams, cross-bars in *talan-gahanavā* to put cross-bars. — Sk. *tulana* weighing, measuring. The original meaning seems to be "scale-beam."

906. **තලය talaya^{1},** s., st. f. *tala,* flat surface; palm (of the hand); blade (of a weapon). — ? lw. = Pk., P., Sk. *tala* ; kśm. *tal* bottom, si. *taru, taro,* g. *taḷ, taḷuṃ,* m. *taḷ, taḷī,* oṛ. *taḷa,* ass. bg. h. pj. *tal, talā,* nep. *talo,* l. *taḷe* below. Cf. *at-tala.*

907. **තලය talaya^{2},** s., st. f. *tala,* land, dry ground. *tala-goyā* land iguana. — Pk., P. *thala,* Sk. *sthala* ; kśm. *thal,* si. *tharu,* g. m. *thaḷ,* oṛ. *thaḷa,* ass. bg. h. nep. pj. l. *thal.*

908. **තලා talā^{1},** s., in *talā-ṭik* (see s.v. *ṭik*) round mark made with ashes etc. on the forehead, either for ornament or sectarian distinction. — P., Sk. *tilaka* ; g. *ṭīlo,* m. *ṭilā,* pj. *til.*

909. **තලා talā^{2},** s., name of the basil plant. *talā-kola* leaves of the basil. — Sk. *tulasī* ; m. *tuḷas, tuḷśī,* si. g. bg. h. pj. *tulsī.*

910. තල් පත **tal-pata,** s., st. f. °*pat*, leaf of the palmyra palm; letter written on such a leaf. — P. *tāla-patta*, Sk. *tāla-pattra*.

911. තල්ල **talla,** s., st. f. *talu*, palate, roof of the mouth. *talu-gahana-vā* to taste, smack. — <*tāluka = Pk. *tālua* ; Pk., P. Sk. *tālu* ; kśm. *tāl*, si. *tārūṃ*, g. *tāḷu*, m. *tāḷū*, oṛ. *tāḷu*, ass. bg. nep *tālu*, h. pj. l. *tālū*.

912. තල් වැට **tal-väṭa,** s., fan. — Pk. *tāla-veṇṭa*, °*voṇṭa*, P. *tāla-vaṇṭa*, Sk. *tāla-vṛnta*.

913. තව **tava**[1], s., religious austerity, asceticism. *tava-päla* hermitage. — Pk. *tava*, P. *tapa*, Sk. *tapas*. Cf. Sinh. *tävilla*, and *pasutäv(illa)*.

914. තව **tava**[2], adv., yet, still, moreover. *tava-ma* id.; *tava-da*, *tava-t* furthermore. — Pk., P. *tāva*, Sk. *tāvat* ; si. *toṃ*, g. *tāv*, m. *taṃv*. h. *tauṃ toṃ*.

915. තවනවා **tavanavā,** v., prt. *tävuvā*, to warm, to foment with warm water etc. Intr. *tävenavā*, prt. *tävuṇā* to be heated ; to hesitate, to repent. — P. *tāpēti* heats, *tappati* is heated, Sk. √*tap*, *tapati*, caus. *tāpayati*, intr. *tapyati* ; kśm. *tāpun* to warm oneself ; si. *tapaṇu*, g. *tāpvuṃ*, m. *tāpṇeṃ* to be warm, oṛ. *tāpibā* to cause to blaze, h. *tāpnā*, nep. *tāpnu* to get warm, pj. *tapāuṇā* to heat, l. *tappaṇ*. Cf. *tambanavā*. Sinh. **taṁbanavā* corresponds to Sk. *tapati*, *tavanavā* to *tāpayati*.

916. තවුතිසා **tavutisā,** s., thirty three in *t°-bhavana* the world or heaven of the 33 inferior gods at the head of whom is Indra (Śakra). — P. *tāvatiṃsa* (*-bhavana* or *-dēvalōka*), Sk. *trayastriṃśa(t)*.

917. තවුර **tavura,** a., solid, firm, immovable. — Pk., P. *thāvar*, Sk. *sthāvara* ; si. *thāṃvaru*, g. *thāvar* ; cf. m. *thāvarṇeṃ* to rest (Bl, T, s.v. *ṭhaharnu*). Sinh. *tahavuru* is a Slw. P.

918. තවුසා **tavusā,** s., st. f. *tavus*, ascetic, religious devotee. *tavus--ves* guise of an ascetic. — Pk. *tāvasa*, P., Sk. *tāpasa*.

919. තළනවා **taḷanavā,** v., prt. *täḷuvā*, to flog, beat, scourge. Caus. *taḷavanavā*, prt. *täḷevuvā*, to cause to flog. — Pk. *tāḍēi*, P. *tāḷēti*, Sk. √*taḍ*, *tāḍayati* ; m. *tāḍneṃ*, g. *tāḍ*, bg. h. pj. *tāṛ-*.

920. තළාව **taḷāva,** s., st. f. *taḷā*, tank, pond. — Pk. *taḷāa*, *talāa*, *taḍāga*, P. *taḷāka*, Sk. *taḍāka*, *taḍāga* ; g. m. *taḷāv*. bg. h. nep. pj. *talāu*.

— තා **tā,** pron., see **tō**.

— තැක් **täk,** s., whey, see **takka**[1].

— තැත **täta**[1], s., see **tata.**

921. තැත **täta**[2], s., st. f. *tät*, aim, effort, endeavour. *tät-karanavā* to attempt or essay. — <MInd. **tatti* = Sk. **tapti*. Cf. P. *tatta*, Sk. *tapta* heated, scorched (by pain or sorrow).

922. **තැතිය tätiya,** s., st. f. *täti*, trembling, fear. *täti-gannavā* to tremble, be agitated from fear. — <MInd. **tatthi* = Sk. **trasti*, √*tras*, *trasati*, *trasta* = Pk. *tasaï*, P. *tasati* ; cf. si. *tarsu*, m. *taras(gāṃḍyā)* coward, h. *taras*, nep. *tarsanu*.

— **තැන täna,** s., see **tana.**

923. **තැනන tänana,** s., thunder. — Sk. *stanana*.

924. **තැන්පත් tän-pat,** a., having come to a place, holding a place or position. *aga-tän-pat* see s.v. *aga*[3]; *tän-pat-karanavā* to deposit, lay up, store ; to bury. — *täna* + *pat* ; P. *thāna* + *patta*, Sk. *sthāna* + *prāpta*.

925. **තැලිය täliya, තලිය taliya,** s., st. f. *täli*, *tali*, dish, plate (metal or earthen). — Pk. *thalliā*, *thālī*, *thāla*, P. *thālī*, *thāla*, Sk. *sthālī*, *sthāla* ; kśm. *thāl*, si. *thārī*, *thāru*, g. *thāḷī*, *thāḷ*, m. *thāḷī*, *thāḷā*, oṛ. *thāḷa*, ass. bg. *thāli*, *thāl*, b. *thārī*, h. pj. *thālī*, *thāl*, nep. *thāli*, *thāl*.

926. **තැවිල්ල tävilla,** s., st. f. *tävili*, fomentation. — Verbal noun of *tavanavā*, q.v.

— **ති ti,** num., see s.v. *tuna*.

927. **තික් tik,** a., sharp, fine. — Pk., P. *tikkha*, Sk. *tīkṣṇa* ; si. *tikho*, g. *tīkhuṃ*, m. *tīkh*, ass. *tikhā* steel, h. *tīkhā*, nep. *tikho*, pj. *tīkhā*, *tikkhā*. Cf. *tiyuṇu*.

928. **තිත් tit**[1], a., bitter, pungent. — Pk. *titta*, P. *tittaka*, Sk. *tikta* ; ass. bg. *titā*, h. *tītā*, nep. *tito*. — Also Sinh. *titta* (lw.).

929. **තිත් tit**[2], s. st. f., heresy, in cpds. like *tit-ganan̆duru* the thick darkness of heresy. — Pk., P. *tittha*, Sk. *tīrtha*. Cf. *toṭa*.

930. **තිත් tit**[3], s., satiation, saturation. — P. *titti*, *titta*, Sk. *tṛpti*, *tṛpta*.

931. **තිත tita,** s., st. f. *tit*, spot, mark ; frequently in cpds. as *tit-vaṭuvā* spotted quail or snipe ; *tit-muvā* spotted deer ; *tit-polan̆gā* spotted viper. — Sk. *tittira*, °*ri* partridge, *tittirīka* spotted like a p. (cf. Bl, s.v. *titar* ; T, s.v. *titro*) seems to be connected with *tita* ; *tit-* may, by dissimilation, alternate with *tik-* : *tik-polan̆gā*.

— **තිබෙනවා tibenavā,** v., see **tabanavā.**

932. **තිඹිරි tim̆biri**[1], a., dark in *tim̆biri-geya* dark room, lying-in room. — Pk., P., Sk. *timira*.

933. **තිඹිරි tim̆biri**[2], s., name of a tree, Diospyros embryopteris. — Pk. *ṭimbaru*, P. *timbaru* ; kśm. *tīṃbar*, *tīṃbrū*, nep. *timur*, *ṭimur*, pj. *timbar*, *tīmrū*.

934. **තිඹිලි tim̆bili,** a., having three creases on the belly. s. °*liyā* a person with such creases. — Sk. *tribalī-ka*. Sinh. has also *ti-vili*, *tun-vili*.

935. **තිමුවා timuvā,** s., leech. — Lit. having three mouths or chaps. Sk. *trimukha* (different meaning).

— **තියනවා tiyanavā, තියෙනවා tiyenavā,** vv., see s.v. *tabanavā*.

936. **තියම්, ti-yam, °මු °mu,** s., t h r e e w a t c h e s (=12 hours) of the day or the night; *tiyamu-räya* the whole night. — P. *ti-yāmā* night, Sk. *tri-yāma*.

937. **තියු tiyu,** s., p r a i s e, in *tiyu-gīya* hymn of praise. — Pk. *thui*, P. *thuti*, Sk. *stuti*.

938 **තියුණු tiyuṇu,** a., s h a r p, p i e r c i n g, p u n g e n t. — P. *tikhiṇa*, Sk. *tīkṣṇa*. Cf. *tik*.

— **තිර tira, තිරු tiru,** a., see **tara.**

939. **තිරය tiraya,** s., st. f. *tira*, c u r t a i n, v e i l. — < **tirya* some thing hung across before another thing. — Cf. AMg. Pk., P. *tiriyaṃ* across, Sk. *tiraḥ*, *tiryak*.

940. **තිරස් tiras** (Cl), adv., h o r i z o n t a l l y. — Pk. *tiriccha*, °*cchi*, Sk. *tiraśca*; g. *tirchuṃ*, m. *tirsā*, *tirkā*, h. pj. *tirchā*, nep. *terso*, *tercho*.

941. **තිරිසනා tirisanā,** s., st. f. *tirisan*, b e a s t, b r u t e. — P. *tiracchāna*. Cf. *tiras*, *tercho*.

942. **තිරෙළුවා tireḷuvā, තිරළුවා tiraḷuvā,** s., st. f. °*ḷu*, r a m, s h e e p. — *tira* + *eḷuvā*.

943. **තිලොව ti-lova,** s., st. f. *ti-lō*, t h e t h r e e w o r l d s. *tilō-guru* teacher of the three worlds, the Buddha. — P. *ti-lōka*, Sk. *tri-lōka*.

944. **තිස tisa, තිහ tiha,** num., st. f. *tis*, t h i r t y; *tis-veni*, *-väni* thirtieth. — Pk. *tīsa*, P. *tiṃsa*, *tiṃsati*, Sk. *triṃśat*; kśm. *trah*, si. *ṭrīha*, g. *trīs*, m. *tīs*, oṛ. *trisa*, ass. bg. *tris*, b. h. *tīs*, nep. *tis*, pj. *tīh*, l. *trīh*.

945. **තිසුල ti-sula,** s., st. f. °*sul*, t r i d e n t, in *tisul-at*, *tisul-avi*, names of god Śiva who bears a trident in his hand (v. *ata*[5]) or as weapon (v. *aviya*). — Sk. *triśūla*.

946. **තුට tuṭa,** s., st. f. *tuṭu*, s a t i s f a c t i o n, g l a d n e s s. *tuṭu-karanavā* to please. — Pk., P. *tuṭṭhi*, *tuṭṭha*, Sk. *tuṣṭi*, *tuṣṭa*.

947. **තුඩ tuḍa,** s., b e a k, b i l l: m o u t h. — Pk., P. *tuṇḍa*, Sk. *tuṇḍa*, *tuṇḍi*, *tundi*; si. *tunī*, g. bg. *ṭuṃḍ*, m. *toṃḍ*, oṛ. *tuṇḍi*, h. *ṭūṃṛī*, pj. *tunnī*.

948. **තුදුස tudusa,** num., st. f. *tudus*, f o u r t e e n (coll. *daha-hatara*). — Pk. *caüddasa*, *coddasa*, °*ha*, P. *catuddasa*, *cuddasa*. Sk. *caturdaśa*: kśm. *codāh*, si. *coḍaṃhaṃ*, g. *cauda*, m. *caudā*, oṛ. *cauda*, h. *caudah*, nep. *cauda*, °*dah*, °*dha*, pj. *caudha*, l. *côdāṃ*.

949. **තුන tuna**[1], num., st. f. *tun*, t h r e e. *tun-veni*, *-väni* third. In compds. *ti-*, *te-* or *tun-*, *tunu-*: *ti-sula* (q.v.); *te-diyata* the three worlds: *tun-kona* triangle (Sk. *tri-koṇa*); *tunu-ruvan* the three gems (Sk. *tri-ratna*). — Pk. *tiṇṇi*, *tiṇṇaṃ*, P. *tīṇi*, *tiṇṇaṃ*, Sk. *trīṇi*; g. *traṇ*, m. *tīn*, oṛ. ass. *tini*, bg. *tin*, h. *tīn*, nep. *tin*, pj. *tinn*.

950. **තුන tuna**[2], s., st. f. *tun*, s t r i n g, c o r d. — Cf. Sk. *tanikā*; h. *tanī*, nep. *tunu*, *tanu*.

951. **තුනු tunu, තුනී tunī,** a., thin, slender, fine. *tunī-kama* thinness ; *tunu-v-aňga* slender body, woman.—Pk. *taṇu*, P. *tanu*, Sk. *tanu* (*tanv-aṅga*).

952. **තුනුව tunuva,** s., st. f. *tunu*, body. *tunu-sapuva* bodily health.—Pk. *taṇū*, P. *tanu*, Sk. *tanū* ; kśm. *tonu*, g. m. nep. *tan*, si. bg. h. *tanu*, pj. *taṇ*.

953. **තුඹ tum̆ba[1],** s., long gourd, Momordica.—Pk., P. *tumba*, Sk. *tumba*(*ka*), *°bī*, *°bikā* ; kśm. *tumba*, *tombu*, si. *tumbo*, *°bī*, g. *tuṃbḍuṃ*, *°ḍī*, m. *tuṃbā*, *tuṃbḍī*, oṛ. bg. *tumbā*, *°bi*, b. *tūmā*, *tumṛī*, h. *tūṃbā*, *toṃbā*, *tomṛī*, nep. *tumbo*, *°bi*, *tummiṃ*, pj. *tummā*, *tūmbā*, *tomrī*, l. *tummaṃ*, *tumba*. Ca : *tumba*.

954. **තුඹ tum̆ba[2],** s., lead.—Pk. *taüa*, P. *tipu*, Sk. *trapu*.

955. **තුර tura[1],** s., st. f. *turu*, tree.—Pk., P., Sk. *taru*.

956. **තුර tura[2],** a., quick, swift.—Sk. *tura*. Cf. Pk. *turia*, P. *turita*, Sk. *tvarita*; Bl, s.v. *turūt*.

957. **තුරු turu[1], තරු taru,** s., star.—Pk. *tāragā*, P. *tārakā*, Sk. *tāraka* or *°kā*; kśm. *tāra*, si. g. nep. *tāro*, m. oṛ. ass. bg. h. pj. *tārā*.

958. **තුරු turu[2],** s., musical instrument, drum.—Pk. *tūra*, P. *turiya*, Sk. *tūrya* ; kśm. si. *turī*, g. *tūr*, *turī*, *turāī*, bg. *turaṛi*, h. *turī*, *turaī*. nep. *turai*, pj. *turhī*.

959. **තුරුක් (තෙල) turuk (-tela),** s., fragrant oil used as one of the four royal perfumes.—Pk. AMg. JM., P. *turukkha*, Sk. *turuṣka* incense.

960. **තුරුණ turuṇa, °ණු °ṇu,** a., youthful, young.—Pk., P., Sk. *taruṇa* ; g. *taruṇ*, m. *tarṇā*, h. *tarun*, nep. *tarunu*, pj. *tarn*.

961. **තුල් tul[1],** a., equal, alike.—Pk. *tulla*, P., Sk. *tulya*.

962. **තුල් tul[2],** a., large, fat, immense.—Pk. *thulla*, P. *thulla*, *thūla*, Sk. *sthūla* ; si. *thulho*, m. *ṭhulā*, ass. *tholokā*, nep. *ṭhulo*, pj. *thullhā*, l. *ṭhullā*.

963. **තුවර tuvara, තෝර tōra,** a species of the Cassia plant.—P. *tagara*, Sk. *sthagara*, *tagara* the shrub Tabernaemontana coronaria, and a fragrant powder prepared of it, *tagaḍa*(*-vallī*) the shrub Cassia auriculata ; m. *tarvaḍ*, *taroḍ*, h. *tarvar* id.

964. **තුසර tusara,** a., cold ; s., mist, dew.—Pk., P. *tusāra*, Sk. *tuṣāra* ; m. bg. h. *tusār*, nep. *tusāro*.

965. **තුසී tusī,** s., name of one of the six heavens, in *tusī-pura* id., *tusī-väsiyā* inhabitant of the heaven T°.—P. *tusita*(*-pura*), Sk. *tuṣita*.

— **තෙ te-,** num., see s.v. **tun.**

966. **තෙත් tet,** a., wet, moist ; s. *teta* moisture. *tet-kanavā* to become wet (lit. to eat moisture).—P. *tinta*, Sk. $\sqrt{}$*tim*, *stim* ; oṛ. *tintā*, bg. *titā*, ass. *titiba* to become wet. Cf. *temanavā*.

967. තෙද **teda,** s., splendour, glory. — Pk. *tēa*, P. *tēja*, Sk. *tējas* ; m. *tevṇeṃ* to beam, burn (?).

— තෙන **tena,** s., see **tana.**

968. තෙනුම් **tenum,** s., theft. — P. *thēna*, Sk. *stēna* thief.

969. තෙනේ **tenē,** s., st. f. *tena*, son. — Pk. *taṇaya*, P., Sk. *tanaya*.

970. තෙපි **tepi,** තෙප් **tep,** pron. pers. 2nd pl., obl. c. *topa*, ye. — Formed in analogy to *api* (q.v.). Cf. Asoka, Dhau. and Jau. inscs. *tuphē*, *tuphēni*, *tuphēhi*, *tuphāka*, *tuphēsu* (Hultzsch, p. CVI) for *tupph°*.

971. තෙමනවා **temanavā,** v., prt. *temuvā*, to wet, moisten. Intr. *temenavā*, prt. *temuṇā*, to become wet. — P. *tēmēti*, Sk. √ *tim*, *timyati*, **tēmayati* ; m. *tevṇeṃ* (T, s.v. *tiun*).

972. තෙර **tera[1],** s., shore, border of a river. — Pk., P., Sk. *tīra* ; kśm. g. m. h. *tīr*, si. *tīru*, oṛ. *tira*, ass. bg. *tir*, nep. *tir*.

973. තෙර **tera[2],** s., aged monk, senior monk. — Pk., P. *thēra*, Sk. *sthavira* ; si. *theru*, m. *ther* old, aged.

974. තෙල **tela,** s., st. f. *tel*, oil. — Pk. *tella*, *tilla*, P. *tēla*, Sk. *taila* ; kśm. *tīl*, si. *telu*, oṛ. *tela*, g. m. ass. bg. b. h. nep. *tel*. Cf. Sinh. snake names *tel-karavalā*, *tel-polaṅgā*.

975. තෙලියා **teliyā,** s., st. f. *teli*, a kind of fish. Lit. the oily one. — P. *tēlika*, Sk. *tailika* ; si. g. m. h. pj. l. *telī*, oṛ. bg. nep. *teli*, ass. b. *teliyā* oil-man.

976. තෙලිස්සා **telissā,** s., st. f. *telisi*, a small kind of viper. — Prob. *teli-* (see *teliyā*) + *issā* (dimin.) ; cf. *poḍiya* : *poḍissa* small quantity (De Lanerolle).

977. තෙවළා **te-vaḷā,** s., lit. the three baskets, the Buddhist sacred scriptures. — P. *ti-piṭaka*, Sk. *tri-piṭaka*.

978. තෙවිදු **te-vidu,** s., the threefold knowledge of an Arahant. — Cf. P. *tē-vijja* possessed of the thr. kn., Sk. *trai-vidya*.

979. තෙසු **tesu,** a., remaining, residual. — By dissimilation for *sesu* (thus also Sinh.) ; Pk., P. *sēsa*, Sk. *śēṣa* ; h. *ses*.

980. තෙළෙස **teḷesa,** num., st. f. *teḷes*, thirteen (coll. *daha-tuna*). — Pk. *tērasa*, *°ha*, P. *teḷasa*, *terasa*, Sk. *trayōdaśa* ; kśm. *truvāh*, si. *teraṃhaṃ*, m. *terā*, g. oṛ. ass. bg. nep. *tera*, h. *terah*, pj. *terāṃ*, l. *tehraṃ*.

981. තොකෙළිය **to-keḷiya,** s., st. f. *°ḷi*, water-sport, fun in the water. — *to* (<*tō-*, q.v.) + *k°*, Sk. *tōya-krīḍā*.

982. තොට **toṭa,** s., ford, ferry (frequently in local names : *ben-toṭa* etc.). *toṭiyā* ferry-man. — <**tūrtha*, oṛ. *tutha* (also dardic *tūrt*, T, s.v. *turnu*); but Pk., P. *tittha*, Sk. *tīrtha*. Cf. *tit[2]*.

983. තොටු **toṭu,** a., heretical. — Sk. *tīrthaka*, cf. Pk. *titthaara*, P. *titthakara*. Cf. *tit[2]* and *toṭa*.

984. **තොතැනිය to-täniya, °න්න °nna,** s., st. f. *°ni*, bed or garden plot so prepared as to keep moisture round the roots of plants.—*tō+täni* = Sk. *sthānaka*, BR, s.v., d.

985. **තොරණ toraṇa,** s., arched gateway, portal.—P. Sk. *tōraṇa*.

986. **තොරතුර toratura,** s., st. f. *°ru*, affair, circumstance.—Cf. P. *antarantarā*, *°rēna*.

987. **තොල tola,** s., st. f. *tol*, lip.—Sk. (lex.) *trōṭi* beak; kśm. *tūṃṭi*, *tōṃth*, si. *ṭoṭī*, g. *ṭoṭo*, m. *ṭoṭī*, bg. *ṭuṭi*, h. *ṭoṃṭ*, *ṭoṭī*, *ṭoṃṭī*, nep. *ṭuṭo*, pj. *ṭūṭī* (various meanings). I expect Sinh. **toḷa*. See also *tuḍa*.

988. **තොස tosa,** s., st. f. *tos*, satisfaction, joy.—Pk. P. *tōsa*, Sk. *tōṣa*.

989. **තොහො toho,** s., chaff or husk of gram.—Sk. *tuṣa*.

990. **තෝ tō¹,** s. (st. f.), water, in *to-keliya*, *tò-täniya*, *°nna*, q.v.—Pk., P., Sk. *tōya*.

991. **තෝ tō²,** pron. pers. 2nd sg., thou. Obl. c. *tā* (dat. *ta-ṭa*, gen. *ta-gē*); pl. *tepi*, q.v —*tō* <Pk., P., Sk. *tava* ; *tā* < Pk. *taē*, P. *tayā*, Sk. *tvayā*. See J. Bloch, L'Indo-Aryen, p. 191.

— **තෝර tōra,** s., see s.v. **tuvara.**

ද D

992. **ද -da,** 1) part. and ; 2) interrog. part. Cf. *mē maga hari eka-da* is this road the right one? *äd-da* is there (enough)? etc.; see sub. *k-*.—Mediaeval forms are *-ij*, *-uj*, *-ud*, *-udu*, *-ut*. Pk., P., Sk. *-ca* ; Sinh. Pk. *-ca*, *-ica* (4th c.).

993. **දකිනවා dakinavā,** v., prt. *duṭuvā*, *däkkā*, to see. *däkuma*, *däkma* seeing, sight. Caus. *dakvanavā*, *dakk°*, prt. *däkvuvā*, *däkk°*, to show.—Pk. *dekkhaï*, P. *dakkhati*, Sk. st. *drakṣ*.—Cf. √ *dṛś* ; si. *ḍekhaṇu*, g. *dekhvuṃ*, m. *dekhṇeṃ*, oṛ. *dekhibā*, ass. *dekhiba*, bg. *dekhā*, h. *dekhnā*, nep. *dekhnu*, pj. *dekhṇā*, l. *ḍekhaṇ*.

994. **දකුණ dakuṇa,** s., st. f. *°ṇu*, gift, present (Ruv 473).—Pk., P. *dakkhiṇā*, Sk. *dakṣiṇā*.

995. **දකුණු dakuṇu,** a., right; southern. s. *°ṇa* the right hand side, south quarter ; *dakuṇu-ata* the right hand or side ; *d°-diga* south quarter.—Pk., P. *dakkhiṇa*, Sk. *dakṣiṇa* ; kśm. *dakhin*, (*dachyunu*), si. *ḍakhiṇu*, h. nep. *dakkhin*, m. *ḍākhiṇ*, pj. l. *dakkhaṇ*.

996. **දක්වා dakvā,** potsp., until, unto, as far as.—Ger. of *dakvanavā*. Cf. *ära*, *tabā* etc.

997. **දඟය daṅgaya,** s., st. f. *daṅga*, calf of the leg.—Pk., P., Sk. *jaṅghā* ; kśm. *zaṅg*, si. *jaṅgha*, g. m. *jāṃgh*, *jāṃg*, oṛ. *jaṅgha*, ass. *zāṅ*, bg. *jāṅ*, h. *jāṃgh*, nep. *jāṃgh*, *jāṃg*, *jāṅ*, pj. *jaṅgh*, l. *jaṅggh*.

998. දඩය **dadaya**[1], s., st. f. *dada*, fine, penalty (mediaeval *dańḍ*, EpZ I 47^{20}, 48^{34}). — Pk., P., Sk. *daṇḍa* ; bg. *dāṃṛ*, *ḍāṃṛ*, ass. h. nep. *ḍāṃṛ*, pj. *ḍann*. Cf. *daṇḍa*.

999. දඩය **dadaya**[2], s., st. f. *dada*, forest, wilderness. In cpds.: *dada-* wild ; cf. *dada-yam* wild sport, hunting.— ? = Sk. *daṇḍaka* name of a district in Dekhan which was a large forest in ancient times.

1000. දණ **dana**, s., knee. *dana-iha* cap of the knee. — Pk. *jāṇu*, P. *jānu*, *jannu*, Sk. *jānu*.

1001. දණ්ඩ **daṇḍa** (<**dańḍḍa*<*dańḍuva*), s., st. f. *dańḍu*, stick, staff, pole. — Pk. *daṇḍaa*, P. *daṇḍaka*, Sk. *daṇḍikā* ; g. m. *ḍāṃḍī*, ass. *ḍāṃri*, oṛ. *dāṇḍi* path, bg. *dāṃri*, *ḍāṃri*, h. *dāṃṛī*, nep. *ḍāṃri*, pj. *ḍaṇḍī*.

— දත් **dat**, pprt., see s.v. **dannavā**.

1002. දත **data**, s., st. f. *dat*, tooth. *dat-katuva* toothpick; *dat-kossa* toothbrush. — Pk., P., Sk. *danta* ; kśm. *dand*, si. *ḍandu*, g. m. *dāṃt*, oṛ. *dānta*, ass. bg. h. nep. *dāṃt*, pj. l. *dand*. Cf. *dätta*.

1003. දත්කූරු කනවා **datkūru-kanavā**, v., to grind or gnash the teeth. — Cf. Sk. adv. *danta-krūram* (to do some thing) fiercely by or with the teeth.

1004. දදය **dadaya**[1], s., st. f. *dada*, cutaneous disease, scurvy. — Pk., P. *daddu*, Sk. *dadrū*, *dardū* ; kśm. *daduru*, si. *dadhu*, g. *dādar*, m. *dād*, oṛ. *dādu*, bg. h. nep. *dād*, pj. *dadd*, *daddarī*, l. *ḍadhar*.

1005. දදය **dadaya** , s., st. f. *dada*, flag. — Pk. *dhaa*, P. *dhaja*, Sk. *dhvaja* ; kśm. *doz*, si. g. *dhaj*, m. pj. *dhaj*, *dhajā*, h. *dhajā*.

1006. දදයා **dadayā**[1], s., st. f. *dada*, fool. — P. *dandha*.

1007. දදයා **dadayā**[2], s., st. f. *dada*, brahmin; bird. — Pk. *dia*, P. *dija*, *dvija*, Sk. *dvija*. Cf. T, s.v. *dādā*.

— දදරයා **dadarayā**, s., see **däduruvā**.

1008. දන් **dan**[1], s., gifts, alms. *dan-väta* regular alms-giving ; *dan-sala* alms-house. — Pk. *dāṇa*, P., Sk. *dāna* ; si. *ḍāṇu*, g. pj. *dāṇ*, oṛ. *dāna*, m. nep. *dān*.

1009. දන් **dan**[2], s., paddy. — Pk. *dhaṇṇa*, *dhanna*, P. *dhānā*, *dhañña*, Sk. *dhānā*, *dhānya* ; kśm. *dāñeṃ*, si. *dhāñu*, g. m. *dhān*, oṛ. *dhāna*, ass. bg. h. nep. *dhān*, pj. *dhāṇ*.

1010. දන් **dan**[3], s., meditation. — Pk. *jhāṇa*, P. *jhāna*, Sk. *dhyāna*. Later Slw. *dahan(a)*.

1011. දන **dana**, s., wealth. — Pk. *dhaṇa*, P., Sk. *dhana* ; kśm. *dana*, si. *dhaṇu*, g. m. *dhaṇ*, ass. bg. h. nep. *dhan*, pj. *dhaṇ*, l. *dhaṇāī*. Sinh. *danavat* rich = Sk. *dhanavant*.

1012. දනනය **dananaya,** s., st. f. *danana*, production, bringing forth.—Pk. *jaṇaṇa*, P., Sk. *janana*.

1013. දනවනවා **danavanavā,** v., prt. *dänevuvā*, to produce.—Pk. *jaṇēi*, P. *janēti*, Sk. √ *jan*, caus. *janayati*. Cf. s.v. *vadanavā*.

1014. දනවා **danavā,** v. intr., prt. *dǟvā*, to burn. Caus. *davanavā*, prt. *dävuvā*, tr. to burn. Intr. of caus. *dävenavā*, prt. *dävuṇā*, to be burnt. — P. *jhāyati*, *jhāpēti*. Cf. Sk. √ *kṣi*, caus. *kṣāpayati*.

1015. දනවුව **danavuva,** s., st. f. *danavu*, inhabited district, country. —P. *jaṇavaa*, P., Sk. *janapada*.

1016. දනා **danā,** s., st. f. *dana*, person; pl. *danō* people.—Pk. *jaṇa*, P., Sk. *jana*; kśm. *zan*, *zonu*, si. *jaṇo*, m. *jaṇ*, oṛ. *jaṇa*, ass. *zanā*, bg. b. *jan*, h. nep. *janā*, pj. l. *jaṇā*. Cf. also *denā*.

1017. දනුව **danuva,** s., st. *danu*, sound.—Pk. *dhuṇi*, P. *dhani*, Sk. *dhuni*, *dhvani* ; si. *dhuni*, g. m. *dhūn*, nep. *dhuni*, pj. *dhuṇ*, *dhun*.

1018. දන්නවා **dannavā,** v., prt. *dattā*, to know, be aware of. Caus. *danvanavā* (double c. *dannavanavā*), prt. *dännuvā* (*dännevuvā*) to make known, notify. Intr. *dänenavā*, prt. *dänuṇā*, to be perceptible of. Cf. *däna-gannavā*, prt. *-gattā* to ascertain, find out.—Pk. *jāṇāi*, caus. *jāṇāvēi*, P. *jānāti*, *jānāpēti*, Sk. √*jñā*, *jānāti*, *jñāpayati* (*jñap°*) ; kśm. *zānun*, si. *jāṇanu*, g. *jāṇvuṃ*, m. *jāṇṇeṃ*, oṛ. *jāṇibā*, ass. *zāniba*, bg. *jānā*, h. *jānnā*, nep. *jānnu*, pj. *jāṇanā*, l. *jāṇaṇ*. The pprt. *dat* is formed after the model of *gat* : *gannavā*.

1019. දප **dapa,** s., st. f. *dap*, pride, arrogance.—Pk., P. *dappa*, Sk. *darpa*+*ka*. Cf. *dap* in nep. *dap-kāunu* to reprimand etc., v. T, s.v.

— දපණ **dapaṇa,** s., see **däpuṇa.**

1020. දපනවා **dapanavā**, v., prt. *däpuvā*, to utter incantations.—Pk. *jampaï*, P. *jappati*, Sk. √*jalp*, *jalpati* ; cf. m. *jāpṇeṃ*, *jāṃpṇeṃ*, nep. *jāp*.

1021. දඹ **daṁba,** s., rose-apple tree, Eugenia Jambos. — Pk., P., Sk. *jambu*, *°bū* ; si. *jamūṃ*, g. *jāṃbu*, m. *jāṃb*, oṛ. *jāmu*, ass. *zāmu*, bg. h. *jām*, nep. *jāmu*, pj. *jammū*.

1022. දඹදිව **daṁba-diva,** s., India.—P. *jambu-dīpa*, Sk. *jambu-dvīpa*.

1023. දඹුවා **daṁbuvā,** s., st. f. *°ṁbu*, jackal.—P. *jambuka*, Sk. *jambūka*.

1024. දම **dama[1],** s., subjugation of one's passions.—Pk., P., Sk. *dama*.

1025. දම **dama[2]**, s., st. f. *dam*, chain. *dam-vāḷa* id.—Pk., P. *dāma*, Sk. *dāma(n)*; g. *dām*, bg. *dām*, *dāmā*, pj. *dāuṃ*, *ḍāuṃ*. Cf. m. *dāvaṇ* (Bl).

1026. දම **dama[3],** s., st. f. *dam* (also later *daham*), law, doctrine; the Buddhist sacred scriptures.—Pk., P. *dhamma*, Sk. *dharma* ; cf. nep. *dhāmi*. Sinh. *peḷa-dam* (SdhRv 28^{32})=P. *pāḷi-dhamma*.

1027. දමනවා **damanavā,** v., prt. *dämuvā,* to subdue, overpower. *dämi* submissive, obedient, *no-dämi* unsubdued. Intr. *dämenavā,* prt. *dämuṇā,* to become subjugated.—Pk. *damēi,* P. *damēti,* Sk. √ *dam,* caus. *damayati, damita* ; nep. *dāunu* (T, Add.).

1028. දම්සක **dam-saka,** s., st. f. °*-sak,* the wheel of the law, supreme harmony of righteousness.—P. *dhammacakka,* Sk. *dharma-cakra.*

1029. දම්සබාව **dam-sabāva,** s., st. f. °*-sabā,* meeting for discussing the Dhamma.—P. *dhamma-sabhā,* Sk. *dharma-sabhā.*

1030. දම්සැරිණිය **dam-säriṇiya,** s., st. f. °*riṇi,* faithful wife.—P. *dhamma-cāriṇī,* Sk. *dharma-cāriṇī.*

1031. දම්සැරියා **dam-säriyā,** s., st. f. °*ri,* religious guide, name of the Buddha.—The meaning shows that the word is not derived from P. *dhamma-cārin,* but from *damma-sārathi* guide of those who must be tamed (*damma*= Sk. *damya*), or that the two words were confounded.

1032. දම්සෙනෙවියා **dam-seneviyā,** s., st. f. °*vi,* religious leader, epithet of Sāriputta Thera.—P. *dhamma-senāpati.*

1033. දර **dara**[1]**,** s., fuel, firewood, *dara-sāya* firewood-pile, funeral pile.—Pk., P., Sk. *dāru* ; h. nep. *dār.*

1034. දර **-dara**[2]**,** a., bearing, wearing, possessing.—Pk., P., Sk. *-dhara.* See *dala-dara.*

1035. දරදි(ය) **daradi(ya),** s., st. f. °*di,* debt.—Pk. *dāridda* poverty, Sk. *dāridrya.* Cf. P. *dalidda* poor.

1036. දරනවා **daranavā,** v., prt. *däruvā,* to bear, suffer; to support.—Pk. *dhārēi,* P. *dhārēti,* Sk. √*dhṛ,* caus. *dhārayati* ; kśm. *darun* to fast, si. *dharaṇu,* g. *dharvuṃ,* m. *dharṇeṃ,* oṛ. *dharibā,* ass. *dhariba,* bg. *dharā,* h. pj. *dharnā,* nep. *dharnu.*

1037. දරය **daraya**[1]**,** s., st. f. *dara,* old age, decrepitude.—Pk., P., Sk. *jarā* (Slw. *jarāva*). Cf. *dunu.*

1038. දරය **daraya**[2]**,** s., st. f. *dara,* earth.—P., Sk. *dharā* (Slw. *darāva*).

1039. දරය **daraya**[3]**,** s., st. f. *dara* (also later *dahara*), torrent, heavy rain; edge or point of a tool.—Pk., P., Sk. *dhārā* ; kśm. *dār,* si. *dhāra,* g. m. *dhār,* oṛ. *dhāra,* ass. bg. h. pj. l. *dhār,* nep. *dhār, dhāro.*

1040. දරුණු **daruṇu,** a., dreadful, terrible. *daruṇu-kama* dreadfulness.—Pk., P., Sk. *dāruṇa.*

1041. දරුවා **daruvā** s., st. f. *daru,* child; fem. *däriya,* st. f. *däri* ; *daru-bara* child-bearing.—Pk. *dāraga, dāraa, dāriyā,* P., Sk. *dāraka, dārikā.*

1042. දල **dala,** s., water. *dala-kaňda* mass of water, i.e. pond, lake.—Pk., P., Sk. *jala* ; kśm. *zal* urine, si. *jaru,* g. m. *jaḷ,* oṛ. *jaḷā,* bg. h. nep. *jalā.*

1043. දලකෙළිය **dala-keḷiya,** s., st. f. °*ḷi*, playing in the water.— Sk. *jala-kēli, jala-krīḍā.*

1044. දලදර **dala-dara,** s., cloud; sea, ocean.—Pk. *jala-hara,* Sk. *jala-dhara* ; bg. *jalahri,* h. pj. *jalahrī,* nep. *jalahari.*

— දලනවා ***dalanavā,** v., see **dalvanavā[1, 2].**

1045 දලබුව **dalabuva,** දලඹුව **dalam̆buva,** s., st. f. °*bu*, °*m̆bu*, womb, embryo, placenta.—P. *jalābu,* (Sk. *jarāyu*). Sinh. also *daḷabuva,* °*m̆buva.*

1046. දල(ය) **dala(ya)[1],** දලුව **daluva,** දල්ල **dalla,** s., st. ff. *dala,* °*lu,* flame of fire, effulgence. *dala-sā* lit. branch of fire, flame.—Pk., P. *jālā,* Sk. *jvālā.* Cf. *dalvanavā[1], dälla, dili, dulu.*

1047. දල(ය) **dala(ya)[2],** s., st. f. *dala.* leaf; division, part, half.—Pk., P., Sk. *dala* ; kśm. *dal, ḍal,* g. m. *daḷ,* oṛ. *daḷa,* ass. bg. h. nep. *dal,* pj. *dal, ḍal,* l. *ḍal.* ? lw. Cf. *däliya[2].*

1048. දලසරයා **dala-sarayā,** s., st. f. °*-sara,* fish.—P., Sk. *jala-cara.*

1049. දලුව **daluva,** දල්ල **dalla,** s., st. f. *dalu,* bud, sprout. *dalu-palā* fresh greens ; *dalu-lanavā* to bud, sprout.—P., Sk. *jālaka* bud. The corresponding words in the MIAVs mean 'net, web' (T, s.v. *jalo,* and Sinh. *däla, däliya[1]*). Also spelt *daḷuva, daḷu.*

1050. දල්වනවා **dalvanavā[1],** prt. *dälluvā,* to kindle, inflame.—Caus. of **dalanavā* to burn, glow=Pk. *jalaï,* P. *jalati,* Sk. √*jval, jvalati*; si. *jaraṇu,* g. *jaḷvuṃ,* m. *jaḷṇeṃ,* oṛ. *jaḷibā,* ass. *zaliba,* h. *jalnā,* nep. *jalnu* ; kśm. *zālun*= P. *jālēti.* Cf. *dilisenavā, dilenavā.*

1051. දල්වනවා **dalvanavā[2],** prt. *dälluvā,* to open (as the mouth).—Caus. of **dalanavā,* to open (intr.)=Pk. *dalaï,* P. *dalati,* caus. *dālēti,* Sk. √*dal, dalati* bursts open, splits, caus. *dālayati* ; kśm. *dalun,* si. *ḍaraṇu,* g. *ḍaḷvuṃ,* m. *daḷṇeṃ,* oṛ. *daḷibā,* ass. *daliba,* bg. *dalā,* h. *dalnā,* nep. *dalnu,* pj. *dalṇā.*

1052. දව **dava,** s., speed.—Pk., P., Sk. *java.* Cf. *duvanavā.*

— දවනවා **davanavā,** v., see **danavā.**

1053. දවය **davaya,** s., st. f. *dava,* forest, wood.—Pk., P., Sk. *dāva-*; g. m. *dāv,* bg. *dāb,* h. *dāṃvā.* Cf. T, s.v. *dāuro.*

1054 දවල **davala,** a., white, pure.—Pk., P., Sk. *dhavala* ; si. *dhauro,* g. *dhoḷuṃ,* m. *dhavaḷ,* oṛ. bg. *dholā,* h. pj. *dhaulā.*

1055. දවස **davasa,** °හ **°ha,** s., st. f. *davas,* day. *davas-patā* daily ; *davas-karanavā* or *yavanavā* to pass one's days. In cpds. *-dā* : *anik-dā, anid-dā* day after to-morrow ; *iri-dā, sam̆du-dā* Sunday, Monday.—Pk. *divasa, diasa, diaha,* P., Sk. *divasa* ; kśm. *doh,* si. *ḍiṃhu,* g. *divas, dīs,* m. *dīs,* nep. *diuṃso,* pj. *diṃh, deh,* l. *ḍeheṃ.*

1056. දස් **das,** a., clever, skilful. *das-kama* dexterity, skill.—<MInd. **daccha* =Sk. *dakṣa* (Pk., P. *dakkha*).

1057. **දසන dasana,** s., st. f. *dasan*, tooth.—Pk. *dasaṇa*, P. *dasana*, Sk. *daśana*. ? lw P.

— **දස(ය)dasa(ya)**[1], num., see **dahaya.**

1058. **දසය dasaya**[2], s., st. f. *dasa*, quarter, side, direction. Sinh. also *disa*, *desa*.—Pk., P. *disā*, Sk. *diśā*. Lww. *dasāva*, *disāva*.

1059. **දසරුව dasaruva,** s., st. f. °*ru*, shoulder.—? < Sk. *dōhśikhara* (metathesis of **dasavura*).—But cf. **dataru* < Sk. *jatru* (De Lanerolle).

1060. **දසු dasu,** s., st. f. *das*, slave; fem. *däsī* female slave. *das-bava* slavery.—Pk., P., Sk. *dāsa*, *dāsī*; kśm. *dās*, si. *dāsu*, g. m. bg. h. *dās*.

1061. **දසුන dasuna,** °**ම** °**ma,** s., st. f. °*sun*, °*sum*, seeing, perceiving.—Pk. *daṃsaṇa*, P. *dassana*, Sk. *darśana*.

1062. **දහ daha**[1], s., in *daha-valla*, skirt or border of a garment.—P. *dasā*, Sk. *daśā*.

1063. **දහ daha**[2], s., lake, pond.—Pk., P. *daha*, Sk. *draha*, *hrada*; bg. h. *dah*, nep. *daha*. ? lw.

1064. **දහන dahana,** s., st. f. *dahan*, burning, fire. *dahan-dälla* flame.—Pk. *dahaṇa*, P., Sk. *dahana*. Cf. Pk. *dahaï*, *ḍahaï* burns, P. *dahati*, *ḍahati*, Sk. √*dah*, *dahati*; si. *ḍahaṇu*, g. *dahvuṃ*, m. *dāhṇeṃ*, oṛ. *dahibā*, ass. *dahiba*, bg. *dahā*, h. *dahnā*, nep. *ḍahanu*, pj. *dahiṇā*.

1065. **දහය dahaya, දසය dasaya,** num., st. ff. *daha*, *dasa*, ten. *daha-tuna*, *daha-hatara* 13, 14, etc.; *daha-veni*, *dasa-veni*, *-väni* tenth.—Pk. *dasa*, *daha*, P. *dasa*, Sk. *daśan*; kśm. *dah*, si. *ḍaha*, g. *das*, m. *das*, *dahā*, oṛ. *dasa*, ass. *dah*, bg. b. h. nep. *das*, pj. *dahā*, l. *dāh*.

1066. **දහර dahara,** a., young, fresh; s. *daharayā* child, youth.—P., Sk. *dahara*. ? lw.

1067. **දහස dahasa, දාස dāsa,** num., st. f. *dahas*, *dās*, thousand.—Pk., P. *sahassa*, Sk. *sahasra*; kśm. *sās*. It seems that *dahasa* stands for *sahasa* (thus also in Sinh.) and has taken the initial *d* from *dasa* ten. J. Bloch, LM, § 224, prefers the derivation from MInd. **dasa-sata*, from which we get (**daha-siya*) *dāsiya* (as in *dāsiya-pattuva* name of a district).

1068. **දළ daḷa**[1], a., thick, coarse, rough. *daḷa-bava* thickness; *daḷa-venava* to become thick or coarse.—Pk. *daḍha*, *diḍha*, P. *daḷha*, Sk. *dṛḍha*; kśm. *doru*, m. *dāḍhā*, oṛ. bg. *daṛa*, h. pj. *diṛh*, nep. *daro*.

1069. **දළ daḷa**[2], s., st. f. *daḷa*, matted hair as worn by ascetics.—Pk. *jaḍā*, P., Sk. *jaṭā*; kśm. *zar*, si. *jaṛhu*, g. m. *jaḍ*, oṛ. *jaṛa*, ass. *zar*, b. *jar*, bg. h. *jaṛ*, nep. *jarv*. Cf. *ḍuḷulu*.

1070. **දළ daḷa**[3], s., st. f. *daḷa*, tusk, fang.—Pk. *dāḍhā*, P. *dāṭhā*, Sk. *daṃṣṭrā*, *dāḍhā*; si. *ḍāṛha*, g. m. *dāḍh*, ass. *dār*, bg. *dāṛ*, h. *dāṛhā*, nep. *dāro*, pj. *dāhṛā*, l. *dāhaṛ*.

1071. **දළදා daḷa-dā,** s., the tooth relic (canine tooth) of the Buddha.—*daḷa*^{2}+*dā*^{3}, P. *dāṭhā-dhātu*.

1072. **දා dā^{1},** a., born, s., son. — Pk. *jāa*, P., Sk. *jāta*. Mediaev. Sinh. also *jā*.

— **දා dā^{2},** s., see s.v. **davasa.**

1073. **දා dā^{3},** s., relic.—Pk. *dhāu*, P., Sk. *dhātu*. Cf. *daḷa-dā*.

1074. **දාගබ dā-gaba** (or *-gäba*, or *-goba*), s., relic-depository, relic-chamber.—P. *dhātu-gabbha*, Sk. *dhātu-garbha*.

1075. **දාය dāya^{1},** s., st., f. *dā*, loss, destruction.—<**jhaya* (P. *khaya*, Sk. *kṣaya*). Cf. s.v. *danavā*.

1076. **දාය dāya^{2}, දාව dāva,** s., birth-story. *dā-vata* id., often in titles like *sasa-dāvata* etc.—P., Sk. *jātaka*.

1077. **දාය dāya^{3},** s., st. f. *dā*, heat.—P., Sk. *dāha*. See s.v. *ḍaha-diya*. There are in Sinh. derivates from MInd. *dah* and *ḍah*.

— **දාස dāsa,** num., see **dahasa.**

1078. **දැඟුම däñguma,** s., st. f. °*um*, moving, motion.—P., Sk. *jaṅgama*.

1079. **දැඩි däḍi,** a., hard, strong. *däḍi-kama* hardness.—? from **daḍḍha*. Cf. *daḷa*^{1}.

1080. **දැත්ත dätta^{1},** s., st. f. *däti*, tooth of a saw.—<MInd. **dantika*. See *data*.

1081. **දැත්ත dätta^{2},** s., st. f. *däti*, name of a plant, Baliospermum axillare.—Sk. *dantikā* (*dantī*, n. of the tree Croton Tiglium).

1082. **දැදිරි dädiri,** a., opened, expanded, in *miṇi-dädiri* (see s.v. *miṇa*).—Pk. *jajjaria*, P. *jajjarita*, Sk. *jarjarita*. Cf. *dädura*.

1083. **දැදුර dädura,** s., st. f. °*ru*, splitting, crack; noise of anything splitting, thunder. *däduru-oya* name of a river.—Sk. *jarjara*. Cf. *dädiri*.

1084. **දැදුරුවා däduruvā, දදරයා dadarayā,** s., st. ff. *däduru*, *dadara*, frog.—Pk., P. *daddura*, Sk. *dardura*; si. *dādur*, ass. *dāduri*, h. *dādur*, nep. *dādarā*, pj. *dādar*, *ḍaḍḍū*, l. *ḍaḍḍū*.

1085. **දැන් dän,** adv., now. *dän-ma* immediately, forthwith.—Pk. *dāṇi(ṃ)*, P. *dāni* (*idāni*), (Sk. *idānīm*); m. *dāṇiṃ*.

1086. **දැපිය däpiya,** s., st. f. *däpi*, pride, arrogance.—<MInd.**dappita*, Pk. *dappiya*, Sk. *darpita*. Cf. Pk., P. *dappa*, Sk. *darpa*. See also *dapa*.

1087. **දැපුණ däpuṇa, දපණ dapaṇa,** s., st. f. *däpuṇu*, °*ṇa*, *dapaṇa*, mirror.—P. *dappaṇā*, Sk. *darpaṇa*.

— **දැමි dämi,** a. pprt., see s.v. **damanavā.**

1088. **දැමිටු dämiṭu,** a., righteous, just.—Sk. *dharmiṣṭha*.

1089. **දැල däla,** s., st. f. *däl*, net, web. *däl-äsa* eye or mesh of a net; *däl-damanavā* to cast nets.—Pk., P., Sk. *jāla*; kśm. *zāl*, si. *jāru*, g. *jāḷ*, m. *jāḷ*, *jāḷeṃ*, or. *jāla*, ass. *zāl*, bg. h. nep. pj. *jāl*, l. *jāḷ*.

1090. දැලිය **däliya**[1], s., st. f. *däli*, sprout, shoot.—Doublet of *daluva*, q.v.

1091. දැලිය **däliya**[2], s., st. f. *däli*, half.—Probably=Sk. *dālita*. Cf. *dalaya*[2].

1092. දැල්කාවා **dälkāvā**, s., st. f. *dälkā*, leech.—Pk. *jalūgā*, P. *jalūkā*, Sk. *jalūkā*, *jalauka(s)* ; si. *jaru*, g. *jaḷo*, m. *jaḷū*, pj. *jalam*. Not quite clear.

1093. දැල්ල **dälla**, s., st. f. *däli*, flame.—P. *jālita*, Sk. *jvālita*. Cf. *dalaya*[1].

1094. දැවය **dävaya**, s., st. f. *däva*, timber, log. *däva-maḍuva* timber shed. —දැව **däva**, දේය **deya**, s., st. ff. *däv*, *dē*, thing, article, pl. *däv*, *dē(val)*. — Pk. *davva*, P. *dabba*, Sk. *dravya*.

1095. දැවි **dävi**, s., spoon (H. Jayatilaka, Eḷu-akārādiya).—Pk. *davvī*, P. *dabbī*, Sk. *dharvī* ; m. *ḍav*. Cf. T, s.v. *dābilo*.

1096. දැළිය **däḷiya**, s., st. f. *däḷi*, moustache, beard.—Pk. *dāḍhiā*, P. *dāṭhikā*, Sk. *dāḍhikā* ; kśm. *doru*, si. *ḍaṛhī*, g. m. *dāḍhī*, oṛ. bg. *dāṛi*, h. pj. *dāṛhī*, nep. *dāri*, l. *ḍāṛhī*.

1097. දා **dā**[1], s. pl., births, sorts, kinds.—Pk. *jāi*, P., Sk. *jāti*. Mediaev. Sinh. also *jäy*.

1098. දා **dā**[2], s., name of a plant, jasmine; also *dā-saman* Jasminum Sambac.—Pk. *jāī*, P. *jāti*, Sk. *jāti* ; si. g. *jāi*, m. *jāī*, oṛ. *jāi*, ass. *zāṃi*, h. *jāī*, nep. *jāi*.

1099. දා **dā**[3], s., in *dā-kätta*, sickle. <**dātrī* ; cf. P. *dātta*, Sk. *dātra*. See *kätta*.

1100. දිග **diga**[1], s., st. ff. *digu*, *dik*, direction, quarter.— ? Slw. from Sk. st. *dik-*, *dig-* of *diś-*.

1101. දිග **diga**[2], දිගු **digu**, දිග් **dig-**, දික් **dik-**, a., long; s. *digā* long-bodied person ; *diga* length ; *dik-dā*, *dig-dā* (v. *dā*[1]) various kinds of serpents as long animals; *dik-*, *diga-*, *digu-karanavā* to lengthen, extend.—Pk. *diggha*, (*dīha*, P. *dīgha*), Sk. *dīrgha* ; si. *ḍrigho*, ass. bg. *digh*, nep. *digho*.

1102. දිගා **dig-ā**, s., longevity. — < MInd. **digghâyu* = P. *dīghâu*, P. *dīghâyu*, Sk. *dīrghâyus*.

1103. දිගැසිය **dig-äsiya**, s., st. f. °*si*, long-eyed one, woman.—<MInd. **digghacchikā*.

1104. දිට **diṭa**, s., st.f. *diṭu*, sight, vision, aspect; view, religious view.—Pk., P. *diṭṭhi*, Sk. *dṛṣṭi* ; kśm. *dreṃth*, m. *dīṭh*, ass. *diṭhak*, *ḍiṭhak*, h. *dīṭh*, *ḍīṭh*, nep. *ḍiṭh*. Cf. *duṭu*. Gr. L 9.

1105. දින **dina**, s., the victor, an epithet of the Buddha.—Pk. *jiṇa*, P., Sk. *jina*.

1106. දිනනවා **dinanavā**, v., prt. *dinuvā*, to win, to gain (victory or prize).—Pk. *jiṇēi*, P. *jināti*, Sk. √*ji*, *jayati* ; kśm. *zēnun*, oṛ. *jiṇibā*, ass. *ziniba*, l. *jiṇaṇ*. Cf. T, s.v. *jitnu*.

1107. දිනය **dinaya,** s., st. f. *dina,* day.—Pk. *diṇa,* P., Sk. *dina* ; si. *diṇu,* g. m. *din,* oṛ. *dina,* ass. bg. h. nep. pj. *din.* ? lw.

1108. දිනිතිය **dinitiya,** s., st. f. °*ti,* mother.—Sk. *janitrī.*

1109. දිනූ **dinū,** a. pprt., that was born.—Pk. *jaṇia,* P., Sk. *janita.*

1110. දිඹුල් **dimbul,** s., name of a tree, Ficus glomerata.—<MInd. **dumbala.* Cf. Pk. *numbara,* P. *udumbara,* Sk. *udumbara,* °*la* ; bg. *ḍumbar, ḍumur,* h. *ḍūmar,* nep. *ḍumri.*

1111. දිය **diya**[1], s., world. *diy-ata* id.; *diya-neta* eye of the world, i.e. the sun.—Pk. *jaa,* P. *jagatī,* Sk. *jagat,* °*tī* ; si. *jagu,* g. m. h. *jag,* pj. *jagg.*

1112. දිය **diya**[2], s., victory. *diya-gosa* shout of victory.—Pk., P., Sk. *jaya.*

1113. දිය **diya**[3], s., bowstring. *dunu-diya* id.—Pk. *jīā,* P. *jiyā,* Sk. *jyā* ; m. h. *jīvā,* cf. h. *jeuṛī,* nep. *jiuri,* pj. *jeuṛā,* °*ṛī.*

1114. දිය **diya**[4], s., water. *diya-kukuḷā* water-fowl ; *diya-dora* water-gate, sluice.—Pk. AMg. *daga* (M.Ś. etc. *uaa*), P. *daka,* (*udaka,* Sk. *udaka*). Cf. T, Add. s.v. *od.*

1115. දිය **diya**[5], imp. of v. *denavā,* q. v., give. *iḍa diya* give (me) room, allow. Also *deva.*

1116. දියනා **diya-nā,** s., lord of the world, name of the Buddha.—Sk. *jagan-nātha.* Cf. *diya*[1].

1117. දියපණ **diya-paṇa,** s., lit. breath of the world, i.e. wind.—Sk. *jagat-prāṇa.* Cf. *diya*[1].

1118. දියරකුසා **diya-rakusā,** s., st. f. °*kus,* water demon.—P. *daka-rakkhasa.* Cf. *diya*[4].

1119. දියුණු **diyuṇu,** a., twofold ; s. *diyuṇuva* advancement, improvement; *diyuṇu-karanavā* to improve, promote.—Pk. *diuṇa, duuṇa,* P. *diguṇa,* Sk. *dviguṇa* ; si. *ḍūṇo,* g. *dūṇuṃ,* m. *duṇa,* ass. bg. *dunā,* h. *dūnā,* pj. l. *dūṇā.* Cf. nep. *dunoṭ.*

1120. දියුල් **diyul,** දුහුල් **duhul,** s., fine cloth of silk or mohair.—Pk. *duūla,* P., Sk. *dukūla.*

1121. දිරනවා **diranavā,** v., to decay, rot. Caus. *diravanavā,* prt. *direvuvā,* to cause to decay.—Pk. *jīraï,* P. *jīrati,* (*jiyyati, jīyati*), Sk. √*jṝ, jīryati* : m. *jirṇeṃ.* Cf. Sinh. *diriṇī* old decrepit woman.

1122. දිරිය **diriya,** s., st. f. *diri,* courage.—Sk. *dhairya* ; m. *dhīr.* Cf. Pk., P., Sk. *dhīra*; si. *dhīru,* g. *dhīruṃ,* m. oṛ. *dhirā,* ass. *dhir,* bg. *dhira,* h. pj. *dhīrā,* nep. *dhiro.*

1123. දිලි **dili,** a. pprt., glittering, shining.—Pk. *jalia,* P. *jalita,* Sk. *jvalita.* Cf. *dulu.*

1124. දිලිහෙනවා **dilihenavā,** දිලිසෙනවා **dilisenavā,** v., prt. *dilisuṇā,* °*huṇā,* to shine, glitter.—*dili*+*ihenavā* ; see *ihinavā.* Sinh. also *diliyenavā.*

1125. දිලෙනවා **dilenavā**, v., prt. *diluṇā*, to shine, glitter.—Intr. of *dalanavā*.

1126. දිව **diva**[1], s., st. f. *divu*, tongue. *uḍu-d°* uvula.—Pk. *jīhā*, P. *jivhā*, Sk. *jihvā* ; kśm. *zēv*, si. *jibha*, g. m. *jībh*, oṛ. *jibha*, ass. *zibhā*, bg. *jibh*, h. *jībh*, nep. *jibro*, l. *jibbh*.

1127. දිව **diva**[2], a., heavenly, divine; s., divine world. *diva-osu* divine medicine.—Pk. *divva*, P. *dibba*, Sk. *divya*.

1128. දිව **diva**[3], s., st. f. *divu*, lamp.—Pk. *dīva*, P., Sk. *dīpa* ; si. *ḍio*, g. *dīvo*, m. *divā*, bg. h. *diyā*, nep. *diyo*, pj. *dīvā*.

1129. දිව **diva**[4], s., st. f. *divu*, island. *lak-diva* the island of Ceylon.—Pk. *dīva*, P. *dīpa*, Sk. *dvīpa*. Gr. L 15.

1130. දිවග **div'-aga**, s., tip of the tongue.—Sk. *jihvâgra*.

1131. දිවමන් **divaman**, a., living, alive.—Pk. *jīvamāṇa*, P., Sk. *jīvamāna*.

1132. දිවයුරු **divayuru**, s., sun.—P., Sk. *divākara*.

1133. දිවස **div'-asa**, දිවැස **div'-äsa**, s., divine eye. *divasin* by divination ; *divas-kiyanavā* to foretell.—Sk. *divyâkṣa*, *°kṣi*.

1134. දිවි **divi**[1], s., life.—Pk. *jīvia*, P., Sk. *jīvita* ; cf. kśm. *zīv*, si. *jīu*, g. m. *jīv*, oṛ. *jiā*, ass. *ziyā*, h. nep. pj. *jiu*=*jīva*.

1135. දිවි **divi**[2], s., oath.—Sk. *divya*, s. n. ordeal, oath, BR, s.v. 4 b, c. Cf. *divuranavā*.

1136. දිවියා **diviyā**[1], s., st. f. *divi*, name of a bird, the blue jay.—Pk. *dīviā*, Sk. *dīvi*.

1137. දිවියා **diviyā**[2], s., st. f. *divi*, leopard, panther.—P. *dīpin*, Sk. *dvīpin* +-*ka*.

1138. දිවුරනවා **divuranavā**, v., prt. *divuruvā*, to swear, take an oath.—*divi*[2]+*uranavā*, lit. to absorb an oath ; cf. Pers. *saugand khvardan* to drink an oath.

1139. දිස **disa**, s., st. f. *dis*, region, quarter. Sinh. also *dasaya*, *desa*.—Pk., P. *disā*, Sk. *diśā*.

1140. දිසි **disi**, a., visible.—P. *dissaka*, Sk. *dṛśya* ; cf. Pk. *dīsaï* is seen, is visible, P. *dissati*, Sk. *dṛśyatē* ; m. *disṇeṃ* etc.

— දිහි **dihi**, s., see s.v. **dī**[1].

1141. දිළිඳු **diḷiňdu**, a., poor; s. *diḷiňdā*, *°ndā* poor person.—Pk. *daridda*, *dalidda*, P. *dalidda*, *daḷidda*, Sk. *daridra*.

1142. දී **dī**[1], s., coagulated milk.—Pk. *dahi*, *dahia*, P., Sk. *dadhi* ; si. *ḍahī*, g. m. *dīṃ*, oṛ. *dahi*, bg. *daï*, b. h. *dahī*, nep. *dahi*, pj. *dahīṃ*, l. *dahī*, B I 267. Mediaev. Sinh. *dihi*, EpZ I 169 C[12], 9th c.

1143. දී **dī**[2], s., vessel, in cpds. as *hambu-dī* gruel vessel, EpZ I 25[6], 9th c.—Sk. -*dhi*.

1144. දු **du-**, pref. implying badness, difficulty etc.—Pk., P. *du-*, *dur-*, Sk. *dus-*, *duṣ-*, *duṭi-*, *duḥ-*, *dur-*. See *duka*, *dugaňda* etc.

1145. දුක **duka**, s., st. f. *duk*, sorrow, pain, misery. Pk. *dukkha*, *duha*, P. *dukkha*, Sk. *duḥkha* ; kśm. *dokh*, si. *ḍukhu*, g. *dukh*, m. *duhī*, *duī*, ass. h. *dukh*, nep. *dukha*, pj. *dukkh*, l. *dukh*.

1146. දුකුළාව **dukuḷāva**, s., misdeed.—Pk. *dukkaa*, P. *dukkaṭa*, °*ta*, Sk. *duṣkṛta*.

1147. දුගඳ **dugaňda**, s., stench, stink.—Pk., P. *duggandha*, Sk. *durgandha*.

1148. දුගී **dugī**, a., poor, indigent; s. *dugiyā* poor person.—Pk. *duggaa*, P. *duggata*, Sk. *durgata*.

1149. දුටු **duṭu**[1], a., evil.—Pk., P. *duṭṭha*, Sk. *duṣṭa*.

1150. දුටු **duṭu**[2], a. pprt., seen.—Pk., P. *diṭṭha*, Sk. *dṛṣṭa*. See *dakinavā*, *diṭa*.

1151. දුත් **dut**, a., crafty, fraudulent, vicious.—Pk., P. *dhutta*, Sk. *dhūrta*. Cf. T, s.v. *dhutnu*.

1152. දුදනා **dudanā**, s., st. f. °*na*, wicked man.—Pk. *dujjaṇa*, P. *dujjana*, Sk. *durjana*.

1153. දුදු **dudu**, s., milk.—Pk., P. *duddha*, Sk. *dugdha* ; kśm. *dod*, si. *ḍudhu*, g. m. *dūdh*, oṛ. *dudha*, ass. bg. *dudh*, b. h. *dūdh*, nep. *dudh*, *dud*, pj. l. *duddh*. B I 286, Gr. L 31.

1154. දුන් **dun**, a. pprt., given.—Pk., P. *dinna*.—See *denavā*.

1155. දුනු **dunu**, a. pprt., old, infirm, decayed. *dunu-vat* old or rotten cloth.—Sinh. Pk. *jiṇa*=Pk. *juṇṇa*, *jiṇṇa*, P. *jiṇṇa*, Sk. *jūrṇa*, *jīrṇa* ; g. *jūnuṃ*, m. *junā*, ass. *zin*, bg. *jina* (cf. Ch I 529), h. *jūnā*, *jīn*.

1156. දුන්න **dunna**, s., st. f. *dunu*, archer's bow. *dunu-sip* archery.—Pk. *dhaṇu*, P. *dhanu*, Sk. *dhanu(s)*+*-ka*.

1157 දුඹුරු **duṁburu**, a., brown, drab, dun.—Pk. *dumma*, Sk. *dhūmra* ; g. *dhumar*, m. *dhumrā*, T, s.v. *dhamilo*. Cf. *duṁbul*.

1158. දුඹුල් **duṁbul**, °ළු °**ḷu**, s., smoke, soot, lamp-black.—Sk. *dhūmala* ; oṛ. *dhumāḷa*, bg. *dhumala*, h. *dhumlā*, *dhumailā*, nep. *dhumilo*, *dhamilo*.

1159. දුඹුලා **duṁbulā**, s., st. f. °*ṁbul*, infirm or weak person.—Pk. *duvvala*, P. *dubbala*, Sk. *durbala* ; si. *ḍubiro*, g. *dubaḷ*, m. *dubḷā*, bg. h. pj. *dublā*, nep. *dublo*.

1160. දුම **duma**[1], s., st. f. °*ma*, °*m*, tree. *duma-rada* tree-king.—Pk., P. *duma*. Sk. *druma*.

1161. දුම **duma**[2], s., st. f. *dum*, smoke, steam. *dum-riya* smoke-car, locomotive ; *dum-gahanavā* to smoke.—Pk., P., Sk. *dhūma* ; g. *dhūm*, m. *dhuī*, oṛ. *dhuāṃ*, ass. *dhuṃvā*, bg. *dhuṃyā*, h. pj. *dhūāṃ*, nep. *dhuvāṃ*, *dhuāṃ*. l. *dhūṃ*.

1162. දුමග **dumaga,** s., st. f. *dumam*, bad or difficult road.—*du-* + *maga*.

1163. දුමන **dumana,** s., bad or sorrowful mind.—Pk. *dummaṇa*, P. *dummana*, Sk. *durmanas*. Cf. *domnas*.

1164. දුමිඳු **dum-iñdu,** s., lord of trees, the bō-tree, Ficus religiosa.—*duma*[1] + *iñdu* ; P. *duminda*.

1165. දුරු **duru**[1], s., cummin seed, fennel.—Pk. *jīraa*, P., Sk. *jīraka* ; kśm. *zyuru*, si. *jīro*, g. *jīruṃ*, *jīrī*, m. *jireṃ*, *jirīṃ*, *jirūm*, oṛ. bg. *jirā*, ass. *zirā*, h. *jīrā*, nep. *jiro*, pj. *jīrā*, *jīrī*.

1166. දුරු **duru**[2], a., far, distant; s. *dura* distance ; *durin* from afar ; *duru-karanavā* to remove, expel ; *dura-diga balanavā* to take a long view.—Pk., P., Sk. *dūra* ; si. *ḍūr*, *dūr*, kśm. g. m. bg. h. pj. *dūr*.

1167. දුලද **dulada,** s., heresy.—Sk. **dur-labdhi* (Ca, Cl) or **dur-labdha*.

1168. දුලබ **dulaba,** a., difficult to obtain, hard to acquire, scarce; s., failure, disappointment.—Pk. *dullaha*, P. *dullabha*, Sk. *dur-labha* ; g. *dulhuṃ* rare, b. *dulhā* bridegroom, h. *dulhā*, *dūlah*, nep. *duloho*, *dulaho* bridegroom.

1169. දුලු **dulu,** a. pprt., shining, glittering.—Doublet of *dili*, q.v.

1170. දුව **duva**[1], s., st. f. *dū*, daughter.—Pk. nom. *duhiā*, *dhīā*, *dhūā*, P. *duhitar*, *dhītar*, Sk. *duhitar* ; si. *dhiu*, *dhiya*, g. *dhī*, m. *dhūv*, oṛ. *jhia*, bg. *jhī*, h. pj. *dhī*, *dhīyā*. Gr. L 9.

1171. දුව **duva**[2], a., firm, stable, fixed.—P. *dhuva*, Sk. *dhruva*.

1172. දුවඟ **duvañga,** දුහඟ **duhañga,** s., the thirteen ascetic practices.—P. *dhūtaṅga*.

1173. දුවද **duvada,** s., bad language, abuse.—P. *dubbaca* abusive, Sk. *dur-vacas*, *durvāc* abuse.

1174. දුවන **duvana,** s., st. f. *duvan*, lap, hip.—Pk. *jahaṇa*, P., Sk. *jaghana*.

1175. දුවනවා **duvanavā,** v., prt. *divuvā*, to run, flee, run away. Caus. *duvavanavā*, prt. *divevuvā*, to cause to run, drive.—P. *javati*, Sk. √*jū*, *javati* (or ? from Sk. √*dru*, *dravati*).

1176. දුසස් **dusas,** s., bad grain, bad harvest.—*du-* + *sas* (v. *as*[3]) ; Sk. **duḥ-sasya*.

1177. දුසිත් **dusit,** a., evil-minded ; s. *dusita* evil mind.—*du-* + *sita* ; Sk. **duś-citta*.

1178. දුසිරි **dusiri,** a., of bad habits ; s., immorality.—Pk. *duccaria*, P. *duccarita*, Sk. *duś-carita*.

1179. දුහුදු **duhudu,** s., enemy.—Sk. *dur-hārd*.

— දුහුල් **duhul,** s., see **diyul.**

1180. **ඩුළුලු duḷulu,** s., ascetic with matted hair.—Pk. *jaḍila,* P., Sk. *jaṭila*. Cf. *daḷa*².

1181. **දූ dū,** s., dice.—Pk. *jūa,* P. *jūta*, Sk. *dyūta* ; si. *jūā*, g. *jūṃvuṃ*, m. *juvā*, bg. *juyā*, h. pj. *jūā*, nep. *juvā*.

1182. **දෙක deka,** num., st. f. *de*, two; s., the two, pair. *de-väni*, *-veni* second; *de-tana* the two breasts. Contr. *dāta* (for *de-ata*) the two hands, *dāsa* (for *de-äsa*) the two eyes.—Pk. *duvē, bē, doṇṇi, dō-*, P. *dvē, duvē-, di-, du-*, Sk. *dvau, dvē, dvi-* ; kśm. *doyi*, si. *ba*, g. *be*, m. *don*, oṛ. ass. bg. b. *dui*, h. *do*, nep. *dui*, pj. *do*.

1183. **දෙට deṭa, දෙටු deṭu,** a., first, eldest, best, pre-eminent; s. *deṭuvā* eminent person, dignitary: *gam-deṭuvā* village headman.—Pk., P. *jeṭṭha*, Sk. *jyēṣṭha* ; kśm. *zyuṭhu*, si. *jeṭhu*, g. *jeṭh*, m. oṛ. *jeṭhā*, ass. *zeṭhā*, bg. *jeṭhā*, h. *jeṭh(ā)*. nep. *jeṭho*, pj. *jeṭṭhā*, l. *jeṭhā*.

1184. **දෙඩුබා deḍubā,** s., st. f. *°bu*, water-snake, Cerberus rhynchops.—P. *deḍḍubha*, Sk. *duṇḍubha, ḍuṇḍhubha, dundubha*.

1185. **දෙණ deṇa, °ණිය °ṇiya,** s., st. ff. *°ṇa, °ṇi*, boat, canoe, trough. Cf. *deṇiya* valley, glen, in local names: *dam̆badeṇiya, pērādeṇiya* etc.—P. *dōṇi*, Sk. *drōṇī* ; g. *doṇī, dohṇī*, m. *don*, bg. *dunī* trough. Cf. kśm. *dran* marshy ground, pj. *dūṇ* valley.

1186. **දෙන dena¹,** s., st. f. *den*, cow; the female of any animal: *eḷa-dena* cow; *divi-dena* female panther.—Pk. *dhēnu*, P. *dhēnu*, Sk. *dhēnā, dhēnu*.

— **දෙන dena²,** s., see **denā.**

1187. **දෙනවා** *denavā*, v., prt. *dunnā*, to give bestow; allow. Caus. *devanavā*, prt. *devuvā*, to cause to give.—Pk. *dēi*, P. *dēti* (*dadāti*), Sk. $\sqrt{}$*dā* (*dadāti*) ; kśm. *dyunu*, si. *ḍianu*, g. *devuṃ*, m. *deṇeṃ*, oṛ, *debā*, ass. *diba*, bg. *denyā*, h. *denā*, nep. *dinu*, pj. *deṇa*, l. *devaṇ*.

1188. **දෙනා denā, °න °na,** s., person (pl. id., *denō*), people. Chiefly with numerals: *apa tun-dena* we three, EpZ I 160 A[19], 10th c.; *soru pas-dena* the four thieves; *tun-denek* three persons; *häma-denā* all persons.—Doublet of *danā*, q.v. Mediaev. Sinh. also *jenā*.

1189. **දෙන්නා dennā,** s., the two persons.—<**dednā*<*de-denā*.

— **දෙය deya, දේ dē, දා dā,** s., see **däva** s.v. **dävaya.**

1190. **දෙරණ deraṇa,** s., earth, ground.—Pk. *dharaṇi*, P., Sk. *dharaṇī* ; cf. nep. *dharan*.

1191. **දෙව deva,** s., st. f. *dev*, cloud, rain. —Pk., P., Sk. *dēva* ; kśm. *dev, div*, si. *ḍeu*, g. m. *dev*, oṛ. *dia*, ass. *deo*, h. nep. pj. *deu*.

1192. **දෙවියා deviyā,** s., st. f. *devi*, god, deity.—Pk *dēvaā*, P. *dēvata, °tā*, Sk. *daivata, dēvatā*.

1193. දෙවොල **devola,** s., st. ff. *devol*, °*vel*, Hindu temple.—Pk. *dēva-ula*, P., Sk. *dēva-kula* ; *devel* perhaps < *dēvâlaya*.

1194. දෙව්තුර **dev-tura,** s., st. f. °*ru*, celestial tree, said to yield whatever is desired.—Sk. *dēva-taru*.

1195. දෙව්දුරු **dev-duru,** s., name of a tree, Pinus Deodora.—P., Sk. *dēva-dāru*.

1196. දෙව්රද **dev-rada,** s., divine king, name of the god Śakra. —P., Sk. *dēva-rājan*.

1197. දෙව්ලොව **dev-lova,** s., st. f. °-*lō*, divine world.—Pk. *dēva-lōga*, P., Sk. *dēva-lōka*.

1198. දෙස **desa,** s., st. f. *des*, country, direction, region.—Pk., P. *dēsa*, Sk. *dēśa* ; kśm. *dīś*, si. *ḍehu*, g. m. *des*, oṛ. *desa*, bg. h. nep. pj. l. *des*.

1199. දෙසනවා **desanavā,** v., prt. *desuvā*, to preach, discourse.—Pk. *dēsēi*, P. *dēsēti*, Sk. √*diś*, caus. *dēśayati*.

1200. දෙස්සා **dessā,** s., teacher, master, in *yak-dessā* exorcist, devil-priest.—P. *dēsaka*, *dēsika*, Sk. *dēśaka*, *dēśika*.

1201. දෙළුම් **deḷum,** s., pomegranate (tree or fruit).—Pk., Sk. *dāḍima*, *dāḷima*, P. *dālima* ; si. *ḍāṛhūṃ*, g. *daḍām*, m. *dāḷimb*, *dāḷīm*, oṛ. *dāṛimba*, *ḍāḷimba*, *ḍāḷima*, ass. *ḍālim*, bg. *dāṛim*, *ḍālim*, h. *dāṛimb*, *dāṛim*, *dālim*, nep. *dārim*. Gr. L 14.

1202. දොම්නස් **domnas,** a., sorrowful, pensive ; s. °*sa* sorrow, melancholy. —P. *dōmanassa*, Sk. *daurmanasya*. Cf. *dumana*.

1203. දොර **dora,** s., door, gate.—Pk. *duvāra*, *dāra*, P., Sk. *dvāra* ; si. *bārī*, g. *bār*, m. *bārī*, oṛ. *duāra*, ass. *duvār*, bg. *duyār*, h. nep. *duvār*, *bār*, pj. *duār*, *bār*, l. *bārī*.

1204. දොරටුව **doraṭuva,** s., st. f. °*ṭu*, gateway, portal. *doraṭu-pālayā* doorkeeper.—*dora*+*aṭuva*, q.v.; essentially=P. *dvāra-koṭṭhaka*.

1205. දොවනවා **dovanavā**[1], දොවිනවා **dovinavā,** v., prt. *devuvā*, to draw milk, to milk.—P. *dōhati*, Sk. √*duh* (*dōgdhi*) ; m. *duhṇeṃ*, *dohṇeṃ*, h. *dohnā*, nep. *duhunu*, pj. *dohnā*, l. *ḍohaṇ*.

1206. දොවනවා **dōvanavā**[2], prt. *devuvā*, to wash, rinse.—Pk. *dhōvaï*, *dhuvaï*, P. *dhōvati*, Sk. *dhāvati*, °*tē* ; si. *dhuaṇu*, *dhāiṇu*, g. *dhovuṃ*, m, *dhuvṇeṃ*, *dhuṇeṃ*, oṛ. *dhoibā*, ass. *dhoiba*, bg. *dhoyā*, h. *dhonā*, nep. *dhunu*, pj. *dhoṇā*.

1207. දොවුන **dovuna,** s., st. f. *dovun*, washing, rinsing, in *dovun-diya* water in which rice has been washed.—P. *dhōvana*, *dhāvana*, Sk. *dhāvana* ; m. *dhuvaṇ*.

1208. දොස **dosa,** s., st. f. *dos*, fault, error, defect. *dos-kiyanavā* to complain.—Pk., P. *dōsa*, Sk. *dōṣa* ; si. *ḍohu*, oṛ. *dosa*, bg. h. nep. *dos*, pj. *doh*, l. *ḍoh*.

1209. **දොළ doḷa,** s., desire, longing, craving (as of a pregnant woman). *doḷa-duka* id.—Pk. *ḍōhaḷa, ḍōhōḷa,* P. *dōhaḷa,* Sk. *dōhala, dōhada, dāuhada* ; m. *ḍohḷā, ḍohāḷā.*

1210. **දොළහ doḷaha, °ස °sa,** num., st. f. *doḷos,* twelve. *doḷos-veni, -väni* twelfth.—Pk. *duvārasa,* P. *dvādasa,* Sk. *dvādaśa.* Cf. *bara*[1].

1211. **දෝ dō**[1]**, දෝහෝ dōhō,** part. expressing doubt, uncertainty. *pin-kamek dōhō-yi* whether (perhaps) it is a meritorious work.—? <**dāhu* =P. *udāhu,* Sk. *utāvā, utāhō.*

1212. **දෝ dō**[2]**,** s., st., f. *dō,* star.—Pk. AMg. *jōī,* P. *jōti,* Sk. *jyōtis, dyōtis* ; cf. Bl, s.v. *jośī,* T, s.v. *jaisi* astrolcger.

න N

1213. **න na,** neg. part., not, un-: contracted *nāra* (<*na-āra*) not except. There are various forms of the particle : 1) *nu-* (before *u* in the following syllable) : *nu-duru* not distant, near ; *nu-nuvaṇa* foolishness ; contr. *nūpan* unborn (<*nu-upan*). 2) *ne-*: *ne-penenavā* to be invisible, to disappear. 3) *no-: no-häki* unable (Sk. *aśakya*) ; *no-bova* do not drink.—A separate word is *nähä, nā* is not, not: *mama dannē nā* I do not know.—Pk. *na, ṇa, ṇu,* P., Sk. *na, nō* ; kśm. *nā, nō, nu,* si. g. *na,* m. *nā, n-,* oṛ. ass. bg. h. nep. *na,* pj. *nā,* l. *na.*

— **නකත nakata,** s., see **näkata.**

1214. **නකු naku,** s., crocodile, alligator.—Pk. *ṇakka,* P. *nakka,* Sk. *nakra* ; h. *nākā.*

1215. **නගනවා naganavā, නඟ° naňga°,** v., prt. *näguvā, näňg°,* to raise, lift up, erect, build. Caus. *naṃvanavā* (for *naňgv°*), prt. *näṃguvā,* (<**näňgguvā* <**näňgvuvā*), to cause to lift up ; intr. *naginavā, naňg°,* prt. *näggā, näṃgā,* or *nägenavā, näňg°,* prt. *näguṇā, näňg°,* to rise, mount, extend.—Mediaev. Sinh. *laňg°,* DhpAGp 60[6], EpZ I 25[10], 10th c. etc.=Pk. *laṅghaï,* P. *laṅghati, laṅghēti,* Sk. √*laṅgh, laṅghati,* caus. *laṅghayati* ; si. *laṅghaṇu,* g. *lāṃghvuṃ,* m. *laṃghṇeṃ,* ass. *laghon,* bg. *laṅghā,* h. *lāṃghnā, nāṃghnā,* nep. *nāṃghnu, nāṃgnu, nāṅnu,* pj. *laṅghṇā,* l. *lagghaṇ.*

1216. **නගා nagā, නඟා naňgā, නංගි naṃgi,** s., younger sister.—Cf. Pk. *ṇagga* naked, P. *nagga,* Sk. *nagna,* (f. *nagnā, nagnikā* a girl before menstruation); g. *nāguṃ* naked, m. *nāgvā, nāgā,* oṛ. bg. h. *nāgā,* nep. *nāgo, nāṃgo,* pj. *naṅgā.*

1217. **නගුට naguṭa, නඟුට naňguṭa,** s., tail.—P. *naṅguṭṭha* ; cf. m. *nāṃḍā, nāṃgoḍā* tail of a scorpion. See also *nagula*[2].

1218. **නගුල nagula**[1]**,** s., st. f. *nagul,* plough—Pk. *ṇaṅgala, laṅgala,* P. *naṅgala,* Sk. *lāṅgala* ; kśm. *laṅgar,* si. *laṅgaru,* m. *nāgār, nāṃgār, °gor,* bg. *nāṃgal,* h. *nāṃgar, nāṃgal, laṃgar.*

1219. නඟුල **nagula²**, s., st. f. *nagul*, tail.—Pk. *ṇaṅgūla*, *laṅg°*, P. *naṅgula*, *laṅgula*, Sk. *lāṅgūla* ; g. *laṅgur*, m. *laṅgul*, or. *lāṅguḷa*, *°ra*, bg. *lāṅgul*. Cf. T, s.v. *laṅgur¹*.

1220. නට **naṭa**, a. pprt., destroyed, perished.—Pk. *ṇaṭṭha*, P. *naṭṭha*, Sk. *naṣṭa* ; kśm. *nōṃṭhu*, g. *nāṭhuṃ*, m. *nāṭ*, ass. *nāṭh*, bg. *nāṭuyā*, h. *nāṭh*. Cf. T, s.v. *nāṭho*.

1221. නටබුන් **naṭabun**, a., devastated, desolate.—*naṭa*+*bun*.

1222. නටයා **naṭayā**, s., st. f. *naṭa*, dancer. Cf. v. *naṭanavā*, prt. *näṭuvā*, to dance.—P. *naṭṭa*, *naṭṭaka* dancer, Abhp 100, 101 (side by side with *naṭana*, *naṭaka*). Cf. m. *nācṇeṃ*, nep. *nācnu*=Pk. *ṇaccati*, P. *naccati*, Sk. *nṛtyati*. See also *naḷuvā*, *näsuma*.

1223. නඩය **naḍaya**, s., st. f. *naḍa*, filth.—P. *laṇḍa*, Sk. *laṇḍa* (*lēṇḍa*=si. *leṇḍu*, *leḍuno*, m. *leṃḍ*, h. *leṃḍ*, *leṃḍi*, nep. *limṛ*).

1224. නත් **nat**, a., endless, infinite.—Pk. *aṇanta*, *ṇanta*, P., Sk. *ananta*. Sinh. also *anat*.

1225. නතුව **natuva**, s., st. f. *natu*, (Ca) inheritance, estate; s. masc. *natuvā* heir.—Sk. *nyasta* (*ni-*+$\sqrt{}$*as²*) deposited ; cf. Sk. *nyāsa*=Pk. *ṇāsa* ; g. *nās*, nep. *nāso*.

1226. නදන **nadana**, නඳන **nañdana**, s., st. f. *°an*, *°un*, joy, pleasure. *nadun-uyana* pleasure garden.—Pk. *ṇandana*, P., Sk. *nandana*. Cf. m. *nāṃdṇeṃ*, nep. *nandnā*.

1227. නන් **nan**, a., several, many, much.—Pk. *ṇāṇā*, P., Sk. *nānā*.

1228. නම **nama¹**, s., honour, in *nama-karanavā*, v., to bow, salute, worship, and in *nam'-añdinavā*, prt. *näm'-ändā*, id.—Pk. *ṇama*, P. *nama*, Sk. *namas* (*namas-kṛ*) ; cf. m. *navas*.

1229. නම **nama²**, s., st. f. *nam*, name. *namäti*, *nam-vū* called (so and so). As particle *-nam* is used for emphasising the preceding word, or it stands at the end of a conditional (*nam-udu*, *nam-ut*, *num-ut*=*nam*+*da*, q.v.) sentence.—Pk. *ṇāma*, P. *nāma*, Sk. *nāman* ; kśm. *nām*, si. *nāmuṃ*, g. *nām*, m. *nāṃv*, *nāv*, cṛ. *nā*, ass. *nāu*, bg. *nām*, h. *nāṃv*, nep. *nāuṃ*, pj. *nāṃ*, l. *naṃ*. Gr. L 16.

— නමනවා **namanavā**, v., see **navanavā**.

1230. නමය **namaya**, නවය **navaya**, num., st. f. *nama*, *nava*, nine. *nama-* (*nava-*) *väni*, *veni* ninth ; *nama-vaka* the ninth day after new or full moon.—Pk. *ṇava*, P., Sk. *nava* ; kśm. *nam*, *nav*, si. *naṃvaṃ*, g. m. *nav*, oṛ. ass. bg. *na*, b. h. nep. *nau*, pj. *nauṃ*, l. *nōṃ*.

1231. නය **naya**, s., mode, manner.—Pk. *ṇāa*, P. *ñāya*, Sk. *nyāya* ; kśm. *nyāy*, si. *niāu*, g. *nyāy*, m. *nyāv*, bg. *nyāy*, h. *niāu*. Sinh. *niyāya* (*niyāva*) is lw. Sk.

1232. **නයා nayā,** s., st. ff. *nay*, *nayi*, *nā*, Cobra Capella. *nayi-kārayā* snake-charmer ; *nayi-gala* snake-stone.—P., Sk. *nāga*.

1233. **නර nara,** a., human.—P., Sk. *nāra* ; Sinh. *narayā* man is probably lw. Sk., P. *nara*.

1234. **නරතුරු naraturu, නිරතුරු niraturu,** a., continual unintermitting.—Pk. *ṇirantara*, P., Sk. *nirantara*.

1235. **නරද narada,** s., arrow.—Pk. *ṇarāa*, P. *nārāca*, Sk. *nārācā*.

1236. **නල nala[1],** s., fire.—Pk. *aṇala*, P., Sk. *anala*.

1237. **නල nala[2],** s., wind.—P., Sk. *anila*.

1238. **නලළ nalaḷa** (also spelt *naḷala*), s., st. f. *nalaḷa* (*naḷal*), forehead. *naḷal-talaya* surface of the forehead.—Pk. *ṇilāḍa*, *ṇalāḍa*, P. *nalāṭa*, *lalāṭa*, Sk. *lalāṭa* ; si. *niraṛu*, m. *niḍāḷ*, *niḍhāḷ*, h. *lilāṛ*, nep. *nidhār*, *nīdār*.

1239. **නව nava,** a., new, fresh. *nava-sañda* new moon.—Pk. *ṇava*, P., Sk. *nava*; kśm. *novu*, si. *naṃoṃ*, g. *navuṃ*, m. *navā*, ass. *na*, bg. *na*, *nai*, h. *navā*, *nayā*, nep. *naulo*, pj. *navāṃ*, l. *navaṃ*.

1240. **නවතනවා navatanavā,** v., prt. *nävatuvā*, to stop (tr.), to cause to cease. Intr. *navatinavā* or *nävatenavā*, prt. *nävatuṇā*, to stop (intr.); caus. *navatvanavā*, prt. *nävätvuvā*, to cause to cease.—*navatanavā*=P. *ni-vattēti*, Sk. *ni-*+$\sqrt{}$*vṛt*, caus. *ni-vartayati*; *navatinavā*=Pk. *ṇi-vattaï*, P. *ni-vattati*, Sk. *ni-vartatē*. Cf. m. *nivaṭṇeṃ* to destroy, kill (Bl), h. *nibaṭnā* to be consumed, pj. *nibiraṇu* to finish.

1241. **නවනවා navanavā, නමනවා namanavā,** v., prt. *nävuvā*, *nämuvā*, to bend (tr.), incline. Intr *nämenavā*, prt. *nämuṇā*, to be inclined.—Pk. *ṇamēi*, P. *nāmēti*, *namayati*, Sk. $\sqrt{}$*nam*, caus. *nāmayati* ; kśm. *namarun*, g. *namāvvuṃ*, oṛ. *nuāṃibā*, bg. *nāmāna*, h. *navānā*, nep. *nuvāunu*. See *nämi*.

— **නවය navaya,** num., see **namaya.**

1242. **නවා navā,** s., rest, passing the night, in *navā-tāna* resthouse, inn.—Not=Sk. *nivṛtta* (WICKREMASINGHE, EpZ I 54, n.7), but=Pk. *ṇivāsa*, P., Sk. *nivāsa*.

1243. **නවාම navāma,** s., st. f. *navām*, new work.—<*nava-kama* ; P. *nava-kamma*.

— **නසනවා nasanavā, නසිනවා nasinavā,** v., see s.v. **nahanavā.**

1244. **නහනවා nahanavā[1], නස° nasa[c],** v., prt. *nähuvā*, *näs°*, to kill, destroy. Caus. *nasavanavā*, prt. *näsevuvā*, to cause to kill ; intr. *nahinavā*, *nas°* or *näsenavā*, prt. *nähuṇā*, *näs°*, to die, to perish.—*nahanavā*=Pk. *ṇāsei*, P. *nāsēti*, Sk. $\sqrt{}$ *naś*, caus. *nāśayati* ; kśm. *nahāvun*, m. *nāsṇeṃ*, bg. *nāsā*, h. *nāsnā*, nep. *nāsnu*. Sinh. *nahinavā*=Pk. *ṇassaï*, P. *nassati*, Sk. *naśyati* ; kśm. *naśun*, g. *nāsvuṃ*, m. *nāsṇeṃ*, h. *nāsnā*, pj. *nassṇā*, l. *nassaṇ*.

— නහනවා **nahanavā²**, v. see **nānavā.**

1245. නහය **nahaya,** s., st. ff. *naha,* nose. *naha-lanuva* nose-string for guiding a bullock.—P., Sk. *nāsā.* Cf. *nǟy.* , *nähäya.*

1246. නහරය **naharaya,** s., st. f. *nahara,* nerve, vein, tendon. *nahara-gäṭaya* knot of a nerve or vein.—Pk. *ṇahāru,* P. *nahāru,* Sk. *snāyu, snāvan*; nep. *nahar.*

1247. නළය **naḷaya,** s., st. f. *naḷa,* tube, reed. *naḷa-karuvā* basket-maker.—Pk. *ṇaḍa, ṇala,* P. *naḷa, nala.* Sk. *naḍa, nala*; kśm. *nari, nal,* si. *naṛu, narī,* g. m. *naḷ,* oṛ. *naṛā, naḷa,* ass. *narā, nal,* bg. h. *naṛ, nal,* nep. *nal,* pj. *naṛā, nal,* l. *naṛ, naḷa.*

— නළල **naḷala,** s., see **nalaḷa.**

1248. නළුවා **naḷuvā,** s., st. f. *naḷu,* dancer.—P., Sk. *nāṭaka.* Cf. *naṭayā.*

1249. නා **nā¹,** s., in *nā-gaha* iron-wood tree, Mesua ferrea.—P., Sk. *nāga.*

1250. නා **nā²,** s., ruler, chief.—Pk. *ṇāha,* P., Sk. *nātha*; m. h. *nāh.*

1251. නානවා **nānavā,** නහනවා **nahanavā,** v., prt. *nǟvā, nähävā,* to bathe (intr.). Caus. *nāvanavā, nahavanavā,* prt. *nǟvuvā, nähävuvā,* to bathe (tr.).—Pk. *ṇhāi,* P. *nahāyati,* caus. *nahāpēti,* Sk. √*snā, snāti,* caus. *snāpayati*; kśm. *nāvun,* g. *nāhvuṃ,* m. *nāhṇeṃ,* h. *nahānā,* nep. *nuvāunu, nuh°,* pj. *nhāuṇā,* l. *nahāvaṇ.*

1252. නාලිය **nā-liya,** s., betel.—See *nā¹.* P. *nāga-latā,* Sk. cf. *nāga-vallī.*

1253. නැකත **näkata,** නකත **nakata,** s., st. f. *°kät, °kat,* star, planet, lunar mansion. *näkättā, näkät-karuvā* astrologer.—Pk. *ṇakkhatta,* P. *nakkhatta.* Sk. *nakṣatra.*

1254. නැගිටිනවා **nägiṭinavā,** v., prt. *nägiṭṭā,* to rise (as from sleep).—Ger. *näga* of v. *naginavā* (see *naganavā*)+*hiṭinavā.* Sinh. also *nägiṭenavā,* prt. *nägiṭuṇā,* to rise, and caus. *näguṭuvanavā,* prt. *nägiṭevuvā,* to raise.

1255 නැණ **näṇa,** s., wisdom, intelligence. *näṇa-vat,* a., wise.—Pk. *ṇāṇa,* P. *ñāṇa,* Sk. *jñāna*; kśm. *zān,* si. *jāṇu,* g. m. *jāṇ,* bg. h. nep. *jān̐,* pj. *jāṇ.*

1256. නැති **näti,** නැත් **nät,** a., adv., not existing, no, not. *näti-deyak* a thing that is not; *näti-venavä* to disappear, to be lost; *näti-karanavā* to lose or cause to disappear. In cpds. not having or possessing: *äs-näti* having no eyes, blind.—Pk. *ṇatthi,* P. *natthi,* Sk. *nâsti*; g. *nathī,* m. *nāthi.* Cf. s.v. *äti.*

1257. නැදී **nädī,** නැඳි **näňdi,** නැන්දා **nändā,** s., paternal aunt; mother-in-law.—*nädī, näňdī*<**nandī*; *nändā* (through **näňddā,* **näňdiyā*) <**nandikā.* Cf. Sk. *nandinī.*

1258. නැබ **näba,** s., st. f. *näba,* navel; nave of a wheel.—Pk. *ṇāhi,* P., Sk. *nābhi*; si. *nāṃhīṃ,* g. *nāiḍī,* oṛ. *nāhi,* ass. bg. *nāi,* b. *nāh,* nep. *nāiṭo.* T, s.v.

1259. **නැබුරු näburu, නැඹුරු nämburu,** a., bent, inclined. *n°-karanavā* to bend.—Sk. *namra*. Cf. *duṁburu* < *dhūmra*.

1260. **නැමි nämi,** a. pprt., bent, curved.—Pk. *ṇavia*, P., Sk. *namita*. See *navanavā*.

1261. **නැව näva,** s., st. f. *näv*, ship. *näv-naginavā* to embark.—Pk. *ṇāvā*, P. *nāvā*, Sk. *nāu*, *nāvā*; kśm. *nāv*, si. *nāuk*, g. m. *nāv*, oṛ. *nā*, ass. *nāu*, b. h. *näv*, nep. pj. *nāu*.

1262. **නැවත nävata, °තත් °ta-t,** adv., again.—*nava* (cf. Engl. *anew*, germ. *von neuem*) + *ata*[1]. Cf. *ihata*, *pahata* etc. De Lanerolle suggests: *nävata* (ger. of v. *navatinavā*) having stopped + *-t* also.

1263. **නැසුම näsuma,** s., st. f. *näsum*, dancing.—<MInd. **naccana*. See s.v. *naṭayā*.

1264. **නැළිය näḷiya,** s., st. f. *näḷi*, a measure of capacity.—P. *nāḷī* tube, pipe, measure of capacity, Pk. *ṇāḍī*, *ṇālī*, Sk. *nāḍī* vein, pulse; cf. Bl, s.v. *nāḍī*, T, s.v. *nāri*.

1265. **නැනා nänā,** s., female cousin, daughter of father's sister or of mother's brother; wife's or husband's sister.—? from *näyā*; a formation like nep. *nātinā*, *nātini* grandson, grand-daughter from *nāti*=Sk. *nāptṛ*. See T, s. vv.

1266. **නැය näya**[1], **නැහැය nähäya,** s., st. f. *nä*, nose.—Sk. *nāsikā*; kśm. *nākh*, si. *naku*, g. m. ass. bg. h. nep. *nāk*, oṛ. *nāka*, pj. l. *nakk*. Cf. *nahaya*.

1267. **නැය näya**[2], s., fitness, justness; name of a philosophical system.—Younger doublet of *naya*, q.v., with particular meaning.

1268. **නැයා näyā,** s., st. f. *nä*, relative, kinsman. *nä-kama* relationship.—Pk. *ṇāi*, P. *ñāti*, Sk. *jñāti*+*-ka*; cf. si. *nāto*, g. *nātuṃ*, m. *nāteṃ*, h. *nātā*, nep. *nāto*, pj. *nāttā*.

1269. **නි ni-,** pref., privative, un-, -less, free from, without. *ni-tätin*, adv., without effort (see *täta*[2]); *ni-kasaḷa*, a., unpolluted.—Pk. *ṇī*, P. *ni-*, Sk. *niṣ-*, *niḥ-*, *niṛ-*. Before verbs and nouns *ni-* may be=Sk. *niṣ-* or=Pk. *ṇi-*, P., Sk. *ni-*.

1270. **නික් nik,** s., goldsmith's weight.—Pk. *ṇikkha*, P. *nikkha*, Sk. *niṣka*.

1271. **නිකම් nikam,** a., unemployed, useless; empty, simple, mere.—Pk. *ṇikkamma*, P. *nikkamma*, Sk. *niṣkarman*; kśm. *nekama*, si. *nikamo*, m. *nikāmī*, oṛ. *nikamā*, h. *nikāmā*, °*mī*, nep. *nikāmi*, pj. *nikkammā*.

1272. **නිකිණිය nikiṇiya, නිකිණිමස nikiṇi-masa,** s., name of the fifth month of the Sinhalese year, July-August.—The old form *nikamaniya*, EpZ III 178[15], 4th c., shows that *nikiṇi* stands for **nikmiṇi*=Sk. **niṣkramaṇīya*. In the 10th c., EpZ III 75 A[14], occurs the form *nikinni* which is perhaps=**nikimni*. Mod. *nikinniya* (Cl).

1273. **නිකුටු nikuṭu,** a., low, base.—P. *nikiṭṭha,* Sk. *nikṛṣṭa* ; oṛ. *nikiṭa,* nep. *nikuṭo.*

1274. **නිකුත් nikut,** a. pprt., gone away, departed, dead. *n°-karanavā* to send away.—Pk. *ṇikkhanta,* P. *nikkhanta,* Sk. *niṣkrānta.*

1275. **නික්මෙනවා nikmenavā,** v., prt. *nikmuṇā,* to come forth, issue. Caus. *nikmavanavā,* prt. *nikmevuvā,* to send forth.—Pk., *ṇikkhamaï,* P. *nikkhamati,* Sk. *niṣ-* + $\sqrt{}$*kram,* *niṣ-kramati.*

1276. **නිගා nigā,** s., insult, in *nigā-karanavā* to insult, revile.—Pk. *ṇiggaha,* P. *niggaha,* Sk. *nigraha.*

1277. **නිගොස nigosa,** s., st. f. *nigos,* sound, noise; echo.—P. *nigghōsa,* Sk. *nirghōṣa.*

1278. **නිති niti,** adv., continually, constantly. *nitin* id.; *nitta,* a., continual.—Pk. *ṇicca,* P. *nicca,* Sk. *nitya.* But *t* ?. See *nisadī.*

1279. **නිදන nidana,** a., poor.—Pk. *ṇiddhana,* P. *niddhana,* Sk. *nirdhana.*

1280. **නිදනවා nidanavā,** **නිඳ° niňda°,** v., to sleep.—Pk. *ṇiddāati,* P. *niddāyati,* Sk. *ṇidrāyati* ; nep. *nidāunu.* See *ninda.*

1281. **නිදර nidara,** a., undecaying, imperishable.—P. *nijjara,* Sk. *nirjara.*

1282. **නිදි nidi,** **නිඳි niňdi,** a. pprt., opprobrious, infamous.—P., Sk. *nindita.*

1283. **නිදු nidu,** a., low, outcast.—Pk. *ṇīa,* P., Sk. *nīca* ; kśm. *nyūcu,* si. *nīcu,* g. m. *nīc,* oṛ. bg. *nica,* ass. *nis,* h. pj. *nīc,* nep. *nic.*

1284. **නිදුක් niduk,** a., sorrowless, happy.—Pk. *ṇiddukkha,* P. *niddukkha,* Sk. *nirduḥkha.*

1285. **නිදොස් nidos,** a., blameless, faultless. *nidos-kama* blamelessness.—P. *niddōsa,* Sk. *nirdōṣa.*

1286. **නින්ද ninda,** s., st. ff. *niňdi, nidi,* sleep. *nidi-* (*niňdi-*) *karavanavā* (or *ganvanavā*) to put to sleep.—Pk. *ṇiddā,* P. *niddā,* Sk. *nidrā* ; kśm. *nendar,* si. *niṇḍra,* g. *nīṃd, nīdar,* m. *nīd,* oṛ. *nida,* bg. *nid,* h. *nīṃd,* nep. *nid,* pj. *nīṃd, nīṃdar,* l. *nindr.*

1287. **නිපදවනවා nipadavanavā,** v., prt. *nipadevuvā,* to produce.—Caus. of **nipadinavā*=Pk. *ṇippajjaï,* P. *nipp(h)ajjati,* Sk. *niṣ-* + $\sqrt{}$*pad,* *niṣpadyatē* ; m. *nipajṇeṃ.*

1288. **නිපන් nipan,** a. pprt., born, produced.—Pk. *ṇipphaṇṇa,* P. *nipphanna,* Sk. *niṣpanna.*

1289. **නිඹ nimba,** s., the Margosa tree, Azadirachta indica.—Pk., P., Sk. *nimba* ; si. *nimu,* m. *niṃb,* h. *nīm,* pj. *nimm.* Cf. T, s.v. *nibu.*

— **නිම nima**[1]**,** s., see s.v. **nimi.**

1290. **නිම nima^{2},** s., st. f. *nim*, rim of a wheel.—P., Sk. *nēmi* ; h. *nev*. B, I 256.

1291. **නිමනවා nimanavā, නිවනවා nivanavā,** v., prt. *nimuvā*, *nivuvā*, to end, finish; to extinguish (tr.), quench, annihilate. Caus. *nimavanavā*, prt. *nimevuvā*, to cause to extinguish ; intr. *nimenavā*, *nivenavā*, prt. *nimuṇā*, *nivuṇā*, to be finished, to be extinguished.—It seems that the meanings of the two verbs MInd. **nimmā*=Sk. *nir-mā* to form, make, and **nivvā*=*nir-vā* to extinguish, were confounded at an early date, as in Sinh. and other MIAVs *m* often alternates with *ṃv*, *v* (Gr.L 16; Ch, BL, I 520; Bl, LM § 137). But formally we may distinguish the derivates of the two verbs in the following manner. Sinh. *nivenavā* may immediately be compared with MInd. **nivvāyati*=P. *nibbāyati*, and *nimavanavā* with Pk. *ṇimmāvēi*, P. *nimmāpēti*, Sk. *nir-māpayati* (with the meaning of **nivvāpēti*, P. *nibbāpēti*), also *nimanavā* with Pk. *ṇimmāi*, Sk. *nir-māti*. But *nivanavā* can, owing to its transitive meaning, hardly be derived from Pk. *ṇivvāi*, P. *nibbāti*, Sk. *nir-vāti* ; it seems to be a new formation, or perhaps haplology of **nivavanavā*.

1292. **නිමි nimi,** a. pprt., finished. Cf. *nima-venavā* to be finished.—Pk. *ṇimmia*, P. *nimmita*, Sk. *nirmita*.

— **නිමිත්ත nimitta, නිමිති nimiti,** see **nivitta, niviti.**

1293. **නිමිස nimisa, නිමෙස nimesa,** s., st. ff. *nimis*, *nimes*, twinkling of an eye, an instant.—Pk. *ṇimēsa*, P. *nimisa*, *nimēsa*, Sk. *nimiṣa*, *nimēṣa*.

1294. **නිය niya^{1},** s., st. ff. *niya*, *nī*, nail of the finger or toe. *niya-kaṭuva* finger-nail pick.—Pk. *ṇaha*, P., Sk. *nakha* ; si. *naṃhuṃ*, h. *nah*, nep. *naṅ*, pj. *nahī*, l. *nauṃh*.

1295. **නිය niya^{2},** s., st. f. *nī*, running water, river.—Pk. *ṇaī*, P., Sk. *nadī*; si. *nāṃīṃ*, m. *naī*, *nahī*, pj. *naī*.

1296. **නිය niya^{3},** s., st. ff. *niya*, *nī*, understanding, prudence.—P., Sk. *naya*. Cf. *nuvaṇa*.

1297. **නිය niya^{4},** s., st. f. *nī*, hidden treasure.—Pk. *ṇihi*, P., Sk. *nidhi*.

1298. **නිය niya^{5},** s., st. f. *nī*, law.—Pk. *ṇīi*, P., Sk. *nīti*.

1299. **නියඟ niyaňga,** s., st. f. *niyaṃ*, drought, summer. *niyaṃ-kala*, *-samaya* dry or hot season.—Pk. *ṇidāha*, P., Sk. *nidāgha* ; nep. *niyānu* hot.

1300. **නියද niyada, °ඳ °ňda,** s., name of a plant, Sanseviera zeylanica.—? Sk. *nagajā*.

1301. **නියන්ගම niyan-gama, නියම්ගම niyam-gama,** s., st. f. *°-gam*, large village, market-town.—*niyan*, *°m*=P., Sk. *nigama*. Cf. *nigama-ggāma*, Mhvs 88.49.

1302. **නියමුවා niyamuvā,** s., st. f. *°mu*, pilot, captain.—Pk. *ṇiāmaga*, P., Sk. *niyāmaka*.

1303. **නියර niyara, නෙර nera,** s., dam, embankment, weir of paddy fields.—For **nivara* ; P., Sk. *nivāra* (*ni-* + √*var*). *nera* is the contracted form.

1304. **නියාව niyāva, °ය °ya,** s., st. f. *niyā*, mode, manner.—lw. Sk. *nyāya*. See *naya*.

1305. **නිරත nirata,** a., attached or devoted to, engaged in, occupied with.—lw. P. id., Sk. *ni-* + √*ram*.

1306. **නිරතු niratu,** a., empty, vacant, void.—P. *nir-attha*(*ka*) vain, useless, Sk. *nir-artha*.

— **නිරතුරු niraturu,** a., see **naraturu.**

1307. **නිරවුල් niravul,** a., unconfused, clear.—P., Sk. *nir-ākula*. See *avul*.

1308. **නිරාව nirāva,** s., st. f. *nirā*, hell, the infernal regions.—P., Sk. *niraya*.

1309. **නිරොද niroda,** a., lacking vitality or power.—<Sk. **nir-ōjas*. See *oda*.

1310. **නිල් nil,** a., blue, green, dark; s. *nila* blueness, greenness, *nilla* verdure; *nil-mē* dark clouds; *nil-karanavā* (or *lanavā*) to make blue.—Pk. *ṇīla*, P., Sk. *nīla* ; si. *nīro*, g. *līlum*, m. *nīḷ*, or. *niḷa*, ass. *nil*, bg. *nila*, h. pj. l. *nīlā*, nep. *nilo*.

1311. **නිල්කට nil-kaṭa,** s., blue-necked one, peacock.—Sk. *nīla-kaṇṭha*.

1312. **නිල්මිණ nil-miṇa,** s., st. f. °*ṇi*, blue gem, sapphire.—Sk. *nīla-maṇi*.

1313. **නිල්වන් nil-van,** a., blue-coloured, blue.—Sk. *nīla-varṇa*.

1314. **නිල්වසන් nil-vasan,** s., blue-clothed one.—Sk. *nīla-vasana*.

1315. **නිවටුවා nivaṭuvā, නුව° nuva°,** s., st. f. °*ṭu*, naked religious mendicant.—P. *nigaṇṭha*. (Sk. *nirgrantha*).

1316. **නිවත් nivat,** s., birth, existence.—P. *nibbatti*, Sk. *nirvṛtti*. Cf. Pk. *ṇivvattēi*, P. *nibbattēti*, °*ati*, Sk. *nir-vartatē*, °*tayati* ; g. *nivaḍvuṃ*, m. *nivaṭṇeṃ*, °*ḍṇeṃ*, h. *nibaṭnā*, °*ḍnā*, pj. *nibbaḍnā*.

1317. **නිවතා nivatā,** s., st. f. *nivat*, poor man.—<MInd. **nivvattha*. *ni* + *vata*[3].

1318. **නිවන nivana,** s., extinguishing; salvation, nirvāṇa.—Pk. *ṇivvāṇa*, P. *nibbāna*, Sk. *nirvāṇa* ; m. *nivāṇeṃ*. Cf. *nimanavā*.

1319. **නිවිය niviya,** s., st. f. *nivi*, waist-fold.—H. Jayatilaka, Eḷu-akārādiya = *neri-paṭa*. Sk. *nivṛta*, *nivīta*. Cf. Ca *nīviya*, *nivi-paṭṭaya*.

1320. **නිවියා niviyā,** s., st. f. *nivi*, agriculturist.—? Pk. *ṇivvua*, P. *nibbuta*, Sk. *nirvṛta* happy, content (agriculture being the most satisfying profession for a Sinhalese).

1321. **නිවිත්ත nivitta, නිමිත්ත nimitta,** s., st. ff. °*viti*, °*miti*, cause, reason, event.—P., Sk. *nimitta.*

1322. **නිවිති niviti, නිමිති nimiti,** s. pl., omens. *niviti-kārayā*, *nim*°, s., soothsayer ; *niviti-(nim°-)ahanavā* to consult the sooth-sayer ; *n°-allanavā* to take signs, to divine.—Sk. *nimittaka.*

1323. **නිවීයනවා nivī-yanavā,** v., prt. *nivī-giyā*, to be extinguished.—*nivī*, ger. of *nivenavā* (see s.v. *nimanavā*) + *y*°.

— **නිවෙනවා nivenavā,** v., see s.v. **nimanavā.**

— **නිසක nisaka,** a., see **nisäka.**

1324. **නිසගය nisagaya,** s., st. f. *nisaga*, nature, natural state.—P. *nisagga*, Sk. *nisarga.*

1325. **නිසදී nisadī** (°*di*), adv., (Ca) continually, constantly.—*nisa*= Pk. *ṇicca*, P. *nicca*, Sk. *nitya*+affix *-d-*. Cf. *niti.*

1326. **නිසන් nisan, නිසල් nisal,** a., near.—Pk. *ṇisaṇṇa*, P. *nisanna*, Sk. *niṣaṇṇa*. See *asan.*

1327. **නිසය nisaya,** s., st. f. *nisa*, night.—P. *nisā*, Sk. *niśā.*

1328. **නිසයුරු nisayuru,** s., moon.—Pk. *ṇisāara*, P. *nisākara*, Sk. *niśākara.*

1329. **නිසර nisara[1],** s., sound, noise.—<Sk. **niḥsvara* ; cf. *niḥsvana* and *nisvana* (Sk. *svara* side by side with *svana*)=P. *nissana.*

1330. **නිසර nisara[2], නිසරු nisaru,** a., unfruitful, empty, useless.—P. *nissāra*, Sk. *niḥsāra.*

1331. **නිසල් nisal[1], °ල °la,** a., non-shaking, firm.—Pk. *ṇiccala*, P. *niccala*, Sk. *niścala* : m. *nical*, h. *niclā*, nep. *nicāl*, pj. *nicall.*

— **නිසල් nisal[2],** a., see **nisan.**

1332. **නිසා nisā,** postp., because of ; conj., because.—P. *nissāya* (PTSPD, s.v.). Cf. *piṇisa.*

1333. **නිසැක nisäka, නිසක nisaka,** a., undoubted, certain. *n°-bava* certainty.—Pk. *ṇissaṅka*, Sk. *niḥśaṅka.*

1334. **නිසි nisi,** a. pprt., suitable, proper.—P. *nissita*, Sk. *niśrita.*

1335. **නිසිණිය nisiṇiya,** s., st. f. *nisiṇi*, ladder, stairs.—Pk. *ṇissēṇi*, *ṇīsaṇiā*, P. *nissēṇi*, Sk. *niḥśrēṇi* ; m. *nisaṇ*, *niśīn*, h. *nisenī*, *nisainī*, *nas*°.

1336. **නිසිරි nisiri,** a., unfortunate.—P. *nissirīka*, Sk. *niḥśrīka.*

1337. **නිසෙස් nises,** a., all.—P. *nissēsa*, Sk. *niḥśēṣa.*

1338. **නිහුණු nihuṇu,** s., whetting, in *nihuṇu-gānavā* to whet, sharpen.—Sk. *niśāna* ; m. *nisṇā* whetstone (Bl).

— **නී nī[1],** s., see **niya[1-5].**

1339. **නී nī[2],** s., name of a tree, Nauclea (or Anthocephalus) Cadamba.—Pk. *ṇīva*, P., Sk. *nīpa.*

1340. **නු nu-,** prefix=Pk. *aṇu-*, P., Sk. *anu-*.

1341. **නුකම nukama,** s., st. f. *nukam*, order, arrangement.—Pk. *aṇukkama*, P. *anukkama*, Sk. *anu-krama*.

1342. **නුග nuga,** s., name of the banyan tree, Ficus altissima.—Pk. *ṇaggōha*, P. *nigrōdha*, Sk. *nyagrōdha*.

1343. **නුපුස් nupus,** a., invaluable.—*nu-* (neg. part., see *na*^{1})+*pus*<MInd. **phussa*=*spṛśya* 'that cannot be touched or reached'.

1344. **නුබ nuba, නුඹ numba,** s., sky.—Pk. *ṇaha*, P. *nabha*, Sk. *nabhas*.

— **නුමුත් numut,** part., see s.v. **nama**^{2}.

1345. **නුරාව nurāva,** s., st. f. *nurā*, love, affection. *nurā-karanavā* to love.—Pk. *aṇu-rāa*, P., Sk. *anu-rāga*.

1346. **නුරුව nuruva**^{1}, s., st. f. *nuru*, parable, simile.—Pk. *aṇu-rūva*, P., Sk. *anu-rūpa*.

1347. **නුරුව nuruva**^{2}, s., st. f. *nuru*, jingling ring on ankle or wrist.—Metathesis of **nuvura*=Pk. *ṇēura* (Ap. *nūura*), P., Sk. *nūpura* ; bg. *neur* (Ch, BL, I 409), h. *nepūr*.

— **නුවටුවා nuvaṭuvā,** s., see **nivaṭuvā**.

1348. **නුවණ nuvaṇa,** s., prudence, intelligence. *nuvaṇ'-äti* intelligent; *nuvaṇa-denavā* to give advice.—The word must be separated from *nuvana* eye. I believe it is =*nuva*, doublet of *niya*^{3} (Sk. *naya*)+suff.-*ṇa* (De Lanerolle, DSL, p. xliii, § 11). Cf. *sevaṇa*, *muhuṇa*.

1349. **නුවන nuvana,** s., st. f. *nuvan*, eye. *nuvan-aga* corner of the eye.—Pk. *ṇaaṇa*, P., Sk. *nayana* ; h. *nain*, *nainū*, nep. *nainu*, pj. *naiṇū*.

1350. **නුවර nuvara,** s., st. f. °*ra*, city, town. *nuvara-väsiyā* inhabitant of a city, citizen.—Pk. *ṇaara*, P., Sk. *nagara* ; g. *-nar*, *-ner*, m. *-ṇer*, bg. *-nar*, *-ner*.

1351. **නුවරා nuvarā, නියරියා niyariyā,** s., st. ff, °*ru*, °*ri*, citizen.—Pk. *ṇāara*. Sk. *nāgara*, *nāgarika*.

1352. **නුවාව nuvāva,** s., st. f. *nuvā*, hem of a Buddhist monk's robe.—P. *anuvāta*.

1353. **නුසරය nusaraya,** s., st. f. °*ra*, remembering.—Cf. Sk. *anu-* +√*smar*, *anu-smarati*, *anu-smaraṇa* ; Pk. *aṇussaraï*, P. *anussarati*.

1354. **නුහුරු nuhuru,** a., incongruous, inapt, clumsy.—*nu-* (see *na*. +*huru*, q.v.

1355. **නුහුව nuhuva,** num., ten thousand.—P. *nahuta*, Sk. *nayuta*.

— **නෙක් nek,** a., see **nē**.

1356. **නෙත neta,** s., st. f. *net*, eye. *net-kona* corner of the eye.—Pk. *ṇetta*, P. *netta*, Sk. *nētra* ; g. *netrum*, or. *neta*, h. *netī*, nep, *neti*, pj. l. *netrā*.

— **නෙපෙනෙනවා ne-penenavā,** neg. v., see s.vv. **na**^{2} and **penenavā**.

1357. **නෙය neya,** s., st. f. *nē*, what should be known, knowledge.—Pk. *ṇēya*, P. *ñeyya*, Sk. *jñēya*.

1358. **නෙරනවා neranavā,** v., prt. *neruvā*, to project, protrude, eject. Caus. *neravanavā*, prt. *nerevuvā*, to cause to protrude.—Pk. *nī-haraï*, P. *nī-harati*, Sk. *nir-* + √*hṛ*, *nir-harati*. Cf. inf. *nernā*, EpZ III 227[18], 10th c.

1359 **නෙරළු neraḷu,** s., coconut tree.—Pk. *ṇāriēla*, *ṇāliara*, P. *nālikēra*, Sk. *nārikēla*, *nālikēra* ; kśm. *norila*, si. *nārelu*, *nāiru*, g. *nāriyal*, m. *nāreḷ*, *nāraḷ*, h. *nāriyal*, nep. *narival*, pj. *nārel*, *narel*. Gr. I 7.

1360. **නෙළුන් neḷun, නෙළුම් neḷum, නෙළුඹු neḷuṁbu,** s., lotus, water lily.—Pk. *ṇaliṇī*, P. *nalina*, Sk. *nalina*, °*nī*.

1361. **නේ nē[1], නෙක් nek, නෙක neka,** a., many. *ne-digin* from many sides.—P. *aṇēa*, P. *anēka*, *nēka*, Sk. *anēka*, *nāika*. Cf. *eka*.

— **නේ nē[2],** s., see **neya.**

— **නො no-,** neg. part., see **na** 3.

ප P

1362. **ප pa-** (*pä-*, *pi-*, *pu-*, *pe-*, *po-*), prefix=Pk., P. *pa-*, Sk. *pra-*.

1363. **පක් pak[1],** s., part, half of a lunar month. *dasa-pak-davas* the tenth day of the half-month, EpZ I 25[11], 10th c.—Pk., P. *pakkha*, Sk. *pakṣa*; kśm. *pach* fortnight, si. *pakhu* id., g. *pāṃkh* wing, side, m. *pākh*, *pāṃkh*, oṛ. *pākha* nearness, ass. *pākhi* feather, bg. *pākh*(*ā*), h. *pākh* wing, *pākhā* side-wall, nep. *pākho*, pj. *pakkh* fortnight, l. *pakkhuṛ* plateau.

1364. **පක් pak[2],** s., bird (Cl).—Pk., P. *pakkhi*, Sk. *pakṣin* ; kśm. *pachin*, si. *pakhī*, bg. *pākhi*, nep. *paṅkhi*, pj. *pakkhī*, *paṅkhī*, l. *pakkhī*.

1365. **පක paka,** s., st. f. *pak*, ripe fruit.— Pk., P. *pakka*, Sk. *pakva* ; kśm. *poku*, *popu*, si. *pako*, g. *pakuṃ*, m. *pikā*, oṛ. *pākalā*, bg. *pākā*, h. *pākal*, nep. *pāko*, pj. l. *pakkā*.

1366. **පට paṭa,** s., band ; plate, slab ; silk cloth, silk. *paṭa-nūl* silk thread ; *paṭa-lanavā* entangle, fold.—Pk., P., Sk. *paṭṭa* ; kśm. *poṭu*, si. *paṭu*, g. *pāṭo*, m. *pāṭ*, oṛ. *pāṭa*, bg. h. nep. *pāṭ*, pj. l. *paṭṭ*.

1367. **පටන් paṭan,** 1) s., beginning, in *paṭan-gannavā* to begin ; 2) postp., beginning from, since (correl. *dakvā*).—P. *paṭṭhāna*, Sk. *prasthāna*. Cf. *päṭi*, *paṭā*.

1368. **පටවනවා paṭavanavā,** v., prt. *päṭevuvā*, to load goods, to impose a tax on.—Pk. *paṭṭhāvei*, *paṭṭhavaï*, P. *paṭṭhapēti*, Sk. *pra-* + √*sthā*, caus. *prasthāpayati* : g. *paṭhāvvuṃ*, m. *pāṭhaviṇeṃ*, oṛ. *paṭhāibā*, ass. *paṭhāiba*, bg. *pāṭhāna*, h. *paṭhānā*, nep. *paṭhāunu*, pj. *paṭhāṇā*.

1369. **පටා paṭā,** postp., beginning from, since (correl. *dakvā*). —ger. P. *paṭṭhāya*, Sk. *pra-sthāya*. Cf. *päṭi*, *paṭan*.

1370. පටිය **paṭiya,** s., st. f. *paṭi,* ribbon, band, belt, girdle.—Pk. *paṭṭaa,* P, Sk. *paṭṭaka, paṭṭikā* ; kśm. *poṭu,* si. *paṭo, paṭī,* bg. *pāṭa, pāṭ,* h. *pāṭā, pāṭī,* nep. *pāṭo, pāṭi,* pj. l. *paṭṭā, paṭṭī.*

1371. පටුන **paṭuna**[1], s., st. f. °*nu,* seaport, town.—Pk. *paṭṭaṇa,* P., Sk. *paṭṭana* ; kśm. *paṭan,* bg. *pāṭan,* oṛ. *pāṭanā* ; m. *pāṭaṇ* and nep. *pāṭan* are names of towns. Sinh. also *patana* city (Ruv 175)=Sk. *pattanā.*

1372. පටුන **paṭuna**[2], s., (mod.) contents of a book.— = ? *paṭuna*[1].

1373. පඩය **paḍaya,** s., breaking wind ; *paḍinavā,* prt. *päḍḍā,* to break wind; *paḍa arinavā* id.—Sk. *pardatē* ; kśm. *pad, padun,* si. *paḍaṇu,* g. *pād, pād-vuṃ,* m. *pād, pādṇeṃ,* oṛ. *pāṛa, pāṛibā,* ass. *pād, pādiba,* bg. *pād, pādā,* h. *pād, pādnā,* nep. *pād, pādnu,* pj. *padd* or *paḍḍ, paddṇā.*

1374. පඬි **paňḍi,** a., learned, erudite.—Pk. *paṇḍia,* P., Sk. *paṇḍita* ; m. *pāṃḍyā,* bg. h. nep. *pāṃṛe,* oṛ. *pāṇḍa,* pj. *paṇḍā.*

1375. පඬු **paňḍu,** a., pale, yellowish. *paňḍu-vana* yellow colour.—Pk., P. *paṇḍu,* Sk. *pāṇḍu.* See *päḍili.*

1376. පඬුර **paňḍura,** පනර **panara,** s., st. ff. °*ru,* ° *ra,* present, offering.—P. *paṇṇâkāra.*

1377. පඬුරු **paňḍuru,** a., white.—P. *paṇḍara,* Sk. *pāṇḍara* ; m. *pāṃḍhar,* g. bg. h. *pāṃḍur.*

1378. පණ **paṇa**[1], s., breath, vitality, life. *paṇa-adinava, -yanavā* to draw the last breath, to expire.—Pk., P. *pāṇa,* Sk. *prāṇa.*

— පණ **paṇa,**[2,3], ss., see **peṇa.**[1,2].

1379 පණත **paṇata,** s., st. f. °*ṇat,* law, ordinance, statute.—P. *paññatta, paññatti, paṇṇatti,* Sk. *prajñapti.* The spelling *panata* alternates with *paṇata.* (But cf. De Lanerolle, DSL, xliii, §4.)

1380. පණර **paṇara,** s., fifteenth day of the lunar month.—Pk. *paṇṇarasa* (Ap. °*raha*), P. *paṇṇarasa* or *panna*° ; kśm. *pandāh,* si. *pandraṃ-haṃ,* g. *pandar,* m. *pandhrā,* oṛ. *pandara,* bg. *panera,* h. *pandrah.* nep. *pandra(h), pandhrā,* pj. l. *pandrāṃ.* Cf. *pahaḷoha.*

1381. පණියා **paṇiyā,** s., st. f. *paṇi,* serpent, cobra.—Pk., P. *phaṇi,* Sk. *phaṇin.* Cf. *peṇa*[2].

1382. පණිවා **paṇivā,** s., st. f. *paṇivā,* taking life. *paṇivā-karanavā* to take life, to kill.—P. *pāṇâtipāta,* Sk. *prāṇâtipāta.*

1383. පණුවා **paṇuvā,** s., st. f. *paṇu,* worm, maggot.—P. *pāṇaka,* Sk. *prāṇaka.*

1384. පත් **pat,** a pprt., arrived at, attained to. *mudun-pat* that has attained the summit ; cf. also *tän-pat-, pat-karanavā* to bring to a place, to appoint.—Pk., P. *patta,* Sk. *prâpta* ; si. *pāto,* m. *pātlā* (T, s.v. *pāunu* and Add.).

1385. පත **pata**[1], s., st. f. *pat,* wing, leaf of a tree or book. *pat-kuḍaya* leaf umbrella.—Pk., P. *patta,* Sk. *pattra* ; kśm. *pathar,* g. *pātruṃ,* oṛ. *pātiā,* m. ass. bg. h. nep. *pāt,* pj. *patt,* l. *pattr.*

1386. පත **pata**[2], s., st. f. *pat,* a measure of grain or liquids.—Pk. *pattha,* Sk. *prastha* ; nep. *pāthi.*

— පතන **patana,** s., see s.v. **paṭuna.**

1387. පතනවා **patanavā,** v., prt. *pätuvā,* to hope, wish, aspire to.—P. *patthēti,* Sk. *prārthayati.*

1388. පතර **patara,** s., anything diffused: powder; assembly, multitude.—Pk. *patthāra,* Sk. *prastāra* ; g. m. *patthārī.* Cf. *patura.*

1389. පතළ **patala,** a. pprt., diffused, spread abroad, public.—P. *patthaṭa,* (Sk. *pra-stīrṇa*).

1390. පතුන් **patun**[1], s., road (Ca).—From st. *panthan,* Sk.*panthānam,* °*ānas* ; cf. Pk., P. *pantha* ; si. h. pj. *paṃth,* m. *pāṃth,* bg. *panthā.*

1391. පතුන් **patun**[2], s., request, asking.—Pk. *patthaṇā,* P. *patthanā,* Sk. *prârthanā.* See *patanavā.*

1392. පතුර **patura,** s., st. f. °*ru,* chip, fragment.—Pk., P. *patthara* stone, Sk. *prastara* ; kśm. *pathur,* si. *patharu,* g. *pāthro,* m. *pāthar,* oṛ. *pathara,* ass. bg. h. *pāthar,* nep. pj. *patthar.* Cf. *patara.*

1393. පතුරනවා **paturanavā,** පතුරුව° **paturuva°,** v., prt. *päturuvā, pätirevuvā,* to diffuse, spread abroad, publish.—Pk. *pattharaï,* P. *pattharati, patthārēti,* Sk. *pra-* + $\sqrt{}$*stṝ* ; g. *pātharvuṃ,* nep. *pathārnu.* See also *pätirenavā.*

— පතුල **patula,** පත්ල **patla,** s., see **palla.**

1394. පත්ත **patta,** s., st. f. *patu,* stake, stick, board.—Pk. *pattaa,* Sk. *pattraka* ; g. *pātruṃ,* m. *pātem,* bg. h. *pātā,* nep. *pāto,* pj. *pattā,* l. *pattrā.*

1395. පදය **padaya,** s., st. f. *pada,* verse.—P. *pajja,* Sk. *padya.*

1396. පදිනවා **padinavā,** v., prt. *päddā,* to paddle, row; drive; swing to and fro. Caus. *paddanavā* (<**padva*°), prt. *pädduvā,* to swing; double caus. *paddavanavā,* prt. *päddevuvā,* to sway, propel; intr. *pädenavā,* prt. *päduṇā,* to swing to and fro.—P. *pâjēti,* Sk. *pra-* + $\sqrt{}$*aj.* Cf. *adinavā.*

1397. පදුල **padula,** a., very bright, brilliant.—Cf. P. *pajjalati,* Sk. *pra-* + $\sqrt{}$*jval.*

1398. පදුවා **paduvā,** පද්දා **paddā,** s., st. f. *padu,* man of a community so called attending to elephants, carrying palanquins etc.—Sk. *prâjaka* driver, coachman. Cf. *padinavā.*

1399. පඳුර **pañdura,** s., st. f. °*ru,* bush, shrub.—The comparison with Pk., P. *pañjara,* Sk. *pañjara, piñjara* cage, skeleton (T, s.v. *piñjarā,* with ?) is phonetically possible, but semasiologically doubtful.

— පන් **pan-**[1], num., see **pan-sälis, pan-sil.**

1400. පන් **pan**[2], s., leaf.—Pk. P. *paṇṇa,* Sk. *parṇa* ; kśm. *pan,* g. m. *pān,* oṛ. *pāna,* ass. bg. h. nep. *pān,* pj. *pannī,* l. *panna.*

1401. පන **pana[1]**, adv., again.—Pk. *paṇa, puṇo*, P. *pana, puna*, Sk. *punar* ; si. *puṇi, piṇi, paṇa*, g. m. *paṇ*, h. *puni*, nep. *pani*.

— පන **pana**, පෙන **pena**, s., see **peṇa.**

— පනට **panata**, s., see **paṇata.**

— පනර **panara**, s., see **paňḍura.**

1402. පනහ **panaha[1]**, °ස **°sa[1]**, num., st. f. *panas*, fifty. *panas-veni, -väni* fiftieth.—Pk. *paṇṇāsaṃ*, P. *paññāsa, paṇṇāsa*, Sk. *pañcāśat* ; kśm. *pañcāh*, si. *pañjāha*, g. *pacās*, m. *pannās*, oṛ. *pañcāsa*, bg. *pañcās*, h. *pacās*, pj. l. *paṃjāh*.

1403. පනහ **panaha[2]**, °ස **°sa[2]**, පනා **panā**, s., the jak tree, Artocarpus integrifolia.—Pk. Mg. *paṇaśa*, P., Sk. *panasa*.

1404. පන්වා **panvā**, s., serpent.—P., Sk. *pannaga*.

1405. පන්සල **pan-sala**, s., leaf-hall, hermitage, monastery.—P. *paṇṇa-sālā*, Sk. *parṇa-śālā*.

1406. පන්සාලිස **pan-sālisa**, num., forty-five.—*pan*<*pañca* (see *paha*)+*sālisa* (see *hataliha*).

1407. පන්සිල් **pan-sil**, s., the five moral precepts.—P. *pañca-sīla*.

1408. පබ **paba**, s., light, brightness.—Pk. *pahā*, P. *pa-bhā*, Sk. *pra-bhā*; g. *poh*, h. *poh, pauh*, pj. *pauh*. See also *pähä, pāna*.

1409. පබඳ **pabaňda**, s., st. f. *°ňda*, connection; literary composition, narrative.—P. *pa-bandha*, Sk. *pra-bandha*.

1410. පබල **pabala**, a., very strong; s., great strength, power.—Pk. *pabala, pavala*, P. *pa-bala*, Sk. *pra-bala* ; nep. *paul* (? T, Add.).

1411. පබළු(ව) **pabaḷu(va)**, පබුළු(ව) **pabuḷu(va)**, s., st. f. *°ḷu*, young bud, sprout; coral.—Pk., P. *pa-vāla, °ḷa*, Sk. *pra-bāla*. See also *pavaḷa*.

1412. පමණ **pamaṇa**, s., degree, quantity. *pamaṇak* only, merely.—Pk. P. *pamāṇa*, Sk. *pramāṇa*.

1413. පමාව **pamäva[1]**, s., st. f. *pamā*, woman.—P. *pamadā*, Sk. *pramadā*.

1414. පමාව **pamäva[2]**, s., st. f. *pamā*, carelessness, indolence; delay.—Pk. *pamāa*, P. *pamāda*, Sk. *pramāda*.

— පමුණුවනවා **pamuṇuvanavā**, v., see **pämiṇenavā.**

1415. පය **paya[1]**, පයස් **payas**, s., st. f. *pā, payas*, fluid, water; milk.—P. *paya*, Sk. *payas*.

1416. පය **paya[2]**, s., st. f. *pā*, cup, bowl. *pā-sivuru* bowl and robes.—Pk. AMg. *pāta*, Pk., P. *patta*, Sk. *pātra*.

1417. පය **paya[3]**, s., st. f. *pā*, foot. *pā-bala* foot-force, infantry.—Pk. *pāa*, P., Sk. *pāda* foot, quarter ; kśm. *pāv*, si. *pāu, pāo*, g. *pāv, pāvlum*, m. *pāv*, oṛ. bg. *pā*, h. *pāv, pāu*, nep. *pāu*, pj. *pāu, paiā, pāvā*, l. *pā, pāva*. Cf. *piya*.

— පර **para**, a., see s.v. **parayā.**

1418. පරණ **paraṇa[1],** s., slave, servant.——Probably a. *para* other + *aṇa* order, command. H. Jayatilaka, Eḷu-akārādiya, translates the word as *anun ayiti aya* a person belonging to others. Ruv (418, 419)=*para-taturu, an-ayin, an-satu* &c., ; see also v. l. *parata* ib.

1419. පරණ **paraṇa[2],** a., old. *paraṇa-kama* oldness.—Pk., P., Sk. *purāṇa* ; kśm. *prōnu*, si. *purāṇo*, g. *purāṇuṃ*, m. *purāṇā*, oṛ. *puruṇā*, ass. *purani*, bg. *purāna*, h. *purānā*, nep. *purānu*, l. *purāṇ*.

1420. පරණ **paraṇa[3],** s., flogging, beating (Ruv 134). H. Jayatilaka =*pahara-dīma*<**pāraṇa*<**paharaṇa*=P. *pa-haraṇa*, Sk. *pra-haraṇa*. Cf. *pahara*.

1421. පරදනවා **paradanavā,** v., prt. *päraduvā*, to defeat, conquer. Intr. *paradinavā* or *päradenavā*, prt. *päraduṇā*, to be defeated ; caus. *para-davanavā*, *paraddanavā*, prt. *päradevuvā*, *pärädduvā*, to defeat.—P. *parā-jayati*, *parā-jēti*, Sk. *parā-*+$\sqrt{}$*ji*, *parā-jayati*, °*tē* defeats, is defeated.

1422. පරපුටුවා **paraputuvā,** s., st. f. °*ṭu*, beggar; cuckoo.—Pk. *para-uṭṭha*, P. *para-puṭṭha*, Sk. *para-puṣṭa*, lit. nourished by another.

1423. පරපුර **parapura,** s., lineage, race.—P., Sk. *paramparā*.

1424. පරමුණුව **paramuṇuva,** s., particle, atom.—P., Sk. *paramāṇu*.

1425. පරයා **parayā,** s., st. f. *para*, outcaste. *para-ballā* pariah dog.— s. of a. *para* other, different, foreign=Pk., P., Sk. *para*.

1426. පරරූ **para-rū,** s., gram. assimilation of a consonant to the following consonant.—Sk. *para-rūpa*.

1427. පරලොව **para-lova,** s., st. f. °*-lō*, the other world, the next life.—P., Sk. *para-lōka*.

1428. පරවියා **paraviyā,** s., st. f. °*vi*, dove, pigeon. *paravi-kūḍuva* dove-cote.—Pk. *pārāvaa*, *pārēvaa*, P. *pārāpata*, *pārēvata*, Sk. *pārāpata*, *pārāvata* ; g. *pārevo*, m. *pārvā*, oṛ. *pārā*, h. nep. *parevā*.

1429. පල **pala,** s., fruit. *pala-ruka* fruit-tree.—Pk., P., Sk. *phala* ; kśm. *phal*, si. *pharu*, g. m. *phaḷ*, oṛ. *phaḷa*, ass. bg. h. nep. pj. l. *phal*.

1430 පලඟ **palaňga,** s., st. f. *palak*, in *palak-baňainavā* to sit cross-legged. —Pk., P. *pallaṅka*, Sk. *paryaṅka*, *palyaṅka* ; kśm. *palaṅg*, *praṅg*, si. *palaṅgu*, g. m. *palaṃg*, oṛ. *palaṅka*, ass. *pāloṅg*, bg. *pālaṅ*, nep. *palaṅ*, pj. *palaṅgh*, l. *palaggh* bed.

1431. පලඳනවා **palaňdanavā,** °ඳිනවා **°ňdinavā,** v., prt. *päländā* (<**ňddā*< **ňduvā*), to put on, wear, don. Caus. *palandanavā* (*nd* <*ňdd* < *ňdv*), prt. *päländuvā*, to adorn (another).—P. *pilandhati*, Sk. *pi-*+$\sqrt{}$*nah*. The spelling with *ḷ* (Ca) is wrong. See De Lanerolle, DSL, p. xliv, §18 a.

1432. පලවනවා **palavanavā,** v., prt. *pälevuvā*, to put to flight, to drive away.—P. *palāpēti*, caus. of *palāyati* (Sk. id.). The ger. of v. intr. **palanavā* to flee = g. *paḷvuṃ*, m. *paḷneṃ*, is preserved in *palā-yanavā*, prt. *palā-giyā* and in the imp. *pala* go on.

1433. පලස් **palas,** s., name of a t r e e, Butea frondosa.—Pk., P. *palāsa*, Sk. *palāśa* ; si. *palāsu*, m. *paḷas*, oṛ. *paḷāsa*, ass. *palāh*, bg. *palās*, b. h. *parās*, nep. *palāṃs*, pj. *palāh*.

1434. පලහනවා **palahanavā,** v., prt. *pälahuvā*, t o b u r n, r o a s t. Intr. *pälahenavā*, prt. *pälahuṇā*, to burn (intr.).—The spelling with *ḷ* seems to be more correct ; **paḷah-* would be derived from MInd. **pa-ḍah*, Sk. √*dah* ; Pk. *ḍahaï*, Sinh. cf. *ḍaha* (-*ḍiya*), q.v. ; internal *ḍ* > *ḷ*.— But cf. Sk. √*pluṣ* ; Sinh. *pulussanavā* is prob. a doublet (DE LANEROLLE).

1435. පලා **palā,** s., h e r b s. *palā-van* green.—Doublet of *palas*, q.v.; Sk. *palāśa* means also ' leaf.'

1436. පලිහ **paliha,** °ස **°sa,** s., st. f. *palis*, s h i e l d.—Pk. *phalaha*, °*ga*, P., Sk. *phalaka* plank ; kśm. *phal*, si. *pharaho*, g. *phaḷ*, m. *phaḷā*, oṛ. *phaḷi*, ass. *phali*, bg. *phalā*, h. *phalī*, nep. *phaliyo*, pj. *phalhā* (*s* in *palisa*, *palis* by false analogy).

1437. පල්ල **palla**[1], s., st. f. *palu*, b u d.—Pk., P., Sk. *pallava* ; si. *palī*, g. *pālav*, m. *pālā*, *pālav*, bg. h. *pālā*, nep. *pāluvā*, pj. *pallhī*.

1438. පල්ල **palla**[2], පත්ල **patla,** පතුල **patula,** s., pl. *patul*, s o l e o f t h e f o o t ; b o t t o m.—P., Sk. *pāda-tala*. Cf. *alla*.

1439. පල්ලා **pallā** (<*paluvā*), s., st. f. *palu*, k e e p e r, g u a r d i a n, in *go-pallā* cattle-keeper.=Pk. *go-vālaa*, P. *gō-pālaka*, Sk. *gō-pāla* ; si. *gavāru*, g. *govāḷ*, m. *govḷā*, oṛ. *goāḷa*, bg. *goyālā*, b. *gvār*, h. *goāl*, *goālā*, nep. *gvālo*, pj. *gavāl*.

1440. පව **pava,** s., st. ff. *pav*, *pā*, s i n, d e m e r i t.—Pk. *pāva*, P., Sk. *pāpa*.

— පවත **pavata,** s., see **puvata.**

1441. පවතිනවා **pavatinavā,** or පැවතෙනවා **pävatenavā,** v., prt. *pävättā*, *pävatuṇā*, t o c o n t i n u e, r e m a i n, e n d u r e. Caus. *pavatvanavā*, prt. *pävättuvā*, to keep, observe (a custom etc.).—Pk. *pa-vaṭṭaï*, P. *pa-vattati*, Sk. *pra-*+√*vṛt*, *pra-vartatē*.

1442. පවන **pavana,** s., st. f. *pavan*, w i n d. *pavan-pata*, lit. wind-leaf, i.e. fan.—Pk. *pavaṇa*, P., Sk. *pavana*. ? lw.

1443. පවර **pavara,** a., c h i e f, n o b l e, p r e - e m i n e n t.—Pk., P. *pavara*, Sk. *pravara*.

1444. පවරනවා **pavaranavā,** v., prt. *pävaruvā*, t o d e v o l v e u p o n, i m p u t e ; t o i n v i t e a n d s e t t l e (a bhikkhu in a place during the rainy season). Intr. *pävarenavā*, prt. *pävaruṇā*, to be imputed.—P. *pa-vārēti*, Sk. *pra-*+√*vṛ*[2], caus. *pra-vārayati*.

— පවස **pavasa,** s., see **puvasa.**

1445. පවසනවා **pavasanavā,** v., prt. *pävasuvā*, t o u t t e r, s a y, r e c i t e.—Sk. *pra-*+√*vac*, cf. *pra-vacana*, P. *pā-vacana*. Or ?=Pk. *pa-gāsēi*, P. *pa-kāsēti*, Sk. *pra-kāśayati*.

1446. පවළ **pavaḷa,** s., red coral.—Pk. *pavāla,* P. *pa-vāḷa,* Sk. *pra-vāḍa* ; ass. *povāl,* bg. *palā,* nep. *puvāṃlo.* See *pabaḷu(va), pabuḷu(va).*

1447. පවා **pavā,** 1) postp., up to, till. *ada-pavā,* DhpAGp 29[17], trsl. of P. *yāva ajja-kālā* ; 2) adv., even.—Ger. of a v. **pavanavā*=Pk. *pāvēi,* P. *pāpēti,* Sk. *prāpayati.* See s.v. *pämiṇenavā.*

1448. පවිටු **paviṭu,** a., sinful. *paviṭu-kama* sinfulness.—P. *pāpiṭṭha,* Sk. *pāpiṣṭha.*

1449. පවුර **pavura,** s., st. f. °*ru,* wall, fortification.—Pk. *pāāra,* P. *pākāra,* Sk. *prākāra* ; cf. Bl, s.v. *pāravḍā* (?)

1450. පවුරුණ **pavuruṇa,** s., st. f. °*ṇu,* a ceremony at the termination of Vassa or Upōsatha.—P. *pavāraṇā,* Sk. *pravāraṇa.*

1451. පවුරුණය **pavuruṇaya,** s., st. f. °*ṇa,* (Ca) literary composition, treatise; chapter.—P. *pakaraṇa,* Sk. *prakaraṇa.*

1452. පවුව **pavuva,** s., st. f. *pavu,* rock, hill.—Pk. *pavvaa,* P. *pabbata,* Sk. *parvata.*

— පස් **pas[1],** see s.v. **paha[1].**

1453. පස් **pas[2],** s., earth, mould, soil. *pas-käṭiya* clod of earth.—Pk., P. *paṃsu,* Sk. *pāṃśu.*

1454. පස **pasa[1],** s., st. f. *pas,* side, neighbourhood.—Pk. *pāsa,* P. *passa,* Sk. *pārśva* ; si. *pasu* side, m. *pās, pāśiṃ,* bg. h. *pās,* pj. *pās, pah* near to. Cf. *paha[2].*

1455. පස **pasa[2],** s., st. f. *pas,* noose, snare.—Pk., P. *pāsa,* Sk. *pāśa* ; oṛ. *pāsa,* bg. *pās,* h. *pāsā,* nep. *pāso[1].*

1456. පස **pasa[3],** s., in *pasa-äṭa* die, dice.—P. *pāsaka,* Sk. *pāśaka* ; g. nep. *pāso[4],* bg. h. *pāsā.*

1457. පස **pasa[4],** s., st. f. *pas,* touch, feeling.—Pk., P. *phassa,* Sk. *sparśa.* Also Slw. *pahasa.*

1458. පසක් **pasak,** a., evident, manifest.—Pk., P. *paccakkha,* Sk. *pratyakṣa.*

1459. පසඟිලි **pas-agili,** °ඟිලි °**ṅgili,** a., having five fingers or divisions.—*pas* (see *paha[1]*) + *äṅgilla.* Cf. Ved. *pañcâṅguri.* See also *pasaṅgul-ruka.*

1460. පසඟ **pasaṅga[1],** s., five divisions or members; tortoise, turtle. °*-turu* five kinds of musical instruments.—P. *pañcaṅga* (°*gika-turiya*) ; Sk. *pañcâṅga.*

1461. පසඟ **pasaṅga[2],** s., minor limbs.—P. *paccaṅga,* Sk. *pratyaṅga.* See s.v. *aṅga[1].*

1462. පසඟුල්රුක **pasaṅgul-ruka,** s., the castor-oil plant.—Sk. *pañcâṅgula.*

1463. පසතුරු **pasaturu,** s., five kinds of musical instruments.—*pasa* (see *paha*)+*turu*, Sk. *pañca-tūrya*.

— පසන් **pasan,** a., see **pahan.**

1464. පසමිතුරා **pasamiturā,** s., st. f. °*ru*, enemy, adversary.—P. *paccāmitta*, Sk. *pratyamitra*.

1465. පස(ය) **pasa(ya),** s., st. f. *pasa*, support, requisite. *sivu-p*° the four requisites offered (to a monk).—Pk. *paccaa*, P. *paccaya*, Sk. *pratyaya*.

1466. පසල් **pasal,** a., neighbouring.—Haplology of **pasasal*=Pk., P. *paccāsanna*, Sk. *pratyāsanna*. Cf. *asal*.

1467. පසවිය **pas-aviya,** s., st. f. °*vi*, aggregate of five weapons. °*viyā*, s., the bearer of five weapons, Cupid. —*pas* (see *paha*[1])+*aviya* ; Sk. *pañcâyudha*.

1468. පසස **pasasa,** s., st. f. °*sas*, praise. *pasasanavā*, v., to praise.—Pk. *pasaṃsā*, *pasaṃsai*, P. *pasaṃsā*, *pasaṃsati*, Sk. *pra-śaṃsā*, *praśaṃsati*. Cf. *päsasuma*.

1469. පසිදු **pasidu,** a., public, well-known.—Pk., P. *pasiddha*, Sk. *pra-siddha*.

1470. පසිඳිනවා **pasiñdinavā,** prt. *pasindā* (<**ñddā* <**ñduvā*), to investigate, examine; to destroy.—Pk. *pacchindaï*, P **pacchindati* (pass. *pacchijjati*), Sk. *pra-*+√*chid*, *pra-cchinatti*.

1471. පසිඳුරු **pas-iñduru,** s., pl., the five senses.—Pk. *pañcindiya*, P. *pañcindriya*, Sk. *pañcēndriya*.

1472. පසිලි **pasili,** s., st. f., monk, recluse (Ruv 321), in *pasili-päl* hermit's hut, EpZ II 271^{38}, 12th c.— P. *paṃsu-kūlika*, Sk. *pāṃśu-k*° one who wears robes made of rags (DE LANEROLLE).

1473. පසු **pasu,** පස් **pas,** adv., after; s. *passa* the hinder part ; *pasu-bata* or *pas-bata* afternoon (time after the meal) ; *pasu-giya* by-gone, past ; *pasu-karanavā* to pass, spend (time).—Pk., P. *pacchā*, Sk. *paścāt* ; (si. *pachoṛu*), g. *pachī*, *pāchuṃ*, (m. *pāsoḍī*), oṛ. *pache*, ass. *pāse*, bg. *pāche*, *pāchu*, h. *pāchai(ṃ)*, nep. *pachi*.

1474. පසුතැවිල්ල **pasu-tävilla,** s., st. f. °*li*, repentance, remorse. *pasutävili-venavā* to repent.—*pasu*+*tävilla*, q.v. Cl quotes also *pasu-täv* (*täv*=Pk. *tāva*, Sk. *tāpa* ; si. *tāu*, g. m. *tāv*, oṛ. *tā*, ass. bg. h. nep. *tāu*, l. *tā*).

1475. පසුතුර **pasutura,** s., st. f. °*ru*, answer. *uturu-pasuturu* question and answer.—P. *uttara* answer, *paccuttara* rejoinder, Sk. *uttara* answer, *praty-uttara* rejoinder.

1476. පසුන් **pasun,** a. pprt., cut; judged, decided. P. *pacchinna*, Sk. *prachinna* ; nep. *pāchin*.

— පසුර **pasura,** s., see **pahura.**

1477. **පසේබුදුන් pasē-budun,** s., pl. hon., a private Buddha.—P. *paccēka-buddha*, Sk. *pratyēka-buddha*.

1478. **පසොස් pasos,** s., early morning, EpZ I 91 A^9, 10th c.; DhpAGp 18^{30}.—Pk., P. *paccūsa*, Sk. *pratyūṣa*.

1479. **පස්කම් pas-kam,** s., the five modes of desire or pleasure.—P. *pañca-kāma*.

1480. **පස්මුල් pas-mul,** s., the aggregate of five roots of plants.—Sk. *pañca-mūla*.

1481. **පස්රස pas-rasa,** s., name of a tree, Phyllanthus emblica.—Lit. containing five flavours; Sk. *pañca-rasā*.

1482. **පස්ලුණු pas-luṇu,** s., five kinds of salt.—Sk. *pañca-lavaṇa*.

1483. **පස්ලෝ pas-lō,** s., five metals.—Sk. *pañca-lōha*.

1484. **පස්වග pas-vaga,** s., five kinds or groups; group of five individuals.—Cf. P. *pañca-vaggiya*, Sk. *pañca-varga*.

1485. **පහ paha[1], පස pasa,** num., st. f. *pas*, five. *pas-veni*, *-väni* the fifth; *pas-vissa* twenty-five. In cpds. (q.v.) before *s* also *pan-*: *pan-siyaya* five hundred. — Pk., P., Sk. *pañca*; kśm. *panc*, *ponju*, si. *pañja*, g. m. *pāṃc*, or. *pāñca*, bg. h. nep. *pāṃc*, pj. l. *pañj*. See *pahaḷoha*.

1486. **පහ paha[2],** adv., away, off. *paha-karanavā* to drive away. — ? from MInd. **passā* = Sk. *pārśvāt*. See *pasa*[1].

1487. **පහටු pahaṭu,** a., pprt., glad, delighted. — Pk., P. *pahaṭṭha*, Sk. *pra-hṛṣṭa*.

— **පහණ pahaṇa** s., see **pāṇa.**

1488. **පහදිනවා pahadinavā** or **පැහැදෙනවා pähädenavā,** v., prt. *pähäduṇā*, to become clear, to be pleased. V. trans. *pahadanavā*, *pād°*, prt. *pähäduvā*, *päd°*, and caus. *pahadavanavā*, prt. *pähädevuvā*, to clear, purge, enlighten. — <MInd. **pasajjati* = Sk. *prasādyatē* (*pra-* + $\sqrt{}$*sad*, caus.). Sinh. *pahadanavā* and *pahadavanavā* are, as the *d* shows, new formations from *pahadinavā*.

1489. **පහන් pahan, පසන් pasan,** a. pprt., pleased, glad. — Pk., P. *pasanna*, Sk. *pra-sanna*.

— **පහන pahana,** s., see **pāna.**

1490. **පහනවා pahanavā, පාහ° pāha°,** v., to solder, weld. — The original meaning seems to be 'to fasten'; cf. mald. *fahan* to sew, Sk. *pāśayati* binds. But the form *pāhanavā*, to which the prt. *pāhuvā* (*pähävuvā*) belongs, is difficult to explain.

— **පහය pahaya,** s., see **pāya.**

1491. **පහර pahara,** s., knock, blow, stroke. — Pk., P. *pahāra*, Sk. *prahāra*.

1492. පහරනවා **paharanavā**[1], v., prt. *pähäruvā*, to stretch out, to expand. — Pk. *pasārēi*, P. *pasārēti* (*no-paharami*, DhpAGp 11[10], trsl. of *na pasāressāmi*), Sk. *pra-* + √*sṛ*, caus. *pra-sārayati* ; g. *pasārvuṃ*, m. *pasārṇeṃ*, bg. *pasārā*, h. *pasārnā*, nep. *pasārnu*, pj. *pasārṇā*.

1493. පහරනවා **paharanavā**[2], v., prt. *pähäruvā*, to smite. — Pk. *paharaï*, P. *paharati*, Sk. *pra-* + √*hṛ*, *pra-harati*.

1494. පහරස් **paharas**, a., hard, solid. — ? Slw. Pk., P. *pharusa* (split aspirate).

— පහස **pahasa**, s., see s.v. **pasa**[4].

1495. පහසු **pahasu**, a., easy, facile, convenient. — ? Slw. P. *phāsuka* (split aspirate).

1496. පහළොහ **pahaḷoha**, පසළොස **pasaḷosa**, num., st. f. °*ḷos*, fifteen. *pahaḷos-veni*, *-väni* the fifteenth ; *pahaḷos-vaka* fifteenth day, day of the full moon. — P. *pañcadasa*, °*sī*, Sk. *pañca-daśa*, °*śī*. Cf. *paṇara*.

1497. පහුර **pahura**, පසුර **pasura**, s., st. f. °*ru*, raft. — P. *paccarī*.

1498. පළඟා **paḷaňgā**, s., st. f. °*ňga*, grasshopper. Cl (wrongly) *palaňga*. Ca *paḷaňgäṭiyā*. — P. *paṭaṅga* (De Lanerolle). See *poḷaňgā*.

1499. පළනවා **paḷanavā**, v., prt. *päḷuvā*, to split, cleave. Intr. *päḷenavā*, prt. *päḷuṇā*, to burst, crack. — Pk. *phāḍēi*. Sk. √*sphaṭ*, caus. *sphāṭayati* ; si. *pharaṇu*, g. *phāḍvuṃ*, m. *phāḍṇeṃ*, oṛ. *phāṛibā*, bg. *phāṛā*, h. *phāṛnā*, nep. *phārnu*, pj. *phāṛnā*. Probably connected with Sk. √*sphal*, caus. (*ā-*)*sphālayati* = Pk. *phālēi*, P. *phālēti* ; kśm. *phālavun* ; m. *phāḷṇeṃ*, ass. *phāliba*, bg. *phālā*, oṛ. *phāḷiā*. See T, s.v. *phārnu*.

1500. පළමු **paḷamu**, a., first ; prior, original — Pk. *paḍhama*, P. *paṭhama*, Sk. *prathama* ; cf. g. *pehluṃ*, m. oṛ. bg. *pahilā*, h. *pahlā*, nep. *pailo*, *pahilo*.

1501. පළල් **paḷal**, පුළුල් **puḷul**, a., wide, broad. *paḷal-karanavā* to widen. — <**paṭhula*, **puṭhula*, P. *puthula*, Sk. *pṛthula*.

1502. පළහය **paḷahaya**, s., st. f. °*ha*, kettle-drum, war-drum. Generally lw. *paṭaha-* (De Lanerolle). — Pk. *paḍaha*, P., Sk. *paṭaha*.

1503. පළිඟුව **paḷiňguva**, s., st. f. °*ňgu*, crystal. — Pk. *phaliha*, *phaḍiha*, P. *phalikā*, Sk. *sphaṭikā* ; g. *phaṭkaḍī*, m. *phaṭkī*, bg. *phaṭikāri*, h. *phaṭkarī*, *phiṭkirī*, nep. *phaṛkiri*, *phaṭkiri*, pj. *phaṭkarī*. Cf. also *piḷi*[1].

1504. පළු **paḷu**, a., sharp, acrid, in the names of plants : *paḷu-kan* Uvaria zeylanica, *paḷu-taṇa* club-rush, Fuirena uncinata. — P., Sk. *paṭu* ; cf. Sk. *paṭu-tṛṇaka*.

1505. පළුපත **paḷu-pata**, s., st. f. °*-pat*, lit. sharp leaf, leaf of a palm tree etc., oar. — Cf. Sk. *paṭu-pattrikā*, name of a shrub.

1506. **පළොල් paḷol,** s., name of a tree, trumpet flower, Stereospermum suaveolens. — Pk. *paḍōla,* P., Sk. *paṭōla* a kind of gourd; m. *paḍoḷ,* or. *pararā,* h. *parvar, palval,* nep. *parvar,* pj. *paṛvāl, parvāl.* In Sinh. a confusion of the word *paṭōla* with *pāṭala* seems to have taken place: *paḷol* means also 'brown' 'pale red' as does Sk. *pāṭala,* and, on the other hand, Sk. *pāṭalā* (°*li*) Bignonia suaveolens is alternatively used for the plant *paḷol.*

— **පා pā[1-3],** ss., see **paya[1-3].**

1507. **පා pā[4],** s., tree. — Pk. *pāava,* P., Sk. *pādapa.*

— **පා pā[5],** s., see **pava.**

— **පා pā[6],** s., see **pāya.**

1508. **පාණ pāṇa, පහණ pahaṇa,** s., stone. *pahaṇa-* or *pāṇa-vässa* hail. — Pk. *pāsāṇa, pāhāṇa,* P. *pāsāṇa,* Sk. *pāṣāṇa*; bg. *pāsān,* h. *pāhān,* pj. *pāhaṇ.* T, s.v. *paharo.*

1509. **පාන pāna, පහන pahana,** s., st. ff. *pān, pahan,* light. — Probably lw. Pk. **pahāṇa* = Sk. *prabhāna,* as in Sinh. *-bh-* between vowels is generally preserved as *b.* Cf. *paba.*

1510. **පානවා pānavā,** v., prt. *pāvā,* to show, display. — <**pahanavā* = Pk. *pakāsēti,* Sk. *pra-* + √*kāś,* caus. *pra-kāśayati.*

1511. **පාමුදු pā-mudu,** s., bangles for the feet, rings worn by women on the toe. — Sk. *pāda-mudrā* means 'foot-print.' See *paya[3]* and *mudda.*

1512. **පාමුල pā-mula,** s., st. f. *-mul,* foot (of a bed or a person), EpZ I 33[6], 10th c. — P., Sk. *pāda-mūla* sole of the foot.

1513. **පාය pāya, පහය pahaya,** s., st. ff. *pā, paha,* palace. — Pk. *pāsāa,* P. *pāsāda,* Sk. *prāsāda.*

1514. **පාළ pāḷa[1], පහළ pahaḷa[1],** a., public, generally known (shortened in *paḷa-karanavā* to publish). — Pk. *pāaḍa,* P. *pākaṭa,* Sk. *prakaṭa*; si. *parghaṭu,* g. m. *pragaṭ,* h. *pargaṭ, pragaṭ,* pj. *pargaṭ.*

1515. **පාළ pāḷa[2], පහළ pahaḷa[2],** a. pprt., struck, smitten. — P. *pahaṭa,* Sk. *prahṛta.*

1516. **පැකම päkama, පැකුම päkuma,** s., st. ff. *päkam,* °*um,* mud. — Blending of P., Sk. *paṅka* and P. *kaddama,* Sk. *kardama.*

1517. **පැකිලෙනවා päkilenavā,** v., prt. *päkiluṇā,* to stumble, trip. Caus. *päkilavanavā,* prt. *päkilevuvā,* to cause to stumble. — P. *pakkhalati,* Sk. *pra-* + √*skhal, praskhalati.*

1518. **පැටිය päṭiya,** s., st. f. *päṭi,* beginning. — ? Sk. *pra-sthiti.* See *paṭan, paṭā.*

1519. **පැටියා päṭiyā, පැටවා päṭavā,** s., st. f. *päṭi,* young one. — Cf. Sinh. *päñcā*; Tam. *piñcu.* (De Lanerolle.)

1520. **පැඩිලි päḍili, පැඬිලි päňḍili,** a., white, pale. — From *paňḍu*, q.v.; cf. *paňḍuru*.

1521. **පැණ päṇa,** s., wisdom; *päṇa-vat* wise, learned. — Pk. *paṇṇā*, P. *paññā*, Sk. *prajñā*. This should be *päna*, with dental *n* (< *ññ*) (De Lanerolle).

1522. **පැණය päṇaya,** s., st. f. *päṇa*, question. *päṇa-visaňdanavā* to answer questions. — Pk. *paṇha*, P. *pañha*, Sk. *praśna*. This should be *pänaya*, with dental *n* (< *ṇh*) (De Lanerolle).

1523. **පැණි päṇi,** s., sweet juice, syrup, honey, molasses. *päṇi-rasa* sweet taste. — P., Sk. *phāṇita*.

— **පැතලි pätali,** a., see **petali.**

1524. **පැතිරෙනවා pätirenavā,** v., prt. *päturuṇā*, to become diffused spread. — Intr. of **paturanavā*. See s.v. *paturuvanavā*.

1525. **පැදකුණු pädakuṇu,** in *p°-karanavā* to perform a reverential salutation. — P. *padakkhiṇā*, Sk. *pradakṣiṇa*.

1526. **පැදුම් pädum,** a., eastern: s. *°ma* east. *pädum-diga* eastern quarter. — P. *pācīna*, Sk. *prācīna*.

1527. **පැදුම päduma,** s., st. f. *°um*, cloud. *pädum-rada* id. — Pk. *pajjuṇṇa*, P. *pajjunna*, Ved. *parjanya*.

1528. **පැන් pän,** s., water. *pän-toṭa* watering place. — Pk. *pāṇia*, P., Sk. *pānīya*; kśm. *pōñu*, si. g. m. *pāṇī*, oṛ. *pāṇi*, ass. bg. nep. *pāni*, h. *pānī*, pj. *pāṇī*.

1529. **පැමිණෙනවා päminenavā,** v., prt. *pämuṇuṇā*, to come, arrive. Caus. *pamuṇuvanavā*, prt. *pämiṇevuvā*, to cause to come, to fetch. — Intr. (caus.) of *pamuṇanavā* for **pavuṇanavā* = P. *pâpuṇāti*, Sk. *pra-* + $\sqrt{}$*āp*, *prâpnōti*. Cf. kśm. *prāvun*, si. *pāiṇu*, g. *pāvuṃ*, m. *pāvṇeṃ*, oṛ. *pāibā*, ass. *pāiba*, bg. *pāoyā*, h. *pānā*, nep. *pāunu*, pj. *pāuṇā*=Pk. *pāvēi*, P. *pāpēti*, Sk. *prâpayati*; cf. Sinh. *pavā*.

1530. **පැරකුම pärakuma,** s., st. f. *°um*, power, might. — P. *parakkama*, Sk. *parākrama*.

1531. **පැල päla,** s., st. f. *päl*, hut, watch-shed. — Sk. *palli*.

1532. **පැවිද්දා päviddā,** s., st. f. *°vidi*, monk. — P. *pabbajita*, Sk. *pra-vrajita*. Cf. Pk. *pavvajjā*, P. *pabbajjā*, Sk. *pravrajyā*.

1533. **පැස päsa, පැහැ pähä,** s., st. f. *päs*, basket. — P. *pacchi*.

1534. **පැසසුම päsasuma,** s., st. f. *°sum*, praise. — Pk. *pasaṃsaṇa*, P. *pasaṃsana*, Sk. *praśaṃsana*. See also *pasasa*.

1535. **පැසි päsi,** a. pprt., cooked, ripe. — P. *pacita*, Sk. *pācita*. See *pihanavā*.

1536. **පැහැ pähä,** s., colour. *pähä-pat* coloured, bright. — ? Doublet of *paba*. See s.v. *pahana*, *pāna*.

1537. පාළ **pāḷa,** s., st. f. *pāḷa,* a measure of capacity still in current use in the villages. — According to PARANAVITANA, EpZ III 184, through **peyaḷa* <*pekaḍa* (ib. III 177[9], 178[10], 4th c.) which itself seems to be metathesis of **peḍaka* = P. *piṭaka* basket.

1538. පිඟු **piṅgu,** a., tawny. — P., Sk. *piṅga.*

1539. පිට **piṭa,** s., st. f. *piṭa,* back, hind part. *piṭa-äṭaya* backbone, dorsal bone. Cf. *piṭa,* adv., outside; postp., on, upon; *piṭin,* postp., from upon; *piṭata* (see *ata*[1]), s., the outside. — Pk., P. *piṭṭha,* Sk. *pṛṣṭha*; g. *pīṭh,* oṛ. ass. *piṭhi,* bg. *piṭh,* h. *pīṭh,* nep. *piṭh,* pj. *piṭṭh.* Derivates of Pk. *paṭṭha* and *puṭṭha* in the MIAVs, see T, s.v. *piṭh.*

1540. පිටි **piṭi,** s., flour, meal. *p°-karanavā* to reduce to powder. — Pk., P. *piṭṭha,* Sk. *piṣṭa*; si. *pīṭho,* g. m. *pīṭh,* oṛ. ass. bg. *piṭhā,* b. h. *pīṭhā,* nep. *piṭho,* pj. *pīṭhī,* l. *pīṭhā.*

1541. පිඩ **piḍa,** s., st. f. *piḍu,* lump, ball (as of boiled rice). — Pk., P., Sk. *piṇḍa*; kśm. *pend,* si. *pinu,* g. *pīṃḍo,* m. *piṃḍ,* oṛ. *piṇḍa,* bg. *piṃṛā,* h. *piṇḍā,* nep. *piṃṛo,* pj. *pinn, pinnā,* l. *pinnaṃ.*

1542. පිඩැල්ල **piḍälla,** s., st. ff. *piḍäli, °ali,* clod, sod. — = *piḍa* + *-l* suffix.

1543. පිණනවා **piṇanavā,** v., prt. *piṇuvā,* to exult, rejoice. Caus. *piṇavanavā,* prt. *piṇevuvā,* to elate, enrapture. — Sk. √*prī, prīṇāti, °ṇītē* (P. caus. *pīṇēti*=Sk. *prīṇayati*). In literature this word occurs always with dental *n*; see DE LANEROLLE, DSL, § 9a, p. xliii.

1544. පිණිස **piṇisa,** postp., for, for the purpose of, in order to. — <MInd. **paṇissāya* (Sk. *pra-ṇi* + √*śri*); see *nisā.*

— පිත් **pit,** s., see s.v. **putā.**

1545. පිත **pita,** s., st. f. *pit,* bile. — Pk., P., Sk. *pitta*; kśm. *peth,* si. *pitu, pito,* g. *pitto,* oṛ. *pitā,* ass. *pit,* h. *pittā,* nep. *pito,* pj. *pit, pittā.*

1546. පිදුරු **piduru,** s., straw. *piduru-hatta* straw-mushroom. — Sk. *piñjara* yellow, tawny.

1547. පින **pina,** s., st. f. *pin,* religious merit. *pin-kama* religious act of merit. — Pk. *puṇṇa* (Mg. *puñña*), P. *puñña,* Sk. *puṇya.*

1548. පිනු **pinu,** පුනු **punu,** a., full, complete. *pinu-* or *punu-pohoya* (see *pōya*) day of the full moon. — Pk., P. *puṇṇa,* Sk. *pūrṇa.* See *pun.*

1549. පිපි **pipi,** a. pprt., expanded, open (as a flower). — Pk. *pupphia,* P. *pupphita,* Sk. *puṣpita.*

1550. පිපෙනවා **pipenavā,** v., prt. *pipuṇā,* to expand, open (as flowers). Caus. *puppanavā* (<**pupv°*), prt. *pippuvā,* to bloat, inflate. — P. *pupphati,* caus. *pupphāpēti,* Sk. √*puṣp, puṣpyati.*

1551. පිය **piya**[1], s., foot, footprint, footstep. *piya-gäṭaya* foot notch, step. — Pk. *paa,* P., Sk. *pada*; but *paya*<*pāda.*

1552. **පිය piya[2],** a., p l e a s i n g, b e l o v e d ; s. fem., w o m a n, w i f e. — Pk. *pia*, P. *piya*, Sk. *priya* ; si. *piyu*, g. *piyuṃ*, m. *piyo*, *pihū*, h. *piyā*, pj. *piyu*, *pīā*.

1553. **පියඟු piyaṅgu,** s., m i l l e t. — P. *piyaṅgu*, Sk. *priyaṅgu* panic seed.

1554. **පියන piyana,** s., st. f. *piyan*, c o v e r, l i d. — Pk. *pihāṇa*, P., Sk. *pidhāna* ; h. nep. *pihān*.

1555. **පියනවා piyanavā,** v., prt. *piyuvā*, *pivuvā*, t o c l o s e, s h u t. Caus. *piyavanavā*, prt. *piyevuvā*, to cause to close, to reject. — P. *pidahati*, ger. *pidhāya* ; Sk. *pi-* + √*dhā*, *pi-dadhāti*, *pidhāya*.

1556. **පියයුර piyayura, පියවුර piyavura,** s., st. f. °*ru*, w o m a n ' s b r e a s t. — Pk. *paōhara*, P., Sk. *payōdhara*.

1557. **පියල් piyal,** s., name of a t r e e, Nephelium longana. — P. *piyāla*, Sk. *priyāla*, *piyāla* Buchanania latifolia.

1558. **පියල්ල piyalla,** s., st. f. *piyali*, r a g, h a l f a g l o b e (as half a coconut), s e e d l o b e. *piyali-karanavā* to reduce any globular seed into halves. — P. *padālēti* cleaves, destroys, Sk. *pra-* + √*dṝ*, caus. *pradārayati* splits, rends, *pradara* splitting, rending.

1559. **පියවර piyavara,** s., f o o t s t e p, i m p r e s s i o n o f t h e f o o t. — < MInd. **padâkāra* form of the foot (*piya*[1] + *ayura*).

1560. **පියවි piyavi,** s., n a t u r e, n a t u r a l f o r m. — Pk. *paaï*, P. *pakati*, Sk. *prakṛti*.

1561. **පියස් piyas,** a., n e a r, p r o x i m a t e ; s. °*sa* neighbourhood. — Pk. *pagāsa*, P. *pakāsa*, Sk. *prakāśa* visible, manifest.

1562. **පියස piyasa, පියෙස piyesa,** s., st. ff. *piyas*, *piyes*, p l a c e, c o u n t r y. — Pk. *paēsa*, P. *padēsa*, Sk. *pradēśa*.

1563. **පියා piyā[1],** s., w i n g of a bird. *piyā-sara* flying. — < MInd. **patāta*, P. *patatta*, Sk. *patatra*.

1564. **පියා piyā[2],** s., st. f. *piya*, f a t h e r. — Pk. nom. *piyā*, P. *pitā*, Sk. *pitṛ*, *pitā* : si. *piu*, pj. *piu*, *piō*, l. *piū*, *peō*, LSI, I 2, p. 123.

— **පියු piyu, පිවු pivu,** a. pprt., see **pī.**

1565. **පියුම piyuma,** s., st. f. *piyum*, l o t u s, Nelumbium speciosum. — Pk. *pauma*, P. *paduma*, Sk. *padma*.

1566. **පියුමසන piyum-asana,** s., st. f. °*-asan*, l o t u s - s e a t, l o t u s - l i k e p o s t u r e. — Sk. *padmâsana*.

1567. **පියුමාරය piyum-āraya,** s., st. f. °*ra*, l o t u s - p o n d. — Sk. *padmâkara*.

1568. **පියුම්ගැබ piyum-gäba,** s., name of the g o d B r a h m ā. — P. *paduma-gabbha*, Sk. *padma-garbha*.

1569. **පියුම්නැබ piyum-näba,** s., name of the g o d B r a h m ā. — Sk. *padma-nābhi*.

1570. **පියුම්නෙත් piyum-net,** s., name of the god Viṣṇu. — Sk. *padma-nētra*.

1571. **පියුම්පණ piyum-paṇa,** s., name of the god Brahmā; sun. — Sk. *padma-pāṇi*. See s.v. *peṇa*[1].

1572. **පියුම්පත piyum-pata,** s., st. f. °*-pat*, leaf of the lotus.— P. *paduma-patta*, Sk. *padma-pattra*.

1573. **පියුම්යොන් piyum-yon,** s., name of the god Brahmā. — Sk. *padma-yōni*.

1574. **පියුම්රා piyum-rā,** s., ruby. — P. *paduma-rāga*, Sk. *padma-rāga*.

— **පියෙස piyesa,** s., see **piyasa.**

1575. **පියෝ piyō,** s., effort; fraud, trick. — Pk. *paōga*, P *payōga*, Sk. *prayōga*.

1576. **පිරි piri**[1]**-,** prefix = Pk., P., Sk. *pari-*.

1577. **පිරි piri**[2]**,** a. pprt., full, filled. *piri-kum̆bu* pot that is full.— Pk. *pūria*, P., Sk. *pūrita*. See *puranavā*[2].

1578. **පිරිකපනවා piri-kapanavā,** s., prt. *-käpuvā*, to divide. Pprt. *piri-käpu* allotted, assigned, EpZ I 49 [51], [53], 10th c. — Sk. *pari-* + √*kḷp*, *pari-kḷpta*, caus. *pari-kalpayati*. See *kapanavā*.

— **පිරිකම pirikama,** s., see **piriyama.**

1579. **පිරිකර pirikara,** s., article, requisite. *aṭa-p°* the eight requisites of a bhikkhu. — P. *parikkhāra*, Sk.*pariṣkāra*.

1580. **පිරිකෙව pirikeva,** s., st. f. °*kev*, surrounding, encircling. — P. *parikkhēpa*, Sk. *parikṣēpa*.

1581. **පිරිත pirita,** s., st. f. °*rit*, protection, a religious ceremony for protection.— P. *parittā*, Sk. *paritrā*.

1582. **පිරිතැසුම piritäsuma,** s., st. f. °*sum*, prayer, request. — P. *pari-tassanā*, *pari-tassati*, Sk. *pari-* + √*tṛs*. Ruv (314) has *piritäsli*. Semasiologically doubtful.

1583. **පිරිනමනවා piri-namanavā,** s., prt. °*-nämuvā*, to set apart. Also *piri-ṇ°*. — P. *pari-ṇāmēti*, Sk. *pari-* + √*nam*, caus. *pari-ṇāmayati*.

1584. **පිරිනිවන් pirinivan,** s., attainment of the highest emancipation. *pirinivanavā*, v., to attain Nirvāṇa. — P. *parinibbāna*, °*bbāyati*, Sk. *parinirvāṇa*, °*vāti* (*pari-niṣ-* + √*vā*).

1585. **පිරිපත piripata,** s., st. f. °*pat*, danger, calamity. — P., Sk. *paripantha*.

1586. **පිරිබඩ piribaḍa,** s., smearing, rubbing on. *p.-karanavā* to smear, rub on. — P. *paribhaṇḍam̥ karōti* makes a house smooth by rubbing it with cowdung.

1587. **පිරිබුන් piribun,** a. pprt., destroyed, extirpated. — P., Sk. *pari-bhinna*.

1588. **පිරිමඩිනවා piri-maḍinavā** or °**දිනවා** °**dinavā,** v., to rub, stroke; to caress.— P. *pari-maddati*, Sk. *pari-* + √*mṛd*, *pari-mardatē*.

1589. **පිරිමහනවා piri-mahanavā,** °**සනවා** °**saṇavā,** v., prt. °*-mähuvā*, °*mäsuvā*, to eke out, make shift. Intr. *piri-mähenavā*, °*s*°, prt. °*huṇā*, °*s*°, to eke out, be barely sufficient. — P. *pari-masati*, Sk. *pari-* + √*mṛś*, *pari-mṛśati*. It is difficult to connect the meanings.

1590. **පිරිමි pirimi,** a., male, masculine; s. *pirimiyā* boy or man. — P. *purimaka*. The male sex is 'preceding' the female sex.

1591. **පිරියත piriyata,** s., completion, end. — P. *pariyanta*, Sk. *paryanta*; or<MInd. **pariyatta*, Sk. *paryāpta*. Cf. Sinh. *piriyata*, a., finished.

1592. **පිරියම piriyama,** °**කම** °**kama,** s., st. ff. °*yam*, °*kam*, adorning, restoring, repairing. — P. *parikamma*, Sk. *parikarman*.

1593. **පිරියස piriyasa,** °**යසුන** °**yasuna,** s., seeking, exploring. — P. *pariyēsaṇā*, Sk. *paryēṣaṇā*.

1594. **පිරිවට pirivaṭa,** s., cloth or garment lent by a washerman.—< MInd. **parivaṭṭa*, P. *parivaṭṭa* turning round, Sk. *parivarta*. Also *piruvaṭa*.

1595. **පිරිවර pirivara,** s., retinue, attendants. *piri-varanavā*, °*-väruvā*, to surround, attend. — Pk., P., Sk. *parivāra*; P. *pari-vārēti*, Sk. *-vārayati*.

1596. **පිරිවැටිය pirivätiya,** s., st. f. °*ti*, over-turning. — MInd. **parivatti*, Sk. *parivṛtti*.

1597. **පිරිවෙන pirivena,** s., st. f. °*ven*, hermitage; college of a monastery. — P. *parivēṇa*.

1598. **පිරිවෙස pirivesa,** s., st. f. °*ves*, halo round the moon or sun. — P. *parivēsa*, Sk. *parivēśa*.

1599. **පිරිස pirisa,** s., retinue, attendants.— Pk., P. *parisā*, Sk. *pariṣat*.

1600. **පිරිසිදු pirisidu,** °**සුදු** °**sudu,** a., clean, pure, chaste. *p*°*-karanavā* to cleanse, clarify.—P. *parisuddha*, Sk. *pariśuddha*.

1601. **පිරිසිඳිනවා piri-siňdinavā,** v., to ascertain; ger. *pirisiňda* having ascertained. Intr. *pirisiňdenavā* to be determined, DhpAGp 25[7], trsl. of P. *paricchijjati*. — P. *pari-chindati*, Sk. *pari-* + √*chid*, *pari-cchinatti*.

— **පිරිසුදු pirisudu,** see s.v. **pirisidu.**

1602. **පිරිසුන් pirisun,** a. pprt., limited, defined. — P., Sk. *paricchinna*.

1603. **පිරිහුන් pirihun,** a. pprt., gone down, wasted away. — Pk., Sk. *parihīṇa*, P. °*na*.

1604. **පිරිහෙනවා piri-henavā,** v., prt. °*huṇā*, to waste away, decline. — *pari-hāyati*, Sk. *pari-* + √*hā*, pass. *pari-hīyatē*.

— **පිරුවට piruvaṭa,** s., see **pirivaṭa.**

1605. **පිල pila,** s., st. f. *pil*, lit. expanded, peacock's feather.— Pk., P., Sk. *phulla*; si. *phulu*, g. m. *phūl*, oṛ. *phula*, ass. bg. *phul*, b. h. *phūl*, nep. *phul*, pj. l. *phull*. Doublet of *pul*, a., expanded (as a flower).

1606 **පිලාව pilāva,** s., spleen. — Pk. nom. *pilihā*, Sk. *plīhan*; oṛ. *pilhāi*, bg. *pilā*, b. *pilhī*, h. *pilhā*, *pilaī*, pj. *pihlā*; but P. *pihaka* = m. *pī*, *pihā*, nep. *phiyo*.

1607. **පිල්ලා pillā, පිලවා pilavā,** s., st. f. *pilav*, young of any animal, grub, maggot. — P. *pillaka*: g. *pīlō*, m. *pilūṃ*, *pillūṃ* (Bl), bg. *pil*, h. *pilū*, *pillā*.

1608. **පිවිටු piviṭu, පුවුටු puvuṭu,** a. pprt., entered.— Pk., P. *paviṭṭha*, Sk. *praviṣṭa*; cf. m. *paiṭhā* entrance.

1609. **පිවිසෙනවා pi-visenavā,** v., prt. °*suṇā*, to enter. — P. *pa-visati*, Sk. *pra-* + √*viś*, *pra-viśati*; si. *pehaṇu*, g. *pesvuṃ*, oṛ. *pasibā*, ass. *pahiba*, bg. *pasā*, h. *paisnā*, nep. *pasnu*.

— **පිවු pivu,** a. pprt., see **pi**.

— **පිසනවා pisanavā,** and **පිසිනවා pisinavā,** vv., see **pihanavā,** and **pihinavā.**

1610. **පිසස් pisas,** s., demon. — Pk. *pisāa*, P. *pisāca*, Sk. *piśāca*. Cf. *pissu*.

1611. **පිසිඹ pisiṁba**(Ca), s., name of the nimba or margosa tree, Azadirachta indica. Also *pisaṁba*, Ruv 212.— Seems to be a blending of Sk. *picumanda* and *nimba* (see *niṁba*).

1612. **පිස්සු pissu,** a., mad, insane; s. *pissā* mad man, *pissī* mad woman; *pissuva* or *pissu-kama* madness. — P. *pisācaka*, Sk. *piśācaka*; m. *pisā* mad, *piseṃ* madness.

1613. **පිහනවා pihanavā, පිසනවා pisanavā,** v., prt. *pihuvā*, *pisuvā*, *pissā*, to cook. Caus. *pisavanavā*, prt. *pisevuvā*, to cause to be cooked; *päsavanavā*, prt. *päsevuvā*, to ripen, mature (tr.); intr. *pähenavā*, *päs*°, prt. *pähuṇā*, *päs*°, to be cooked, to ripen. — P. *pacati*, Sk. √*pac*, *pacati*. The corresponding verbs in the MIAVs are intr. and derived from P. *paccati*, Sk. *pacyatē*, T, s.v. *pacnu-*. The Sinh. caus. and intr. *päs*° make us assume a base-form **pasanavā*. See *päsi*.

1614. **පිහිට pihiṭa,** s., help, assistance, favour. *p°-venavā* to help. — Pk. *païṭṭhā*, P. *patiṭṭhā*, Sk. *pratiṣṭhā*.

1615. **පිහිටනවා pihiṭanavā, පිහිටෙනවා pihiṭenavā,** v., prt. *pihiṭiyā*, *pihiṭuṇā*, to be established. Caus. *pihiṭavanavā*, *pihiṭuvanavā*, prt. °*ṭevuvā*, to establish, place. — P. *pati-ṭṭhāti*, °*ṭṭhāpēti*; Sk. *prati-* + √*sthā*, caus. *pratiṣṭhāpayati*.

1616. **පිහිටි pihiṭi,** a. pprt., fixed, established. — Pk. *païṭṭhia*, P. *patiṭṭhita*, Sk. *pratiṣṭhita*.

1617. **පිහිනවා pihinavā, පිසි° pisi°**, v., prt. *pissā*, t o w i p e, r u b o f f. — Pk. *puñchaï*, P. *puñchati*, Sk. *pra-* + √*uñch*, *prōñchati* ; g. *puṃchvuṃ*, m. *pusṇeṃ*, oṛ. *pocchibā*, bg. *puṃchā*, h. *poṃchnā*, nep. *puchnu*, *pochnu*, pj. *pūṃjhṇā*, l. *pūjhaṇ*.

1618. **පිළ piḷa[1]**, s., l e d g e along the side of a house to sit on. — Pk. *pīḍha(a)*, P., Sk. *pīṭha(ka)* ; kśm. *pīru*, si. *pīṛhī*, g. *pīḍhiyuṃ*, m. *piḍheṃ*, oṛ. *piṛhā*, ass. *pirā*, h. *pīṛhā*, nep. *pirā*, *pirhā*, pj. *pīhṛā*, l. *pīṛhā*.

1619. **පිළ piḷa[2]**, s., t r o u b l e, p a i n. — Pk. *pīḍā*, *pīrā*, P. *pīḷā*, Sk. *pīḍā* ; si. *pīra*, g. *pīḍ*, m. cf. *pīḍṇeṃ*, h. *pīṛ*, *pīr*, nep. *pir*, pj. l. *pīṛ*.

1620. **පිළි piḷi**, s., in *piḷi-miṇa* c r y s t a l. — See s. v. *paḷiňguva*.

1621. **පිළි- piḷi-**, prefix = Pk. *paḍi-*, P. *paṭi-*, Sk. *prati-*. P. *pati-* > Sinh. *pihi-* in *pihiṭa* etc.

— **පිළිකම piḷikama**, s., see **piḷiyama.**

1622. **පිළිකුල් piḷikul**, a., f o u l, a b o m i n a b l e. *p*°-*karanavā* to abhor.— P. *paṭikūla*, Sk. *pratikūla*.

1623. **පිළිකෙව piḷikeva**, s., st. f. °*kev*, o p p o s i n g, r e f u s i n g. *piḷikev-karanavā* to reject. — P. *paṭikkhēpa*, Sk. *pratikṣēpa*.

1624. **පිළිගන්නවා piḷi-gannavā**, v., to a c c e p t, r e c e i v e. Caus. *piḷi-ganvanavā* to cause to accept, to present. — P. *paṭi-gaṇhāti*, Sk. *prati-gṛhṇāti*. See *gannavā*.

1625. **පිළිතුර piḷitura**, s., st. f. °*ru*, r e j o i n d e r, r e p l y. — <MInd. **paṭiyuttara* ; Sk. *pratyuttara*, (P. *paccuttara*).

1626. **පිළිදගිනවා piḷi-daginavā**, v., t o c h e r i s h, f o s t e r, s u p p o r t. *piḷidägīma*, °*guma*, s., cherishing etc., protection. — P. *paṭi-jaggati*, *paṭijaggana*, (Sk. *prati-* + √*jāgṛ*, *prati-jāgarati*).

1627. **පිළින piḷina**, s., st. f. °*na*, p r o m i s e, a g r e e m e n t. *piḷina-denavā* to promise. — Pk. *paḍiṇṇā*, P. *paṭiññā*, Sk. *pratijñā* ; m. *paiṇ*. Cf. T, Add., s.v. *jānnu*.

— **පිළිපක් piḷipak**, a., see **piḷivak.**

1628. **පිළිපදිනවා piḷi-padinavā**, v., prt. °*päddā*, t o k e e p, o b s e r v e. — P. *paṭi-pajjati*, Sk. *prati-* + √*pad*, *prati-padyatē*.

1629. **පිළිපන් piḷipan**, a. ppt., o b s e r v e d, a r r i v e d, a t t a i n e d. — P. *paṭipanna*. Sk. *pratipanna*. See also *piḷivan*, *puḷuvan*.

1630. **පිළිබඳ piḷibaňda**, a., c o n n e c t e d w i t h, a t t a c h e d t o. — For °*bada* (thus EpZ III 227[15], 10th c.), P. *paṭibaddha*, Sk. *pratibaddha*.

1631. **පිළිබිඹුව piḷibiṁbuva**, s., l i k e n e s s, i m a g e. — Pk. *paḍibīmba*, P. *paṭibimba*, Sk. *pratibimba*.

1632. **පිළිමය piḷimaya**, s., st. f. °*ma*, l i k e n e s s, i m a g e, p i c t u r e. — Pk. *paḍimā*, P. *paṭimā*, Sk. *pratimā*.

1633. **පිළිය piḷiya,** s., st. f. *piḷi*, cloth. — P., Sk. *paṭī, paṭikā*.

1634. **පිළියම piḷiyama, පිළිකම piḷikama,** s., st. ff. °*yam*, °*kam*, refitting, mending. — Pk. *paḍikamma*, P. *paṭikamma*, Sk. *pratikarman*.

1635. **පිළිරැව් piḷiräv,** s., resonance, echo. — P. *paṭirava*, Sk. *pratirava*.

1636. **පිළිරුව piḷiruva,** s., st. f. °*rū*, likeness, image; metaphor. — Pk. *paḍirūva*, P. *paṭirūpa*, Sk. *pratirūpa*.

1637. **පිළිවක් piḷivak, පිළිපක් piḷipak,** a., hostile, antagonistic. — Pk. *paḍivakkha*, P. *paṭipakkha*, Sk. *pratipakṣa*.

1638. **පිළිවදන piḷivadana,** s., st. f. °*dan*, reply. — Pk. *paḍivaaṇa*, P. *paṭivacana*, Sk. *prativacana*.

— **පිළිවන් piḷivan,** a., see **puḷuvan.**

1639. **පිළිවිසිනවා piḷivisinavā,** v., prt. *piḷivissā*, to inquire, question. — P. *paṭi-pucchati*, Sk. *prati-* + √*pṛch*, *pratipṛcchati*. Cf. *puḷuvut*.

1640. **පිළිවෙත piḷiveta,** s., st. f. °*vet*, ceremony, observance. — Pk. *paḍivatti*, P. *paṭipatti*, Sk. *pratipatti*.

1641. **පිළිවෙළ piḷiveḷa,** s., arrangement, order. — P. *paṭipāṭī*.

1642. **පිළිසඳ piḷisaňda,** s., re-birth. *piḷi-siňdenavā*, prt. °*ňduṇā*, to be conceived in the womb. — P. *paṭisandhi*, Sk. *pratisaṃdhi*, v. *prati-saṃdhīyatē*.

1643. **පිළිසඳර piḷisaňdara,** s., friendly greeting, friendliness. — P. *paṭisanthāra*, Sk. *prati-*+*saṃstāra*.

1644. **පිළිසන් piḷisan, °සුන් °sun,** a. pprt., covered, hidden. — P. *paṭicchanna*, Sk. *praticchanna* (*prati-* + √*chad*).

1645. **පිළිසරණ piḷisaraṇa,** s., aid, favour, patronage. — P. *paṭisaraṇa*, Sk. *pratisaraṇa*.

1646. **පිළිසිඹියාව piḷisiṁbiyāva,** s., st. f. °*yā*, discriminating or universal knowledge. — P. *paṭisambhidā*.

1647. **පිළිසෙව piḷiseva,** s., st. f. °*sev*, prohibition. — P. *paṭisēdha*, Sk. *pratiṣēdha*.

1648. **පිළිහසුන piḷihasuna,** s., st. f. °*sun*, written reply. — P. *paṭisāsana*, Sk. *pratiśāsana*.

1649. **පි pi, පියු piyu, පිවු pivu,** a. pprt., shut, closed. — P., Sk. *pihita* (*pi-* + √*dhā*).

1650. **පුඟුලා puňgulā,** s., st. f. °*ňgul*, person, individual. — Pk., P. *puggala*, Sk. *pudgala*.

1651. **පුට puṭa,** s., in *puṭa-pāka* refining or sublimating vessel, for preparing drugs. — P., Sk. *puṭa*, lw. (De Lanerolle).

1652. පුටුපය **puṭupaya,** s., in *puva-puṭup°* and *uturu-puṭup°* names of the 25th and 26th lunar mansions. — P. *poṭṭhapāda,* Sk. *prōṣṭhapada.*

1653. පුටුව **puṭuva,** s., st. f. *puṭu,* chair, seat. — Sk. *prōṣṭha.*

1654-1658. —

1659. පුතා **putā,** s., st. ff. *put, pit,* son. — Pk., P. *putta,* Sk. *putra* ; kśm. *pothar,* si. *putru,* g. m. *pūt,* oṛ. *puta,* ass. bg. *put,* h. *pūt,* nep. *put,* pj. *putt, puttar,* l. *puttur.*

1660. පුද **puda,** s., offering, oblation. *p°-karanavā* to offer. — Pk. *pūā,* P., Sk. *pūjā.*

1661. පුදනවා **pudanavā,** v., prt. *piduvā,* to offer, present. — Pk. *pūēi,* P. *pūjēti,* Sk. *pūjayati.*

1662. පුන් **pun,** a., full. *pun-sañda, pun-sisi* full moon. — Doublet of *pinu, punu,* q.v.

— පුන **puna,** adv., see **pana.**

1663. පුනරුත් **punar-ut,** a. pprt., repeated, reiterated. — P. *punar-utta,* Sk. *punar-ukta.*

1664. පුප් **pup,** s., flower. — Pk. P. *puppha,* Sk. *puṣpa.* Cf. *pipenavā.*

1665. පුපුර **pupura,** s., spark of fire. *pupuranavā,* v., prt. *pipuruvā,* to burst, crack ; caus. *pupuravanavā,* prt. *pipirevuvā,* to burst (tr.), rupture. — Intens. of Sk. √*sphur, sphurati* ; si. *phuraṇu,* g. *phurvuṃ,* m. *phurṇeṃ,* nep. *phurṇu.* P. *pharati* < Sk. *spharati* (derivates in the MIAVs see T, s.v. *pharpharāunu*).

— පුප්පනවා **puppanavā,** v., see s.v. **pipenavā.**

— පුබුදිනවා **pubudinavā,** etc., v., see **kubudinavā.**

1666. පුබුදු **pubudu,** a. pprt., awake; expanded, open (as a flower). — Pk., P. *pabuddha,* Sk. *prabuddha.*

— පුර **pura^{1},** postp., see **pera.**

1667. පුර **pura^{2},** a., full in *pura-sañda* full moon. — Pk., P., Sk. *pūra* ; nep. *pur.*

1668. පුරනවා **puranavā^{1},** v., prt. *piruvā,* to begin, start, initiate. — Denom. of *pura^{1}.* Cf. √*pur* precede, in the Dhātup.

1669. පුරනවා **puranavā^{2},** v., prt. *piruvā,* to fill. Caus. *puravanavā,* prt. *pirevuvā,* id. — Pk. *pūrēi,* P. *pūrēti, pūrāpēti,* Sk. √*pṝ, pūrayati* ; kśm. *pūrun,* si. *pūraṇu,* g. *pūrvuṃ,* m. *purṇeṃ, puraviṇeṃ,* oṛ. *purāibā,* ass. *puriba, purāiba,* h. *pūrnā, purānā,* nep. *purnu. purāunu,* pj. *pūrnā, purāuṇā,* l. *pūraṇ.*

1670. පුර(ය) **pura(ya),** s., st. f. *pura,* city. *pura-dora* city-gate. — Pk., P., Sk. *pura* ? lw.

1671. පුරිස් **puris,** s., man. — Pk., P. *purisa,* Sk. *puruṣa* ; si. *purihu,* h. nep. *pursā.* ? lw.

1672. පුරු **puru,** s., st. f. *puru,* pollen. — P., Sk. *parāga.*

1673. පුලිඟුව **puliṅguva,** s., st. f. °*ṅgu,* spark.— Pk., P. *phuliṅga,* Sk. *sphuliṅga;* nep. *philiṅgo,* °*luṅgo.*

1674. පුලිඳා **puliṅdā,** s., st. f. °*ṅdu,* forest-dweller, Väddā.— P., Sk. *pulinda.*

1675. පුලුටු **puluṭu,** a. pprt., burnt, fried, grilled.—P. *piluṭṭha,* Sk. *pluṣṭa.* See *pulussanavā, palahanavā.*

1676. පුලුදු **puludu,** s., desire, cupidity (H. Jayatilaka, Eḷu-akārādiya, s.v. = *itā-lol-bava*). — Sk. *pra-* + $\sqrt{}$*lubh,* pprt. *pra-lubdha* ; P. cf. *palōbhēti.*

1677. පුලුස්සනවා **pulussanavā,** v., prt. *pilissuvā,* to burn up, bake, roast. Intr. *pilissenavā,* prt. *pilissuṇā,* to become roasted. — *puluss*° < *pulusv*°, caus. of. **pulusanavā* = Sk.$\sqrt{}$*pluṣ, pluṣyati* ; nep. *pilsinu.* See *palahanavā.*

— පුල් **pul,** a., see **pila.**

1678. පුව **puva**[1]**,** s., st. f. *pū,* a kind of cake.—Pk. *pūa,* P. *pūpa, pūva,* Sk. *pūpa* ; m. *puvā,* h. *pū, pūā,* nep. *puvā.*

1679. පුව **puva**[2]**,** a., preceding, previous, former. — Pk. *puvva,* P. *pubba,* Sk. *pūrva.*

1680. පුවක් **puvak,** s., areca-nut. — P., Sk. *pūga* + *pak* ripe fruit.

1681. පුවඟු **puvaṅgu,** s., name of a plant, Sinapis nigra. — P. *piyaṅga,* Sk. *priyaṅgu.*

1682. පුවත **puvata,** පවත **pavata,** s., st. f. °*vat,* continuance; narrative, account. — Pk. *pavitti,* P. *pavatti,* Sk. *pravṛtti.*

1683. පුවස **puvasa,** පවස **pavasa,** s., thirst. — Pk. *pivāsā, piāsā,* P., Sk. *pipāsā* ; kśm. g. m. *pĕ̄ǝs,* ass. *piyāh,* bg. h. nep. *piyās.*

1684. පුවළ **puvaḷa,** a., hard, firm, great. — Generally compared with Sk. *prāuḍha.* We have to assume a MInd. **pavūḷha,* pprt. of *pra-* + $\sqrt{}$*vah.*

1685. පුවුටු **puvuṭu,** a. pprt., see **piviṭu.**

1686. පුවෙණි **puveṇi,** පෙවෙණි **peveṇi,** s., braid of hair. — P. *pavēṇi,* Sk. *pravēṇi.*

1687. පුස **pusa,** s., in *pusa-näkata* name of the 8th lunar mansion.— Pk. *pussa,* P. *phussa,* Sk. *puṣya*; kśm. *poh, puh,* m. *pūs,* oṛ. *pusa,* ass. *puh,* h. *pūs,* nep. *pus.*

1688. පුහුණු **puhuṇu,** a., accustomed, practised, proficient; s. *puhuṇuva* advancement, proficiency. — Cf. Sk. *praguṇa* (DBJ).

1689. පුහුදුනා **puhudunā,** s., o r d i n a r y p e r s o n. — P. *puthujjana,* Sk. *pṛthag-jana.*

1690. පුළ **puḷa,** s., n o s t r i l. — Pk. *puḍa* bag, hollow of the hand, P. *puṭa* basket, Sk. *puṭa* pocket, nostril (*nāsā-puṭa*). The derivates in the MIAVs have various meanings, see Bl, s.v. *puḍā* ; T, s.v. *purā.*

1691. පුළුන් **puḷun,** s., c o t t o n, f l u f f. — ? = P. *phuṭana* tearing, bursting, Sk. *sphuṭana* ; cf. kśm. *phuṭun,* si. *phuṭaṇu,* g. *phuṭvuṃ,* m. *phuṭṇeṃ,* oṛ. *phuṭibā,* ass. *phuṭiba,* bg. *phuṭā,* h. *phūṭnā,* nep. *phuṭnu,* pj. *phuṭṭṇā,* l. *phuṭṭaṇ.*

— පුළුල් **puḷul,** a., see **paḷal.**

1692. පුළුවන් **puḷuvan,** පිළිවන් **piḷivan,** a., a b l e, c a p a b l e; p o s s i b l e. *puḷuvan-kama* ability ; *p°-karanavā* to enable ; *p°-venavā* to become able. — Doublet of *piḷipan,* q. v., with different meaning.

1693. පුළුවුත් **puḷuvut,** a. pprt., i n q u i r e d. — Sk. *prati-pṛṣṭa.* See *piḷivisinavā.* Cf. *puḷuvusnā* inquiring.

1694. පූ **pū[1],** a. pprt., w i n n o w e d, in *pū-karanavā* to winnow. — Pk. *pūa,* P., Sk. *pūta* (√*pū*).

— පූ **pū[2],** s., see **puva[1].**

1695. පෙකණිය **pekaṇiya,** s., st. f. *pekaṇi,* n a v e l. *pekaṇi-väla* navel string.— Pk. *pekkhaṇijja,* Sk. *prēkṣaṇīya.* Lit. the 'visible' part of the body between the jacket and the sarong. In the Roḍiyā-dialect : *pekiṇitia* the part of the body above the navel.

1696. පෙණ **peṇa[1],** පණ **paṇa[2],** s., h a n d. — Pk., P., Sk. *pāṇi.*

1697. පෙණ **peṇa[2],** පණ **paṇa[3],** s., the extended h o o d o f a c o b r a. — Pk., P., Sk. *phaṇa* ; kśm. *phan,* si. *phaṇi,* g. *pheṇ, phaṇī,* m. *phaṇ,* oṛ. *phaṇā,* ass. *phanā,* bg. h. *phan,* nep. *phani,* pj. *phaṇ.*

1698. පෙණ **peṇa[3],** s., f r o t h, f o a m. — Pk., P. *phēṇa,* Sk. *phēṇa, phēna* ; kśm. *phīna,* si. *phīṇu,* g. m. *pheṇ,* oṛ. *pheṇa,* ass. bg. nep. *phen,* h. *phenā.*

1699. පෙණෙල **peṇela,** s., d r a i n, g u t t e r. — P. *paṇālī, panālī,* Sk. *praṇālī, pranālī.*

1700. පෙත් **pet,** s., in *pin-pet* t r a n s f e r e n c e o f m e r i t. — P. *patti,* Sk. *prâpti.*

1701. පෙත **peta,** s., st. f. *pet,* r o w, l i n e. — Pk. *pantī,* P. *panti,* Sk. *paṅkti* ; g. m. *pāṃt,* ass. bg. *pāṃti,* h. *pāṃt,* nep. *pāṃti.*

1702. පෙතලි **petali,** පැතලි **pätali,** a., f l a t, l e v e l, p l a i n.— Sk. *patrala* thin; si. *patiro,* °*lo,* g. *pātḷuṃ,* m. *pātaḷ,* oṛ. *pātaḷa,* ass. bg. *pātal,* h. pj. l. *patlā,* nep. *pātalo.* Semasiologically doubtful

1703. පෙත්ත **petta,** s., st. f. *peti,* s l i c e, any thin piece of wood. — Pk. *pattiā,* P. *pattikā,* Sk. *pattrikā* ; g. *pātrī,* m. *pātī,* bg. *pāti,* h. *pātī,* nep. *pāti,* pj. *pattī, pattrī.*

1704. **පෙඳ peňda,** s., 1) t a i l of a bird ; 2) b a l l. — T compares it 1) with h. pj. *peṃdā* bottom, nep. *piṃd, piṃdh* bottom, bullocks, and 2) with kśm. *pend,* m. *peṃd* ball.

1705. **පෙනෙනවා penenavā,** v., prt. *penuṇā,* t o b e v i s i b l e, a p p e a r. Caus. *penvanavā,* prt. *pennuvā,* to show, display. — Pk. *paṇṇāyaï, paṇṇāvēi,* P. *paññāyati, paññāpēti,* Sk. *pra-* + √*jñā, pra-jñāyatē, pra-jñāpayati.* Cf. T, Add. s.v. *jānnu.*

1706. **පෙම pema,** s., st. f. *pem,* l o v e. *at-pema* self-love. — Pk. *pemma,* P. *pēma,* Sk. *prēman.*

1707. **පෙර pera,** a., f o r m e r, f i r s t ; a n c i e n t ; e a s t e r n. *pera-bata* (forenoon) midday meal ; *perä rajun davasä* during the time of former kings, EpZ I 132[22], 12th c. ; *pera-diga* eastern quarter. *pera* or *pura,* postp., in front of. — Sk. *purā* (the vocalism is not clear). Compounded with *puva* = Sk. *pūrva* : cf. *perāduru* former teachers = P. *pubbâcariyā.* See also *peraṭu.*

1708. **පෙරටු peraṭu,** a., s t a n d i n g i n f r o n t ; °*ṭuva,* ° *ṭuven,* adv., preceding, before, in front. — *pera* + *ṭu,* q.v. Cf. Sk. *pūrva-stha.*

1709. **පෙරතු peratu,** a., i n f r o n t ; °*tuva,* adv., before. — Cf. P. *puratthā,* Sk. *purastāt.*

— **පෙරවනවා peravanavā,** v., see **poravanavā.**

1710. **පෙරවියා peraviyā, පෙරෙ° pere°,** s., st. f. °*vi,* p r i m e m i n i s t e r, r o y a l c o u n s e l l o r. — Pk. *purōhia,* P., Sk. *purōhita.*

1711. **පෙරහර perahara[1],** s., p r o t e c t i o n, s a f e t y. — Pk., P., Sk. *parihāra.*

1712. **පෙරහර perahara[2], °හැර °hära,** s., f e s t i v a l, p r o c e s s i o n. — P. **pārihāriya,* Sk. *pārihārya* (different meaning).

1713. **පෙරුම peruma,** s., st. f. °*rum,* h o p e, w i s h. — P. *pāramī.* Cf. P., Sk. *pāramitā.*

1714. **පෙල්ල pella,** s., st. f. *peli,* t e s t i c l e. *peli-pāranavā* to destroy the testicles by crushing. — Sk. *pēlaka.*

— **පෙවෙණි peveṇi,** s., see **puveṇi.**

— **පෙහෙ pehe, පොහො poho,** s., see **pōya.**

1715. **පෙහෙරා peherā,** s., w e a v e r. — P. *pēsakāra,* Sk. fem. *pēśaskārī.*

1716. **පෙහෙවස් pehe-vas,** s., r e l i g i o u s f a s t. — P. *upōsatha-vāsa.*

1717. **පෙළ peḷa[1],** s., r o w, l i n e ; t e x t of a book. *peḷak* a row, a number of, some. — Pk., P. *pāli, pāḷi,* Sk. *pāli* ; g. m. *pāḷ,* bg. *pāli,* h. *pālī,* nep. *pāli,* pj. *pāl.*

1718. **පෙළ peḷa[2],** s., b o x. — Pk. *pēḍā,* P. *pēḷā,* Sk. *pēṭā.* Cf. < **peṭṭa* : si. *peṭu,* g. m. *peṭ,* or. *peṭa,* ass. bg. h. nep. pj. *peṭ.*

1719. පෙළනවා **peḷanavā,** v., prt. *peḷuvā,* to molest, trouble, harass. Intr. *peḷenavā,* prt. *peḷuṇā,* to be harassed, afflicted. — Pk. *pīḷēi,* P. *pīḷēti,* Sk. √*pīḍ, pīḍayati* ; si. *pīṛanu,* g. *pīḍvuṃ,* m. *pilṇeṃ,* ass. *piriba,* bg. *piṛā,* h. *peṛnā,* nep. *pirāunu,* pj. *pīṛṇā.*

1720. පෙළහර **peḷahara,** s., miracle. — Pk. *pāḍihēra,* P. *pāṭihāriya,* °*hēra,* °*hīra,* Sk. *prātihārya.* Sinh. *peḷahara* also used for *perahara*[2].

1721. පේ **pē,** s., departed spirit.— Pk. *pēa,* P. *pēta,* Sk. *prēta.*

1722. පොකුණ **pokuṇa,** s., st. f. °*ṇu,* pond, reservoir. — Pk. *pokkhariṇī,* P. *pokkharaṇī,* Sk. *puṣkariṇī.*

1723. පොකුර **pokura,** s., st. f. °*ru,* 1) lotus; 2) tip of an elephant's trunk. *pokuru-däli* edible lotus root. — Pk. *pokkhara, pukkhara,* P. *pokkhara,* Sk. *puṣkara* ; m. *pokhar,* oṛ. *pokhuri,* bg. *pūkūr,* h. pj. *pokhar.*

1724. පොත **pota,** s., st. f. *pot,* book. *pot-pat* books and papers, literature.—Pk. *potthiā,* P. *potthaka,* Sk. *pusta(ka)* ; kśm. *pūthi,* si. g. m. *potī,* oṛ. *pothā,* ass. bg. *puthī,* h. pj. *pothī,* nep. *pothi.*

1725. පොරවනය **poravanaya,** පොරෝනය **porōnaya,** s., st. f. °*vana,* °*ōna,* cloak, robe. — Sk. *prāvaraṇa,* P. (metathesis of *r*) *pārupana.*

1726. පොරවනවා **poravanavā,** පෙරවනවා **peravanavā,** v., prt. *perevuvā,* to wrap around, enrobe. — Sk. *pra-ā-* + √*vṛ,* caus. *prâ-vārayati,* P. *pārupati.*

1727. පොරෝව **porova,** පොරව **porava,** s., st. f. *porō,* axe, hatchet. *porō-kārayā* axeman, wood-cutter.— Pk., P. *pharasu, parasu,* Sk. *paraśu* ; g. *pharśī,* m. *pharas,* bg. h. nep. *pharsā.*

1728. පොලඹනවා **polaṁbanavā,** v., prt., *pelaṁbuvā,* to instigate, invite, impel (Cl : to desire, decoy, cheat, induce). — Sk. *pra-* + √*labh, pra-lambhayati* cheats, deceives, P. *pa-lambhēti* id.

— පොවනවා **povanavā,** v., see s.v. **bonavā.**

1729. පොවුවා **povuvā,** s., st. ff. *pov, pō,* young animal. — P. *pōa,* P., Sk. *pōtaka* ; kśm. *pūtu,* m. *povā,* oṛ. *puā,* bg. *poyā,* h. *poā,* nep. *pothi,* pj. *poā* (in the MIAVs of young animals or plants).

1730. පොසොන් **poson**[1], s., flowers (pl.). — Sk. *prasūna.*

1731. පොසොන් **poson**[2], s., name of the month June-July. *poson-vī* variety of paddy (harvest in June-July). — <**puva-savana,* P. *pubba* + *sāvana,* Sk. *pūrva* + *śrāvaṇa.*

— පොහො **poho**[1], s., see **pōya.**

1732. පොහො **poho**[2], a., able, competent. — Pk. *pahu,* P. *pabhū,* Sk. *prabhu.* ? lw. Pk. see s.v. *pāna.*

1733. පොළ **poḷa,** s., boil, tumor, cataract on the eye; spot. — Pk. *phōḍa(a),* P. *phōṭa(ka),* Sk. *sphōṭa(ka)* ; si. *phoṛa,* g. *phoḍlo,* m. *phoḍ,* oṛ. *phoṛi,* bg. h. pj. *phoṛā,* nep. *phor, phoro.*

1734. **පොළඟා polaṅgā,** s., st. f. *poloṅ*, general name for the viper. — According to De Lanerolle < *pola* (meaning spot) + *aṅga* having a spotted body; not = P. *pataṅga* which is in Sinh. *palaṅgā*.

1735. **පොළනවා poḷanavā,** v., prt., *peḷuvā*, to winnow, sift. — Pk. *phōḍēi*, P. *phōṭēti*, Sk. √*sphuṭ*, caus. *sphōṭayati*; kśm. *phōrun*.

1736. **පොළොව poḷova, පොළව poḷava,** s., st. f. *poḷō*, earth. — Pk. *puḍhavi*, P. *puṭhavī*, *paṭhavī*, Sk. *pṛthivī*.

— **පෝ pō,** s., see **povuvā.**

1737. **පෝය pōya, පොහොය pohoya,** st. ff. *poho*, *pehe*, *pō*, any of the four quarter days of the moon, the Buddhist holy day of the week. *poho-dina*, *pō-dina* id.; see *pehe-vas*. — Pk. *pōsaha*, P. *upōsatha*, Sk. *upavasatha*.

බ B

1738. **බඟහර baṅgahara,** s., toddy, intoxicant. — *baṅga* = Pk. *bhaṅgā*, P. *bhaṅga*, Sk. *bhaṅgā* hemp, Caunabis sativa; kśm. *baṅga*, si. *bhaṅga*, g. m. *bhāṃg*, oṛ. *bhāṅga*, ass. bg. *bhāṅ*, b. h. *bhāṃg*, nep. *bhāṅ*, pj. *bhaṅg*.

1739 **බට baṭa,** a. pprt., descended, sunk. *baṭa-hira* set sun, west. — Pk., P. *bhaṭṭha*, Sk. *bhraṣṭa* (√*bhraṃś*). See *bahinavā*.

1740. **බටු baṭu,** s., egg-plant, Solanum melagena. — Sk. *bhaṇṭākī*, (P., Sk. *bhaṇḍākī*). See also *vam-baṭu*.

1741. **බඩ baḍa,** s., belly, abdomen, womb. *baḍa-daru* pregnant. Original meaning 'pot': in *baḍu-hala* pottery, *baḍa-hälayā* potter. — Pk., P. *bhaṇḍa*, Sk. *bhāṇḍa* pot; kśm. *bāna*, si. *bhānī*, g. *bhāṃḍuṃ*, m. *bhāṃḍ*, oṛ. *bhāṇḍa*, bg. *bhāṃṛ*, h. *bhāṃṛā*, nep. *bhāṃro*, pj. *bhāṃḍā*.

1742. **බඩහැරියා baḍahäriyā, බඩැරියා baḍäriyā,** s., storekeeper, treasurer. — Pk. *bhaṇḍâgāria*, P. *bhaṇḍâgārika*, Sk. *bhāṇḍâgārika*; g. *bhaṃḍārī*, m. *bhāṃḍārī*, oṛ. *bhaṇḍāri*, ass. *bhaṃrāli*, bg. *bhāṃrāri*, b. *bhaṃrārī*, h. pj. *bhaṇḍārī*, nep. *bhaṃrāri*.

1743. **බඩුව baḍuva,** s., st. f. *baḍu*, article, thing; pl. *baḍu* articles, goods, effects. — P. *bhaṇḍaka*, cf. Sk. *bhāṇḍikā*.

1744. **බණ baṇa[1],** s., arrow. — Pk., P., Sk. *bāṇa*; si. *bāṇu*, g. m. *bāṇ*, oṛ. *bāṇa*, ass. bg. h. nep. *bān*, pj. *bāṇ*.

1745. **බණ baṇa[2],** s., recitation, word; the word of the Buddha. *b.-kiyanavā* to preach. — P., Sk. *bhāṇa*.

1746. **බණනවා baṇanavā, බණි° baṇi°,** v., prt. *biṇuvā*, to speak, deliver an address. Caus. *baṇavanavā*, prt. *bäṇevuvā*, to speak to, address. The v. *baṇinavā*, prt. *biṇuvā*, means 'to abuse, revile'. — Pk. *bhaṇaï*, P. *bhaṇati*, Sk. √ *bhaṇ*, *bhaṇati*; g. *bhaṇvuṃ*, oṛ. *bhaṇibā*, ass. *bhaniba*, h. *bhannā*, nep. *bhannu*.

1747. බණවර **baṇa-vara,** s., a turn at reading *baṇa,* a portion for recital. *pirit-satar-baṇvar* the four sections of the paritta, EpZ I 48^{3a} 10th c. — P. *bhāṇa-vāra.*

1748. බත **bata,** s., st. f. *bat,* boiled rice, meal. *bat-piṅḍa* lump of b. r.— Pk., P. *bhatta,* Sk. *bhakta* ; kśm. *bata,* si. *bhatu,* g. m. *bhāt,* oṛ. *bhāta,* ass. bg. b. h. nep. *bhāt,* pj. *bhattā.*

1749. බද **bada,** a. pprt., bound, joined, united : in cpds. belonging to. — Pk., P., Sk. *baddha* ; si. *badho,* pj. l. *baddhā.* See *bañdinavā.* In early mediaeval Sinh. *bad* alternates with *baj.*

— බදන **badana,** s., see **baduna.**

1750. බදිනවා **badinavā,** v., prt. *bäddā,* to fry, grill, roast. Intr. *bädenavā,* prt. *bäduṇā,* to become fried. — Pk. *bhajjaï,* P. *bhajjati,* Sk. √*bhrajj, bhṛjjati;* kśm. *bazun,* si. *bhujaṇu,* m. *bhājṇeṃ,* oṛ. *bhājibā,* ass. *bhāziba,* bg. *bhājā,* h. *bhājnā,* pj. *bhujjṇā.* T, s.v. *bhāji.*

1751. බදුන **baduna,** බදන **badana,** s., vessel, utensil, pot. — Pk. *bhāaṇa,* *bhāṇa,* P., Sk. *bhājana.*

1752. බදුරු **baduru,** බඳුරු **bañduru,** a., good, fortunate, auspicious. — Slw. Sk. *bhadra* (with split *-dr-*). Or ? = Sk. *bandhura* delightful, handsome.

1753. බද්ද **badda,** s., st. f. *badu,* tax, lease, rent. *badu-denavā* to give on lease. — Sk. *bandhaka* pledge ; g. *bāṃdho,* m. bg. *bāṃdhā,* nep. *bāṃdho.*

1754. බඳ **bañda,** s., body. — Pk., P., Sk. *bandha.* As to the meaning 'body' see BR, s.v. *bandha* 12. The corresponding words in the MIAVs m. bg. b. h. nep. *bāṃdh,* generally mean 'embankment, dam'.

1755. බඳිනවා **bañdinavā,** v., prt. *bändā* (<**bäñddā*), to bind, tie. Intr. *bäñdenavā,* prt. *bäñduṇā,* to become bound together, adhere ; to bind one's self. — Pk. *bandhaï,* P. *bandhati,* Sk. √*bandh* (*badhnāti*) ; si. *bandhaṇu,* g. *bāṃdhvuṃ,* m. *bāṃdhṇeṃ,* oṛ. *bāndhibā,* ass. *bāndhiba,* bg *bāṃdhā,* b. *bāṃdhab,* h. *bāṃdhnā,* nep. *bāṃdhnu,* pj. *bannhṇā,* l. *bannhaṇ.*

1756. -බඳු **-bañdu,** a., such, such like. *e-bañdu* such as that. — Pk., P., Sk. *bandhu* relative.

1757. බප **bapa**[1]**,** s., father. — Pk. *bappa* ; g. *bāpā,* oṛ. *bāpa,* m. ass. bg. h. nep. *bāp,* l. *bāpū.*

1758. බප **bapa**[2]**,** s., st. f. *bap,* tear. — Pk. *bappha,* P. *bappa,* Sk. *bāṣpa* ; si. *bāpha,* g. m. *bāph,* oṛ. *bāmpha,* h. nep. *bāph.* Gr. L 31.

1759. බඹගොස **bam̆ba-gosa,** s., st. f. *-gos,* excellent voice, the voice of the Buddha. — P. *brahma-ghōsa.*

1760. බඹය **bam̆baya,** s., st. f. *bam̆ba,* a fathom (measure of the extended arms). — P. *byāma,* alternating with *vyāma* (Sk. *vyāma*). See *vāma.*

1761. බඹරය **bam̆baraya,** බමරය **bamaraya,** s., st. f. °*ra*, humming top. — Sk. *bhramaraka*.

1762. බඹරා **bam̆barā,** බමරා **bamarā,** s., st. f. °*ra*, large black bee, wasp. — Pk., P. *bhamara*, Sk. *bhramara* ; kśm. *bombur*, si. *bhaum̥ru*, g. *bhamar*, m. *bhom̥var*, or. *bhaam̥ra*, ass. *bhomorā*, bg. *bhomar*, h. *bhaum̥rā*, nep. *bhumaro*, *bhum̥varo* etc., pj. *bham̥var*.

1763. බඹලොව **bam̆ba-lova,** s., st. f. -*lō*, the Brahma world. — Pk. *bambha-lōa*, P., Sk. *brahma-lōka*.

1764. බඹසර **bam̆ba-sara,** a., celibate. *bam̆basara-vasa* living in the state of celibacy. — Pk. *bambha-cāri*, P., Sk. *brahma-cārin*.

1765. බඹා **bam̆bā,** s., st. f. *bam̆ba*, the god Brahmā. In cpds. best, excellent: *bam̆ba-gosa* excellent voice. — Pk. *bambha*, P. *brahmā*, Sk. *brahman*. See *bamuṇā*. Cf. *baram*.

1766. බඹුරු **bam̆buru[1],** a., twisted or curled, curly, as hair. — Sk. *bhramaraka* ; si. *bhaum̥rī*, g. *bhamar*, m. *bhom̥r*, h. *bhaum̥rī*, nep. *bhumari*, pj. *bham̥var* (various meanings). See *bam̆baraya*.

1767. බඹුරු **bam̆buru[2],** බමර **bamara,** a., tawny. — Probably Slw. Sk. *babhru* brown (with split aspirate). Cf. m. *bhurā* (Bl), nep. *bhuro* (T).

1768. බම **bama,** s., whirling, giddiness. — P. *bhama*, Sk. *bhrama*.

1769. බමකරුවා **bama-karuvā,** s., st. f. °*ru*, turner. — P. *bhama-kāra* + -*ka* ; Cf. Sk. *bhrama-karman*.

1770. බමණ(ය) **bamaṇa(ya),** s., st. f. °*ṇa*, going round, revolving, whirling. — Pk., P. *bhamaṇa*, Sk. *bhramaṇa*.

1771. බමනවා **bamanavā,** v., prt. *bämurā*, to go round, revolve, whirl. Intr. *bämenavā*, prt. *bämuṇā*, to revolve, whirl. — Pk. *bhamaï*, P. *bhamati*, Sk. √*bhram*, *bhramati* or *bhrāmyati* ; kśm. *bramun*, si. *bham̥vaṇu*, g. *bham̥vum̥*, m. *bhom̥vṇem̥*, h. *bhaunā*, pj. *bhaum̥ṇā*, l. *bhem̥vaṇ*. T, s.v. *bhayāunu*.

— බමර **bamara,** °රය **°raya,** °රා **°rā,** ss., see s.vv. **bam̆buru[1-2], bam̆baraya, bam̆barā.**

1772. බමුණා **bamuṇā,** s., st. f. °*ṇu*, brahmin. *bämiṇī* a brahmin woman. — P. *bambhaṇā*, °*ṇī*, P., Sk. *brāhmaṇa*, °*ṇī* ; si. *bām̥bhaṇu*, °*bhiṇī*, g. *bāmaṇ*, °*mṇī*, m. *bāmaṇ*, °*mhṇī*, ass. *bāmun*, bg. *bāman*, °*mani*, bg. *bāman* or *bābhan*, h. *bāmhan*, °*mhni*, nep. *bāun* or *bāhun* or *bāvan*, °*ni*, pj. *bāmhaṇ* or *barāhmaṇ*, °*ṇī*. See *bam̆bā*, *baram*.

— බය **baya,** s., see **biya.**

1773. බර **bara[1],** num., twelve. — Pk. *bārasa*, °*ha*, P. *bārasa* ; kśm. *bāh*, si. *bāram̥ham̥*, g. *bār*, m. *bārā*, or. ass. bg. *bārā*, h. *bārah*, nep. *bāra(h)*, pj. *bārām̥*, l. *bāhrām̥*. Gr. L 9. Cf. *doḷaha*.

1774. බර **bara²**, බැර **bära**, a., heavy, weighty, important; s., weight, load.— Pk., P., Sk. *bhāra* ; g. m. *bhār*, oṛ. *bhāra*, ass. bg. h. nep. pj. l. *bhār*.

1775. බරණා **baraṇā**, s., st. f. °*ṇa*, serpent. — Sk. √ *bhur*, *bhurati* moves rapidly ; cf. *bhuraṇa*, *bhuraṇyu*.

1776. බරම් **baram**, s., the god Brahmā.—P. *brahmā*, Sk. *brahman*. Cf. *bam̆bā*.

1777. බරවය **baravaya**, s., elephantiasis. — P. *bhāra-pādatā*.

1778. බරියා **bariyā**, s., carrier, porter.— Pk. *bhāria*, P., Sk. *bhārin*, *bhārika* ; ass. bg. *bhāri*, h. *bhārī*, nep. *bhāriyā*.

1779. බරුව **baruva**, s., st. f. *baru*, a weight attached to a fishing net. — P., Sk. *bhāraka* load.

1780. බල් **bal**, a., young (Ruv 271), ignorant, foolish. — Pk., P., Sk. *bāla* ; kśm. *bāla*, si. *bāru*, g. m. *bāḷ*, oṛ. *bāḷa*, bg. *bāl*, h. pj. *bāla*, l. *bāl*. T, s.v. *bālakha*.

1781. බල **bala**, s., cave, hole (Cl). — Pk., P., Sk. *bila* ; si. *biru*, m. *bīḷ*, bg. h. *bil*.

1782. බලනවා **balanavā**, v., prt. *bäluvā*, to look, view, superintend.— Pk. *bhalaï* (Hem 4.74 ; Pischel, Hem II 140) remembers, Sk. √*bhal*, *bhalatē* ; g. *bhāḷvuṃ* to observe, m. *bhalṇeṃ*, *bhārṇeṃ* to charm, oṛ. *bhāḷibā*, ass. *bhāliba*, h. *bhālnā*, pj. *bhalṇā*, l. *bhālaṇ*, nep. *bhāl* heed, attention.

1783. බලය **balaya**, s., st. f. *bala*, strength, power. — ? lw. Pk., P., Sk. *bala* ; kśm. *bal*, g. m. *baḷ*, oṛ. *baḷa*, ass. bg. h. nep. pj. *bal*.

1784. බලස **balasa** (Ca), s., fish-hook.— ? lw. Pk., P. *balisa*, Sk. *baliśa*. Cf. *biḷiya*.

1785. බලා **balā**, s., a species of crane. — P., Sk. *baḷākā*.

1786. බල්ලා **ballā**, s., st. f. *balu*, dog.— Sk. *bhalluka* bear or dog ; m. *bhālū(k)*, oṛ. *bhālu*, ass. bg. *bhāluk*, bg. *bhāul*, h. *bhālū*, nep. *bālu*. Sinh. *balu-mäkkā* flea, cf. *mäkkā*.

1787. බව **bava**, s., st. ff. *bava*, *bav*, *bäv*, the fact that, that. *hulan̆ga tada bava däka* seeing that the wind was strong. — Pk., P., Sk. *bhāva* ; kśm. *bāv*, si. *bhāu*, g. m. *bhāv*, oṛ. bg. *bhāu*, h. *bhāv*, nep. pj. *bhāu*.

— බස **basa**, s., බසිනවා **basinavā**, v., see s. vv. **baha, bahinavā.**

1788. බහ **baha**, බස **basa**, s., st. f. *bas*, word, speech, language. — Pk., P. *bhāsā*, Sk. *bhāṣā* ; nep. *bhās*.

1789. බහල **bahala**, a., much, many. — Pk., P., Sk. *bahula*.

1790. බහිනවා **bahinavā,** බසි° **basi°**, or බැහෙනවා **bähenavā,** බැසෙ° **bäse°**, prt. *bässā*, *bähuṇā*, to descend, to set (as the sun etc.). Caus. *basvanavā*, *bass°*, double caus. *bassavanavā*, prt. *bässevuvā*, to cause to descend, lower. *basnā-ira* setting sun, west; s. *basnāva* ebb, ebb tide. — Pk. *bhaṃsaï*, *bhassaï*, P. *bhassati*, Sk. √*bhraṃś*, *bhraṃśatē*, *bhraśyati*; nep. *bhāsnu*.

— බළ **baḷa,** s., see s.v. **beḷē.**

1791. බළලා **baḷalā,** s., st. f. *baḷal*, cat. — Pk. *biḍāla*, *bilāla*, *birālaa*, P. *biḷāra*, *°la*, Sk. *biḍāla*; kśm. *brōru*, g. *bilāḍo*, oṛ. *biṛāḷa*, *bilāra*, ass. *birāl*, bg. *biṛāl*, *bilāl*, h. *bilār*, *billāṛ*, nep. *birālo*. Gr. L 21. Sinh. *baḷal-luṇu*, lit. cat-salt, i.e. saltpetre, nitre, cf. P. *bilāla* a kind of salt.

1792. බා **ba[1],** s., arm, hand. *pärakumbā* nom. pr. = *Parākramabāhu*. — Pk., P., Sk. *bāhu*; kśm. *bāū*, si. *bāṃha*, g. *bāhu*, m. *bāhī*, oṛ. *bāhā*, bg. *bāh*, b. *bāṃhuṃ*, h. pj. l. *bāṃh*, nep. *bāṃh*, *bāṃhāṃ*.

— බා **bā[2],** a., see **biya.**

1793. බා **bā[3],** s., share, part. — Pk. *bhāa*, P., Sk. *bhāga*; l. *bhā*. Cf. Sinh. *bāya*, s., half.

1794. බානවා **bānavā,** v., prt. *bāvā*, to lower, set down; to cut (the hair). — Seems to be contraction of **bahanavā* which is derived from Sk. *bhraṃśayati*, caus. of √*bhraṃś*.

1795. බැගින් **bägin,** adv., at the rate of, each. — <**bhaggēna*; cf. Pk., P. *bhagga*, Sk. *bhāgya*; si. *bhāgu*, g. ass. bg. h. nep. pj. *bhāg*.

1796. බැති **bäti,** s., st. f. *bäti*, devotion, piety. — Pk., P. *bhatti*, Sk. *bhakti*; si. *bhati*, g. *bhāt*, m. h. *bhāṃt*, h. nep. *bhāṃti* ('sort, manner').

1797. බැම **bäma,** s., eyebrow. — Pk. *bhamuha*, P. *bhamu(ka)*; kśm. *bum*, g. *bhavuṃ*, m. *bhaṃvaī*, bg. *bhomā*, h. *bhauṃ*, pj. *bhauṃh*.

1798. බැම්ම **bämma,** s., bond, ligament; retaining wall; dam. — <**bäňdma* < *bäňduma*; v. *baňdinavā*.

— බැර **bära,** a., s., see **bara.**

1799. බැරි **bäri,** a., unable, impossible. — In my Sinh. Etym[1], I have derived *bäri* from Sk. *apārya* (cf. *tad-vaktuṃ na pāryatē* it is impossible to say that, cf. BR., s.v. *par[2]*). But in this case we should rather expect **väri*. Cf., however, *burul*, *buhuru*, *beṭṭa*, *boruva*. Is perhaps *bäri*=P., Sk. *bhārika* heavy?

1800. බැරිණි **bäriṇi,** s., st. f. *°ṇi*, pregnant woman. — Sk. *bhāriṇī*, fem. of *bhārin* bearing.

1801. බැවින් **bävin,** conj., because, lit. from the fact. *saturan näti bävin* because he had no enemies, EpZ I 131[19], 12th c. — Instr. of *bava*, Sk. *bhāvēna*.

— බැහැ **bähä,** a., see **bā.**

1802. බැහැර **bähära,** a., outer, exterior; s., exterior place. *b°-yanavā* to go out. — Pk., P. *bāhira* (cf. Sk. *bahis*); si. *bāhari,* g. m. *bāher,* oṛ. *bāhāra,* ass. bg. h. *bāhir,* nep. *bāira.* See *bǟrak.*

1803. බැළය **bäḷaya,** s., st. f. *bäḷa,* hire, wage, pay; s. *bäḷayā* worker for wages. — Pk. *bhāḍaa,* Sk. *bhāṭa, bhāṭi*; si. *bhāṛo, bhāṛi,* g. *bhāḍ, bhāḍuṃ,* m. *bhāḍ, bhāḍeṃ,* bg. h. pj. *bhāṛ, bhāṛā,* nep. *bhārā.*

1804. බෑ **bǟ,** බැහැ **bähä,** a., impossible. *ma-ṭa mēka karan-ṭa bǟ* it is impossible for me to do this, I cannot do this. — ? Pk. *bāhia,* P., Sk. *bādhita* (√*bādh*) abolished, restricted.

1805. බෑනා **bǟnā,** බැහැනා **bähänā,** s., nephew, sister's son, son-in-law. — Pk. *bhāiṇēa,* °*ṇejja,* °*nijja,* P. *bhāgineyya,* Sk. *bhāginēya*; si. *bhāṇiju,* °*ṇejo,* g. *bhāṇo, bhāṇiyo,* °*ṇej,* m. *bhācā,* oṛ. *bhāṇiji,* h. *bhāṃjā,* nep. *bhānij,* pj. *bhāṇjā,* l. *bhāṇeā.*

— බෑය **bǟya,** s., see s.v. **bā[3].**

1806. බෑයා **bǟyā,** s., st. f. *bǟ,* brother. — Pk. *bhāā, bhāi, bhāu, bhāua,* P. *bhātar, bhātika, bhātuka,* Sk. *bhrātṛ, bhrātṛka*; kśm. *bōyu,* si. *bhāī, bhāu,* m. *bhāī, bhāū,* oṛ. ass. bg. *bhāi,* h. pj. *bhāī,* nep. *bhāi,* l. *bhrā.*

1807. බෑරක් **bǟrak,** s., an exterior place. °*ka,* °*ka-ṭa* to an ex. pl., in *bǟrak-da* or *b°-yanava-da* are you going far ? where to ? = where are you going ? (polite question). — Contraction of *bähära* + indef. art. *-ak.*

1808. බික් **bik,** s., 1) community of bhikkhus, 2) mendicant, bhikkhu. —Pk., P. *bhikkhā, bhikkhu,* Sk. *bhikṣā, bhikṣu*; kśm. *bēcha,* si. *bhikhyā,* g. *bhīkh,* m. *bhīk,* oṛ. *bhika,* bg. nep. *bhik,* h. *bhīkh,* pj. *bhikkh,* Gr. I 3.

1809. බික්සඟ **bik-saňga,** s., community of bhikkhus, Buddhist monks. — P. *bhikkhu-saṅgha.*

1810. බිඟු **biňgu[1],** බිඟ **biňga,** s., name of a plant, Eclipta alba (Ca) or Verbesina prostrata (Cl). — Pk. *bhaṅgaraa,* Sk. *bhṛṅgāra, bhṛṅgarāja*; h. *bhaṃgrā, bhaṃgrā, bhaṃgrāj,* g. *bhāṃgro.* Cf. T, s.v. *bhāṅro.*

1811. බිඟු **biňgu[2],** s., wasp, large black bee. *biňgu-peḷa* row or line or swarm of wasps. — Pk. *bhiṅga,* Sk. *bhṛṅga*; h. *bhuṅgā, bhaṅgā.*

1812. බිත **bita,** s., st. ff. *bitu, bit,* wall. *bitu-sitiyama* wall picture, fresco. — Pk., P., Sk. *bhitti*; si. *bhito,* g. m. *bhīṃt,* bg. *bhit,* b. *bhīt.* h. *bhīt, bhīṃt,* nep. *bhit.*

— බිදි **bidi,** s., see s.v. **budinavā.**

1813. බිඳ **biňda,** s., st. f. *biňdu,* drop (of any fluid). — Pk., P., Sk. *bindu*; kśm. *bimd,* si. g. bg. h. *bimdu,* m. *bimd.*

1814. බිඳිනවා **biňdinavā,** v. tr., prt. *bindā,* to break, fracture. Caus. *biňdavanavā, biňdu°,* prt. *biňdevuvā,* and double caus. *bindavanavā* (< **biňdd° <*biňdv°*), prt. *bindevuvā,* to cause to break ; intr. *biňdenavā,* prt. *biňduṇā,* to break, crack.—Pk. *bhindaï,* P. *bhindati,* Sk. √*bhid, bhinatti.*

1815. බිබිළ **bibiḷa,** බිබුළ **bibuḷa,** බුබුළ **bubuḷa,** s., st. ff. *bibiḷi,* °*buḷu,* bubble, pimple, pustule; water-spring (*bibuḷa*). — Pk. M. *bubbua,* P. *bubbuḷa(ka),* Sk. *budbuda.*

1816. බිඹු **bimbu,** s., disk (of the sun or moon) ; image, statue.— Pk., P., Sk. *bimba.*

1817. බිම **bima,** s., st. f. *bim* (*bin, biṃ*), ground, floor. *bim-mala* mushroom, lit. ground-flower ; *bin-*(or *biṃ-*)*taṁburu* see s.v. *taṁbara* ; *bin-*(or *biṃ-*) *geya* underground chamber, tunnel. — Pk., P., Sk. *bhūmi* ; kśm. *bum,* si. *bhuṃi,* g. *bhoṃ, bhoṃy,* m. *bhūṃ,* or. *bhuiṃ,* ass. *bhuṃi,* bg. *bhui,* h. *bhūṃ, bhūīṃ,* nep. *bhuiṃ,* pj. *bhūṃ,* l. *bhoeṃ.*

1818. බිය **biya,** බය **baya,** s., st. ff. *biya, baya, bā,* fear. *biya-pat* frightened. — Pk., P., Sk. *bhaya* ; kśm. *bay,* si. *bhai,* g. *bhe,* m. *bheṃ,* or. *bhe,* bg. *bhay,* h. pj. *bhai.*

1819. බියල්ල **biyalla,** s., st. f. *biyali,* division of a seed, seed globe. *bayali* beans, EpZ III 177[6], 4th c., PARANAVITANA, p. 184-5.—P., Sk. *bidala.*

1820. බියෙස් **biyes,** a., near, neighbouring. — P. *abhyāsa,* Sk. *abhyāśa.*

1821. බිරි **biri,** බිරු **biru,** a., frightful, terrific. *biru-sara* bear, lit. having a terrific voice (Ca). — Pk., P., Sk. *bhīru.*

1822. බිරිය **biriya,** s., f., wife. — P. *bhariyā,* Sk. *bhāryā.*

1823. බිලියම **bili-yama,** s., st. f. °*-yam,* making offerings (to propitiate demons or spirits). — P. *bali-kamma,* Sk. *bali-karman.*

1824. බිල්ල **billa,** s., st. f. *bili,* offering (to demons or spirits). *bili-puṭuvā* crow, lit. nourished by bili.— Pk., P., Sk. *bali* + suff. *-ka* ; kśm. *bal,* g. *baḷī,* m. *baḷ,* or. *baḷi,* ass. bg. nep. *bali,* h. *bal,* pj. *balī.*

1825. බිල්ලා **billā,** s., kidnapper, bogey to frighten children. Sk. *bhilla* name of a wild mountain tribe + *-ka.*

1826. බිසක් **bisak** (Ca), s., doctor. — ? Slw. P. *bhisakka.*

1827. බිසව **bisava,** s., st. ff. *bisav, bisō,* queen.— ? <Sk. *abhisēcitā* inaugurated ; cf. Pk. *abhisēa,* P. *abhisēka,* Sk. *abhiṣēka.*

1828. බිස්ස **bissa,** s., st. ff. *bisi, bihi,* rug, bundle of straw as door-mat (Ruv 323). — Pk., P. *bhisī,* Sk. *bṛsī* ; m. *bhīṃs.*

1829. බිහි **bihi,** adv., a., outer, outside. *bihi-venavā* to be born. — P. *bahi(ṃ),* Sk. *bahis.* See s.vv. *bähära, bārak.*

1830. බිහිදොර **bihi-dora,** s., o u t e r d o o r, p o r t i c o in front of a house. — Sk. *bahir-dvāra*.

1831. බිහිණි **bihinī,** s., st. f. °*ni*, e l d e r s i s t e r; also *buhunā*, °*naṇī*. — P., Sk. *bhaginī*; kśm. *beñe*, si. *bheṇu*, g. *bahen*, m. *bahīṇ*, oṛ. *bhauṇi*, ass. *bhani*, bg. *bain*, h. *bahin*, *bahnī*, nep. *baini*, pj. *bhaiṇ*, l. *bhēṇ*.

1832. බිහිරි **bihiri,** බිරි **bīri,** a., d e a f; s. °*rā*. °*rī* deaf person (male, female).— Pk. *bahira*, P., Sk. *badhira*; g. *beheruṃ*, m. *bahirā*, bg. *baherā*, h. *bahirā*, nep. *bairo*.

1833. බිළිය **biḷiya,** s., st. f. *biḷi*, b a i t. *biḷi-kaṭuva* bait-hook, fish-hook. — Pk. *baḍisa*, *balisa*, Sk. *baḍiśa*; ass. *barahi*, bg. *baṛsi*, nep. *balsi*, *balchi*. Cf. *balasa*.

— බී **bī,** බීමත් **bī-mat,** see s.v. **bonavā.**

1834. බුත් **but,** s., e a t i n g (H. Jayatilaka, Eḷu-akārādiya=*välaňdīma*). — Pk., P. *bhutti*, Sk. *bhukti*.

1835. බුදිනවා **budinavā,** v., t o e a t. s. *bidi* e a t i n g, m e a l. — Pk. *bhuñjaï*, P. *bhuñjati*, Sk. √*bhuj*, *bhuñjatē*. — *bidi* ? <MInd. **bhuñjita*.

1836. බුදු **budu,** s., st. f. *budu*, *but*, t h e B u d d h a. Generally the c. obl. pl. *budun* is used to denote the B. Cf. *but-saraṇa* title of a book ' Refuge in the B°.' — Pk., P., Sk. *buddha*.

1837. බුදුබව **budu-bava,** s., B u d d h a h o o d. — P. *buddha-bhāva*.

1838. බුන් **bun,** a. pprt., 1) b r o k e n, 2) e x p a n d e d (as flowers). *sun-bun* see s.v. *sun*; *bun-käbali* broken bits, refuse. — Pk., P., Sk. *bhinna* (√*bhid*).

1839. බුන්න **bunna,** s., st. f. *bun*, r o o t of a tree (Ruv 199 *bun*).— Pk. *bundha*, P. *bunda*, Sk. *budhna*; kśm. *bon* down, g. *buṃdhuṃ* bottom of top, m. *buṃdh*. Cf. T, s.v. *bundi*.

— බුබුළු **bubuḷu,** s., see **bibiḷa.**

1840. බුමු **-bumu,** s., s t o r e y, in *de-bumu*, *tun-bumu* two-, three-storeyed etc.— P. *bhūmaka* (*dve-bh°*, *ti-bh°*).

1841. බුරුල් **burul,** a., s l a c k, l o o s e, l a x; s. *burula* slackness. — Pk., P., Sk. *virala*. But b ? Cf. *buhuru*, *beṭṭa*, *boruva*.

1842. බුලත් **bulat,** s., b e t e l (plant or leaf). — Metathesis of **tabul* (Roḍiyā-dial. *tabala*), Pk. *tambōla*, P. *tambūla*, °*lī*, Sk. *tāmbūla*, °*lī*; g. *taṃbol*, m. *tāṃbūl*, oṛ. *tāmbuḷa*, ass. *tāmol*, bg. *tāmbul*, h. *taṃbol*, nep. *tamol*, *taṃbol*.

1843. බුස **busa,** s., c h a f f of corn; d r y c o w - d u n g; s o u r c u r d s; w e a l t h. — Pk., P. *bhusa*, Sk. *busa*, *buśa*, *buṣa*; kśm. *bosu*, si. *buhu*, g. *bhuṃsuṃ*, m. *bhūṃs*, oṛ. *bhusi*, bg. *bhusā*, *bhusi*, b. *bhūs*, h. *bhus*, *bhūṃs*, nep. *bhus*, pj. *bhoh*, *bhussī*, l. *bhoh*.

— බුහු **buhu,** a., see **bō.**

— බුහුනා **buhunā,** °නණී °**naṇī,** s., see s.v. **bihinī.**

1844. බුහුමන් **buhuman,** s., great honour, respect. *b°-karanavā* to reverence. — Pk. *bahumāṇa,* P., Sk. *bahumāna.*

1845. බුහුරු **buhuru,** s., st. f., hole, pit. — ? Pk., P., Sk. *vivara*; h. *bīar,* T, Add. s.v. *bārnu.* But *b* ? Cf. *burul, beṭṭa, boruva.*

1846. බූ **bū**[1], s., world.— lw. Sk. *bhū* in cpds. as *bū-nā* lord of the world, Śiva, etc.

1847. බූ **bū**[2], s., demon. — Pk. *bhūa,* Pk., Sk. *bhūta.*

1848. බූ **bū**[3], a., hairy (of plants), hispid. In names of plants as *bū-avariya* hairy-indigo, Indigofera hirsuta, etc. (Ca, App.). — Bg. *bhuyā* mildew, b. *bhūā* a hairy worm, h. *bhūā̤* caterpillar, nep. *bhuvā* the fine down on the body of a young animal (T).

1849. බෙට්ට **beṭṭa,** s., st. f. *beṭi,* ball or lump of dung. — Sk. *viṣṭā*; si. *viṭhi,* m. *vīṭ* disgust, h. *bīṭh, bīṭ,* pj. *biṭṭh, viṭṭh,* l. *viṭṭh.* (T, s.v. *biṭulo*). But *b* ? Cf. *burul, buhuru, boruva.*

1850. බෙඬිවල **beňḍivala,** බෙඬු° **beňḍu°**, s., staff, pike. — Pk. *bhiṇḍivāla,* P. *bhindipāla,* Sk. *bhiṇḍipāla* or *°nd°.*

1851. බෙම් **bem,** s., demon, devil. — Pk., P., Sk. *bhīma* dreadful.

1852. බෙය **beya,** s., st. f. *bē,* division, destruction. — Pk. *bhēa,* P., Sk. *bhēda.* Cf. *bēdaya.*

1853. බෙරය **beraya,** s., st. f. *bera,* drum. *bera-kārayā* tom-tom beater.— P., Sk. *bhēri.*

1854. බෙරවායා **bera-vāyā,** s., st. f. *bera-vā,* drummer. — <**bhēri-vādaka.* Cf. P. *bhēriṃ vādēti,* Jā II 110[7].

1855. බෙලි **beli,** s., wood-apple, Aegle Marmelos. — Pk., P. *billa,* Sk. *bilva*; kśm. *bil,* g. *bīluṃ,* m. *bel,* oṛ. *bela,* ass. bg. *bel,* h. *bīl, bel,* nep. *bel.* The forms with *e* probably from **bella* = Sk. *bāilva.*

1856. බෙහෙද **beheda,** °ත **°ta,** s., st. f. *behet,* drug, medicament. *behet-velendā* druggist, apothecary. — P. *bhēsajja,* Sk. *bhāisajya.*

1857. බෙළේ **beḷē,** s., st. f. *baḷa,* fighter, soldier. *baḷa-äṇiya* army. — Pk. *bhaḍa,* P., Sk. *bhaṭa.*

1858. බේදය **bēdaya,** s., st. f. *bēda,* division, variance, discord, schism. — P., Sk. *bhēda* (Slw). Cf. *beya.*

1859. බේරනවා **bēranavā,** v., prt. *bēruvā,* to separate, distinguish, to sort.— < *bē-karanavā* (HSm).

1860. බොක්ක **bokka,** s., st. f. *boku,* stomach, belly; pl. *boku* intestines. — T, s.v. *boknu,* compares Sk. *bukkā* (lex.); kśm. *bokh,* si. *bukī,* m. *bokā,* oṛ. *buka,* ass. bg. *buk,* l. *bukkī.* The words mean 'heart' or 'kidney.'

1861. බොදු **bodu** (Ca), s., boiled rice.— Pk., P. *bhojja,* Sk. *bhōjya*; oṛ. *bhoja.* ass. bg. h. nep. pj. *bhoj.*

1862. බොදුන **boduna,** s., st. f. *bodun,* food, meal. *bodun-paya*[2] food-dish, plate, bowl. — Pk. *bhōaṇa,* P., Sk. *bhōjana.*

1863. බොනවා **bonavā,** v., prt. *bivuvā, bīvā,* to drink. Ger. *bī* having drunk, *bī-mat* (see *mat*[1]) drunk, intoxicated. Caus. *povanavā,* prt. *pevuvā,* to cause to drink. — Pk. *piaï,* P. *pibati,* Sk. √*pā, pibati* ; kśm. *pivun,* si. *piaṇu,* g. *pīvuṃ,* m. *piṇeṃ,* oṛ. *piibā,* ass. *piba,* bg. *piyā,* hi. *pīnā,* nep. *piunu,* pj. *pīṇā,* l. *pīvaṇ.*

1864. බොරුව **boruva,** s., st. f. *boru,* falsehood, lie. *boru-kiyanavā* to tell lies. — Derived from Sk. *aparādha* by P. Goldschmidt. But *b* ? Cf. *burul, buhuru, beṭṭa.* See also *varada.*

1865. බෝ **bō**[1], බොහෝ **bohō,** බුහු **buhu,** a., much, many. *bō-karanavā* to multiply ; *buhu-man,* q.v. — Pk. *bahua,* P., Sk. *bahu(ka)* ; si. *bahūṃ,* g. oṛ. ass. bg. pj. *bahu,* l. *bahūṃ* ; cf. nep. *bahut.*

1866. බෝ **bō**[2], s., wisdom, supreme enlightenment. *bō-gaha* name of the sacred tree Ficus religiosa. — Pk. *bōhi,* P., Sk. *bōdhi.*

1867. බෝමැඩ **bō-mäḍa,** s., terrace round a Bō-tree. — P. *bōdhi-maṇḍa.*

ම M

— ම් **m-,** st. of pron. dem. in **mē, mū,** q.v.

— ම **ma-,** st. of pron. pers. 1. sg. see **mama.**

1868. ම **-ma,** encl. part. emphasising the preceding word. *ohu-ma* he himself; *boho-ma* very, exceedingly ; *e-dā-ma* that day itself, etc. — Pk. *ēa,* P. *ēva, -yēva, 'va,* Sk. *ēva* (*v* and *m* alternate in Sinh.) ; (kśm. *-y, -uy,* bg. h. *-i,* nep. *-i, -ai*).

— මං **maṃ** (= *maṅ*), s., see **maga.**

1869. මකනවා **makanavā,** v., prt. *mäkuvā,* to erase, expunge. Intr. *mäkenavā,* prt. *mäkuṇā,* to become erased. — Pk. *makkhēi,* P. *makkhēti,* Sk. √*mrakṣ, mrakṣati,* caus. *mrakṣayati* ; si. *makhaṇu,* m. *mākhṇeṃ* (Bl), oṛ. *mākhibā,* bg. *mākhā.* Gr. L 24.

1870. මකුණා **makuṇā,** s., st. f. °*ṇu,* bug. — P. *maṅkuṇa,* °*ṇa,* Sk. *matkuṇa* ; kśm. *mōṃkun,* g. *mākaṇ,* h. *makhūn.* Cf. T, s.v. *makunu.*

1871. මකුළු **makuḷu,** s., a kind of white clay, pipe-clay. — Sk. *makkula, makkōla* red chalk.

1872. මකුළුවා **makuḷuvā,** s., st. f. °*ḷu,* 1) monkey; 2) spider. — Pk. *makkaḍa,* P. *makkaṭa,* Sk. *markaṭa* monkey, spider ; si. *makaṛu,* g. *mākḍuṃ* monkey, *mākḍī* bug, m. *mākaḍ* monkey, oṛ. *mākaṛa* monkey, *mākaṛasā* spider, bg. *mākaṛ,* h. *makṛā* spider, nep. *mākal* monkey, *mākuro* spider, pj. *makkṛī* spider, l. *makkuṛ* locust.

1873. **මග maga, මඟ mañga,** s., st. f. *maṃ, maga,* way, road. s. *magiyā* traveller. *maga-arinavā* to get out of the way, give way, keep aloof. — Pk., P. *magga,* Sk. *mārga* ; si. *māgu.*

1874. **මගුරා magurā,** s., st. f. °*ru,* a river fish, sheat-fish.—P. *maggura,* Sk. *madgura.*

1875. **මගුල magula, මඟුල mañgula,** s., st. f. °*ul,* happiness, good fortune, festival. *magul-bata* festival meal, wedding feast. — Pk., P., Sk. *maṅgala* ; si. *maṃgalu,* g. m. *maṃgal,* bg. h. *maṃgal,* nep. *māgal, māṅal,* pj. *maṃggal.* Sinh. *magul-ätā* the royal elephant, state-elephant = P. *maṅgala-hatthin.*

1876. **මට maṭa,** a., pprt., polished, smooth. — Pk. *maṭṭha,* P. *maṭṭha, maṭṭa,* Sk. *mṛṣṭa* (√*mṛś*) ; si. *maṭho,* g. *māṭhuṃ,* m. *māṭhā,* oṛ. *maṭhuā,* ass. *māṭh,* bg. *māṭha,* h. *māṭhā, maṭṭhā,* nep. *māṭho,* pj. l. *maṭṭhā.*

1877. **මඩ maḍa,** s., scum, mud, mire, dirt. *maḍa-bima* muddy place, swamp. — Pk., P., Sk. *maṇḍa* ; kśm. *monḍu* gruel, g. *māḍo,* m. *māṃḍā,* or. *manḍa,* ass. *mār,* bg. *māṛ,* b. h. *māṃṛ,* nep. *māṛ, māṃṛ.*

1878. **මඩනවා maḍanavā, මඩිනවා maḍinavā, °ඬිනවා °ñḍinavā,** v., prt. *mänḍā, mäḍḍā,* to trample, press out, thresh. Caus. *maḍavanavā,* prt. *mäḍevuvā* to cause (oxen) to trample (ground or corn) ; intr. *mäḍenavā,* prt. *mäḍuṇā,* to be trampled. — Pk. *maḍḍaï,* P. *maddati,* °*ddēti,* °*ddāpēti,* Sk. √*mṛd, mardati,* caus. °*dayati* ; kśm. *māṃḍun,* g. *māḍaṇ,* oṛ. *māṛibā,* ass. *māriba,* bg. *māṛā,* h. *māṃṛnā,* nep. *māṛnu, māṃṛnu,* pj. *maddhṇā.*

1879. **මඩය maḍaya,** s., st. f. *maḍa,* ornament. — Sk. *manḍa* (BR, s.v. 4) ; cf. P. *manḍana,* m. *māṃḍṇeṃ* to arrange ; T, s.v. *maṛer.*

1880. **මඩුල්ල maḍulla, මැඩිල්ල mäḍilla,** s., st. ff. °*ulu,* °*iḷi,* circle, ring. — Pk., P., Sk. *manḍala* ; kśm. *mandal,* m. *māṃḍaḷ,* oṛ. *manḍala,* h. *maṃḍlī,* nep. *māṛo, māṃṛo,* pj. *manḍal.*

1881. **මඩුව maḍuva,** s., st. f. *maḍu,* shed, temporary building. — Pk. *manḍava,* P., Sk. *manḍapa* ; si. *maṃḍapu,* g. *māṃḍavī,* m. *māṃḍav,* h. *maṃḍuā.* A Sinh. doublet *maḍiya,* EpZ III 227[12], 10th c.

1882. **මඩුවා maḍuvā, මැඩියා mäḍiyā,** s., st. ff. *maḍu, mäḍi,* frog. — Pk. *manḍukka,* P., Ved. *manḍūka.*

1883. **මත් mat,** a. pprt., intoxicated. *bī-mat* id. (see *bonavā*) ; *bī-mat-kama* drunkenness. — Pk., P., Sk. *matta* (√*mad*) ; kśm. *motu,* si. *mato,* g. *mātuṃ,* m. bg. *māt,* h. *mātā,* pj. *mattā.*

1884. **මත mata,** s., head, summit, top. — Sk. *masta,* side by side with *mastaka* (see *matta*).

1885. **මතු -matu,** adv., only. — P. *mattaṃ,* Sk. *-mātram.*

1886. මතුරු **maturu,** s., mystical incantation, spell, charm. v. *maturanavā*, prt. *mäturuvā*, to mutter magical incantations. — Slw. Sk. *mantra* (cf. *yatura*) ; kśm. *momthar*, si. *mandru*, l. *mandr*.

1887. මත්ත **matta,** s., st. f. *matu*, head, upper part; future time. *matu*, adv., in future ; *matuyehi*, *mattehi*, *mattē*, postp., above, after. — Pk. *matthaa*, P. *matthaka*, Sk. *mastaka*; si. *mathu*, *matho*, g. *māthuṃ*, m. *māthā*, or. *mathā*, ass. h. *māth*, *māthā*, bg. *māthā*, nep. *māth*, l. *matthā*.

1888. මද **mada,** මඳ **mañda,** s., slight, scanty, little, few. *madak* a little ; *mada-venavā* to diminish. — Pk., P., Sk. *manda*; kśm. *mondu*, si. *mando*, m. g. bg. h. pj. *maṃd*. Sinh. *madi*, *mañdi*, probably <*mandaka*.

1889. මදට **madaṭa,** s., small red berries (used as jeweller's weight), the seeds of the tree *madaṭiya*, Adenanthera pavonina. — Pk. *mañjiṭṭha* red, °*ṭṭhā* madder, P. *mañjeṭṭha*, °*ṭṭhī*, Sk. *mañjiṣṭha*, °*ṣṭhā*; kśm. *mazēṭh*, si. *mañuṭha*, h. *maṃjīṭh*, nep. *majiṭho*, *maṃjiṭho*, pj. *majīṭh*, *maṃjīṭh*.

1890. මදය **madaya**[1], s., st. f. *mada*, kernel, pulp, flesh of a fruit. — Pk., Sk. *majjan*. Also *madula*, °*lu*. Cf. *midulu*.

1891. මද(ය) **mada(ya)**[2], s., st. f. *mada*, intoxicating liquor, arrack (Ca). — Pk., P. *majja*, Sk. *madya* ; m. *māj*, h. *māṃj*, *mājā*, *maṃjhā* (different meaning, see Bl, s.v.).

— මදර **madara**[1], මඳර **mañdara,** see **maduru.**

1892. මදර **madara**[2], s., the coral tree, Erythrina indica. — Pk. *mandāla*, P. *mandārava*, Sk. *mandāra(va)*. See *mädiriya*.

1893. මදිනවා **madinavā,** v., prt. *mäddā*, to smooth, polish. Double caus. *maddavanavā* (<**madv°*), prt. *mäddevuvā*, to cause to polish; intr. *mädenavā*, prt. *mäduṇā*, to become polished. — Pk. *majjaï*, P. *majjati*, Sk. √*mṛj*, *mārjati* ; si. *mājaṇu*, g. *māṃjvuṃ*, m. *māṃjṇeṃ*, or. *mājibā*, h. *māṃjnā*, pj. *māṃjṇā*. See *amadinavā*.

1894. මදිරා **madi-rā,** s., intoxicating liquor. — *madi* (see *madaya*[2]) + *rā* (see *raha*).

1895. මදු **madu,** in *madu-raṭa* a country in India. — P. *madda*, Sk. *madra*.

1896. මදුරු **maduru,** මදර **madara,** මඳර **mañdara,** nom. propr., the Mēru, mountain. — P., Sk. *mandāra*.

1897. මදුරුවා **maduruvā,** s., st. f. °*ru*, mosquito. — ? < Sk. *mandra* the 'humming' fly.

1898. මදොස **madosa,** s., st. f. °*dos*, box, chest, trunk; *mandos*, EpZ I 222[34], 10th c. — P. *mañjūsā*, Sk. *mañjūṣā* ; m. *māṃdūs*.

1899. මද්දාන **maddāna,** මද්දහන **maddahana,** s., st. ff. °*āna*, °*ahan(a)*, midday, noon. — Pk. *majjhaṇha*, P. *majjhanha*, Sk. *madhyâhna*.

1900. මන් **man,** s., pride, haughtiness. — Pk. *māṇa*, P., Sk. *māna* ; kśm. *mān*, si. *māṇu*, ass. bg. h. nep. *mān*, pj. l. *māṇ*.

1901. **මන mana,** s., mind. *mana-ram* delightful ; *mana-hara* captivating the mind. — Pk. *maṇa (maṇa-hara)*, P. *mana (manō-rama, °-hara)*, Sk. *manas*; kśm. ass. bg. h. nep. *man*.

1902. **මනා manā,** a., good, pleasing, delightful. — P. *manāpa*, Sk. *mana-āpa*. See *mänava*.

1903. **මනිනවා maninavā,** v., prt. *männā*, to measure. Double caus. *mannavanavā* (<**manv°*), prt. *männevuvā*, to cause to measure ; intr. *mänenavā*, prt. *mänuṇā*, to measure (so much).—P. *mināti*, Sk. √*mā*, *mināti*. See *mavanavā*.

— **මනුමරක manumaraka,** s., see **munuburā.**

1904. **මම mama,** pron. pers. 1. sg. ; cas. obl. *mā*, dat. *ma-ṭa*, gen. *ma-gē*, abl. *ma-gen*, loc. *mā kerehi*. — Pk., P. acc. *maṃ*, *mamaṃ*, instr. *mayā* ; Sk. *mām*, *mayā*, *mama*, *mahyam* ; si. *muṃ*, g. *mēṃ*, m. *mā* (Bl, LM § 208), oṛ. *muṃ*, ass. *maï*, bg. *mui*, *mo-* (Ch, BL II, § 539), b. *mēṃ*, h. *maiṃ* etc.

1905. **මයිලා mayilā,** s., st. f. *°yil*, maternal uncle.— Pk. *māula(ga)*, P., Sk. *mātula*.

— **මයුරා mayurā,** s., see **miyurā.**

1906. **මර mara,** s., death. *mara-haňḍa* death-cry. — Pk., P., Sk. *mara* ; g. *maro*, bg. *marā*, nep. *maro*. See also *maru*.

1907. **මරනවා maranavā,** v., prt. *märuvā*, to kill, destroy. Caus. *mara-vanavā*, prt. *märevuvā*, to cause to kill ; intr. *märenavā*, prt. *märuṇā*, to die, expire. — Pk. *mārēi*, P. *mārēti*, Sk. √*mṛ*, caus. *mārayati* ; kśm. *mārun*, si. *māraṇu*, g. *mārvuṃ*, m. *mārṇeṃ*, oṛ. *māribā*, ass. *māriba*, bg. *mārā*, h. pj. *mārnā*, nep. *mārnu*, l. *māraṇ*.

1908. **මරා marā,** a., green. — Cf. P. *maragaa*, *°gada*, Sk. *marakata* emerald.

1909. **මරු maru**[1], a., deadly, fatal ; s. *maruvā* death (personified) ; *maru-pahara* fatal blow.— Pk. *māra(ga)*, P., Sk. *māra(ka)* ; kśm. *mār*, si. g. *mār*, *māro*, m. bg. *mār*, h. nep. *mār*, *mārā*, pj. *mār*.

1910. **මරු maru**[2], s., wind. — Pk. *maru*, *mārua*, P. *maru*, *māruta*, Sk. *marut*, *māruta*.

1911. **මල mala**[1], s., excretion of the body, faeces. *mala-maga* anus. — Pk., P., Sk. *mala* ; kśm. *mal*, si. *maru*, g. m. *maḷ*, oṛ. *maḷa*, ass. bg. h. nep. pj. *mal*, l. *maḷ*.

1912. **මල mala**[2], s., st. f. *mal*, drinking cup. — P. *mallaka*, Sk. *malla* (BR, s.v. 1d).

1913. **මල mala**[3], s., st. f. *mal*, flower. *mal-asuna* flower-altar ; *mal-dama* garland ; *mal-gannavā* to bloom, flower. — Pk., P., Sk. *mālā*.

1914. **මල mala**[4], s., a., wild, savage. *mala-daru* Väddā (Ruv 400). See *malaya*.

1915. මලදු **maladu,** a., wild, savage. — Pk. *miliccha,* Sk. *mlēccha.* Cf. *milis.*

1916. මලය **malaya,** a., mountainous, wild. *malaya-raṭa* a hilly district of Ceylon. — *malaya* a mountainous region in India.

1917. මල් කරුවා **mal-karuvā,** s., st. f. °*ru,* florist, worker in flowers. — P., Sk. *mālā-kāra* + suff. *-ka.*

1918. මව **mava,** s., st. f. *mav,* mother. *mav-piyō* parents. — Pk. *māā,* P. *mātā,* Sk. *mātā (mātṛ)* ; g. m. oṛ. ass. bg. nep. *mā,* h. pj. *māṃ,* l. *mā.*

1919. මවනවා **mavanavā,** v., prt. *mävuvā,* to bring into existence, to create. Intr. *mävenavā,* prt. *mävuṇā,* to be created. — Pk. *māvēi,* P. *māpēti,* Sk. √*mā,* caus. *māpayati* ; si. *māiṇu,* g. *māvuṃ,* m. *māvṇeṃ*; cf. g. m. ass. bg. h. nep. *māp* measure.

— මස් **mas^{1}, ^{2},** ss., see **maha^{1}, ^{2}.**

1920. මස **masa^{1},** s., st. f. *mas,* beard.— Pk. *massū, maṃsu,* P. *massu,* Sk. *śmaśru.*

— මස **masa^{2},** s., see s.v. **maha^{3}.**

— මසනවා **masanavā,** v., see **mahanavā.**

1921. මසා **masā,** s., st. f. *mas,* fish. *mas-päsa* fish-basket. — Pk., P. *maccha,* Sk. *matsya* ; kśm. *mach,* si. *machu,* g. *māchlī,* m. *māsā,* oṛ. *mācha,* ass. *mās,* bg. *māch,* b. *machlī,* h. *māch, machlī,* nep. *mācho,* pj. *macch.* Gr. L 4, 26.

1922. මසුරු **masuru,** a., parsimonious, niggardly; s. °*rā* niggard. *masuru-kama* niggardliness. — Pk. *macchara,* P. *macchara,* °*cchariya,* Sk. *matsara, mātsarya.* Cf. T, s.v. *macchar.*

1923. මස් දිව **mas-div,** s., fisherman. — Sk. *matsya-jīvin.*

1924. මස්ස **massa,** s., st. f. *masu,* an ancient coin, gold equal to the weight of a madaṭiya seed. *masu-ran* id. — P. *māsaka,* Sk. *māṣaka* bean, a weight, a coin.

— මහ **maha^{1}-,** a., see **mā-.**

1925. මහ **maha^{2},** s., st. f. *mas,* flesh, meat.— Pk., P. *maṃsa,* Sk. *māṃsa* ; kśm. *mās, māz,* si. *māṃsu, māhu,* g. *māṃs,* m. *māṃs, mās,* h. pj. l. *mās,* nep. *māsu.* Gr. L 39.

1926. මහ **maha^{3},** මස **masa^{2},** s., st. f. *mas,* month. — Pk., P., Sk. *māsa* ; kśm. *mās,* si. *māṃhu,* g. m. *mās,* oṛ. *māsa,* ass. *māh,* bg. b. h. nep. *mās,* l. *maṃh.*

1927. මහඔසු **maha-osu,** s., ginger, lit. the great medicine. — P. *mahōsadha,* Sk. *mahāuṣadha.*

1928. මහගු **mahagu,** මහඟු **mahaṅgu,** a., very valuable, precious.— Pk., P. *mahaggha,* °*gghiya,* Sk. *mahârgha,* °*rghya* ; si. *mahāṃgo,* g. *mohoṃ-guṃ,* m. *mahāg, mhāg,* ass. *mahaṅgā,* bg. *māhāṅgā,* h. *mahaṅgā,* nep. *mahaṃgo.*

1929. මහණව **mahaṇava,** s., the great ocean. — P. *mahaṇṇava,* Sk. *mahârṇava.*

1930. මහණා **mahaṇā,** s., st. f., °*ṇa,* ascetic, Buddhist monk; f. *meheṇa* nun. — Metathesis of **hamaṇa* : Pk., P. *samaṇa,* °*ī,* Sk. *śramaṇa,* °*ī.*

1931. මහත **mahata,** s., st. f. *mahat,* bulk, size, magnitude. — Sk. *mahattva.*

1932. මහතා **mahatā,** s., master, gentleman. — P. *mahattā,* Sk. *mahâtmā.*

1933. මහදිව **maha-diva,** s., st. f. °*-div,* the great Island (one of the four dvīpas by which the Mēru mountain is surrounded). — P. *mahā-dīpa.*

1934. මහනවා **mahanavā,** මස° **masa°,** v., prt. *mähuvā,* °*s*°, to fetter, chain, sew. — ? from a caus. of Ved. √*myakṣ* to be fixed on or in. T's explanation s.v. *macāunu* is semasiologically difficult.

1935. මහමුහුණා **maha-muhuṇā,** s., st. f. °*ṇu,* owl. — P., Sk. *mahā-mukha,* lit. the big-faced one.

1936. මහරට **maha-raṭa,** s., the Marāṭha country. — Pk. *marahaṭṭha,* P. *mahā-raṭṭha,* Sk. *mahā-rāṣṭra* ; g. *marāṭho,* m. *marāṭhā,* h. *marhaṭṭā,* nep. *marāṭhi.*

1937. මහරු **maharu,** a., precious, good, excellent. — P. *mahâraha,* Sk. *mahârha.*

1938. මහලු **mahalu,** a., aged, old; s. *mahallā* old man, senior; fem. *mähälla,* °*llī, mehelī* aged woman. — P., Sk. *mahallaka,* °*llakī.*

1939. මහසත් **maha-sat,** s., the Great Being, the Bodhisattva. — Pk., P. *mahā-satta,* Sk. *mahā-sattva.*

1940. මහසල් **maha-sal,** a., noble. — P. *mahā-sāla,* Sk. *mahā-śāla.*

1941. මහසුන **mahasuna,** s., st. f. °*n,* throne, chair of state. — P., Sk. *mahâsana.*

— මහි **mahi,** s., see **mihi, mī.**

1942. මළ **maḷa,** a. pprt., dead. *maḷa-kaňda* dead body, corpse. — Pk. *maa, maḍaa,* P. *mata, maṭaka,* Sk. *mṛta* ; kśm. *moru,* si. *maṛhu,* g. *maḍuṃ,* m. *maḍ, maḍeṃ,* oṛ. *maṛā,* ass. *marā,* bg. *maṛā,* nep. *moro, muro.* Gr. L 5.

1943. මළුව **maḷuva,** s., st. f. *maḷu,* courtyard, enclosure. — P. *mālaka, māḷaka.* Otherwise T, s.v. *maro*^{2}.

1944. මා **mā^{1}-,** මහ **maha-,** a., great, in cpds. as *maha-gama, mā-gama* name of a village, lit. large village. The title *mahayā* in mediaev. inscrs. means 'the Great one' (Greater India Soc. Journ. II 108). It is added to *āpā* (q.v.) or to a name: *udā mahayā,* EpZ I 186^{2}. — Pk., P., Sk. *mahā* ; m. *mahā-mhā-,* etc.

1945. **මා mā**[2], s., m o o n. *mā-räs* moon beams. — P. *mā*, Sk. *mās*. Cf. *maha*[3].

1946. **මාගම māgama,** s., st. f. °*gam*, w o m a n. — P. *mātu-gāma*, Sk. *mātṛ-grāma* the aggregation of mothers, womankind.

1947. **මාරුක mā-ruka, මහරුක maha-ruka,** s., st. f. °*-ruk*. c o c o n u t t r e e. —Lit. the great tree, P. *mahā-rukkha*, Mhvs 72.9, Sk. *mahā-vṛkṣa*.

1948. **මාවත mā-vata,** s., st. f. °*-vat*, h i g h r o a d. — *mā*+*vata*[2].

1949. **මාවතා mā-vatā** (*mā-vat*, Ruv 244), s., st. f. °*vat*, o w l. — Sk. *mahā-vaktra*, lit. the big-faced one.

1950. **මැක්කා mäkkā,** s., st. f. *mäki*, f l y, in *balu-mäkkā* f l e a, lit. dog-fly.— Pk. *makkiā*, P. *makkhikā*, Sk. *makṣikā* ; si. *makhi*, *makho*, g. *mākh*, *mākhī*, *mākho*, ass. *mākhi*, h. *mākhī*, nep. *mākho*, pj. *makkh*, *makkhī*, l. *makkhī*. See *mässā*.

1951. **මැගුම mäguma,** s., st. f. *mägum*, l o o k i n g. Nom. verb. of *maganavā* = Pk. *maggaï*, P. *maggati*, Sk. *mārgayati* seeks ; kśm. *maṅgun*, g. *māgvuṃ*, m. *māgṇeṃ*, oṛ. *māgibā*, ass. *māgiba*, bg. *māgā*, *māṅgā*, h. *māṃgnā*, nep. *māgnu*, *māṃgnu*, *māṅnu*, pj. *maṅgṇā*, l. *maṅgaṇ*.

1952. **මැට්ට mäṭṭa,** s., st. f. *mäṭi*, c l a y. — Pk. *maṭṭiā*, P. *mattikā*, Sk. *mṛttikā* ; si. *miṭī*, g. *māṭī*, m. *māṭī*, oṛ. ass. bg. *māṭi*, b. *māṭī*, h. *māṭī*, *maṭṭī*, *miṭṭī*, nep. *māṭo*, *māṭi*, pj. *miṭṭī*, l. *maṭṭ*.

1953. **මැඩයා mäḍayā,** s., st. f. *mäḍa*, h e - g o a t. — Pk. *meḍḍha*, *meṇḍha*, *meṇḍa*, P. *meṇḍa*, Sk. *mēḍhra*, *mēṇḍha* ; g. *meṃḍho*, m. *meṃḍhā*, oṛ. *meṇḍā*, ass. *mer*(*-sāg*), bg. *meṛā*, b. *meṃṛhvā*, h. *meṛhā*, *meṃḍhā*, nep. *meṛo*, pj. *meṃḍhā*.

1954. **මැඩි mäḍi,** a. pprt., c r u s h e d, o p p r e s s e d.—Pk. *maddita*, Sk. *mardita*. See *maḍanavā*.

— **මැඩියා mäḍiyā,** s., see **maḍuvā.**

— **මැඩිල්ල mäḍilla,** s., see **maḍulla.**

— **මැණ mäṇa,** s., see **miṇa.**

1955. **මැණික mäṇika,** s., st. f. °*ik*, g e m, j e w e l. — Sk. *māṇikya*. Cf. *mäṇa*, *miṇa*.

1956. **මැණික්කටුව mäṇik-kaṭuva,** s., st. f. °*ṭu* w r i s t. — Tam. *maṇi-kkaṭṭu*.

1957. **මැතියා mätiyā,** s., st. f. *mäti*, c o u n c i l l o r. — Pk., P. *mantin*, Sk. *mantrin*. Cf. *ämatiyā*.

1958. **මැද mäda,** a., c e n t r a l, m i d d l e : s., c e n t r e.—*mäda-desa* middle part of the body, waist. — Pk., P. *majjha*, Sk. *madhya* : kśm. *manz*, si. *mañjhu*, g. *mojhār*, m. *māj*, oṛ. *mājhi*, ass. *māz*, bg. *māj*. h. nep. *mājh*, pj. *majhlā*, l. *majjh*.

1959. **මැදඇඟිල්ල mäd'-aṅgilla, මැදැඟිල්ල mäd'-äṅgilla,** s., st. f. °*ili*, m i d d l e f i n g e r. — Sk. *madhyâṅguli* : nep. *mājhi-auṃli*.

1960. **මැදහත් mädahat,** a., standing between, interposing mediating. — Pk. *majjhattha,* P. *majjhatta,* Sk. *madhya-stha.*

1961. **මැදි mädi,** a., middle; s. *mädda* centre. — Sk. *madhya* + suff.-*ka.*

1962. **මැදින්දින mädindina,** s., name of the month March-April, the last month of the Sinhalese year. — *mädim* + *dina* ; Sk. *madhyaṃdina* Wednesday.

1963. **මැදිම් mädim, මැදුම් mädum,** a., middle, central. *mädum-yuma* middle watch of the night. — Pk., P. *majjhima,* Sk. *madhyama* ; kśm. *mazyumu,* ass. *māziu.*

1964. **මැදිරිය mädiriya[1], මැදුර mädura,** s., st. f. °*ri*, °*ru,* house. —Pk., P., Sk. *mandira.*

1965. **මැදිරිය mädiriya,** s., st. ff. -°*ri,* name of a tree. *kaḷu-mädiriya* false calamander, Diospyros oppositifolia.—Sk. *mandāra* (cf. *madara*[2]) or perhaps = Sk. *mañjarī* (BR, s. v. 3).

1966. **මැදිරි(යා) mädiri(yā),** s., st. ff. °*ri,* cat (Ruv 239). — Pk., P. *majjāra,* Sk. *mārjāra* ; g. *māṃjar,* m. *māṃjar, mājar,* h. *maṃjār, maṃjāḍ.* Gr. L 13.

1967. **මැනව mänava, °වි °vi,** part., it is good, it would be well if, used in a respectful entreaty after a pprt. — Undoubtedly connected with *manā,* q.v. ; it seems that a form of *venavā* is annexed to it.

1968. **මැය mäya** (Ca), s., st. f. *mā,* juggling, jugglery. —P., Sk. *māyā, māyākāra* ; m. *māv.*

1969. **මැර māra[1],** s., st. f. *märu,* ray of light (Ca). — P., Sk. *marīci.* But cf. Sinh. *merada* id. (De Lanerolle).

1970. **මැර mära[2],** s., st. f. *märu,* boundary (Ruv 187). — P. *mariyādā,* Sk. *maryādā* ; g. m. *mer.*

1971. **මැළි mäli,** a., lazy, indolent. *mäli-karanavā* to act lazily, hesitate. — Probably from √*mlā* ; Pk. *milāṇa* withered, P. *milāyati* languishes, *milāta,* Sk. *mlāyati, mlāta* or *mlāna.* According to traditional orthography this word is always spelt with *ḷ* (De Lanerolle).

1972. **මැසි mäsi,** or **මැසිසුනු mäsi-sunu** (Ca), s., dark coloured mineral used medicinally.— *mäsi*=Pk., P. *masi,* Sk. *maṣi* ; si. *masu,* g. *masī, mes,* m. *maśī,* oṛ. *masi,* ass. *mahi,* bg. *masi,* h. *masī,* nep. *masi,* pj. l. *mass*+ *sunu* (see *hunu*).

1973. **මැසිරිගල mäsirigala,** s., a kind of gem, cat's eye. — P. *masāragalla,* Sk. *musāragalva,* cf. *masāragalvarka* (BR, s.v. *masāra*).

1974. **මැස්ස mässa,** s., st. f. *mäsi, mähi,* stage, scaffold, platform. —Pk., P., Sk. *mañca*+suff.-*ka* ; si. *mañjo,* g. *mācḍo, māṃcḍo,* m. *māc,* oṛ. *mañcā,* bg. *mācā,* b. *māṃc,* h. *mācā, māṃcā,* nep. *māc, māṃc,* pj. *mañjā,* l. *mañjī.*

1975. මැස්සා **mässā,** s., st. f. *mäsi, mähi,* fly; fem. *mässī* female fly. — Pk. *macchiā*, Sk. *makṣikā* ; kśm. *machi*, m. *māśī*, oṛ. bg. *māchī*. Cf. also *mäkkā*. Sinh. has alternating forms (Sk. *kṣ* > *kkh* or *cch*) like Pk., Hindī.

— මෑ **mā**[1], s., see **mäya.**

— මෑ **mā**[2], මෑත **māta,** see s.v. **mē.**

1976. මෑ **mā**[3], s., beans, pulse. — Pk., P. *māsa*, Sk. *māṣa* ; kśm. *māh*, si. *mamhī*, ass. *māh*, bg. nep. *mās*, pj. *māṃh*, l. *mamh*.

1977. මිට **miṭa,** s., st. f. *miṭi*, fist, handful; handle. — Pk., P. *muṭṭhi*, Sk. *muṣṭi* ; kśm. *mŏṭh*, si. *muṭhi*, g. m. *mūṭh*, oṛ. ass. *muṭhi*, bg. nep. *muṭh*, b. h. *mūṭh*, pj. l. *muṭṭh*.

1978. මිටිය **miṭiya,** s., st. f. *miṭi*, hammer. — MInd. *muṭṭhi* + *-ka*, Sk. *muṣṭika*.

1979. මිට්ටා **miṭṭā,** s., st. f. *miṭi*, dwarf. — From *miṭa* fist, lit. fist high. Cf. Eng. tom-thumb, Germ. Däumling.

1980. මිඩි **miḍi,** මිඩිය **miḍiya,** s., female servant or slave. — Lit. "the shaved one"; Sk. *munḍitā, munḍayati* shaves, shears, P. *munḍēti* ; Cf. PARKER, Village Folk Tales of Ceylon I 84.

1981. මිණ **miṇa,** මැණ **mäṇa,** st. f. *mini*, gem, precious stone. *miṇi-dama* gem-chain. — Pk., P., Sk. *maṇi* ; si. g. *maṇi*, m. *maṇī*, h. *man, maṇ*, pj. *maṇī*.

1982. මිණිදඬු **miṇi-daňḍu,** in *m.-d.-väṭa* lamps or torches having handles set with jewels. — Sk. *maṇi-daṇḍa*.

1983. මිණිපලඟ **miṇi-palaňga,** s., gem-set-throne over which a war was caused among the Nāgas. — P. *maṇi-pallaṅka*, Mhvs I 44 sq.

1984. මිණිබිම **miṇi-bima,** s., ground or locality where gems are found. — Sk. *maṇi-bhūmi*.

1985. මිණිමුතු **miṇi-mutu,** a., lit. sheath-freed, opened, expanded (as a flower). — Sk. *maṇi-mukta*.

1986. මිත් **mit,** s., friend. — Pk., P. *mitta*, Sk. *mitra* ; kśm. *mĕthar*, si. *miṭru*, oṛ. *mita*, ass. bg. *mitā*, nep. *mit*, h. *mīt*, pj. *mitrāī* friendship. Sinh. also (with split *-tr-*) *miturā*, st. f. *°ru*, fem. *miturī*.

1987. මිතුදම **mitu-dama,** s., friendship. — P. *mitta-dhamma*.

1988. මිදි **midi,** s., grape vine, in cpds.: *m°-pala* grapes; *m°-vatta* vineyard, etc. — P. *muddikā*, Sk. *mṛdhvīkā*.

1989. මිදුලු **midulu,** s., marrow. — P. *miñjā* ; si. *miñā*. Suff. *-la*. Cf. *madaya*[1] : *madulu*.

1990. මින් **min,** s., fish. — Sk. *mīna*.

1991. මිනිසත් බව **minisat-bava,** s., state of being human, manhood. — *minisat* = P. *manussatta*, Sk. *manuṣyatva* + *bava*.

1992. **මිනිස්ලොව minis-lova,** s., world of men. — P. *manussa-lōka*, Sk. *manuṣya-lōka*.

1993. **මිනිහා minihā, °සා °sā,** s., st. f. *minis*, man; pl. *minissu* people, folk, persons. *minis-piya* human region, inhabited country (cf. P., Sk. *janapada*). *miniya*, st. f. *minī*, human corpse. — Pk. *maṇussa*, *mānusa*, P. *manussa*, *mānusa*, Sk. *manuṣya*, *mānuṣa* ; si. *māṇhū*, g. *māṇas*, m. *māṇūs*, oṛ. *miṇisa*, ass. *mānuh*, bg. h. *mānus*, nep. *mānis*, pj. *māṇas*.

1994. **මිය miya, මිහිය mihiya**, s., st. ff. *mihi*, *mī*, earth. *mihi-talaya* surface of the earth. — Pk., P., Sk. *mahī*.

1995 **මියනවා miyanavā**, v., prt. *miyuvā*, to die. — Pk. *mijjaï*, P. *mīyati*, *miyyati*, Sk. $\surd$*mṛ*, *mriyate*. In the MIAVs there are derivatives of Pk. *maraï*, P. *marati*, Sk. *marate*. See Bl, s.v. *marṇeṃ*, T, s.v. *marnu*.

— **මියු miyu,** s., see s.v. **mīvā.**

— **මියුරා miyurā,** s., see **mōrā.**

1996. **මියුරු miyuru, මිහිරි mihiri,** a., pleasant, sweet; s. *mihira* sweetness. *miyuru-sara* sweet voice ; *mihiri-diya* fresh water. — Pk. *mahura*, P., Sk. *madhura*. Sinh. *miri* sweet (see *mirijja*) seems to stand for *mīri* = *mihiri*.

1997. **මියුලා miyulā,** s., deer. *miyuläsa*, *°si* the deer-eyed one, woman. — MI. **miga*<Sk. *mṛga* (cf. *muvā*) + suff. *-la*.

1998. **මිරිඟු miriṅgu,** s., mirage. *m°-pän* appearance of water produced by the mirage. — Cf. P., Sk. *marīcikā*.

1999. **මිරිජ්ජ mirijja,** s., fresh-water. — for *miri* (see s.v. *miyuru*) + *diya*.

2000. **මිරිස් miris,** s., st. f. id., cayenne pepper, chillies. *miris-gala* chillie-stone, stone for grinding chillies. — Pk. *maria*, *miria*, P., Sk. *marica*; kśm. *marc*, *maric*, si. *mirī*, g. m. *marī*, oṛ. *marica*, ass. *maris*, bg. *maric*, b. *maric*, *maricā*, *mircā*, h. *maric*, *miric*, *mirc*, *mirī*, nep. *maric*, pj. *marcām̐*, *miric*, *mirc*.

2001. **මිල(ය) mila(ya),** s., st. f. *mila*, price, money. *mila-aḍu* low-priced, cheap. — Pk. *mulla*, *mūlia*, P. *mulla*, *mūlya*, Sk. *mūlya* ; kśm. *mŏl*, si. *mulhu*, g. *mūl*, pj. *mul* (m. ass. h. nep. l. *mol* < Sk. *maulya*).

2002. **මිලි mili,** a., filthy; s., filth, dirt. — Seems to be derived from **malita*. Cf. *mala*[1].

2003. **මිලිදු milidu, මිලිඳු miliṅdu,** a., savage, wild.—Pk. *miliccha*, Sk. *mlēccha*. Cf. *maladu*, *milis*.

2004. **මිලින milina,** a., dirty, filthy. — Pk. *maliṇa*, P., Sk. *malina* ; m. *maḷiṇ*, ass. bg. h. nep. *malin*, pj. *malīn*.

2005. **මිලිස් milis,** s., barbarian, wild, savage. — Pk. *miliccha*, Sk. *mlēccha*. Cf. *maladu*, *milidu*.

2006. මිස **misa**^{1}, a., u n t r u e, f a l s e. — Pk., P. *micchā*, Sk. *mithyā* ; m. *mīs*, bg. h. *michā*.

2007. මිස **misa**^{2}, postp., u n l e s s, e x c e p t, s a v e.—P. *muñciya*, ger. of v. *muñcati*, Sk. *mucya*. Cf. *mut*.

2008. මිසදිටු **misa-diṭu**, a., o f f a l s e v i e w s, h e r e t i c a l. — P. *micchā-diṭṭhi(ka)*, Sk. *mithyā-dṛṣṭi*.

2009. මිසහැර **misahära**, a., u n f a i t h f u l, a d u l t e r o u s.— P. *micchâcāra*, Sk. *mithyâcāra*.

— මිහි **mihi**, s., see **mī**^{1}.

2010. මිහිඟුව **mihiṅguva**, s., st. f. °*ṅgu*, a k i n d o f d r u m. — Pk. *muiṅgu* (Hem 1.46), P. *mutiṅgu*, Sk. *mṛdaṅga*.

2011. මිහිදුම **mihi-duma**, මීදුම **mī-duma**, s., f o g, m i s t, lit. earth smoke. — *mihi* (cf. *miya*) + *duma*^{2}.

— මිහිරි **mihiri**, a., see s.v. **miyuru**.

2012. මී **mī**^{1}, මිහි **mihi**, s., h o n e y.—Pk. *mahu*, P., Sk. *madhu* ; oṛ. *mahu*, ass. bg. h. *mau*, nep. *maha*.

2013. මී **mī**^{2}, s., in *mī-gaha*, n a m e o f a t r e e, Bassia longifolia ; *mī-pala* fruit of B.l. — Pk. *mahua*, P. *madhuka*, Sk. *madhūka* ; g. *mahuḍo*, *mauḍo*, m. *moh*, *mohā*, *mhoṃv*, h. *mahūā*, nep. *mauvā*, *mahuvā*, l. *mahūā*, *mahvā*.

— මීමා **mīmā**, s., see s.v. **mīvā**.

2014. මීමැස්සා **mī-mässā**, s., st. f. *mäsi*, b e e, lit. honey-fly. — *mī*^{1} + *mässā* ; P. *madhu-makkhikā*, Sk. *madhu-makṣikā*.

2015. මීයා **miyā**, s., st. f. *mī*, m o u s e, r a t. *mī-ugula* rat-trap. — Pk. *mūsia*, °*saa*, P. *mūsika*, Sk. *mūṣika*, °*ṣaka* ; h. *mūsā*, nep. *muso*.

2016. මීවා **mīvā**, මීමා **mīmā**, s., st. ff. *miyu*, *mivu*, *mī*, b u f f a l o. *mī-kiri* buffalo's milk ; *mī-gonā* buffalo bull ; *mī-dena* buffalo cow ; *mī-vässī* female buffalo calf.— Pk., P. *mahisa*, Sk. *mahiṣa* ; kśm. *maiṃś*, *mūṃś*, si. *memhi*, g. *bheṃs*, m. *mhais*, bg. b. h. *bhaiṃs*, nep. *bhaiṃsi*, pj. *maiṃh*.

2017. මුං **muṃ** (for *muṅ*), මුඟු **muṅgu**, s., a kind of p u l s e, Phaseolus mungo. — Pk., P. *mugga*, Sk. *mudga* : kśm. *mŏṅg*, si. *muṅu*, g. *mag*, m. *mūg*, oṛ. *muga*, bg. *mug*, b. h. *mūṃg*, nep. *muṅ*, *mug*, *muṃg*, pj., l. *muṅg*.

2018. මුක් **muk**^{1}, s., d e m o n. — Probably < Pk., P. *mukka* for *mutta*, Sk. *mukta*, lit. one who is free from bodily bonds.

2019. මුක් **muk**^{2}, a., d u m b. — Pk. *mukka* (alternating with *mūa*, *mūga*), P. *mūga*, Sk. *mūka* ; m. *mukā*, bg. *muka*, h. *mūk*, nep. *muk*.

2020. මුගටියා **mugaṭiyā**, s., m o n g o o s e, Herpestes griseus. — Certainly connected with P. *muṅgusa* (perhaps borrowed from Telugu ?), but the termination *-aṭi* is difficult to explain. Cf. HOBSON JOBSON, s.v. mungoose.

2021. මුගුර **mugura,** s., st. f. °*ru*, club, staff, mace. — Pk. *muggara, moggara*, P. *muggara*, Sk. *mudgara* ; sī. *muṅiro*, g. *mogrī*, m. *mogar*, oṛ. *mugura*, bg. *mugur*, b. *mumgrā*, h. *mūgrā*, *mogrā*, nep. *muṅro*, *mugro*, pj. *muṅgalī*, *moglā*, l. *muṅglī*.

2022. මුඩු **muḍu,** a., shaved, bald, bare.— Pk., P., Sk. *muṇḍa* ; kśm. *mŏṇḍu*, si. *muno* (g. of *mumḍvum* to shave), m. *muḍā*, oṛ. *muṇḍā*, ass. *murā*, bg. *muṛa* (h. *mūmḍnā* to shave), nep. *muṛo*, *muṛho*, *mumṛo*.

2023. මුත් **mut[1],** s., liberation, salvation. H. Jayatilaka, Eḷu-akārādīya =*midīma*. — Pk., P. *mutti*, Sk. *mukti*.

2024. මුත් **mut[2],** postp., except, besides. — <MInd. **muttā* = Sk. *muktvā*. Cf. *misa*[2].

2025. මුතු **mutu,** s., pearls. *mutu-dama* string of pearls. — Pk., P. *muttā*, Sk. *muktā*. The words of the MIAVs are all derived from Pk. *mottia*, Sk. *mauktika*. See Bl, s.v. *motiṃ*. T, s.v. *moti*.

2026. මුතුදැල **mutu-däla,** s., pearl-net, network of pearls. — Sk. *muktā-jāla*.

2027. මුතුහර **mutu-hara,** s., pearl necklace. — P. *muttā-hāra*, Sk. *muktā-hāra*.

2028. මුදනවා **mudanavā,** v., prt. *miduvā*, to release, set free. Caus. *mudavanavā*, prt. *midevuvā*, to cause to be released ; intr. *midenavā*, prt. *miduṇā*, to get free. — Pk. *mucaï*, P. *muñcati*, Sk. √*muc*, *muñcati*. According to W. Printz < caus. *mōcēti*, Bull. School Or. St. VIII, 701.

2029. මුදලිඳු **mudaliṅdu,** s., name of a tree and of a Nāga King.—P. *mucalinda*, Sk. *mucilinda*.

2030. මුදිඟිල්ල **mudiṅgilla,** s., st. f. °*li*, ring-finger. — *mudu* (v. *mudda*) +*äṅgilla* ; MInd. **mudraṅguli* + *-ka*.

2031. මුදුන **muduna,** s., st. f. °*dun*, top, summit. *mudun-äṭaya* backbone, spine ; *rivi-muduna* summit of the sun, midday ; *m°-karanavā* to place at the top. — Pk. *muddha*, *muḍḍha*, *muṇḍha*, P. *muddhan*, Sk. *mūrdhan* ; si. *muṇḍhu*, g. *muḍī*, m. *mumḍ*, *mumḍhī* oṛ. *muṇḍa*, ass. *mur*, bg. *muṛ*, h. *mūmṛ*, nep. *muṛ*. pj. *muṇḍ*, l. *mūṇḍh*. The nasalized form *munduna* in inscrs., e.g., EpZ I 33[17], 10th c.

2032. මුදුවරයා **muduvarayā** (Ca), s., goldsmith, jeweller (Ruv 395, *muduvaru*). — *mudu* (v. *mudda*) + *kara*, *karu*, MInd. **muddā-kāraka*.

2033. මුද්ද **mudda,** මුදුව **muduva,** s., st. f. *mudu*, finger-ring. — Pk. *muddā*, °*ddiā*, P. *muddā*, °*ddikā*, Sk. *mudrā*, °*drikā* ; si. *muṇḍra*, °*ḍrī*, m. *mudī*, oṛ. *muda*, °*di*, bg. *mudā*, b. *mumdan*, h. *muṇḍrī*, *mūdrī*, nep. *mundri*, *munri*, pj. *mundar*, *mumdrī*, l. *mundrī*.

2034. මුනුබුරා **munuburā,** s., st. f. *°ru,* grandson; fem. *minibirī* grand-daughter. — <**munum̆burā.* The form in Sinh. Pk. is *maṇumaraka,* EpZ I 211[2], or *manum°,* AIC Nr. 5, 10, by metathesis < **manuramaka*=Pk. *maṇōrama,* P., Sk. *manōrama.* Regarding the meaning, cf Sk. *nandin* son (pleasing the father).

2035. මුපත **mupata,** s., birth, origin (Ruv 92). — Sk. *samuppatti* ; cf. Pk., P. *samuppanna.*

— මුය **muya,** s., see s.v. **muva.**

2036. මුරු **muru,** s., an immortal, god. — Pk., P., Sk. *amara* (*àmára*).

2037. මුල **mula,** s., st. f. *mul,* root, origin, source. *mul-piyā* first ancestor, primogenitor; *m°-adinavā* (*-allanavā, -basinavā*) to take root. — Pk., P., Sk. *mūla* ; kśm. *mūl,* si. *mūru, °rī,* g. *mul, °ḷo,* m. *mūḷ, °ḷā,* oṛ. *muḷā,* ass. *mul, mulā,* bg. *mulā,* b. *mūr, mūl,* h. pj. *mūl, °lī,* nep. *mulo,* l. *mūḷ.*

2038. මුල්කරුණ **mul-karuṇa,** s., original reason, chief cause. — Sk. *mūla-kāraṇā.*

2039. මුව **muva,** මුය **muya,** s., mouth, face. *muva-dora* mouth of a river ; lit. mouth-door. — Pk. *muha,* P., Sk. *mukha* ; si. *muṃhuṃ,* g. *moṃh,* m. *mohaḷ,* h. *muṃh,* nep. *muhuṛā, muhuṃṛā, mohoṛā,* pj. *mūṃh,* l. *muṃh.* Cf. *muhuṇa.*

2040. මුවත් **muvat,** a., sharp; s., *muvata* sharpness. — I derived the word from *muva* + *ata* = Sk. *anta* ; but how can we explain the forms *muvahat, muvāt,* quoted in Cl and Ca ? Cf. *yaṭat, yaṭahat.*

2041. මුවතණ **muva-taṇa,** s., mirage. — P. *miga-taṇhikā,* Sk. *mṛga-tṛṣṇā.*

2042. මුවදුත් **muva-dut,** s., jackal. — Sk. *mṛga-dhūrta.*

2043. මුවනැබ **muva-näba,** s., musk. — Sk. *mṛga-nābhi.*

2044. මුවරද **muvarada,** s., pollen of flowers. — P., Sk. *makaranda.*

2045. මුවරදද **muvara-dada,** s., name of Cupid. — Sk. *makaradhvaja* having the shark as flag. Cf. *mōrā.*

— මුවරා **muvarā,** s., see s.v. **mōrā.**

2046. මුවා **muvā,** s., st. f. *muva,* male deer. *muva-dena* female deer ; *m°-mas* venison ; *m°-hama* deer-skin. — Pk. *maya,* P. *maga,* Sk. *mṛga.*

2047. මුස **musa**[1], s., error, delusion.—Pk., P. *musā,* (AMg. *musaṃ*) Sk. *mṛṣā-.* The *musā-* in cpds. like Pk. *musā-vāa* taken as subst.

2048. මුස **musa**[2], s., fainting. *musa-pat* fainted, unconscious. — Pk., P. *mucchā,* Sk., *mūrchā*; nep. *much* mixing.

— මුසු **musu,** a., see s.v. **muhu**[2].

2049. මුස්ස **mussa** (Ca), s., horripilation, erection of the hair; *musa,* in Ruv 122.—Perhaps P. *samucchaya,* Sk. *samucchraya* raising aloft.

— මුහු **muhu**[1], a., see **mū**[3].

2050. මුහු **muhu**[2], මුසු **musu**, a., mixed. *m°-karanavā* to mix. — Pk., P. *missa*, Sk. *miśra* ; m. *misaḷ*.

— මුහුණ **muhuṇa**, s., see **mūṇa**.

— මුහුද **muhuda**, s., see **mūda**.

2051. මුහුළු **muhuḷu**, s., hair of the head. *m°-miṇa* gem in a crest. — Pk. *mauḍa*, P. *makuṭa*, Sk. *makuṭa*, *mukuṭa* top knot of hair, diadem. Sinh. *muhula* (*muhul*) hair of the head, is only modern and belongs to a time when *l* and *ḷ* were no longer differentiated.

2052. මුළු **muḷu**[1], a., deceived, EpZ I 130[5], 12th c.; s. *muḷāva* error, delusion. —Pk. *mūḍha*, P. *mūḷha*, Sk. *mūḍha* ; kśm. *muḍa* (?), si. *mūṛho* (T, s.v. *mujinu*).

2053. මුළු **muḷu**[2], a., all, entire; s. *muḷa* multitude, group, congregation (of monks), fraternity. — Sk. *samūḍha*, *samūḷha* (*sam* + $\sqrt{}$*ūh*). For the meaning of s. *muḷa*, cf. that of Pk., P., Sk. *samūha*.

2054. මූ **mū**[1], pron. dem., this one, said of animals or low persons. — *m-* + *ū*, *ō*. Cf. also Pk., P., Sk. *amu-*; Pk. *amuga*, P., Sk. *amuka*.

2055. මූ **mū**[2], s., urine.—Pk. AMg. *mūya*, Pk., P. *mutta*, Sk. *mūtra* ; kśm. *mathar*, si. *mutru*, g. *mūtar*, m. *mūt*, bg. *mut*, b. h. *mūt*, nep. *mut*.

2056. මූ **mū**[3], මුහු **muhu**, a., ripe, matured. — P. *mudu*, Sk. *mṛdu*.

2057. මූණ **mūṇa**, මුහුණ **muhuṇa**, s., st. f. *°ṇu*, face. — Sk. *mukha* (see *muva*) + suff. *-ṇa*. De Lanerolle, DSL p. xliii, §11.

2058. මූද **mūda**, මුහුද **muhuda**, s., st. f. *°du*, ocean. *mūdu-hatta* sea-fungus, sponge. — Pk., P. *samudda*, Sk. *samudra*.

2059. මෙත **meta**, s., st. f. *met*, kindness, pity.— Pk., P. *mettī*, Sk. *maitrī* ; P. also *mettā*, *metyā*, Sk. *maitra*, *maitrya*.

2060. මෙන් **men**, adv., a., like, similarly, exactly as. *rivi-mañḍulu-men* just like the orb of the sun, EpZ I 130[4], 12th c. — P., Sk. *samēna*.

2061. මෙර(ය) **mera(ya)**, s., st. f. *mera*, spirituous liquor, toddy. — P. *mēraya*, Sk. *mairēya*.

2062. මෙල **mela**, මෙලා **melā**, s., meeting, union, assemblage. — Pk., P., Sk. *mēla* ; kśm. *mēl*, si. *meru*, *meṛo*, g. *meḷ*, *meḷo*, m. *meḷ*, *meḷā*, oṛ. *meḷā*, ass. *mel*, bg. h. nep. pj. *mel*, *melā*, l. *melā*.

2063. මෙලි **meli**, a., very rich, opulent (Ruv 417).—? from MInd. **mollaka* ; cf. Pk. *molla* (= Sk. *maulya*) price (m. ass. h. l. *mol*), *mūli*, *mūlilla* rich.

2064. මෙවුන් **mevun**, s., sexual intercourse; pair, couple. — Pk. *mēhuna*, P. *mēthuna*, Sk. *māithuna* ; m. *mehuṇ*.

2065. මෙවුන්දම **mevun-dama**, s., sexual intercourse. — P. *mēthunō dhammō* ; Sk. cf. *māithunu-dharmin*.

2066. **මෙවුල mevula,** s., st. f. *mevul*, g i r d l e, n e c k - c h a i n. *mevul-dama* (d^{o2}) id.—Pk. *mēhalā*, P. *mēkhalā*, Sk. *mēkhalā*.

— **මෙහෙණ meheṇa,** s., see s.v. **mahaṇā.**

2067. **මෙහෙය meheya,** s., st. f. *mehe*, *mē*, s e r v i c e, w o r k. *mehe-vara* (*m°* + *kāra*) id.; *mehe-karuvā* servant, servitor.— Cf. Sk. √*śram*, *śrāmyati*; *śramaṇa* : *mahaṇa* (De Lanerolle).

— **මෙහෙලි mehelī,** s., see s.v. **mahallā.**

— **මෙළෙක් meḷek,** a., see s.v. **moḷok.**

2068. **මේ** $\textbf{mē}^{1}$**, මෙ me,** pron. dem., t h i s. *meccara*, *me-vitara*, *me-vicara* this much; *me-täna* this place; *me-tek* thus far; *me-dā* this day, the present time; *me-vak* this time; *mäta* (<*mē ata*) this side, near. Inflected : 1) m. *meyā*, f. *mä*, n. *meya*; 2) m. *mēkā*, f. *mēkī*, n. *mēka*. — *m-* + *ē*.

2069. **මේ** $\textbf{mē}^{2}$**,** s. pl., c l o u d s. *mē-kala* rainy season; nom. pr. *sala-mey-van*, *sala-me-van* (P. *silā-mēgha-vaṇṇa*). — Pk. *mēha*, P., Sk. *mēgha*; si. *mīṃhu*, g. *meh* (*mehulo*), (m. *mehuḍā*,) h. pj. *meṃh*.

2070. **මොක්** $\textbf{mok}^{1}$**,** a., p r i m a r y, p r e e m i n e n t (Ruv 426).— P. *mokkha*, Sk. *maukhya*.

2071. **මොක්** $\textbf{mok}^{2}$**,** s., st. f. *mok*, l i b e r a t i o n, f i n a l e m a n c i p a t i o n. *mok-äduru* name of the Buddha. — Pk., P. *mokkha*, Sk. *mōkṣa*; si. *mokhu*.

2072. **මොර mora,** s., c r y, s h o u t. *mora-hañḍa* id.; *m°-gasanavā* to cry aloud. — < **muvara*; Pk. *muhala*, P., Sk. *mukhara*.

2073. **මොහොත mohota,** s., st. f. *mohot*, m o m e n t, i n s t a n t. — Pk., P. *muhutta*, Sk. *muhūrta*.

2074. **මොහො(ය) moho(ya), මෝ(ය) mō(ya),** s., st. f. *moho*, *mō*, i g n o r a n c e, f o l l y. *moh'-añdura* darkness of folly.— Pk., P., Sk. *mōha*; si. *mohu*, g. *moh*, m. *moh*, *moho*, bg. h. *moh*.

2075. **මොහොර mohora,** s., g r e a t r a m p a r t. — Perhaps <**mahavavura* <*maha-* + *pavura*, q.v.

2076. **මොළොක් moḷok, මෙළෙක් meḷek,** a., s o f t, t e n d e r. — I have preferred the spelling *molok*, *melek* (Cl) and explained the word by metathesis of **komol* = Pk., P., Sk. *kōmala*; kśm. *kumolu*, si. *kuṃaro*, g. *komaḷ*, *kumḷuṃ*, m. *koṃvḷā*, oṛ. *kaaṃḷā*, ass. *kumḷīyā*, nep. *kamalo*, pj. *kūmal*, (*kūlā*, l. *kūlā*). But the historical spelling seems to be that with *ḷ* (Ca). This makes my etymology dubious. De Lanerolle, DSL p. xliv, §.16, derives *moḷok* from **muḍu-kka* < Sk. *mṛdu-ka*.

2077. **මෝ(ය) mō(ya), මොහො(ය) moho(ya),** s., st. ff. *mō*, *moho*, i g n o r a n c e, f o l l y. *moh'-añdura* darkness of folly. — Pk., P., Sk. *mōha*; si. *mohu*, m. *moh*, *moha*, g. bg. h. *moh*.

2078. **මෝරා mōrā[1], මුවරා muvarā**, s., st. f. °*ra*, shark. — Pk. *maara*, P., Sk. *makara*.

2079. **මෝරා mōrā[2], මියුරා miyurā, මයුරා mayurā**, s., st. ff. °*ru*, peacock. —Pk. *maūra*, P., Sk. *mayūra* ; si. *moru*, g. m. *mor*, ass. *mairā*, bg. *maur*, h. pj. *mor*, nep. *mujur*.

2080. **මෝල mōla, මොහොල mohola**, s., st. f. *mōl*, *mohol*, large pestle, pounder. *mōl-gaha* id. — Pk. *mŭsala*, P., Sk. *musala* ; kśm. *muhulu*, si. *muhurī*, g. *musḷuṃ*, m. *musaḷ*, oṛ. *musaḷa*, ass. *muhal*, bg. *musal*, b. *mūsar*, h. pj. *mūsal*, nep. *musal*.

ය Y

2081. **ය ya**, s., iron. *ya-kaḍa* id.; *ya-dora* iron door.— P. *aya*, Sk. *ayas*.

2082. **යකා yakā**, s., st. f. *yak*, demon, devil. *yakadurā* or *yak-dessā* exorcist, devil-priest. — Pk. *jakkha*, P. *yakkha*, Sk. *yakṣa* ; kśm. *yochu*, nep. *jakkhu*, pj. *jakkh*.

2083. **යකිනි yakinī, යකින්න yakinna**, st. f. °*ṇi*, female demon. — P. *yakkhinī*, Sk. *yakṣiṇī* ; h. *jakhnī* ogress.

2084. **යකුළ yakuḷa**, s., st. f. °*ḷu*, sledge hammer. — *ya* + *kuḷa*.

2085. **යට yaṭa**, adv., postp., under, beneath, below ; s. *yaṭasa* (*y*° + *asa*[2]) the lower part ; *yaṭa-ṭa*, *yaṭin* below, down; *yaṭa-karanavā* to put under, suppress. — <**àyáṭa* = Sk. *adhastāt*. Cf. P. *heṭṭhā*.

2086. **යටත් yaṭat, යටහත් yaṭahat**, a., humble, submissive, low. *yaṭatē*, adv., postp., under, subject to ; *yaṭat-(yaṭahat-)kama* humbleness, lowness ; *y°-väsiyā* any subject of a kingdom ; *y°-karanavā* to humble, subdue ; *y°-venavā* to surrender, become humble. — *yaṭa* + *ata*[1].

— **යටිය yaṭiya**, s., see s.v. **yäṭiya.**

2087. **යතුර yatura[1]**, s., st. f. *yaturu*, going, journey. — Pk. *jattā*, P., Sk. *yātrā*. Cf. Bl, s.v. *varāt*, T, s.v. *bari-yāṃt*=Sk. *vara-yātrā*.

2088. **යතුර yatura[2]**, s., st. f. °*ru*, machine, instrument. *yaturu muduva* key of a lock ; *y°-lanavā* or *yatullanavā* to lock (a door). — Later form than *yatta*, q.v.

2089. **යතුරාව yaturāva**, s., st. f. *yaturu*, journey, voyage.— Later form than *yatura*[1], q.v.

2090. **යත්ත yatta**, s., st. f. *yatu*, carpenter's plane. *yatu-gānavā* to plane. — Pk. *janta*, P. *yanta*, Sk. *yantra* ; kśm. *yēndar*, si. *janḍru*, m. *jāṃt*, oṛ. *jāṃti*, ass. *zāṃt*, bg. h. *jāṃtā*, nep. *jāṃto*, pj. *jand*, *jandar*, l. *jandar*, *jandrā*.

2091. **යදිනවා yadinavā**, v., prt. *yäddā*, to pray, beseech, imprecate. —P. *jāai*, P. *yācati*, Sk. √*yāc*, *yācatē* ; si. *jāçaṇu*, g. *jācvuṃ*, m. *jācṇeṃ*, bg. *jācā*, h. *jāṃcnā*, nep. *jāṃcnu*, pj. *jacṇā*.

2092. යන **yana,** යනු **yanu,** යන්න **yanna,** (also *yannak, yanuvak, yannehi, yanuven* &c.) part. corresponding to Pk. *iya*, P. *iti, ti*, Sk. *iti*, after a sentence or a single word or name. — Pprs. of *yanavā*. Cf. *yi*.

2093. යනවා **yanavā,** v., prt. *giyā*, ger. 2 *gos*, to go, proceed. Caus. *yavanavā*, prt. *yävuvā*, to send. — Pk. *jāi*, P. *yāti*, Sk. √*yā*, *yāti* ; kśm. *yinu*, g. *jāvuṃ*, m. *jāṇeṃ*, oṛ. *jibā*, ass. *zāiba*, bg. *jāoyā*, h. *jānā*, nep. *jānu*, pj. *jāṇā*, l. *jā* go thou. Cf. *gos*.

— යපෙනවා **yapenavā,** v., see s.v. **yäpenavā.**

2094. යම් **yam,** part. with correlative meaning: *yam-sē da* . . . .*e-men* in whatsoever manner . . . . in that manner ; *yam-lesa* . . . . *ē-lesak* id., SdhRv 47^{5-6} ; *yam-tāk da* . . . . *ē-tāk* as much . . . . as ; *yam-tamak*, trsl. of P. *yaṃ-vā taṃ-vā*, DhpAGp 18^{28-30}. With indef. meaning : *yam-kisi* some, any.— No doubt a survival of the pron. rel. st. *ya*-, probably the loc. sg. = Pk. *jammi*, P. *yamhi*, *yasmiṃ*, Sk. *yasmin*.

2095. යම **yama,** s., st. f. *yam*, watch (of the night) ; *alu-yama* (the last watch of the night) daybreak (v. *alu*); *mändin-yamä* at midnight, EpZ II 271^{30}, 12th c. — Pk. *jāma*, P., Sk. *yāma*.

2096. යල **yala,** s., the lesser harvest (September harvest). — < **àyála* = P., Sk. *akāla*.

2097. යලක් **-yalak,** ECpds., times: *tun-yalak* three times, *sat-y°* seven times, etc. *yala* (originally after a vowel) = *kālam* + indef. article *-ak*.

2098. යව් **yav,** part., till, as many as. *yav amat bamaṇan* as many brahmins as there are bowls. — Pk. *jā*, P. *yāva*, *yāvaṃ*, *yāvat* ; g. *jav*, m. *jaṃv*, *joṃ*, h. *jab* quand, pj. *jau* comme.

2099. යව **yava,** s., barley. *yava-piṭi* barley meal. — Pk. *java*, P., Sk. *yava* ; si. *jau*, g. m. *jav*, oṛ. *jaa*, ass. *zâ(-dhān)*, bg. *ja*, b. h. pj. nep. *jau*, l. *jô*.

2100. යව්දිව් **yav-div,** a., life-long. — Pk. *jā-jīvaṃ*, P. *yāvā-jīvaṃ*, Sk. *yāvaj-jīvam*.

2101. යහ **yaha,** යස **yasa,** a., good, excellent; s., fame, glory. *yasa-sirin yut* endowed with the fortune of glory, EpZ I 130^{3}, 12th c. ; *yaha-pat* good, excellent (v. *pat*) ; *yehen*, adv., well, excellently.—Pk. *jasa*, P. *yasa*, Sk. *yaśas* ; si. *jasu*, g. m. h. pj. *jas*. Cf. also Sinh. *yehe*, s., something good ; *yeheka*, °*ki* it is good, all right.

2102. යහන **yahana,** s., st. f. *yahan*, bed, couch. *yahan-tala* id. — Metathesis of **hayán* = Pk. *sayaṇa*, P. *sayana* (*sēna*), Sk. *śayana*. Cf. *äñda*.

2103. යාළ **yāḷa,** යහළ **yahaḷa,** s., a measure of capacity, cart-load. *ak-y°*, see s.v. *aga*[3].— According to PARANAVITANA, EpZ III 183, from Pk. AMg. *sagaḍa*, *saaḍha*, Mg. *śaaḷa*, P. *sakaṭa*, Sk. *śakaṭa*. MInd. *sakaṭa* becomes Sinh. Pk. *hakaḍa* (4th c., EpZ III $177^{5, 6}$)> **hayaḍa*>*yahaḍa* (Metathesis, inscr. of the 5th or 6th c.)>*yahaḷa*.

2104. **යාළු yāḷu, යහළු yahaḷu,** a., friendly, intimate; s. *°ḷuvā* friend; fem. *yeheḷī*. — Metathesis of **hayaḷu*<**hu.aḷu* < **suhaḍa* = P. *suhada*, Sk. *suhṛd*. Cf. *ḷa*.

2105. **යැටිය yäṭiya, යටිය yaṭiya,** s., st. f. *yäṭi, yaṭi,* stick, walking-stick. —Pk. *jaṭṭhi*, P. *yaṭṭhi*, Sk. *yaṣṭi*; but kśm. *loṭhu*, si. *lāṭhi*, g. *lāṭhī*, m. *lāṭh*, oṛ. ass: bg. *lāṭhi*, b. h. *lāṭh*, nep. *lāṭho*, pj. l. *laṭṭh*, from MInd. **laṭṭhi*.

2106. **යැපෙනවා yäpenavā, යපෙනවා yapenavā,** v., prt. *yäpuṇā*, to keep going, maintain. *yäpīma, yap°*, s., satisfaction, maintenance, livelihood. — P. *yāpēti*, Sk. *yāpayati*. The Sinh. verb is either derived from a form **yappēti* or it is a Slw.

2107. **යි -yl,** part. at the end of 1) a quotation or 2) a sentence. — Pk. *-ti, -tti*, P. *-ti, -iti*, Sk. *iti*. Cf. *yana*.

2108. **යු yu,** s., season, in *sa-yu* the six seasons.— Pk. AMg. *uu*, P. *utu*, Sk. *ṛtu*.

2109. **යුගය yugaya,** s., pair.—P. *jua*, P., Sk. *yuga*; m. *jūṃ* yoke, bg. *ju*, b. *juā*, h. *jū*, nep. *juvā*.

2110. **යුණු -yuṇu,** a. ECpds., multiplied. — Pk., P., Sk. *guṇa* (*g* > *y* after a vowel). See *diyuṇu*.

2111. **යුත් yut,** a. pprt., endued with, having, containing. — Pk. *jutta*, P. *yutta*, Sk. *yukta*. Cf. T, s.v. *juto* (different meaning).

2112. **යුත yuta,** s., multitude. — Pk. *jūha*, P., Sk. *yūtha*; Eastern h. *jathā* (Hoernle 45). The base-form must be **yuttha*.

2113. **යුතු yutu,** a., fit, proper, becoming. *yutta*, s., what is right, propriety; justice. — Sk. *yukta* + *-ka*. Cf. *yut*.

2114. **යුදය yudaya,** s., st. f. *yuda*, war, battle, contest. — Pk. *juddha*, P., Sk. *yuddha*; kśm. *yŏd*, cf. g. *jhuj-*, *jhujh-*, m. *jujṇeṃ*, *juṃjṇeṃ*, *jhujṇeṃ* etc., h. *jūjh-*, nep. *judhāunu*, *jud-*, pj. *jūj-*, *jūjh-*. Gr. L 27.

2115. **යුරු -yuru,** a. ECpds., like, similar. — Sk. *ākāra*. Cf. *ayura* (*-yuru* after a vowel). G.: 49. 397.

2116. **යුවරද yuva-rada,** s., sub-king, viceroy. — *yuva* = Pk. *juvāṇa*, P., Sk. *yuvan* + *rada*, q.v.; P., Sk. *yuvarāja*.

2117. **යුවල yuvala,** s., st. f. *yuvala*, pair. *yuval'-äsa* the two eyes. — P. *juala*, P., Sk. *yugala*. Ca spells *yuvaḷaya*.

2118. **යුවලපත් yuvala-pat,** s., name of a tree, Bauhinia purpurea. — Lit. paired-leaf, *yuvala* + *pata*[1]; cf. Sk. *yuga-pattra*.

2119. **යුස yusa,** s., juice. — Pk. *yūsa*, Sk. *yūṣa*.

— **යෙහෙන් yehen,** adv., see s.v. **yaha.**

— **යෙහෙළි yeheḷi,** s., see s.v. **yahaḷu.**

2120. යෙළ **yeḷa,** යේළ **yēḷa,** a., one and a half. *yeḷa-siyayak* one hundred and fifty ; *y°-gavu* one and a half gavu. — By Edw. MÜLLER compared with P. *diyaḍḍha*, but the etymology is very doubtful.

2121. යොත **yota,** s., st. f. *yot*, cord, line, rope. — Pk. *jotta*, P. *yotta*, Sk. *yōktra* ; si. *joṭro*, g. *jotar*, *jotruṃ*, m. *jot*, oṛ. *jota*, ass. *zoṃt*, bg. *jot*, b. *joṭā*, h. nep. *jot*, pj. *jotar*.

2122. යොදනවා **yodanavā,** v., prt. *yeduvā*, to put together, construct, form. Caus. *yodavanavā*, prt. *yedevuvā*, to cause to construct ; intr. *yedenavā*, prt. *yeduṇā*, to become formed. — Pk. *jōēi*, P. *yōjēti*, *yōjāpeti*, Sk. $\sqrt{}$*yuj*, caus. *yōjayati* ; pj. *joṇa*, l. *jovaṇ* to yoke. Cf. T, s.v. *jokhnu* (Add.).

2123. යොදුන **yoduna,** s., st. f. *yodun*, a measure of distance about 16 miles. — Pk. *jōaṇa*, P., Sk. *yōjana*.

2124. යොන් **yon,** s., womb, origin.— Pk. *jōṇī*, P., Sk. *yōni* ; bg. *joni*, h. *jon*.

2125. යොන **yona,** s., young woman. — Cf. P. *juvāṇa*, P. *yuvān*, Sk. *yuvan*. Cf. *yovun*.

2126. යොනා **yonā,** s., Moorman. —P. *yavana*, *yōna*, Sk. *yavana*. Cf. E. R. AYRTON, Ceylon Notes and Queries, I, 1913, p. viii.

2127. යොවුන් **yovun,** s., youth. — Pk. *jovvaṇa*, P. *yobbana*, Sk. *yāuvana* ; m. h. nep. *joban*, pj. *jobaṇ*, l. *joban*.

2128. යෝ **yō**[1], s., union (Cl).— Pk. *jōa*, P., Sk. *yōga* ; ass. *zo* preparations, bg. *jo* opportunity, nep. *joha* arrangement.

2129. යෝ **yō**[2], s., warrior. — Pk. *jōha*, P., Sk. *yōdha*.

ර R

2130. රක **raka,** s., protection, preservation. — P. *rakkhā*, Sk. *rakṣā* ; m. g. h. pj. *rākh*.

2131. රකිනවා **rakinavā,** v., prt. *räkkā*, to guard, protect. Intr. *räkenavā*, prt. *räkuṇa*, to be protected, to live, receive sustenance. — Pk. *rakkhaï*, P. *rakkhati*, Sk. *rakṣati* ; (kśm *rachun*,) si. *rakhanu*, g. *rākhvuṃ*, m. *rākhṇeṃ*, oṛ. *rakhibā*, ass. *rākhiba*, bg. *rākhā*, h. *rākhnā*, nep. *rākhnu*, pj. *rakkhṇā*, l. *rakhan*.

2132. රකුසා **rakusā,** රකුස්සා **rakussā,** s., st. ff. *rakus*, *°su*, demon; fem. *rakusī* female demon. *rakusu*, a., diabolic, hellish. — Pk., P. *rakkhasa*, Sk. *rākṣasa* ; g. *rākhas*. m. *rākhis-*, b. nep. *rākas*, h. *rākhas*, pj. *rākhas*, *rākas* (cf. nep. pop. *rāchesi*, *rāchisi* ogress). Sinh. *rakusu*, *°ssā*, from *r°+-ka*.

2133. රක්නාව **raknāva,** s., preservation, protection. — P. *rakkhana*, Sk. *rakṣaṇa*. Cf. *rakinavā*.

2134. රඟ **raṅga,** s., colour; manner, style; dancing, acting. — Pk., P., Sk. *raṅga*; kśm. *raṅg*, oṛ. bg. *rāṅgā*, h. *rāṃg*, nep. *raṅ*, *raṅg*, pj. l. *raṅg*.

2135. රඟබිම **raṅga-bima,** s., place for acting, theatre, arena. — Sk. *raṅga-bhūmi*.

2136. රඟමඬල **raṅga-maḍala,** s., place for acting, theatre. — Sk. *raṅga-maṇḍala*.

2137. රට **raṭa,** s., country, province, district. — Pk., P. *raṭṭha*, Sk. *rāṣṭra*. Cf. s.v. *maha-raṭa*.

2138. රටවැසියා **raṭa-väsiyā,** s., inhabitant or native of a country. P. *raṭṭha-vāsī*, Sk. *rāṣṭra-vāsin*.

2139. රත් **rat,** a., red; hot; s. *rata*, st. ff. *rat*, *ratu*, red colour, blood. *rat-ran*, s., wrought gold; *rat-venavā* to become hot. — Pk., P. *ratta*, Sk. *rakta*; si. *rato*, g. *rātuṃ*, m. *rātā*, ass. *rātul*, h. *rātā*, nep. *rāto*, pj. l. *rattā*.

2140. රතනුවන **rata-nuvana,** s., red-eyed one, buffalo, Indian cuckoo, pigeon. — *rat* + *n*°, q.v., Sk. *rakta-nayana*.

2141. රතැස් **ratäs,** s., red-eyed one, buffalo. — P. *rattakkhi*, °*kkha* (a demon), Sk. *raktâkṣi*, °*kṣa* red-eyed one, buffalo.

2142. රතු **ratu,** a., red; s. *rattā* the red one, red-ant. *ratu-käṭaya* red gem, ruby. — Sk. *raktaka*. Cf. *rat*.

2143. රත්මිණ **rat-miṇa,** රත්මැණ **rat-mäṇa,** s., red gem, ruby. — *rat*+*m*°, P. *ratta-maṇi*.

2144. රද **rada**[1], s., king. — Pk. *rāā*, P. *rājā*, Sk. *rājan*; kśm. *rāy*, si. *rāu*, g. *rāy*, *rāv*, m. *rāy*, oṛ. *rāya*, bg. *rāy*, h. *rāy*, *rāo*, nep. *rāi*, pj. *rāi*, *rāu*.

2145. රද **rada**[2], s., st. f. *rada*, dust. — P. *raja*, Sk. *rajas*.

2146. රදනිය **rada-niya**(Ca), s., statesmanship, politics.—Sk. *rāja-nīti*.

2147. රදය **radaya**[1] (Ruv 404), රොද්ද **rodda**(Ca), st. f. *rada*, *rodu*, cord, string, rope. — Pk., P., Sk. *rajju*.

2148. රදය **radaya**[2], st. f. *rada*, pain. — P., Sk. *rujā*.

2149. රදවා **radavā,** s., st. f. *radā*, washerman. — P., Sk. *rajaka*.

2150. රඳනවා **raňdanavā,** v., prt. *räňduvā*, to colour. — Pk. *rañjēi*, P. *rajati*, *rañjēti*, Sk. √*raj*, caus. *rañjayati*. It is difficult to connect with the meaning "to colour" the other meaning "to stay, to remain." One is inclined to believe that we must refer to Sk. *rajyati* is pleased, attached (to feel well somewhere); but cf. intr. *räňdenavā*, prt. *räňduṇā*, to collect in one place, accumulate, become massed or stopped.

2151. රණ **rana**[1], s., st. f. *ran*, forest. — Pk. *araṇṇa*, *raṇṇa*, P. *arañña*, Sk. *araṇya*; si. *riṇu*, *rañ*, *riñ*, g. *rān*, m. *rāṇ*, *rān*, h. *rān*. The spelling *raṇa* is wrong. Cf. DE LANEROLLE, DSL p. xliii, § 5.

2152. රණ **rana**[2], s., st. f. *ran*, gold. *ran-miṇi* gold and gems. — Pk. *hiraṇṇa*, P. *hirañña*, Sk. *hiraṇya*.

2153. රන්කරුවා **ran-karuvā**, s., goldsmith. — Sk. *hiraṇya-kāraka*.

2154. රන්ගැබ **ran-gäba**, s., 1) gold-mine; 2) name of god Brahmā. — Sk. *hiraṇya-garbha* god Brahmā.

2155. රන්මය **ranmaya**, රන්මුවා **ranmuvā**, a., made of gold, golden. — Sk. *hiraṇyamaya*, *hiraṇmaya*.

2156. රන්වන් **ran-van**, a., golden-coloured. — Sk. *hiraṇya-varṇa*.

2157. රඹ **raṁba**, s., plantain. — Pk., P., Sk. *rambhā*.

2158. රම් **ram**, a., agreeable, pleasing. — Pk., P. *ramma*, Sk. *ramya*; cf. nep. *rāmro*. Sinh. *rama* delightful, *ramā* wife, lww. Sk.

2159. රසන් **rasan**, s., in *rasan-dama* (woman's) girdle. — P. *rasanā*, Sk. *raśanā* + *dama*[2]. Cf. *rähäna*.

2160. රහ **raha**, රා **rā**, රස **rasa**, s., st. ff. id., juice, taste, flavour.—Pk., P., Sk. *rasa*; kśm. *ras*, si. *raho*, g. m. *ras*, oṛ. *rasa*, ass. *rah*, bg. h. nep. *ras*, pj. *rahā*. Sinh. also *rasa-ya* with all the meanings of Sk. *rasa*. In this form probably lw.

2161. රහත් **rahat**, s., saint, Arahant. — Pk. *arihā*, P. *arahā*, °*haṃ*, Sk. *arahant*.

— රා **rā**[1], s., noise, see s.v. **räv**.

— රා **rā**[2], s., see s.v. **raha**.

2162. රා **rā**[3], s., passion, desire. — Pk. *rāa*, P., Sk. *rāga*.

2163. රා **rā**[4], s., Ascending node. — Pk., P., Sk. *rāhu*.

2164. රා(ව) **rā(va)**, s., st. f. *rā*, pond, lake. — Perhaps the true Sinhalese derivative of Sk. *hrada* (cf. s.v. *daha*). In nep. there is *raha* side by side with *daha*.

2165. රැකවලා **räka-valā**, s., st. f. °*val*, watchman, keeper, guardian. *räkaval-karanavā* to watch (*rakval-k*°, EpZ II 233 B[20], 9th c.). — Pk. *rakkhavāla*, Sk. *rakṣapāla*; g. *rakhvāḷ*, oṛ. *rakhuāḷa*, bg. *rākhāl*, b. *rakhvār*, h. *rakhvār*, °*vāl*, °*vālā*, nep. *rakhvālo*, pj. *rakhvāl*.

2166. රැඟුම **räṅguma**, s., st. f. °*ṅgum*, dance, play, theatrical performance. *räṅgum-dakvanavā* (or *-penvanavā*) to perform theatrically. — See s.v. *raṅga*; cf. Sk. *raṅgaṇa* dancing.

2167. රැය **räya,** s., st. f. *rä,* night. — Pk. *rāī,* (*ratti,* P. *ratti,*) Sk. *rātrī* ; (kśm. *rāth,* si. *rāti,* g. m. *rāt,* oṛ. ass. *rāti,* bg. h. nep. pj. l. *rāt*).

2168. රැල්ල **rälla,** s., st. f. *räli,* fold, wrinkle; wave. *räli-gahanavā* to pucker, ruffle; *r°-naginavā* to rise as waves. — Doubtful. Perhaps Metathesis of **läri*<**lāri,* Pk. *laharī,* Sk. *lahari* (Ed. Müller) ; si. *lahari,* °*ro,* g. *lār, ler,* m. *lahar,* or. *lahaṛā,* ass. bg. *lahari,* h. nep. *lahar,* pj. *lahir.* In this case the spelling *räḷi* waves and the distinction between it and *räli* folds would be incorrect. Ca has also *raḷa* wave, Cl *rala.*

2169. රැව **räv,** රා **rā,** s., noise, sound. *räv-denavā* to give forth sounds. — Pk. *rava,* P., Sk. *rāva.*

2170. රැස **räsa[1],** s., st. f. *räs,* ray of light. *räs-vihiduvanavā* to send out rays. — Pk. *rassi,* P. *rasmi, raṃsi,* Sk. *raśmi.* With the meaning " cord, rein ": si. *rasī, raso,* g. b. h. nep. *rās,* pj. *rassī, rassā,* l. *rassā.*

2171. රැස **räsa[2],** රැහැ **rähä,** s., st. f. *räs,* mass, heap, multitude. *räs-karanavā* to collect; *räs-venavā* to assemble. — Pk., P. *rāsi,* Sk. *rāśi* ; si. *rāhi,* g. m. *rās,* oṛ. *rāsi,* bg. b. h. nep. pj. *rās.*

2172. රැස්මඬල **räs-maḍala,** s., disk or ring of rays of the sun or moon. — Sk. *raśmi-maṇḍala.*

2173. රැන **räna,** රැහැන **rähäna,** s., st. f. *rän,* cord, rope.— Parallel form of *rasan* (q.v.) < Sk. *raśanā.*

— රික **rika,** රිකිල්ල **rikilla,** ss., see s.v. **ruka.**

2174. රිට **riṭa,** s., st. f. *riṭi,* stick, long pole used as oar. — With cerebralisation = P. *aritta,* Sk. *aritra.*

2175. රිටි **riṭi,** s., in *riṭi-gaha,* Upas tree, Antiaris innoxia. See Hobson-Jobson, s.v. *Upas.* — Pk. *ariṭṭha, riṭṭha-ga,* P. *ariṭṭha,* Sk. *ariṣṭaka* ; g. *rīṭh,* m. *riṭhā, rimṭhī,* bg. oṛ. *riṭhā,* h. *rīṭhā,* nep. *riṭho,* pj. *rīṭhā, reṭhā.*

2176. රිටුවා **riṭuvā,** s., st. f. *riṭu,* crow. — P. *ariṭṭha,* Sk. *ariṣṭa.*

2177. රිට්ටාව **riṭṭāva,** s., st. f. *riṭṭā,* name of the fourth, ninth or fourteenth day of the lunar fortnight, said to be unlucky. — Connected with P. *riṭṭha,* Sk. *riṣṭa, riṣṭi* misfortune ; cf. si. g. m. *rīs,* h. nep. pj. *ris.*

2178. රිත් **rit,** a., empty, void.— Pk., P. *ritta,* Sk. *rikta* ; m. *ritā,* h. *rītā,* nep. *ritto, rīto,* pj. *rītī.*

2179. රිදී **ridi,** s., silver. — Pk. *raaa,* P., Sk. *rajata.*

2180. රිදීමුවා **ridīmuvā,** a., made of silver. — P., Sk. *rajatamaya.*

2181. රිදෙනවා **ridenavā,** v., prt. *riduṇā,* to be painful, ache. Caus. *riddanavā, rudd°,* prt. *ridduvā,* and double caus. *riddavanavā,* prt. *riddevuvā,* to cause to ache, to give pain. — P. *rujati,* Sk $\sqrt{}$*ruj, rujati.*

2182. රිය **riya[1],** s., name of the wife of Cupid. — Pk. *raī,* P., Sk. *rati.*

2183. **රිය riya[2]**, s., carriage. *riy'-adurā*, *r°-ädurā* coachman. — Pk. *raha*, P., Sk. *ratha*.

2184. **රියඉස riya-isa, රියහිස riya-hisa**, s., hood of a carriage. — Sk. *rathaśīrṣa* the fore-part of a carriage.

2185. **රියකරුවා riya-karuvā**, s., (mod.) driver of a vehicle, coachman (for *riy'-ädurā*).— Sk. *ratha-kāraka*.

2186. **රියඟ riyañga[1]**, s., any part of a carriage, carriage wheel. — Sk. *rathâṅga*.

2187. **රියඟ riyañga[2]**, s., ruddy goose (Ruv 246 = *sak-vā*).— Sk. *rathâṅga*.

2188. **රියන riyana**, s., cubit (=18 inches). — Pk. *arattī*, P. *ratana*, Sk. *aratni*.

2189. **රියසක riya-saka**, s., carriage wheel. — Sk. *ratha-cakra*.

2190 **රියසරි riya-sari** (Ca), **රියසැරි riya-säri** (Ca), s., coachman. — Cf. P. *rathacara*, Sk. **ratha-cārin*.— Prob. for *rivi-säri* (Sk. *ravi-sārathi*) the sun's charioteer, name of Aruṇa. De Lanerolle.

2191. **රිවි rivi**, s., sun. *rivi-maga* sun's path, sky. — Pk., P., Sk. *ravi*.

2192. **රිවිදින rivi-dina**, s., Sunday. — P., Sk. *ravi-dina*.

2193. **රිවිපුත් rivi-put** (or *-pit*), s., planet Saturn. — Sk. *ravi-putra*.

2194. **රිවිමඬල rivi-mañḍala**, s., disk of the sun. — Sk. *ravi-maṇḍala*.

— **රිවිසැරි rivi-säri**, s., see s.v. **riya-sari**.

2195. **රිසිය risiya, රිස්ස rissa**, s., st. f. *risi*, pleasant taste; wish, desire. *risi-venavā* to desire.—Pk. *rui*, *ruiya*, P. *ruci*, Sk. *ruci*, *-rucitā*. Cf. *russanavā*.

2196. **රිහිරි rihiri** (contr. *rīri*), s., st. f. *rihiri*, *rīri*, blood. *rīri-yakā* a demon (Parker, Anc. Ceylon, p. 145). — Cf. s.v. *urira*.

2197. **රුක ruka[1]**, s., st. f. *ruk*, sorrow, affliction (Ruv 135). — Pk. *rukkha*, *lukkha*, P. *lūkha*, Sk. *rūkṣa*, *lūkṣa* dry, barren, rough; kśm. *lochu*, si. *rukho*, g. *lūkhuṃ*, m. oṛ. bg. *rukhā*, h. *rūkhā*, nep. *rukho*, pj. l. *rukkhā*. Semasiologically doubtful.

2198. **රුක ruka[2], රික rika**, s., st. f. *ruk*, tree. *rikilla* twig, sprig (=*ruk*+ diminutive suff. *-la*). — Pk., P. *rukkha*, Sk. *vṛkṣa*; g. m. h. *rūkh*, nep. *rukh*, pj. l. *rukkh*.

2199. **රුක්දෙවියා ruk-deviyā**, s., sylvan deity. — P. *rukkha-dēvatā*, Sk. *vṛkṣa-dēvatā*.

2200. **රුක්මුල ruk-mula**, s., foot of a tree.—P. *rukkha-mūla*, Sk. *vṛkṣa-mūla*.

2201. **රුතිය rutiya**, s., st. f. *ruti*, wish, desire. — From a MInd. **rutti*, Sk. **rukti*, $\sqrt{}$*ruc*.

2202. **රුදැව rudäva**, s., pain, ache. — P., Sk. *rujā* (? Slw.).

2203. **රුදු rudu,** a., fierce, cruel, savage. — Pk., P. *rudda*, Sk. *rudra*, *raudra*. With split *-dr-* Sinh. *ruduru* the god Śiva.

2204. **රුප්පය ruppaya** (or *°pē*), s., foot of a tree. — < *ruk-paya* = MInd. **rukkhapāda*.

2205. **රුව ruva,** s., st. f. *rū*, form, image, comeliness, beauty. *rū-bara* beautiful ; *rū-kaḍaya* puppet, dancing doll (v. *kaḍa*). — Pk. *rūvu*, P., Sk. *rūpa* ; m. *-ruṃ* (cf. Bl, s.v.), oṛ. ass. bg. *-ru*, b. h. nep. pj. *-ru*.

2206. **රුවන ruvana,** s., st. f. *ruvan*, gem, jewel. *ruvan-räsa* heap of gems. — Pk. *raaṇa*, P. *ratana*, Sk. *ratna*.

2207. **රුවනවා ruvanavā,** v., prt. *rivuvā*, to thrust in, put in between, insert. — Pk. *rövēi*, P. *rōpēti*, Sk. *rōpayati*, √*ruh* ; m. *rovṇeṃ*, oṛ. *roibā*, ass. *roiba*, bg. *royā*, nep. *ropnu*.

2208. **රුවනාර ruvan-âra,** s., gem-mine, i. e. ocean. — P. *ratanâkara*, Sk. *ratnâkara*.

2209. **රුවල ruvala,** s., st. f. *ruval*, sail. *ruval-näva* sailing boat. — Metathesis of **luvar*=P. *lakāra* (indones. *layar*), HSm., Bull. Soc. de Lingu. xxxiv, fasc. 2, nr. 102, 1933.

2210. **රුසිරු rusiru,** a., pleasant, beautiful. — Pk. *ruira*, P., Sk. *rucira*.

2211. **රුස්සනවා russanavā,** v., prt. *rissuvā*, to bear, enjoy, like. — <**rusvanavā*, caus. of **rusanavā*=Pk. *ruccaï*, P. *ruccati*, Sk. **rucyatē* (√*ruc*) is pleasant, is liked ; si. *rucaṇu*, g. *rucvuṃ*, m. *rucṇeṃ*, oṛ. *rucibā*, ass. *rusiba*, bg. *rucā*, h. *rucnā*, nep. *rucnu*, pj. *rucṇā*. Cf. *risiya*.

2212. **රෙද්ද redda,** s., st. f. *redi*, cloth, garment. *redi-kaḍa* piece of cloth. — I think the word must be derived from √*raj* to dye, pprt. caus. *rañjita*.

2213. **රෙනවා renavā,** v., prt. *rivuvā*, *runnā*, to evacuate by stool (vulgar). —Sk. √*rī* ; Pk. *rīaï* moves, Sk. *riyati* lets run. In the Iranian languages cf. MP. *rītan*, NP. *rīdan* cacare. Horn, Neupers. Etymologie, p. 142.

2214. **රෙහෙණ reheṇa,** s., the fourth lunar asterism. — P., Sk. *rōhiṇī*.

2215. **රේ rē,** part. expressive of disrespect. — P., Sk. *rē* ; kśm. *rē* (used after the name of a person addressed), si. g. m. oṛ. ass. bg. h. *re* (T, s.v. *re*).

2216. **රේමස් rē-mas, රෙහෙමස් rehe-mas,** s., sheatfish. — Pk. *rōhia*, P., Sk. *rōhita* ; m. *rohī*, oṛ. *rohi*, ass. *rau*, bg. *rui*, h. *rohū*, *rehū*, *rahū*, nep. *revā*, pj. *rohū*, *rehū*.

— **රොද්ද rodda,** s., see s.v. **radaya**[1].

2217. **රොන rona,** s., st. f. *ron*, dust, pollen. — Pk., P., Sk. *rēṇu* ; g. *reṇ*, nep. *ren* (?), pj. *ren*.

2218. **රොස rosa,** s., st. f. *ros*, anger. — Pk., P. *rōsa*, Sk. *rōṣa*.

2219. **රෝ rō,** s., disease, illness. — P., Sk. *rōga*.

ල L

— ල **la,** a., see s.v. **lā.**

— ලං **laṃ,** s., a., see s.v. **laṅga.**

2220. ලක **laka**[1] (or *lak-diva*), name of Ceylon. — P. *laṅkā, laṅkādīpa,* Sk. *laṅkā, laṅkādvīpa.*

2221. ලක **laka**[2], s., st. f. *lak,* mark. — Pk., P. *lakkha,* Sk. *lakṣa.* In the MIAVs g. m. h. nep. *lākh* etc., num. = 100,000 (Bl, T, s.v.).

2222. ලකර **lakara,** s., st. f. *lakara,* beauty. — Pk. *alaṃkāra,* P. *alaṅkāra,* Sk. *alaṃkāra.*

2223. ලකළ **lakaḷa,** a., beautiful. — Pk. *alaṃkia,* P. *alaṅkata,* Sk. *alaṃkṛta.*

2224. ලකුණ **lakuṇa,** s., st. f. °*ṇu,* mark, sign. *lakuṇu-karanavā* to mark. —Pk., P. *lakkhaṇa,* Sk. *lakṣaṇa.*

2225. ලගිනවා **laginavā,** v., prt. *läggā,* to abide, lodge, lie down. Double caus. *laggavanavā,* prt. *läggevuvā,* to give lodging, to cause to lie down. — Pk. *laggaï,* P. *laggati* (*lagati,* Sk. √*lag, lagati*) ; kśm. *lagun,* si. *lagaṇu,* g. *lāgvuṃ,* m. *lāgṇeṃ,* oṛ. *lāgibā,* ass. *lāgiba,* bg. *lāgā,* h. *lāgnā,* nep. *lāgnu,* pj. *laggṇā,* l. *laggaṇ.* Gr. 50.25.

2226. ලඟ **laṅga,** ලං **laṃ** (for *laṅ*), s., a., near, proximate; *laṅga-ṭa* to the vicinity of ; *laṃ-maga* short way. — Pk., P. *lagga,* Sk. *lagna* ; si. *lagi,* m. *lāgīṃ,* oṛ. bg. nep. *lāgi,* h. *lāgī, lāge* (H p. 225, LSI I. 2, p. 215). The word is often spelt *ḷaṅga* (Ca), but, I think, incorrectly. — The traditional spelling is always with *ḷ* (De Lanerolle).

— ලඟනවා **laṅganavā,** v., see s. v. **naganavā, läṅgi.**

2227. ලටපට **laṭapaṭa,** s., medley (of things) ; nonsense. — g. m. oṛ. bg. h. *laṭ-paṭ.* Cf. Turner, s.v. *laṭṭi-paṭṭi.*

2228. ලටි **laṭi,** ලටු **laṭu,** s., liquorice plant, Abrus precatorius. — P. *laṭṭhi, laṭṭhikā* (also *madhu-laṭṭhikā*) ; kśm. *loṭhu,* si. *lāṭhi,* g. *lāṭhī,* m. *lāṭh,* oṛ. ass. bg. *lāṭhi,* b. h. *lāṭh,* nep. *lāṭho,* pj. l. *laṭṭh* (in the MIAVs generally "stick, pole"). Sinh. *laṭṭa* is a name of the *mī-gaha* Bssia longifolia.

2229. ලඩු **laḍu,** s., confectionery made of jaknuts, coconut and treacle. —Pk., Sk. *laḍḍu.*

— ලත් **lat,** a. pprt., see s.v. **lada**[4].

2230. ලතු **latu,** s., gumlac, red dye. *latu-van* lac colour.— Pk. *alattaya,* P. *alattaka, lattaka,* Sk. *alaktaka, laktaka.*

2231. ලද **lada**[1], a., young, tender. — Sk. *navaja.* See s.v. *lā.*— The traditional spelling is always with *ḷ* (De Lanerolle).

2232. ලද **lada**[2], s., shame. — Pk., P., Sk. *lajjā* ; kśm. *laz,* si. *laja,* g. m. *lāj,* oṛ. *lāja,* ass. *lāz,* bg. h. nep. *lāj,* pj. *lajj.*

2233. ලද **lada**[3], s., fried grain. — Pk. *lāyā,* P. *lājā,* Sk. pl. *lājāḥ* ; kśm. *lāy,* oṛ. *liā,* b. h. nep. *lāvā.*

2234. ලද **lada^{4},** ලත් **lat,** a. pprt., r e c e i v e d. — Pk., P. *laddha*, Sk. *labdha* ; si. *ladho*, l. *laddhā*, cf. g. *lādhvuṃ*, m. *lādhṇeṃ*, pj. *laddhṇā*. See *labanavā*.

2235. ලනවා **lanavā,** v., prt. *lāvā*, t o p u t, p l a c e, l a y. Caus. *lavanavā*, prt. *lävuvā*, to cause to place. — Pk. *lāya* taken, *lēi* (Hem 4.238) takes ; g. *levuṃ*, m. *leṇeṃ*, ass. *laïba*, bg. *laoyā*, h. *lānā*, *lenā*, nep. *lānu*.

2236. ලබනවා **labanavā,** v., prt. *läbuvā*, t o g e t, r e c e i v e. Intr. *läbenavā*, prt. *läbuṇā*, to receive.— Pk. *lahaï*, P. *labhati*, Sk. *√labh*, *labhatē* ; si. *lahaṇu*, g. *lābhvuṃ*, m. *lābhṇeṃ* (cf. T, s.v.), h. *lahnā*, nep. *lahanā*, pj. *lahiṇā*.

2237. ලබ්බ **labba,** s., st. f. *labu*, p u m p k i n, g o u r d. — Pk. *alāu*, *lāu*, P. Sk. *lābu*, *alābu*+-*ka* ; oṛ. ass. bg. *lāu*, b. h. pj. *laukā*, nep. *lauko*.

2238. ලඹ **lam̆ba,** a., h a n g i n g ; s. *lam̆baya* plummet, plumb ; *lam̆ba-lanuva* plumb-line. — Pk., P., Sk. *lamba* hanging, long ; si. *lāma* length, g. *lāṃbuṃ*, m. *lāṃb*, or. *lambā*, h. *lāṃb*, *lambā*, nep. *lāmu*, pj. l. *lammā*.

2239. ලම්බෝරා **lam̆bōrā,** s., b i g - b e l l i e d o n e, n a m e o f G a ṇ ē ṣ a. — Sk. *lambôdara*.

2240. ලල **lala,** a., d e s i r i n g. — P. *lālasā* desire, Sk. *lālasa* ; cf. si. *lālici*, g. m. bg. h. pj. *lālac*.

2241. ලවන **lavana,** s., st. f. °*an*, l i p. —Pk. *lavaṇa*, P., Sk. *lapana*. Sinh. also *lavanata* = *l*° + *ata*.

2242. ලවා **lavā,** postp., b y m e a n s o f, t h r o u g h. — Ger. of v. *lavanava*, v.s.v. *lanavā*.

2243. ලස් **las,** a., i d l e. — Pk., P., Sk. *alasa* ; kśm. *ālaci*, si. *ārisu*, °*sī*, g. *āḷas*, *āḷsuṃ*, m. *āḷas*, *ālśī*, ass. *ālāh*, bg. *ālse*, h. *ālas*, *ālasī*, nep. *alsi*, pj. *ālas*, *ālasī*. Cf. *läsi*.

2244. ලස **lasa,** s., st. f. *las*, b r i b e. — Pk., P., Sk. *lañca* ; si. g. m. h. *lāṃc*. Cf. *atlasa*, *allasa*.

2245. ලහ **laha,** s., t a b l e t, t i c k e t, l a b e l. Cf. *lahā(-bat)*, EpZ I 25^{16}, 10th c. — Metathesis of **hala* = Pk. *salāyā*, P. *salākā*, Sk. *śalākā* ; si. *sarāī*, m. *saḷaī*, bg. *salā*, b. h. pj. l. *salāī*, nep. *salāi*.

2246. ලා **lā-** (generally *la-*), a., n e w, y o u n g, f r e s h. *la-daru* infantile ; *la-daruvā* babe ; *la-pata* tender leaf ; *lā-daḷuva* young bud ; *la-hiru* early sun, newly risen sun ; *lā-pala* young fruit. — Ca spells *ḷā*, but I believe that *lā* is = P., Sk. *nava* (Pk. *ṇava* ; kśm. *novu*, si. *namoṃ*, g. *navuṃ*, m. *navā*, ass. *na*, bg. *na*, *nai*, h. *navā*, *nayā*, nep. *naulo*, pj. *navāṃ*, l. *navaṃ*), and is shortened in cpds. as *sē* white becomes *se-* ; see *lada^{1}* = *navaja* ; *la-hiru*, cf. *navôdita sūrya* ; *la-daruvā*=**nava-dāraka* etc. Sinh. *nava* new is lw. — According to traditional spelling *ḷa-*, *ḷā-*, *ḷa-daru*, *ḷa-daḷu*, *ḷa-hiru* &c., &c., are always spelt with *ḷ*. See DSL p. xliv, § 16. Also cf. Tam. *iḷa-nilā* (Sinh. *ḷa-sam̆da*) crescent moon. DE LANEROLLE.

2247. ලැඟි **läňgi,** a. pprt., gone beyond, transgressed, lifted up.—Pk. *laṅghia*, P., Sk. *laṅghita*. Cf. *laňganavā*.

2248. ලැදි **lädi,** a., inclined to, devoted to.—P. *laddhika* ; cf. Sk. *labdhi*: si. *lādhi*.

2249. ලැසි **läsi,** a., lazy, idle. — Sk. *alāsya* ; cf. *las*.

2250. ලික්කාවා **likkāvā,** s., young louse, nit.—Pk. *likkhā*, Sk. *likṣā* ; kśm. *lach*, *lich*, si. *līkha*, g. m. *līkh*, oṛ. *nikha*, ass. *lekhi*, bg. *likkā*, h. pj. *līkh*, nep. *likho*. Perhaps lw. Widespread also in the Iranian languages (P. HORN, Neup. Etym. s.v. *rišk*).

2251. ලිත **lita,** s., almanac, calendar.—Pk., P. *litta*, Sk. *lipta*, √*lip* ; cf. Bl, s.v. *limpṇeṃ*, T, s.v. *lipnu*.

2252. ලිය **liya**[1], s., st. f. id., creeper ; (poet.) woman.— Pk. *laā*, P., Sk. *latā*.

2253. ලිය **liya**[2], s., dwelling house.—Sk. *laya* rest, repose, place of rest ; cf. *layana* = *gṛha*, *āsana*.

2254. ලිය **liya**[3], s., weariness, loss, destruction.—Sk. *laya* melting away, reduction, destruction.

2255. ලියනවා **liyanavā,** v., prt. *livuvā*, to write. Caus. *liyavanavā*, prt. *liyevuvā*, to cause to write ; *liyannā* clerk.—Pk. *lihaï*, P. *likhati*, caus. *likhāpēti*, Sk. √ *likh*, *likhati* ; si. *lekhaṇu*, g. *lekhvuṃ*, m. *lehṇeṃ*, *lihiṇeṃ*, ass. *lekhiba*, bg. *lekhā*, h. *lekhnā*, nep. *lekhnu*.

2256. ලිහිණියා **lihiṇiyā,** s., st. f. °*ṇi*, bird. ECpds. : *ula-lihiṇiyā* a kind of stork; *säḷa-l*° the maina bird etc.—? from √*las*, *lasati* moves rapidly ; cf. *lāsin* moving to and fro. Also spelt *ḷihiṇi*, DhpAGp 30[23]

— ලිහිල් **lihil,** ලිල් **lil,** a., see s.v. **ihil.**

2257. ලුණු **luṇu,** s., salt. *luṇ'-amba*, *luṇu-diya* salt-water.—Pk., P. *lōṇa*, Sk. *lavaṇa* ; kśm. *nūn*, si. *lūṇu*, g. *luṇ*, m. *loṇ*, oṛ. *luṇa*, *nuṇa*, bg. *nun*, h. *lon*, *lūn*, *non*, *nūn*, nep. *nun*, pj. *lūṇ*, *nūṇ*. Gr. 50.15.

2258. ලුහු **luhu,** a., light, short, brief, swift. *l*°-*dana* poor people. — Pk. *lahua*, *halua*, P. *lahu*, *lahuka*, Sk. *laghu*, *laghuka* ; g. *haḷu*, m. *haḷū*, h. *halū*, nep. *halaum*.

2259. ලුහුඬු **luhuňḍu,** a., short, brief, deficient. — *luhu*-+*aḍu*, q.v., cf. pj. *lahuḍā* young.

2260. ලුහුනු **luhunu,** ලූනු **lūnu,** s. pl., onions.— Pk. *lasuṇa*, P. *lasuna*, Sk. *laśuna* ; kśm. *ruhun*, g. m. *lasaṇ*, oṛ. *rasuṇa*, bg. *rasun*, b. *lahsun*, *rasun*, h. *lasun*, *lhasun*, nep. *lasun*, pj. *lasaṇ*.

2261. ලෙය **leya,** s., st. f. *lē*, row, line. *sand-leyak-bandu* like a crescent moon. EpZ I 186[4], 10th c.—Pk. *lēhā*, P., Sk. *lēkhā* ; si. *līha*, pj. *līh*.

— ලෙව් **lev,** s., see s.v. **lova.**

— ලෙවකනවා **leva-kanavā,** ලෙවිනවා **levinavā,** v., see s.v. **lovinavā.**

2262. ලෙස **lesa,** s., manner, method. — *-lesa, -lesa-ṭa, -lesin* are used (a) to form adverbs, or (b) to express final propositions: *me-lesa, me-lesin* thus; *balana-lesa* in order to see.—P. *lēsa,* Sk. *lēśa* trick, stratagem. Ca gives for Sinh. *lesa* also the meaning "deception" (cf. Muv 10).

2263. ලෙළ **leḷa,** a., shaking, quavering. *leḷa-denavā* to shake, quaver.—In P. *lōḷa* alternates with *lōla* (v. PTSPD), and in Sk. √*luḍ, luṭ* with *lul.* Cf. kśm. *lolɨ* and g. *loḷo* tongue, si. *rolo* wandering, m. *loḷ* rolling over, oṛ. *loḷi* and nep. *lolā* hanging ear-ornament, ass. *lolā* and bg. *lola* loose, pj. *lol* flap of skin (on a bull).

2264. ලෙළෙනවා **leḷenavā,** v., prt. *leḷuṇā,* to shake (intr.). Caus. *leḷavanavā,* prt. *leḷevuvā,* v. tr., to shake, agitate.—Pk. *loṭṭaī,* Sk. √ *lul* : *lōlati* ; *luḍ* : *lōḍati* ; *luṭ* : *lōṭatē, luṭyati* ; *luṭh* : *luṭhati* ; si. *leṭaṇu,* g. *leṭvuṃ, loṭvuṃ,* m. *leṭṇeṃ, loṭṇeṃ,* oṛ. *loṭibā,* ass. *leṭiba, loṭiba,* bg. *loṭā,* h. pj. *leṭnā, loṭnā,* nep. *leṭnu, loṭnu,* l. *leṭaṇ.*

2265. ලේ **lē,** s., blood. *lē-van* blood-colour, red.—Pk. *lōhia,* P., Sk. *lōhita* ; si. *lohū,* g. *lohī,* bg. *lau,* h. *lohū, lehū, lahū,* nep. *lohu.*

2266. ලොත්ගහ **lot-gaha,** s., name of a tree, Symplocos racemosa. — Pk. *loddha,* P. *lodda,* Sk. *lōdhra* ; kśm. *lôdu,* si. *loḍru,* g. *lodhar,* m. *lodh, lod,* oṛ. *lodha,* bg. h. *lodh,* nep. *rudhilo,* pj. *lodh, lodar.*

2267. ලොබ **loba,** s., covetousness, desire. — Pk., P., Sk. *lōbha* ; m. *loho.*

2268. ලොම් **lom,** s., hair, wool, fur. *lom-roda* lock of hair. — Pk., P. *lōma* (*rōma*), Sk. *lōman* (*rōman*) ; (kśm. *rum*), si. *lūṃ, luaṃ* (*rūm*), g. *lom* (*rom, ruṃuṃ*), m. *loṃ, loṃv,* (oṛ. *roma,*) ass. *nom,* (bg. *roṃ,* h. *roāṃ, rūāṃ,* nep. *rauṃ, ruṃ,*) pj. *lūīṃ* (*rom, roāṃ, rūāṃ*), l. *luṃ.* Cf. *uṇu-lom.*

2269. ලොව **lova,** s., st. f. *lō,* world. *lō-väḍa* public good. —Pk. *lōa, lōga,* P., Sk. *lōka* ; MIAVs lw. *lok.*

2270. ලොවග **lovaga,** s., chief of the world, i. e. the Buddha.—P. *lōkagga.*

2271. ලොවනා **lova-nā,** ලෝනා **lō-nā,** s., lord of the world, i.e. the Buddha. — P., Sk. *lōkanātha.*

2272. ලොවිනවා **lovinavā,** v., prt. *levuvā,* to lap, lick. — P. *lēhati,* Sk. √*lih, lēḍhi, lihati.* Cf. Sinh. *leva-kanavā* to lick ; Ca quotes also *levinavā* besides *lov°.*

2273. ලොහො **loho,** s., st. f. *loho, lō,* metal. *lō-kaḍa* bronze.—Pk., P., Sk. *lōha* ; si. *lohu,* g. *loh,* m. *loh, lokhaṃḍ,* oṛ. *luhā,* ass. *lo,* bg. h. nep. pj. l. *lohā.*

2274. ලෝකරුවා **lō-karuvā,** ලොහොකරුවා **loho-karuvā,** °කුරුවා **°-kuruvā,** s., iron-worker, blacksmith.—Pk. *lōhāra,* P., Sk. *lōhakāra*(*-ka*) ; si. *luhāru,* g. *luhār,* m. *lohar,* bg. h. nep. l. *lohār,* pj. *luhār.*

2275. **ලෝදා lō-dā,** s., world sphere. — P. *lōka-dhātu.*

ව V

2276. **ව va[1]-,** prefix = Pk. *ava-*, P., Sk. *apa.* Cf. *varada*[1], *vasmara.*

2277. **ව va[2]-,** prefix = Pk., P., Sk. *ava-.* See *vaguranavā, vaṭana*[1], *vahasa*[2].

2278. **ව va[3]-,** prefix = Pk. *uva-*, P., Sk. *upa-.* See *vaḍaya*[1], *varada*[2], *vahara*[1]. Cf. also *uva-.*

2279. **ව va[4]-, වි vi-,** prefix = Pk., P., Sk. *vi-.* See *vataḷa, vadanavā* ; *vikuṇanavā* etc.

2280. **වක් vak,** a. crooked, curved; s. *vakaya* curve flexure ; *vak-venavā* to become bent or contorted.—Pk. *vaṅka,* P. *vakka, vaṅka,* Sk. *vakra* ; kśm. *vakar,* si. *vaṅga, viṅgo,* g. *vāṃkuṃ,* m. *vāṃkā,* oṛ. *baṅkā,* bg. h. *bāṃkā,* nep. *bāṅgo, bāṅño,* pj. *biṅgā, viṅgā.*

2281. **වක vaka[1],** s., st. f. *vak,* period, lunar day.— The same as *pak*[1] (q.v.), originally in cpds. after a vowel. Cf. *aṭa-vaka* eighth day after the new or full moon. — <MInd. **aṭṭha-pakkha.*

2282. **වක vaka[2],** s., st. f. *vak,* in *vak-niya,* name of a tree, from the fibres of which bow strings are made, Sanseviera zeylanica. — (Pk., P. *vakkala*) Sk. *valka* (*valkala*) ; g. m. *vāk,* (ass. bg. *bākal,* h. *baklā,* nep. *bokro,*) pj. *bakk* + *niya* (cf. *niyaňda*).

2283. **වකනවා vakanavā,** v., prt. *väkuvā,* to daub, smear, rub on. — Intr. *väkenavā,* prt. *väkuṇā,* to become smeared with. — Seems to be a parallel form of *makanavā,* q.v. P. *makkhēti.*

2284. **වකුගඩුව vaku-gaḍuva,** s., kidney. — *vaku* = P. *vakka,* Sk. *vṛkka* ; kśm. *bokh,* si. *bukī,* m. *bokā,* oṛ. *buka,* ass. bg. *buk,* l. *bukkī* + *gaḍuva,* q.v.

2285. **වග vaga[1],** s., sort, class, group; matter, affair. *vaga-kiyanavā* to state a matter, give account, to find fault with.—Pk., P. *vagga,* Sk. *varga* ; si. *vagu,* g. *vāgh,* pj. l. *vagg* ; cf. h. *bagār,* nep. *bagāl.*

2286. **වග vaga[2],** s., tiger. — Pk. *vaggha,* P. *vyaggha,* Sk. *vyāghra* ; si. *vāghu,* g. m. *vāgh,* oṛ. *bāgha,* ass. bg. h. nep. pj. *bāgh.*

2287. **වගු vagu,** °ඟු **°ňgu,** s., name of Bengal. — P., Sk. *vaṅga.*

2288. **වගුරනවා vaguranavā,** v., prt. *väguruvā* (or *vaguḷā*), to pour out, shed, spill. Caus. *vaguruvanavā,* prt. *vägirevuvā,* id. ; intr. *vägirenavā,* prt. *vägiruṇā,* to flow, fall off. — Sk. *ava-* + $\sqrt{}$*ghṛ, gharati.*

2289. **වගුළ vaguḷa, වගළ vagaḷa,** a. pprt., outpoured. — < MInd. **ava-ghaṭa,* or *vi-ghaṭa,* Sk. **ava-ghṛta, vi-ghṛta.* Cf. *vaguranavā.*

2290. **වට vaṭa,** a., round, circular; s. *vaṭaya* circle.—Pk., P. *vaṭṭa,* Sk. *vṛtta.*

2291. වටන **vaṭana**[1], s., st. f. *vaṭan*, position, standing place. — Pk. *avatthāṇa*, P. *avaṭṭhāna*, Sk. *avasthāna* : si. *vathāṇu*, m. *vaṭhān*, bg. *bāthān*, b. nep. *bathān*, h. *bathān*, *baṭhān*.

2292. වටන **vaṭana**[2], s., st. f. *vaṭan*, attending upon, waiting on. *vaṭana labanuyē*, trsl. of P. *upaṭṭhiyamāno*, DhpAGp 32[1]. — Pk. *uvaṭṭhāṇa*, P. *upaṭṭhāna*, Sk. *upasthāna*. Cf. Sinh. *vaṭā* = P. *upaṭṭhāka*.

2293. වටනවා **vaṭanavā**, v., to turn round. — P. *vaṭṭēti*, Sk. √*vṛt*, caus. *vartayati* ; kśm. *vaṭun*, si. *vaṭaṇu*, g. *vāṭvuṃ*, oṛ. *bāṭibā*, ass. *bāṭiba*, bg. *bāṭnā*, h. *baṭnā*, nep. *bāṭnu*, pj. *baṭṭnā*, *vaṭṭnā*, l. *vaṭaṇ*. Cf. *vaṭinavā*, *väṭenavā*.

— වටය **vaṭaya**[1], s., see s.v. **vaṭa**.

2294. වටය **vaṭaya**[2], s., rain. — P. *vaṭṭa* (pprt. of *vassati*), Sk. *vṛṣṭa*. Cf. *vässa*.

2295. වටිනවා **vaṭinavā**, v., to be worth, merit, deserve. *vaṭinā*, a., worth. — Pk. *vaṭṭaï*, P. *vaṭṭati* behoves, is right, Sk. √ *vṛt*, *vartatē*. Cf. *vaṭanavā*. In the older language also a v. *vaṭinavā*, prt. *väṭiyā*, to attend, wait on, seems to have existed = P. *upaṭṭhāti*, Sk. *upa* + √*sthā* : in the DhpAGp 14[2], P. *upaṭṭhahiṃsu* is translated by *väṭiyō*.

2296. වටුවා **vaṭuvā**, s., snipe in general (also sand-piper etc.).—Pk. *vaṭṭaa*, P. *vaṭṭakā*, Sk. *vartikā*, *vartakā* ; kśm. *bāṭuru*, bg. *bāṭuyā*, h. pj. *baṭer*, nep. *baṭṭāi*.

2297. වඩනවා **vaḍanavā**, v. tr., prt. *väḍuvā*, to increase, augment; to take up (and carry a child in the arms). Intr. *vaḍinavā*, prt. *väḍiyā*, to increase, (hon.) to proceed, go ; *väḍenavā*, prt. *väḍuṇā*, to increase, grow. — *vaḍanavā* < Pk. *vaḍḍhēi*, P. *vaḍḍhēti*, Sk. √*vṛdh*, caus. *vardhayati* ; *vaḍinavā* < *vaḍḍhaï*, *vaḍḍhati*, *vardhatē* : *väḍenavā* < MInd. **vaḍḍhiyati*. Cf. kśm. *baḍun*, si. *vadhaṇu*, g. *vādhvuṃ*, *vuḍhvuṃ*, m. *vāḍhṇeṃ*, oṛ. *baṛhibā*, ass. *bāriba*, bg. *bāṛā*, h. *bāṛhnā*, nep. *baṛnu*, *baṛhnu*, pj. *vaddhṇā*, l. *vaddhaṇ* (meanings in the MIAVs "to increase" and "to proceed, go").

2298. වඩබාදිය **vaḍa-bā-diya**, s., flow and ebb of the tide, the tide.— *vaḍa* (v. *vaḍanavā*)+*bā* (v. *bahinavā*)+*diya* (q.v.). Sinh. *vaḍa-diya* flood tide.

2299. වඩය **vaḍaya**[1], s., part, half. — P. *upaḍḍha* (Sk. *upa*+*ardha*).

2300. වඩය **vaḍaya**[2], s., cutting; headless trunk. – Sk. √*vṛdh*, *vardhayati* cuts ; cf. g. *vāḍh*, *bāṛh*, h. *bāṛh*, *bāṛ* edge of a knife, nep. *bāṛ*.

2301. වඩුවා **vaḍuvā**, s., st. f. *vaḍu*, carpenter; *vaḍu-äduṛā* id. ; *v°-maḍuva* carpenter's shed.—Pk. *vaḍḍhaïa*, P. *vaḍḍhaki*, Sk. *vardhaka*, °*ki* ; m. *vāḍhāyā*, oṛ. *baṛhāi*, ass. *bārai*, bg. *bāṛaï*, h. *baṛhaī*, nep. *baṛaï*, *baṛahi*, pj. *vāḍḍhī*.

2302. වණය **vaṇaya**, s., st. f. *vaṇa*, sore, ulcer. *vaṇa-venavā* to become ulcerous.—Pk., P. *vaṇa*, Sk. *vraṇa* ; m. *vaṇ*.

2303. වට **vata¹**, s., st. f. *vat*, face. — P. *vatta*, Sk. *vaktra* ; si. *vātu*, l. *vāt* mouth. Cf. *mā-vatā*.

2304. වට **vata²**, s., st. f. *vat*, road, way. *mā-vata* highway.—< MInd. **vattan* = Pk. *vaṭṭā*, P. *vaṭuma*, Sk. *vartman* ; kśm. *vath*, si. *vāṭa*, g. m. *vāṭ*, oṛ. *bāṭa*, ass. bg. h. *bāṭ*, nep. *bāṭo*, pj. *bāṭ*, *vāṭ*, l. *vāṭ*.

2305. වට **vata³**, s., st. f. *vat*, substance, wealth. *vat-kama* id. — Pk., P. *vatthu*, Sk. *vastu* ; si. *vathu*.

2306. වට **vata⁴**, s., st. f. *vat*, cloth, garment. — Pk., P. *vattha*, Sk. *vastra*.

2307. වට **vata⁵**, s., st. f. *vat*, religious rite, ceremony. *vat-karanavā* to perform rites.—Pk., P. *vatta*, Sk. *vṛtta* ; kśm. *bāth*, g. *vāt*, h. *bāt* news, si. *vātu*, nep. *bāt*, pj. *bāt*, *vāt* talk.

2308. වටළ **vataḷa**, a. pprt., spread abroad, diffused.—Pk., P. *vitthata*, Sk. *vi-* + $\sqrt{}$*stṛ*. Cf. *vaturanavā*.

2309. වතුර **vatura**, s., st. f. *vaturu*, flood; (coll.) water. — The original meaning is "spread, extension, flood" (m. *vithar*). Cf. the book-title *amā-vatura* flood of ambrosia ; *gaṃ-vatura* high-water. Pk., P. *vitthāra*, Sk. *vistāra* (B. Gunasekara). Wickremasinghe's derivation from Sk. *vartarūka* (EpZ I 27, n. 2) is improbable. The vocalism *a.u.* in *vatura* is irregular. Cf. *vitara*.

2310. වතුරනවා **vaturanavā**, v., prt. *vatuḷā*, *väturuvā*, to spread. Intr. *vätirenavā*, prt. *väturuṇā*, to lie extended, to overflow.—Pk. *vitthārēi*, P. *vitthārēti*, Sk. *vi-* + $\sqrt{}$*stṛ*, caus. *vi-stārayati* ; kśm. *vatharāvun*, h. *bithārnā*.

2311. වත්ත **vatta**, s., st. f. *vatu*, garden, plantation. *vatu-kumburu* gardens and fields.—P. *vatthu*, Sk. *vāstu* + *-ka*.

2312. වද **vada¹**, s., fault.—P. *vajja*, Sk. *varjya* ; cf. Pk. *vajjēi*.

2313. වද **vada²**, s., leather thong. — Sk. *vardhra* ; cf. P. *vaddha-maya* leathern.

— වද **vada³** (= *vācā*), see s.v. **vadāranavā**.

2314. වද **vada⁴**, s., cattle-pen, sheepfold. *go-vada* (*-vuda*) cattle pen.— P. *vaja*, Sk. *vraja*.

2315. වදන **vadana**, s., st. f. *vadan*, saying, word.—Pk. *vaaṇa*, P., Sk. *vacana*.

2316. වදනවා **vadanavā**, v., prt. *väduvā*, to bring forth young.— Pk. *viaaï*, P. *vijāyati*, Sk. *vi-* + $\sqrt{}$*jan*, *vi-jāyatē* ; g. *viāvuṃ*, m. *viṇeṃ*, bg. *biyā*, h. *byānā*, nep. *biyāunu*, l. *viāvaṇ*.

2317. වදය **vadaya**, s., st. f. *vada*, punishment, torture. *vada-karuvā* executioner, torturer ; *v°-karanavā* to torture. — Pk., P. *vajjhā*, Sk. *vadhyā*.

2318. වදාරනවා **vadāranavā,** v., prt. *vadāḷā*, *vädāruvā*, to speak, say, tell.—*vada* = Pk. *vāā*, P. *vācā*, Sk. *vāc*, *vācā*+*karanavā* (HSm).

2319. වදිනවා **vadinavā,** වැදෙනවා **vädenavā,** v., prt. *väduṇā*, to strike against; to enter, intrude. Ger. *vädä*, EpZ I 33[25].—Caus. *vaddanavā*, prt. *vädduvā*, to cause to enter, to put in, in *as-v°* to till, cultivate (the ground); double caus. *vaddavanavā*, prt. *väddevuvā*, in *as-v°* to get tilled.—Pk. *vaaï*, P. *vajati*, Sk. √*vraj*, *vrajati*.

2320. වදුර **vadura,** විදුර **vidura,** s., st. f. *°ru*, diamond, thunderbolt. — Pk. *vaïra*. P. *vajira*, Sk. *vajra*; cf. nep. *bajr̥āṃṭh* (T).

2321. වදුරවි **vadur'-avi,** විදු° **vidu°,** s., name of god Sakka as thunderer. — P. *vajirâyudha*, Sk. *vajrâyudha*.

2322. වදුල **vadula,** s., arbour, bower.—? P. *vañjula* ratan, Sk. *vañjula* name of several plants.

2323. වඳ **vaňda,** a., barren; s. *vaňdī* barren female; *vaňda-karanavā* to make barren, spay.—Pk., P. *vañjhā*, Sk. *vandhyā*; si. *vāṃjha*, g. *vāṃjh*, m. *vāṃjhā*, bg. *bāṃjhā*, b. h. *bāṃjh*, nep. *bāṃjho*, pj. *bañjh*.

2324. වඳිනවා **vaňdinavā,** v., prt. *vändā*, to bow, worship. — Pk. *vandaï*, P. *vandati*, Sk. √*vand*, *vandatē*.

2325. වඳුරා **vaňdurā,** s., st. f. *°ru*, monkey. — Pk. *vāṇara*, P., Sk. *vānara*; kśm. *vāṃdur*, si. *vānaru*, m. *vāṃdar*, ass. *bāndar*, bg. h. *bāṃdar*, nep. *bāṃdar*, *bāṃdhar*, *bānar*, pj. *bandar*, *bāṃdar*.

2326. වන් **van¹,** a. pprt., entered, arrived at. Cf. *as-van* (s. vv. *as* and *vadinavā*), EpZ I 47[22.24], 169 C[21]; *nidanna-ṭa vannī* (she) having fallen asleep, AmāV 8[3]. Inflected *senna-ṭa* (*vapna-ṭa*) *vanha*, lit. they entered into laughing (weeping), AmāV 13[12,15]. — Appears to be pprt. of v. *vadinavā*, but I cannot explain the form.

2327. වන **vana,** s., st. f. *van*, colour. *ran-van* gold-coloured. Ecpd. *-van* similar, resembling.—Pk., P. *vaṇṇa*, Sk. *varṇa*; m. *vān*, *vāṇ*, g. *vān*, h. *bān* habit, nep. *bāni* habit, pj. *bāṇā* profession. The spelling *vaṇa* is incorrect as the st. f. *van-* shows.

2328. වනනවා **vananavā,** v., prt. *vänuvā*, to describe, praise, eulogise. —Pk. inf. *vaṇṇiuṃ*, P. *vaṇṇēti*, Sk. *varṇayati*; kśm. *vınun*, m. *vaṇṇeṃ*, *vāṇiṇeṃ*.

2329. වනස **vanasa,** s., st. f. *vanas*, destruction, death. — Pk. *viṇāsa*, P. *vināsa*, Sk. *vināśa*; si. *viṇāhu*, h. nep. *bināś*, pj. *vaṇāh* murder.

2330. වනසනවා **vanasanavā,** v., prt. *vänasuvā*, to devastate, destroy. Intr. *vänasenavā*, prt. *vänasuṇā*, to be destroyed.—Pk. *viṇāsēi*, *viṇassaē*, P. *vināsēti*, *vinassati*, Sk. *vi-*+√*naś*, *vi-nāśayati*, *vinaśyatē*; cf. si. *vaṇasvuṃ*.

2331. වප **vapa,** s., st. f. *vap*, sowing. *vap-magula* sowing feast; *vap-masa* name of the month October-November which is the chief sowing time. — P. *vappa*, Sk. *vapra* sown field. According to TURNER s.v. *ubāunu* (Add.), < Sk. *vāpya.*

2332. වපුරනවා **vapuranavā,** v., prt. *väpuruvā*, *vapuḷā*, to sow.—*vap*+*puranavā.*

2333. වම් **vam,** a., left, sinistral; s. *vama* the left side; *vam-äsa* the left eye; *vam-pasa* the left side.—Pk., P., Sk. *vāma*; g. m. *vām*, oṛ. *bāṃ*, ass. *bāuṃ*, bg. *bāṃ*, h. *bāvāṃ*, *bāyāṃ*, nep. *bāuṃ.*

2334. වම **vama,** s., st. f. *vam*, armour, coat of mail.—Pk., P. *vamma*, Sk. *varman.*

2335. වමන් **vaman,** s., st. f. *vaman*, disrepute, dishonour.—Pk. *avamāṇa*, P., Sk. *avamāna* (or P., Sk. *apamāna*).

2336. වමාරනවා **vamāranavā,** v., prt. *vämāruvā*, to vomit.—*vama* vomiting + *karanavā* (HSm); cf. P. *vamati*, Sk. √*vam*, *vamati*; m. *vamṇeṃ*, h. *bamnā.*

2337. වමිය **vamiya,** s., white-ant hill.—P. *vammia* (Hem 1-101), P. *vammīka*, Sk. *valmīka.*

2338. වමී **vamī,** s., woman. — Sk. *vāma* desirable, pleasing, *vāmā* woman.

2339. වම්බටු **vam-baṭu,** s., egg-plant, Solanum melongena.—*vam*<**vaṅ* (cf. *vagu*)=P. *vaṅga*, Sk. *vaṅga* 1) Bengal, 2) egg-plant; m. *vāṃgī* (Bl, s.v.), pj. *vaṅgā* (T, s.v. *baigun*) + *baṭu*, q.v.

— වය **vaya,** වැය **väya,** s., see s.v. **viya**[4].

2340. වයනවා **vayanavā,** v., prt. *väyuvā*, to play on a musical instrument. — Pk. *vāēi*, P. *vādēti*, Sk. √*vad*, caus. *vādayati*; intr. P. *vajjati*, Sk. *vādyate*; see T, s. v. *bajnu.*

2341. වයබ **vayaba,** වයඹ **vayaṁba,** s., North-West. — Sk. *vāyavī.*

2342. වයම **vayama,** s., st. f. *vayam*, labour, effort. — P. *vāyāma*, Sk. *vyāyāma.* Sinh. also *väyama.*

2343. වර **vara,** s., time, occasion. *varak* once; *de-varak* twice; *tun-varak* three times etc. — Pk., P., Sk. *vāra*; kśm. *vār*, si. *vāra*, g. m. *vār*, oṛ. *bāra*, ass. bg. h. nep. *bār*, pj. *bār*, *vār.*

2344. වරටයා **varaṭayā,** s., foreigner, barbarian (Ca). — ? Haplology of **vararaṭayā*<Pk. *avara*, P., Sk. *apara* + *raṭa*, q.v.

2345. වරණයා **varaṇayā,** s., st. f. *varaṇa*, tusked elephant. — P., Sk. *vāraṇa.*

2346. වරද **varada**[1], s., wrong, fault, error, crime. *v°-karanavā* to do wrong; *v°- tabanavā* or *-naganavā* to lay blame upon, accuse. — Pk. *avaraddha*, P. *aparaddha*, Sk. *aparāddha* (*apa* + √*rādh*, pprt.).

2347. **වරද varada[2],** s., st. f. *°da*, heir apparent, sub-king. — P., Sk. *uparāja.* See W. Geiger, Journ. Greater India Soc. II 105-7.

2348. **වරදිනවා varadinavā,** or **වැරදෙනවා väradenavā,** v., prt. *väraduṇā*, to err, do wrong, mistake. Caus. *varaddanavā*, prt. *värädduvā*, to err; double caus. *varaddavanavā*, prt. *väräddevuvā*, to cause to err, mislead. — Pk. *ava-rajjhaï*, P. *apa-rajjhati*, Sk. *apa* + *√rādh*, *apa-rādhyati.*

2349. **වරනවා varanavā,** v., prt. *väruvā*, to stop, cease, intermit. — Pk. *vārēi*, P. *vārēti*,, Sk. *√ vṛ*, caus. *vārayati*; kśm. *vārun*, si. *vāraṇu*, g. *vārvuṃ*, m. *vārṇeṃ*, h. *bārnā*, nep. *bārnu*, pj. *bārnā*, *vārnā*.

2350. **වරළු varaḷu,** a., bent, crooked (Ruv 434); s. *varaḷa* bunch or knot of hair; *varallā* thief, robber. — Cl and Ca spell *varalu*; but I believe the word is a metathesis of **vaḷaru*=Sk. *vaṭara*, *vaṭhara*, in the kōśas=*vakra* crooked, *caura* thief.

2351. **වරා varā,** s., pig, hog. — Pk., P., Sk. *varāha.*

2352. **වල් -val,** suff. of pl. in nouns of the neutral declension. The older form is *-var* (EpZ I 93 A[44], 10th c. etc.) = Sk. *vāra* (not "turn" but) "multitude" (BR s.v. 5). Cf. *bāṇa-vāra* mass of arrows.

2353. **වල vala[1],** s., st. f. *val*, wood, jungle. In cpds. *val-* wild: *val-kaha* wild turmeric; *val-ūrā* wild hog etc.; *vali-* in *vali-kukuḷā*, v. below. — Pk. *vaṇa*, P., Sk. *vana*, mald. *vaḷi*; kśm. *van*, si. *vaṇu* tree; oṛ. *baṇa*, ass. bg. b. h. nep. *ban*, pj. *baṇ*.

2354. **වල vala[2],** s., st. f. *val*, hair. — Pk., P. *vāla*, Sk. *vāla*, *vāra*; kśm. *vāl*, si. *vāru*, g. *vāḷ*, oṛ. *bāla*, ass. bg. h. nep. *bāl*, pj. *vāl*, *bāl*, l. *vāl*.

2355. **වලග val-aga,** s., tail. — P. *vālagga*, Sk. *vālâgra*. With elision of *a* in the 2nd syllable, Sinh. *valgaya*, *valgē* tail; also *valigē*.

2356. **වලඳ valaňda,** s., sign, mark. — P. *valañja* (*pada-v°* footprint). Cf. the next word.

2357. **වලඳනවා valaňdanavā,** v., prt. *välaňduvā*, to use, enjoy, eat. — P. *valañjēti*. The historical spelling, however, is *vaḷaňd°* (cf. EpZ I 47[27], 10th c.) with cerebral.

2358. **වලපිනවා valapinavā, වැලපෙනවා välapenavā,** v., prt. *välapuṇā*, to weep, lament, wail.—Sk. *vi-*+*√ lap*, *vi-lapati*, P. *vi-lapati*; m. *viḷavṇeṃ*, h. *bilāpnā*, pj. *vilapṇā*.

2359. **වලහා val-ahā,** s., bear. — *vala*[1] + *ahā*, q.v.

2360. **වලා valā[1],** s., bracelet (with suff. *-la* also *valalla*, st. f. *valalu*). — Pk. *valaa*, P., Sk. *valaya*; not from Sk. *vālaka* (T, s. v. *bālo*) which would become **valu*, nom. sg. **valuva*, **valla* in Sinh.—The traditional spelling is always *vaḷā*, with cerebral *ḷ* (De Lanerolle).

— **වලි vali,** a., see s.v. **vili.**

2361. **වලිකුකුළා vali-kukuḷā,** s., jungle cock. — P., Sk. *vana-kukkuṭa.*

2362. **වල්කෙහෙල් val-kehel,** s., wild banana. — Sk. *vana-kadalī.*

2363. **වල්නා val-nā,** s., (Ca) jackal, fox. — *vala*+*nā*^{2} ruler of the forest.

2364. **වල්මීමා val-mīmā,** s., wild buffalo, Bosgavaeus. — *val*+*mīmā, mīvā,* P. *vana-mahisa.*

2365. **වල්මීයා val-mīyā,** s., moose deer. — Lit. rat of the wood, see s.v. *mīyā.*

2366. **වල්විදුනාව val-vidunāva,** s., whisk made of the tail of a yak. — P. *vāla-vījanī.* Cf. *vala*^{2}.

2367. **වල්සර val-sara,** a., wild, barbarous; s. *val-sarayā* wild man, Väddā. — Pk. *vaṇayara,* P. *vana-cara(ka),* Sk. *vana-cara.*

2368. **වවනවා vavanavā,** v., prt. *vävuvā,* to cultivate (the ground), plant (trees). Intr. *vävenavā,* prt. *vävuṇā,* to vegetate, grow. — Pk., *vavaï,* P. *vapati,* Sk. *√vap, vapati* ; kśm. *vavun,* ass. *baïba,* bg. h. *bonā.*

— **වස් vas,** s., see s. v. **vässa.**

2369. **වස vasa**^{1}, s., st. f. *vas,* 1) bamboo, flute; 2) race, lineage. *vas-karuvā* flute-player, piper. — Pk., P. *vaṃsa,* Sk. *vaṃśa* ; kśm. *baiṃs,* g. *vāṃs,* m. *vāṃsā,* oṛ. *bāuṃsa,* ass. *bāṃh,* bg. b. h. nep. *bāṃs.*

2370. **වස vasa**^{2}, s., st. f. *vas* year. — P. *vassa,* Sk. *varṣa.*

2371. **වස vasa**^{3}, s., st. f. *vā,* word, speech. — Pk. *vāā,* P., Sk. *vācā.* See s.v. *vadāranavā.*

2372. **වස vasa**^{4}, s., st. f. *vas,* dwelling, living, abiding. — Pk., P., Sk. *vāsa* ; kśm. g. m. *vās,* oṛ. *bāsa,* ass. *bāh,* bg. b. *bāsā,* h. nep. pj. *bās.*

— **වස vasa**^{5}, s., see s.v. **vaha.**

2373. **වසත් vasat,** s., in *vasat-kala* the spring time. — Pk., P., Sk. *vasanta.*

2374. **වසන vasana**^{1}, **වස්න vasna,** s., st. ff. *vasan, väsan,* clothing, garment. — P., Sk. *vasana.*

2375. **වසන vasana**^{2}, s., st. f. *vasan,* dwelling. — P., Sk. *vasana.*

2376. **වසන vasana**^{3}, **වැසන väsana,** s., st. f. *vasan, väsan,* injury, calamity. — Pk. *vasaṇa,* P., Sk. *vyasana.*

2377. **වසනවා vasanavā,** v., prt. *visuvā,* to dwell, reside, inhabit. —Pk. *vasaï,* P. *vasati,* Sk. *√vas, vasati* ; g. *vasvuṃ,* m. *vasṇeṃ,* oṛ. *basibā,* ass. *bahiba,* bg. *basā,* h. *basnā,* nep. *basnu,* pj. *bahiṇā, vahiṇā.* Also Sinh. *vesenavā.*

2378. **වසම් vasam,** a., 1) unequal, irregular; 2) vicious, bad, wicked. — Pk., P. *visama,* Sk. *viṣama* ; with meaning 2) also Sinh. *visam̆ba,* q. v.

2379. **වසර vasara,** s., st. f. *vasara*, year. — Pk., P. *vacchara*, Sk. *vatsara*.

2380. **වස්සා vassā,** s., st. f. *vasu*, *vahu*, male calf. *vässī* female calf. — Pk. *vaccha*, P. *vacchaka*, Sk. *vatsa(ka)*; kśm. *vochu*, si. *vacha*, bg. b. h. *bāchā*, nep. *bācho*, *bãccho*, pj. *bacchā*, *vacchā*, l. *vacchā*.

2381. **වහ vaha, වස vasa^{5}, විස visa,** s., poison, venom. — Pk., P. *visa*, Sk. *viṣa*; kśm. *vĕh*, si. *vihu*, oṛ. *bisa*, ass. *bih*, bg. h. nep. *bis*, pj. *bih*, *vih*, l. *vihuṃ*. Cf. *äs-vaha*.

2382. **වහන vahana,** s., st. f. *vahan*, sandal, shoe. — *vahan-saňgaḷa* pair of sandals. — (Pk. *uvāṇahā*,) P. *upāhanā* (Sk. *upānah*; h. *panhī*, *panaī*). Cf. *vahansē*.

2383. **වහනය vahanaya,** s., vehicle, raft, boat; bearing, conveying.— Pk. *vāhaṇa*, P., Sk. *vāhana* (? +*ka*); g. m. *vāhan*, m. *vāhṇeṃ* current, ass. bg. h. *bāhan*, nep. *bāhān*, l. *vāhṇ* mountain torrent.

2384. **වහන්සේ vahansē,** s., honorific in *maha-terun-vahansē* the Great Thera; *rajjuruvan-vahansē* His Majesty the King etc. — <*vahana*+*sē* form of the sandal, i.e. footprint. See Bull. of School of Or. Studies VIII, 1936, p. 557. The honorific *unnānsē* "he" (said of monks) is a contraction and assimilation of *un-vahan-sē*.

2385. **වහය vahaya,** s., vehicle. — P., Sk. *vāha*.

2386. **වහර vahara^{1},** s., help (Ruv 448). — Pk. *uvagāra*, P., Sk. *upakāra*. Also *vahala* help.

2387. **වහර vahara^{2},** s., usage, practice. — Pk. *vavahāra*, P. *vōhāra*, Sk. *vyavahāra*; pj. *buhār*, *vuhār*.

— **වහල vahala,** s., see s. v. **vahara^{1}.**

2388. **වහලා vahalā,** s., st. f. *vahal*, slave. *vahalī* female slave; *vahal-meheya* slavery, servitude. — P. *vasala*, Sk. *vṛṣala*. Cf. also Sinh. *vasalayā* outcast.

2389. **වහස vahasa^{1},** s., abuse. — Sk. *apahāsa*, cf. Pk. *ava-hasaï*. Sinh. *vahasi*, *vahasi(-basa)* abusive language is derived from Sk. *apa-hasita*.

2390. **වහස vahasa^{2},** s., advantage. — Sk. *avakāśa*. In Sinh. *vahasa* and *ovas*, q.v., as in P. *avakāsa* and *ōkāsa*.

2391. **වහස vahasa^{3},** s., laughter. — Pk., Sk. *vihāsa*.

2392. **වහිනවා vahinavā, වසිනවා vasinavā,** v., prt. *vässā*, to rain. Caus. *vasvanavā*, *vassa°*, prt. *vässuvā*, and double caus. *vassavanavā*, prt. *vässevuvā*, to cause to rain. — Pk. *vassaï* (A. AMg. *varisaï*), P. *vassati*, Sk. √*vṛṣ*, *varṣati* (; g. *varasvuṃ*, m. *varasṇeṃ*, oṛ. *barasibā*, ass. *barahiba*, h. *barasnā*, nep. *barsanu*, pj. *varhṇā*).

2393. **වළ vaḷa,** s., hole, pit. *v°-lanavā* to bury. — Sk. *avaṭa*; cf. P. *āvāṭa*.

2394. වා **vā,** s., st. f., wind. — Pk. *vāa,* P., Sk. *vāta*; kśm. *vāv,* si. *vāu,* g. *vā,* m. *vāv,* oṛ. ass. *bā,* bg. *bāi,* h. *bāv, bāī,* nep. *bā,* pj. l. *vā.* Possibly also < Sk. *vāyu.*

2395. වාරය **vāraya,** s., st. f. *vāra,* day, turn. — Sk. *vāsara.*

2396. වැකි **väki,** a. pprt., smeared on, rubbed on. — P. *makkhita,* Sk. *mrakṣita.* See s.v. *vakanavā.*

2397. වැට **väṭa,** s., fence, hedge. *väṭa-baňdinavā* to fence. — Pk., P. *vaṭṭi,* Sk. *varti.* The corresponding words in the MIAVs for "fence" are derived from Sk. *vāṭa.* Cf. Bl, s.v. *vāḍā*; T, s.v. *bāṛ.*

2398. වැටිය **väṭiya**[1], s., st. f. *väṭi,* border, bank, dam. — The same as *väṭa* + suff. *ka.*

2399. වැටිය **väṭiya**[2], s., st. f. *väṭi,* lit. something twisted, lamp-wick. *väṭi-karanavā* to twist, twine; *kes-väṭiya,* v. *kesa.* — Pk. *vaṭṭiā* (*vattiā*), P. *vaṭṭikā,* Sk. *vartikā*; si. *vaṭi,* g. *vāṭ,* m. *vāt,* oṛ. *bati,* ass. bg. *bāti,* b. h. *bātī,* nep. *bāti,* pj. *battī.*

2400. වැටෙනවා **väṭenavā,** v., prt. *väṭuṇā,* to fall, drop, fall down.— Pass. (with peculiar meaning) of *vaṭanavā*; P. **vaṭṭiyati,* Sk. *vartyatē.*

2401. වැඩ **väḍa**[1], honorific before a verb: *v°-innavā* or *v°-siṭinavā* to be seated; *v°-vasanavā* to reside, etc. (when speaking of venerable persons).—Ger. of *vaḍinavā,* see s.v. *vaḍanavā.*

2402. වැඩ **väḍa**[2], s., st. f. *väḍa,* increase, good result, profit; *°ḍaya,* work, business. *väḍaka-ṭa näti* good-for-nothing; *väḍa-karuvā* workman, servant; *v°-karanavā* to work; *a-väḍa* harm, injury.— Pk. *vuḍḍhi,* P. *vaḍḍhi,* Sk. *vṛddhi*; kśm. *vuḍ,* g. *vadh,* m. *vāḍh,* bg. *bāṛ,* h. *bāṛh,* nep. *baṛ, baṛh,* pj. *vaddh* increase.

2403. වැඩි **väḍi,** a. pprt., increased, grown, greater. *v°-karanavā* to increase, multiply; *v°-denā* the greater number of persons, the majority. — Pk. *vaḍḍhia,* P. *vaḍḍhita,* Sk. *vardhita*; si. *vadhi,* nep. *baṛi, baṛhi* more.

2404. වැත්ත **vätta,** s., st. f. *väti,* occasion, opportunity. — Pk. *vatti* (*vitti, vutti,* P. *vutti*), Sk. *vṛtti* (*vṛtta*;) (h. *būt, būtā,* nep. *butā* power, pj. *buttā* means) + suff. *-ka.* Sinh. *vät* similarity seems to be = *vṛtti* without suff. *-ka.*

2405. වැද **väda,** in *väda-hovinavā* to lie down, *väda-ot* (*-hot*) lying down, reclining. — Ger. of *vadinavā* to enter.

2406. වැඳි **vädi,** s., st. f., panegyrist, public bard (Ruv 360). —P. *vandi,* Sk. *vandin.*

2407. වැද්දා **väddā,** s., st. f. *vädi,* archer, Väddā (Ruv 400). — The derivation from Pk. *vāha,* P., Sk. *vyādha* hunter is phonologically impossible. Perhaps we must assume Sk. *veddhar* "piercer, perforator" as base-form.

2408. **වැණි väni,** a., like, such, similar *me-väni* such as this; s. *vänna* a similar thing, sort, class. — P. *vaṇṇin*, Sk. *varṇin*.

2409. **වැම väma,** s., a fathom.—Alternating with *bam̆baya*, q.v., as in P. *vyāma* with *byāma*.

— **වැය väya,** s., see s.v. **viya**[4].

2410. **වැර vära, වෙර vera,** s., strength, force, might.— Pk. *vīria*, P. *viriya*, Sk. *vīrya* ; m. *vir*, *virī*.

2411. **වැරැල්ල värälla,** s., st. f. *väräli*, slight rain, drizzling.— P., Sk. *vāri* + dimin. suff. *-li*.

2412. **වැල väla**[1], s., st. f. *väl*, creeper. — Pk. *vallī*, *velli*, P., Sk. *vallī*; si. *vali*, g. m. *vel*, bg. h. nep. *bel*, pj. *bel*, *vel*, l. *val*, *valh*.

2413. **වැල väla**[2], s., st. f. *väl*, necklace. — Sk. *vālikā* ; g. m. *vāḷī*, bg. *bāli*, b. *bāri*, h. *bālī*, nep. *bāli* (T, s.v.), pj. *vālī*, l. *vāḷī* ring. The traditional spelling of this word is always with *ḷ* (De Lanerolle).

2414. **වැල්ල välla,** s., st. f. *väli*, sand, sandy place. *väli-gala* sandstone ; *v°-bima* sandy soil. — Pk. *vāluā*, P. *vālukā*, *vālikā*, Sk. *vālukā* ; si. *vārī*, g. *vāḷu*, m. *vāḷū*, or. ass. bg. *bāli*, h. *bālū* (, nep. *bāluvā*), pj. *bālū*.

2415. **වැව väva,** s., st. ff. *väv*, *vä*, tank, large pond, lake. *väv-sorovva* lake-outlet. — P., Sk. *vāpī*.

— **වැසන väsana,** s., see s. v. **vasana**[3].

2416. **වැසි väsi**[1], s., ordure, dung. *väsi-kiḷiya* privy. — P. *vacca*, *vacca-kuṭī*, Sk. *varcas*.

2417. **වැසි väsi**[2], a., dwelling, residing; s. *väsiyā* inhabitant. — Pk. *vāsi*, P. *vāsin*, *vāsika*, Sk. *vāsin*.

2418. **වැස්ස vässa,** s., st. ff. *väsi*, *vähi*, rain. *väsi-kala* rainy season ; *vähi-lihiṇiyā* rain-bird, swallow. Also Sinh. *vas* in *vas-vasanavā* to sojourn during the rainy season ; *vas-vasavanavā* to lodge (a monk) during the r.s. — *vas* =P. *vassa*, Sk. *varṣa* ; kśm. *vośu*, si. *vasa*, nep. *bāsi*. Sinh. *vässa* the same + suff.-*ka*.

2419. **වැහැප් vähäp,** s., bull. — Pk. *vasaha*, P. *vasabha*, Sk. *vṛṣabha* ; b. *basahā*, h. *basah*, nep. *basāhā*.

2420. **වෑය vǟya,** s., st. f. *vǟ*, adze. — Pk. *vāsī*, P. *vāsi*, Sk. *vāśī* ; bg. *bāsi*. Cf. si. *vāholo*, g. *vāṃslo*, b. *basūlā*, h. *basolā*, *basūlā*, nep. *basulo*, *basilo*, l. *vaholā*.

2421. **වෑයම vǟyama,** s., st. f. *vǟyam*, trying, endeavour, attempt. *vǟyam-karanavā* to try. — Pk., P. *vāyāma*, Sk. *vyāyāma*. T, Add. s.v. *jamnu*.

— **වි vi-,** pref., see **va**[4].

2422. **විකප vikapa** (Ruv 736), s., doubt, option, alternative. — Pk. *viyappa*, P. *vikappa*, Sk. *vikalpa*.

2423. **විකපිය vikapiya,** s., consideration. — P. *vikappita*, Sk. *vikalpita*.

2424. **විකුණනවා vikuṇanavā,** v., prt. *vikuṇuvā*, to sell. Intr. *vikiṇenavā*, prt. *vikuṇuṇā*, to be sold.— Pk. *vikkēi*, P. *vikkiṇāti*, Sk. *vi-* + $\sqrt{}$*krī*, *vi-krīṇītē*; si. *vikaṇu*, m. *vikṇeṃ*, oṛ. *bikibā*, ass. *bikiba*, bg. *bikā*, h. *biknā*, nep. *biknu*, pj. *bikṇā*, *vikṇā*, l. *vikaṇ*.

2425. **විකුම vikuma, වික්ම vikma,** s., might, power, heroism. — Pk., P. *vikkama*, Sk. *vikrama*.

2426. **විකෙව් vikev,** s., doubt, uncertainty, perplexity. — Pk. *vikkhēva*, P. *vikkhēpa*, Sk. *vikṣēpa*.

2427. **විගහ vigaha,** s., separation; encounter, war (Ruv 361).— Pk. *viggaha*, Sk. *vigraha* (; ? g. *vi-ghuṃ*, *viṃghuṃ*, oṛ. ass. bg. *bighā*, b. h. *bīghā*, nep. *bighā*, pj. *bīgāh*, *vigghā*, l. *vigghā* a measure of land).

— **විට viṭa**[1], in *ō-viṭa*, s., see s.v.

2428. **විට viṭa**[2], s., time, opportunity. *de-viṭak* twice ; *viṭin-viṭa* from time to time. At the end of a temporal sentence : *ohu giya viṭa* when he went. Ved. *viṣṭā*, *viṣṭhā*, *viṣṭi*, cf. *tri-viṣṭi* three times.

2429. **විටි viṭi**[1], s., wages.— Pk. *viṭṭhi* (*veṭṭhi*), Sk. *viṣṭi* (; g. m. *veṭh*, oṛ. *beṭh*, nep. *beṭhi*).

2430. **විටි viṭi**[2], s., rain (Ruv 625).—Pk., P. *vuṭṭhi*, Sk. *vṛṣṭi* ; h. *-vaṭh* (T, Add. s.v. *barsanu*).

2431. **විත vita,** s., drinking vessel. — P. *vittha*, Dhp-a III 66^{22}, cf. *surā-vittha*, Jā V 427^{33}. PTSPD, s.v.

2432. **විතර vitara,** s., breadth, extent. — Pk., P. *vitthāra*, Sk. *vistāra*.

2433. **විදි vidi,** s., the god Brahmā (Ruv 16). — Sk. *vi-* + $\sqrt{}$*dhā*, *vidhi*. Slw.

2434. **විදිත(ය) vidita(ya),** s., (conquered) country or district. — P., Sk. *vijita*. Slw.

2435. **විදිනවා vidinavā,** v., prt. *viddā*, to bore, pierce, shoot (an arrow). Double caus. *viddavanavā*, prt. *viddevuvā*, to cause to pierce ; intr. *videnavā*, prt. *viduṇā*, to become pierced. — Pk. *vijjhaï*, P. *vijjhati*, Sk. $\sqrt{}$*vyadh*, *vidhyati* ; si. *vijhaṇu*, h. *bījhnā*, nep. *bijhnu*.

2436. **විදිනිය vidiniya, විජි° viji°,** s., st. ff. °*ni*, fan. Pk. *vīaṇa*, P. *vījanī*, Sk. *vījana* ; s. *viñiṇu*, *viṃjṇo*, m. *vijnā*, *vijṇā*, h. *bijnā*, *benā*.

2437 **විදු vidu**[1], s., lightning. — Pk., P. *vijju*, Sk. *vidyut* ; si. *viju*, g. *vīj*, m. *vīj*, *vijū*, pj. *bijj*, l. *vījj*.

2438. **විදු vidu**[2], s., knowledge, learning. — Pk., P. *vijjā*, Sk. *vidyā* ; si. *vija* (T, s. v. *bijuvā*).

— විදුර **vidura,** s., s.v. **vadura.**

2439. විදුරස්න **vidur'-asna** (or *-asuna*), s., the Buddha's throne, a particular posture. — P. **vajirâsana*, Sk. *vajrâsana*.

2440. විදුලිය **viduliya,** s., st. f. *°li*, lightning. — Pk. *vijjuliā*, P. *vijjullatā*, Sk. *vidyullatā* ; g. *vijḷī*, oṛ. *bijuḷi*, ass. *bizuli*, bg. *bijli*, h. *bijulī*, *bijlī*, nep. *bijuli*, pj. *vijlī*, l. *vijjlī*.

2441. විඳිනවා **viňdinavā,** v., prt. *vindā*, to feel; to enjoy, possess; to suffer. Caus. *viňduvanavā*, prt. *viňdevuvā*, to cause to suffer pain. —P. *vindati*, Sk. *√vid*, *vindati*.

2442. විනා **vinā[1],** postp., without, except. — lw. P., Sk. *vinā*.

2443. විනා **vinā[2],** s., leader, the Buddha. — P., Sk. *vināyaka*.

2444. විනිස **vinisa,** s., judgment. — P. *vinicchaya*, Sk. *viniścaya*.

2445. විප් **vip,** s., brahmin. — Pk., P. *vippa*, Sk. *vipra*.

2446. විපක් **vipak,** a., opposed, hostile. — P. *vipakkha*, Sk. *vipakṣa*.

2447. විපත **vipata,** s., st. f. *vipat*, misfortune, calamity. — P., Sk. *vipatti*.

2448. විපිළිසර **vipiḷisara,** s., st. f. id., regret, repentance; perplexity. — P. *vippaṭisāra*, Sk. *vipratisāra*.

2449. විමන **vimana,** s., st. f. *viman*, residence, palace. — Pk. *vimāṇa*, P., Sk. *vimāna* ; h. *bevān*.

2450. විය **viya[1],** s., yoke. *gäl-viya*, see s.v. *gäl* ; *viya-gaha* yoke. — Metathesis of **yiva* = Pk. *jua*, P., Sk. *yuga* ; si. *ju(-haru)*, m. *jūṃ*, bg. *ju*, b. *juā*, h. *jūā*, nep. *juvā*.

2451. විය **viya[2],** s., age. *viya-pat* arrived at age. — Pk. *vaa*, P., Sk. *vayas* ; kśm. *vaiṃs*, nep. *baiṃs*.

2452. විය **viya[3],** bird (Ruv 480). — Sk. *vi*, *vayas*.

2453. විය **viya[4],** වැය **väya,** වය **vaya,** s., expenditure, loss, decline. *viya-dama* expenditure. — P. *vyaya*, *vaya*, Sk. *vyaya*.

2454. විය **viya[5],** s., illness (Ruv 480). — Pk. *vāhi*, P., Sk. *vyādhi*.

2455. විය **viya[6],** s., st. f. *vī*, paddy, rice. *vī-äṭaya* grain of paddy. — P. *vīhi*, Sk. *vrīhi*.

2456. වියත් **viyat,** a., clear, manifest; learned; s. *viyatā*, *°ttā* learned man, scholar. — P. *vyatta*, Sk. *vyakta*.

2457. වියත **viyata,** s., st. f. *viyat*, the span of the hand. — Pk. *vihatthi*, P. *vidatthi* (see Geiger, P. Gr. 38[3]), Sk. *vitasti* ; si. *vithi*, g. *veṃt*, m. *vīt*, *vīth*, h. *bītā*, *bittā*, nep. *bittā*, pj. *bitth*, *vitth*, l. *vitth*.

2458. වියන **viyana,** s., st. f. *viyan,* canopy. *viyan-baňdinavā* to fix a canopy. — Pk. *viāṇa,* P., Sk. *vitāna.*

2459. වියනවා **viyanavā,** v., prt. *viyuvā,* to weave, plait. Caus. *viyavanavā,* prt. *viyevuvā,* to get woven. — Sk. √*vā, vayati* (Cf. P. *vināti,* pass. *vīyati*) ; kśm. *vōnun,* si. *uṇaṇu,* g. *vaṇvuṃ,* m. *viṇṇeṃ,* oṛ. *buṇibā,* bg. *bunā,* h. *bunnā, binnā,* nep. *bunnu, bannu,* pj. *buṇṇā, vuṇṇā, biṇṇā,* l. *uṇan.*

2460. වියරණ **viyaraṇa,** s., st. f. °*ṇa,* grammar. — P., Sk. *vyākaraṇa.*

2461. වියරු **viyaru,** a., demented, insane; s. °*ruva* madness ; °*ruvā* mad man : *viyaru-väṭenavā* to run mad. — Pk. *viāra,* P., Sk. *vikāra.* Cf. Germ. *verrückt.*

2462. වියල(යා) **viyala(yā),** s., panther, tiger (Ruv 236). — P. *viyāla,* Sk. *vyāla.* ? Slw.

2463. වියවුල් **viyavul,** a., confused; s. °*la* confusion, disorder ; *viyavul-karanavā* to confuse. — P., Sk. *vyākula.* Cf. T, s.v. *baulāhā.*

2464. වියසන **viyasana** (Ruv 135), s., distress, misfortune, calamity. — P., Sk. *vyasana.* See *vasana*[3], *väsana.*

2465. වියු **viyu,** a., pprt., said, uttered. — P., Sk. *vādita.*

2466. වියෝ **viyō,** s., separation. *viyō-ginna* fire of separation, i.e. pain of s. ; *v-venavā* to be separated. — P., Sk. *viyōga.*

2467. විරහි **virahi,** a. pprt., separated, absent. — P., Sk. *virahita.*

2468. විරා **virā,** a., free from desire, passionless. — P., Sk. *virāga.*

2469. විරිත **virita,** s., abstinence from what is forbidden. — The prototype seems to be **varitta.* Cf. P. *vāritta.*

2470. විරිදු **viridu,** °රුදු °**rudu,** a. pprt., opposed, hostile. — Pk., P., Sk. *viruddha.*

2471. විරූ **virū,** a., deformed, ugly. — P., Sk. *virūpa.*

2472. විරෙනවා **virenavā,** v., prt. *viruṇā,* to become liquid, melt. — Cf. Sk. √*lī* (see s.v. *vilin*), Pk. *virāi* ; m. *virṇeṃ.* Sinh. *virī-yanavā* to melt away is a composite of v. *virī* (ger. of *virenavā*) and *yanavā.*

2473. විල **vila,** s., st. f. *vil,* hole, pit, lake. *vil-tera* lake shore. — Pk., P., Sk. *vila.*

2474. විලඳ **vilaňda,** s., fried grain. — Cf. Pk. *lāyā,* P. *lājā,* Sk. pl. *lājāḥ.* See *laďa*[3].

2475. විලවුන් **vilavun,** s. pl., scented unguents. — Pk. *vilēvaṇa,* P., Sk. *vilēpana.*

2476. විලසී **vilasī,** s., st. f. *vilas,* dallying woman. — Pk., P., Sk. *vilāsinī.*

2477. විලි **vili,** වලි **vali,** a., wild (living, growing etc. in the jungle). *vili-(vali-) kukuḷā* jungle cock. — Sk. *vanin.*

2478. **විලින් vilin,** a. pprt., liquid. — Pk. *viliṇa*, P., Sk. *vilīna*. Cf. Pk. *vilijjaï*, P. *vilīyati*, Sk. *vilīyatē* ; nep. *bilinu*.

2479. **විලිමුවා vili-muvā,** s., monkey, ape (lit. the wrinkle-faced one). — P. *valīmukha*, Sk. *valīmukha*.

2480. **විලිය viliya,** s., st. f. *vili*, wrinkle. — Pk., P., Sk. *vali*+-*ka*. Simple *vali* is Sinh. *vila*, st. f. *vil*. Cf. *vil-muvā* alternating with *vili-muvā*.

2481. **විවන vivana,** a., colourless, pale. — Pk., P. *vivaṇṇa*, Sk. *vivarṇa*.

2482. **විවස් vivas,** a., manifest, clear. — Sk. *vikāśa* ; cf. P. *vikāsin*.

2483. **විවසුන් vivasun,** s., spiritual insight. — P. *vipassanā*.

2484. **විවා vivā,** s., marriage. *vivā-magul* marriage-ceremony. — Pk. *viāha*, P., Sk. *vivāha* ; si. *vihāṃu*, g. m. *vivāh*, ass. *biyā*, bg. *bihā*, h. *bivāh*, *byāh*, nep. *bie*, *bihe*, pj. *biāh*, *viāh*.

— **විස visa,** s., see s.v. **vaha.**

2485 **විසකුණු visakuṇu,** a., learned, wise. — Pk. *viakkhaṇa*, P. *vicakkhaṇa*, Sk. *vicakṣaṇa*.

2486. **විසඳනවා visaňdanavā,** v., prt. *visaňduvā*, to explain, reply, define.—Pk. *visajjēi*, P. *visajjēti*, *vissajjēti* emits, replies, Sk. *vi*-+√*sṛj*, caus. *visarjayati* discharges, utters.

2487. **විසඹ visaṁba[1],** a., wicked, vicious. — See s.v. *vasam*.

2488. **විසඹ visaṁba[2],** s., confidence, trust (Ruv 337). — Pk., P. *vissambha*, Sk. *viśrambha*.

2489. **විසර visara[1],** s., investigation, examination. — Pk. *viāra*, P., Sk. *vicāra*.

2490. **විසර visara[2],** s., spreading, expanding. — Sk. *visāra* ; cf. Pk. *visārēi*, P. *visārin*. Sinh. *visara* multitude, flock (Ruv 254), is lw. Sk. *visira*. Cf. *visiri*.

2491. **විසල් visal,** a., wide, extensive, large.— Pk., P. *visāla*, Sk. *viśāla*.

2492. **විසා visā[1],** s., name of a lunar asterism. — Pk. *visāhā*, P. *visākhā*, Sk. *viśākhā*.

2493. **විසා visā[2],** s., district; refuge, asylum. — Pk., P. *visaya*, Sk. *viṣaya*.

2494. **විසි visi[1],** s., word, speech. — P. *vacī*, but *vasa*[3] (q.v.) < *vācā*.

— **විසි visi[2],** num., see s.v. **vissa.**

2495. **විසි visi[3],** s., street. — P. *visikhā*, Sk. *viśikhā*.

2496. **විසිකිස් visikis,** s., doubt. — P. *vicikicchā*, Sk. *vicikitsā*.

2497. **විසිතුරු visituru,** s., particoloured, variegated; beautiful.— Pk. *vicitta*, P. *vicitta*, °*tra*, Sk. *vicitra*. H. JAYATILAKA, Eḷu-akārādiya, quotes also a Sinh. *visit*.

2498. **විසින් visin,** postp., b y, t h r o u g h. Can hardly be separated from P. *vasena*, Sk. *vaśena*, but the vocalism is irregular.

2499. **විසිරි visiri, විසුර visura,** a., e x t e n d e d, s c a t t e r e d ; s. *visiriya* fan. — Cf. P. *visara*, *visārin*, Sk. *visara*, *visārin*, *visārita*.

2500. **විසිරෙනවා visirenavā,** v., prt. *visiruṇā*, t o b e s p r e a d or s c a t t e r e d. Caus. *visuruvanavā*, prt. *visirevuvā*, to scatter, disperse. — Sk. *vi-* + √*sṛ*, *vi-sarati*. We must assume as basis a Sinh. v. **visuranavā*.

2501. **විසුදු visudu,** s., p u r i t y ; h o l i n e s s. — Pk., P. *visuddhi*, Sk. *viśuddhi*.

2502. **විසුණු visunu** (Ca, °*ṇu*), s., p o w d e r. — P. *vicuṇṇa*, Sk. **vicūrṇa* in *vicūrṇī-bhū* to become powder.

2503. **විසුළ visuḷa,** a. pprt., s p r e a d, e x t e n d e d, l a r g e — P. *visaṭa*, *visata*, Sk. *visṛta* (T, s.v. *sarnu*). Ca and Cl erroneously spell *visula*.

2504. **විසෙණිය viseṇiya,** s., t h e f i f t h d a y after the new or full moon. — Cf. P. *visāṇa*, Sk *viṣāṇa* horn (the moon having the shape of a horn). The prototype must be *viṣāṇikā*. See WICKREMASINGHE, EpZ I, p. 39, n. 1.

2505. **විස්ස vissa,** num., st. f. *visi*, t w e n t y. *visi-veni*, *-väni* twentieth. — Pk. *vīsaï*, *vīsaṃ*, P. *vīsati*, *vīsaṃ*, Sk. *viṃśati*, *-viṃśat* ; kśm. *vuh*, si. *vīha*, g. *vīś*, m. *vīs*, oṛ. *bimsa*, ass. *biha*, bg. *bis*, h. *bīs*, nep. *bis*, pj. l. *vīh*. Gr. 50.17.

2506. **විහිදනවා vihidanavā,** v., prt. *vihiduvā*, t o d i f f u s e (tr.), s p r e a d o u t, o p e n w i d e. Caus. *vihidavanavā*, °*duv*°, prt. °*devuvā*, to cause to diffuse ; intr. *vihidenavā*, prt. °*duṇā*, to spread, become diffused, open.—P. *vissandāti*, Sk. *vi-* + √*syand*, caus. *viṣyandayati*.

2507. **විහිදි vihidi, °දු °du,** a. pprt., d i f f u s e d, e x p a n d e d. — P. **vissandita*, Sk. **viṣyandita*.

2508. **විළිය viḷiya,** s., st. f. *viḷi*, s h a m e, m o d e s t y. — Sk. *vrīḍa*, *vrīḍita*.

— **වී vī,** s., p a d d y, see s.v. **viya**[6].

2509. **වුරුණු vuruṇu,** a. pprt., l i q u e f i e d, d e c o c t e d. *v°-tela* scum of the flesh.—pprt. of *virenavā*, q.v.

2510. **වුවන vuvana,** s., st. f. *vuvan*, f a c e (H. JAYATILAKA). — Pk. *vaaṇa*, P., Sk. *vadana*.

2511. **වුහුට vuhuṭa, °ටු °ṭu,** a. pprt., c a s t, s e n t, i s s u e d. — P. *vissaṭṭha*, Sk. *visṛṣṭa*.

2512. **වූ vū,** a. prt., t h a t h a s b e c o m e. — Pk. *bhūa*, *hūa*, P., Sk. *bhūta* ; h. *hūā*, nep. *bhayo*.

2513. **වෙණ veṇa,** s., st. f. id., l u t e, h a r p. *v°-tata* string of a lute. — Pk., P., Sk. *vīṇā* ; ass : bg. *bin*, b. h. *bīn*, nep. *bin*, pj. *bīn*.

— **වෙණෙඳා veṇeňdā,** see s.v. **veḷeňdā.**

2514. **වෙට veṭa**[1], a., or postp., n e a r. *veṭa-ṭa* near to ; *veṭin* from the presence or vicinity of.— P. *upanti*, *upantika*, Sk. *upānta*, *upāntika*.

2515. වෙත **veta**[2], s., st. f. *veta*, cane, reed (H. Jayatilaka).— Pk., P. *vetta*, Sk. *vētra* ; m. *vet*, oṛ. *beta*, bg. h. nep. pj. *bet*. See *veya*.

2516. වෙදසල **veda-sala,** °හල **°-hala,** s., medical hall, hospital. — P. *vejja-sālā*.

2517. වෙදා **vedā,** s., st. f. *veda*, doctor, physician. *veda-satara* medical science.—Pk., P. *vejja*, Sk. *vaidya* ; si. *veju* (, nep. *bijuvā*).

— වෙන් **ven,** වෙන **vena,** see s.v. **ven-karanavā.**

2518. වෙනවා **venavā,** v., prt. *vuṇā*, to become.—Pk. *bhōi*, *hōi*, P. *bhavati*, *hōti*, Sk. *bhavati* ; kśm. *bŏvun*, si. *huaṇu*, g. *hovuṃ*, m. *hoṇeṃ*, oṛ. *hebā*, ass. *hāba*, bg. *hoyā*, b. *hoeb*, h. *honā*, nep. *hunu*, pj. *hoṇā*, l. *hovaṇ*.

2519. වෙනු **venu,** s., the god Vishnu —Pk., P. *viṇhu*, Sk. *viṣṇu*.

2520. වෙන්කරනවා **ven-karanavā,** v., to separate, sunder, sever; *ven-venavā*, v., to become separated.—Sk. *vinā-karōti*, *-bhavati*, cf. P. *vinābhāva* (cf. Pk. *viṇā*, P. *vinā* ; kśm. *vĕn*, g. *viṇ*, m. *vīṇ*, *viṇeṃ*, oṛ. *binu*, ass. *bine*, h. *bin*, nep. *-binu*, p. *biṇ*). In Sinh. *vena* other, different (*venas* id. = *vena* + *asa*[2]), has become an adj.

— වෙය **veya**[1], see s.v. **vē**[1].

2521. වෙය **veya**[2], s., st. f. *vē*, bamboo cane. *vē-väla* id. — Pk. *vēaa*, P., Sk. *vētasa* ; nep. *baiṃs*.

— වෙර **vera**[1], s., see. s.v. **vära**.

2522. වෙර **vera**[2], s., hatred. — Pk., P. *vēra*, Sk. *vaira* ; si. *veru*, m. *vair*.

2523. වෙරළුමිණ **veraḷu-miṇa,** s., cat's-eye gem. — *veraḷu* = Pk. *vērulia*, *vēluria*, *vēḷuria*, P. *vēḷuriya*, Sk. *vaiḍūrya*.

2524. වෙල **vela,** s., shore, beach. — Pk., P., Sk. *velā* ; kśm. *vela*, si. *vera*, g. m. *veḷ*, oṛ. *bela*, ass. *beli*, h. *ber*, *bel*, nep. *ber*, pj. *ber*, *vel*, l. *vel*, *väla*.

2525. වෙවුලනවා **vevu-lanavā,** v., prt. *vevuluvā*, to shiver, tremble. Caus. *vevulavanavā*, prt. *vevulevuvā*, to shake (tr.).— *vevu* : from Sk. √*vip*, *vēp*, *vēpatē*. Cf. Pk. *vēvaï* ; P. *vēpa*, *vēpana*, *vēpathu*, Sk. *vēpa*, *vēpas*, *vēpana*, *vēpathu*.

— වෙස් **ves**[1], s., see s.v. **vessā.**

2526. වෙස් **ves**[2], in *ves-aṅgana*, *ves-aṁbuva* harlot, prostitute. — Pk. *vēsā*, P. *vēsī*, *vēsiyā*, Sk. *vēśyā* ; m. *vesvā*, h. *besvā*, pj. *vesvā*.

2527. වෙස **vesa,** s., st. f. *ves*, form, appearance; disguise, mask. *ves-mūṇa* mask, visor ; *ves-pānavā* to disguise one's self, to perform theatrically.—Pk., P. *vēsa*, Sk. *vēṣa* (; ? m. *bheś*, *bhes*, h. nep. *bhes*, *bheṣ*, pj. *bhekh*, *bhes*).

— වෙසෙනවා **vesenavā,** v. = **vasanavā,** q. v.

2528. **වෙස්සා vessā,** s., st. f. *ves,* merchant or agriculturist. *ves-kula* mercantile caste. — Pk. AMg. *vessa,* P. *vessa,* Sk *vaiśya.*

2529. **වෙහෙර vehera,** s., temple.—Pk., P., Sk. *vihāra.* Cf. the name of the Indian province *bihār.*

2530. **වෙහෙස vehesa,** s., st. f. id., fatigue, trouble. *vehesa-karanavā* to fatigue ; *v°-venavā* to become fatigued. — P. *vihēsa,* P., Sk. *vihiṃsā.*

2531. **වෙහෙසනවා vehesanavā,** v., prt. *vehesuvā,* to fatigue, trouble. Intr. *vehesenavā,* prt. *vehesuṇā,* to be troubled, to take trouble. — Pk. *vihiṃsaï,* P. *vihiṃsati,* Sk. *vi-*+√*hiṃs, vi-hinasti, vi-hiṃsanti.*

— **වෙළඳ veḷaňdā,** s., see s.v. **veḷeňdā.**

2532. **වෙළනවා veḷanavā,** v., prt. *veḷuvā,* to wrap, entwine. Intr. *veḷenavā,* prt. *veḷuṇā,* to wind round.—Pk. *vēḍhēi,* P. *vēṭhēti,* Sk. √*vēṣṭ,* caus. *vēṣṭayati* ; kśm. *vurum,* si. *veṛhaṇu,* m. *veḍhṇeṃ,* oṛ. *beṛhibā,* ass. *beriba,* bg. *beṛā,* h. *beṛhā,* nep. *bernu, berhuu.* Cf. g. *veḍh* ring, pj. *veṛhā courtyard,* l. *vehṛ* enclosure.

2533. **වෙළඹ veḷaṁba, වෙළෙඹ veḷeṁba,** s., mare. — P. *vaḷavā,* Sk. *vaḍabā, °vā.*

2534. **වෙළෙඳ veḷeňdā, වෙළඳ veḷaňdā,** s., st. ff. *°ňda,* merchant. — Pk. *vāṇia,* P., Sk. *vāṇija* ; si. *vāṇyo,* g. *vāṇiyo,* m. *vāṇī,* oṛ. *baṇiyā,* ass. *baniyā,* bg. *bāniyā,* b. h. nep. *baniyā,* pj. *bāniyā.* Sinh. has several forms : with *ḷ* : *veḷendā* (<**veḷeňddā* <**veḷeňduvā* = *vāṇijaka*) ; with *ṇ* : *veṇeňdā,* st. f. *veṇeňda.*

2535. **වෙළෙඳාම veḷeňdāma, වෙළඳාම veḷaňdāma,** s., st. ff. *°ňdām,* trade, traffic, commerce. — <**veḷeňda-ama* = *veḷeňda*+*kama.*

2536. **වෙළෙප veḷepa, වෙළප veḷapa,** s., st. f. *veḷep,* branch of a tree, bush. — P., Sk. *viṭapa* (? *p*).

2537. **වේ vē[1], වෙය veya,** s., street. — Pk. *vīhiā,* P., Sk. *vīthi.*

2538. **වේ vē[2],** s., st. f., speed. — Pk. *vēa,* P., Sk. *vēga.*

— **වේ vē[3],** s., see s.v. **veya[2].**

2539. **වේ vē[4],** s., st. f., the Veda. *vē-guru* teacher of the Veda. — Pk. *vēa,* P., Sk. *vēda* ; cf. h. nep. *(cau-)be.*

2540. **වේණ vēṇa,** s., horn, in *kaga-vēṇā,* q. v. — <**veheṇa,* Pk., P. *visāṇa,* Sk. *viṣāṇa.*

— **වොටුන්න voṭunna,** s., see s.v. **oṭunna.**

— **වොටුවා voṭuvā,** s., see s.v. **oṭuvā.**

ස S

2541. **ස- sa-,** pref., with, together with. In cpds. : *sa-dos* faulty (see *dosa*) — Pk., P., Sk. *sa-*.

2542. **සක් sak,** s., a number, multitude. *a-sak* innumerable (see *asak*²). — Pk., P. *saṅkhā*. Sk. *saṅkhyā*.

2543. **සක saka¹,** s., st. f. *sak*, wheel, disk. — Pk., P. *cakka*, Sk. *cakra*; si. *caku*, g. m. *cāk*, or. *caka*, ass. *sāk*, *sākā*, bg. b. h. *cāk*, nep. *cāko*, pj. *cakk*, l. *cakkar*.

2544. **සක saka²,** s., st. f. *sak*, eye. — Pk., P. *cakkhu*, Sk. *cakṣus*.

2545. **සකත් sak-at, සක්අත් sak'-at,** s., name of god Vishnu. — Sk. *cakra-hasta*.

2546. **සකප sakapa,** s., st. f. *sakap*, consideration, opinion (Ruv 94). — Pk., P. *saṃkappa*, Sk. *saṃkalpa*.

— **සකර sakara¹,** s., see s.v. **hakuru.**

2547. **සකර sakara²,** s., preparing, perfection, embellishment; t.t. "formations."—Pk. *sakkāra* (Hem 1.28), P. *saṃkhāra*, Sk. *saṃskāra*.

2548. **සකර sakara³,** s., kind treatment, hospitality. — P., Pk. *sakkāra*, Sk. *satkāra*.

2549. **සකස් sakas,** a., good, excellent. *s°-karanavā* to put in good order. — P. *sakkacca*, Sk. *satkṛtya*.

2550. **සකිනු sakinu,** a. pprt., scattered, confused, mixed. — P. *saṃkiṇṇa*, Sk. *saṃkīrṇa*.

2551. **සකු saku,** s., Sanskrit language. — Pk. *sakkaa*, P. *saṃkata*, °*ṭa*, Sk. *saṃskṛta*.

2552. **සකුළු sakuḷu, සැකුළු säkuḷu,** a., hard, strong; harsh, rough.— ?= Pk. *saṃkaḍa*, P., Sk. *saṃkaṭa*; g. *sāṃkḍuṃ*, m. *sāṃkaḍ*, *sāṃkḍā*, h. *sāṃkar*, nep. *sāṃguro* narrow.

2553. **සකෙව් sakev, සැ° sä°,** s., abridgement, abbreviation. *säkevin* in short.— P. *saṃkhēpa*, Sk. *saṃkṣēpa*.

2554. **සක්දෙව් sak-dev,** s., the god Indra or Śakra. — Pk., P. *sakka*, Sk. *śakra*.

2555. **සක්නැබ sak-näba,** s., hub or nave of a wheel. — Sk. *cakra-nābhi*.

2556. **සක්නිය sak-niya,** s., a drug. — Sk. *cakra-nakha* a kind of perfume.

2557. **සක්පණ sak-paṇa,** s., name of god Vishnu. — P. *cakka-pāṇi*, Sk. *cakra-pāṇi*.

2558 **සක්ලකුණ sak-lakuṇa,** s., mark of a wheel on the foot of the Buddha.—P. *cakka-lakkhaṇa*.

2559. **සක්වළ sakvaḷa,** s., a world, a sphere. — P. *cakkavāṭa*, Sk. *cakravāla*.

2560. **සක්වා sakvā,** s., name of a bird, the ruddy goose.—Pk. *cakkavāa*, P. *cakkavāka*, Sk. *cakravāka* ; kśm. *cakav*, si. *cakuo*, g. m. *cakvā*, oṛ. *cakuā*, ass. *sakovā*, h. pj. *cakvā*, nep. *cakhevā*.

2561. **සක්විති sakviti,** s., universal sovereign. — Pk. *cakkavaṭṭin*, P. *cakkavattin*, Sk. *cakravartin*.

2562. **සග saga[1],** s., chapter, section. — Pk., P. *sagga*, Sk. *sarga*.

2563. **සග saga[2],** s., heaven. — Pk., P. *sagga*, Sk. *svarga*.

2564. **සගවැසියා saga-väsiyā,** s., st. f. °*vāsi*, inhabitant of heaven, a god.—P. *sagga-vāsin* ; cf. Sk. *svarga-vāsa*.

2565. **සඟ saṅga,** s., multitude, assembly; the community of bhikkhus.—P. *saṅgha*, Pk., Sk. *saṃgha*.

2566. **සඟරම saṅgarama,** s., st. f. °*am*, war, battle.—(Pk. *saṃgāma*, P. *saṅgāma*,) Sk. *saṃgrāma*.

2567. **සඟහ saṅgaha,** s., compilation, compendium; entertainment of persons.—Pk. *saṃgaha*, P. *saṅgaha*, Sk. *saṃgraha*. Sinh. also *saṅgarāva* compendium.

2568. **සඟළ saṅgaḷa,** s., pair, couple. *saṅgaḷa-sivura* double robe worn by a Buddhist monk. — Pk. *saṃghāḍa*, °*ḍī*, P., Sk. *saṃghāṭa* ; g. *saṃghāḍo*, m. *sāṃgaḍ*, b. *siṃghāṛā*, h. *siṃghāṛā*, nep. *saṅār*, *saṃghār*, etc., with different meaning. Cf. *aṅguḷa*.

2569. **සඟිය saṅgiya,** s., collection (of Buddhist sacred books).—P. *saṅgīti*, Sk. *saṃgīti*.

2570. **සටහන saṭahana,** s., st. f. °*han*, mark, sketch; note, record, register. *s°-pota* note-book.—Pk. *saṃṭhāṇa*, P. *saṇṭhāna*, Sk. *saṃsthāna*. Cf. m. *sāṃṭhṇeṃ*, h. *sāṃṭhnā*.

2571. **සණ saṇa, සැණ säṇa,** s., moment, instant. *säṇen*, *säṇekin* immediately, soon.—P. *khaṇa*, Sk. *kṣaṇa* ; m. *saṇ*, h. *chan*, *chin*, pj. *chin*. See also *kaṇa[2]*, *keṇehi*.

2572. **සත් sat,** a., being, existing. — Pk., P. *santa*, Sk. *sant*.

2573. **සත sata[1], සැත säta[1],** s., st. ff. °*t*, umbrella. — Pk., P. *chatta*, Sk. *chattra* ; kśm. *chathar*, si. *chaṭru*, oṛ. *chatā*, ass. *sāti*, bg. h. nep. *chātā*, l. *chattar*.

2574. **සත sata[2], සැත säta[2],** s., st. ff. °*t*, weapon, instrument. — Pk., P. *sattha*, Sk. *śastra*.

2575. **සත sata[3],** s., st. f. *sat*, science.—Pk., P. *sattha*, Sk. *śāstra*.

2576. **සතාත් sat-at,** s., name of god Brahma.— *satā* (q.v.) + *at* = Pk., P. *attan*, Sk. *ātman*.

2577. **සතන satana,** s., st. f. *satan*, spreading, extension. — Pk. *saṃtāṇa*, P. *santāna*, Sk. *saṃtāna*.

— සතප්පනවා **satappanavā,** සතප්වනවා **satapvanavā,** v., see s.v. **sätapenavā.**

2578. සතා **satā,** s., pl. *sattu,* living being, irrational animal. — Pk., P. *satta,* Sk. *sattva* : kśm. *sath,* m. *sat,* pj. *satt* truth, nep. *sāto* spirit.

2579. සතු **satu,** a., belonging to. *an-satu* belonging to another. — Pk. *santia,* P., Sk. *santaka.*

2580. සතුටු **satuṭu,** a., satisfied, content: s. °*ṭa* satisfaction, gladness; *satuṭu-karanavā* to satisfy.—Pk. *saṃtuṭṭha,* P. *santuṭṭha,* Sk. *saṃtuṣṭa.*

2581. සතොස **satosa,** s., st. f. *satos,* satisfaction, gladness. — Pk. *saṃtōsa,* P. *santōsa,* Sk. *saṃtōṣa.*

2582. සත්දල **sat-dala** or සත්පත් **sat-pat,** s., name of a tree, Alstonia (or Echites) scholaris.—Lit. seven leaves. *sat* (v. *hat*)+*dala* (Sk. lw.), *pata*[1]; cf. P. *satta-paṇṇa.* Sk. *saptaparṇa* : m. *sātvaṇ. sātvīṇ.*

2583. සත්වා **satvā,** s., caravan-leader, merchant, trader.—Pk., P. *sattha-vāha.* Sk. *sārtha-vāha.* Cf. kśm. *sāth* company, si. *sāthu* caravan, m. h. pj. *sāth* company: Pk. *satthia,* P. *satthika,* Sk. *sārthika* belonging to a caravan. oṛ. *sāthi,* si. g. m. h. pj. *sāthī,* nep. *sāthi* comrade.

2584. සද **sada,** s., sound, word. — Pk., P. *sadda.* Sk. *śabda* : kśm. *sada,* si. *sado.* g. m. h. *sād.* pj. *sadd.*

2585. සදනවා **sadanavā,** v., prt. *sädūvā,* to prepare, adorn. Intr. *sädenavā,* prt. *säduṇā.* to be adorned, adorn one's self. — Pk. *sajjēi,* P. *sajjēti,* Sk. *sajjayati* : g. *sājruṃ,* m. *sājṇeṃ,* oṛ. *sajāibā,* ass. *xazāiba,* bg. *sājā,* h. *sajānā.* nep. *sajāunu,* pj. *sajāuṇā.*

2586. සදනා **sadanā,** s., st. f. *sadana,* good person. — P., Sk. *sajjana.* Cf. *su-danā.*

2587. සදහම **sadahama,** s., the true doctrine (i.e. of the Buddha). — P. *saddhamma,* Sk. *saddharma.*

2588. සදුල **sadula,** s., arrow-grass, Heteropopogon hirtus. — P. *saddala* the dubba (Sk. *dūrvā*) grass, Sk. *śādvala* turf.

සඳ **sañda**[1], s., see s.v. **hañda.**

2589. සඳ **sañda**[2], s., desire, love. — Pk., P., Sk. *chanda.*

2590. සඳ **sañda**[3], s., combination, joint. — Pk. *saṃdhi,* P. *sandhi.* Sk. *saṃdhi* : kśm. *sand.* si. *sandhu,* g. m. *sāṃdh,* ass. *xāṃdhi,* nep. *sāṃdh,* *sāṃd.*

2591. සඳ **sañda**[4], සැඳෑ **säñdä,** s., evening. — Pk., P. *sañjhā,* Sk. *saṃdhyā* ; si. *sañjha,* g. *sāṃj,* m. *sāṃjh,* oṛ. *sañjha,* ass. *xāṃz,* bg. h. *sāṃjh,* nep. *sāṃjh, sāṃj,* pj. *sañjh.*

2592. සඳකත **sañda-kata,** s., a kind of gem. — Sk. *candra-kānta.*

2593. සඳමඬුල්ල **sañda-maḍulla,** s., disk of the moon. — P. *canda-maṇḍala,* Sk. *candra-maṇḍala.*

2594. සඳල්ල **sañdalla,** s., st. f. *sañdalu,* balcony. — H. JAYATILAKA = Sk. *candra-śālā.*

2595. සඳහස **sañda-hasa,** s., sword, sabre. — Sk. *candra-hāsa.*

2596. සඳා **sañdā** (also *sañdahā*), postp., on account of, for the purpose of. — P. *sandhāya,* Sk. *sam-* + √*dhā,* ger. *saṃdhāya.*

2597. සඳෑස **sañd'-äsa,** s., st. f. *sañdäs,* eye in a peacock's feather. — *sañda* (v. *hañda*) + *äsa,* q.v. Cf. P. *candaka,* Sk. *candraka.*

2598. සන් **san,** a. pprt., covered, hidden. *san-piyesa* secret place.— Pk. *chaṇṇa,* P., Sk. *channa* ; si. *chano,* g. *chānū,* nep. *chānu* roof, pj. *chann* thatched shed.

2599. සන **sana**[1]**,** s., st. f. *san,* mark, sign. *san-karanavā* to make signs. — Pk. *saṇṇā,* P. *saññā,* Sk. *saṃjñā* ; g. bg. h. nep. *sān,* pj. *sann.*

2600. සන **sana**[2]**,** s., st. f. *san,* sound. — Sk. *svāna* ; pj. *sān* (T, s.v. *sankanu*). Not from *svana* ; in this case the st. f. would be **sana.*

2601. සනද **sanada,** s., armour, mail (Ruv 352). — Pk., Sk. *saṃnaddha,* P. *sannaddha.*

2602. සනහ **sanaha**[1]**,** s., bathing. — Perhaps from a Sk. **siṣṇāsā* from the des. *siṣṇāsati* of √*snā.*

2603. සනහ **sanaha**[2]**,** s., oil, grease, affection. — Pk. *siṇēha,* P. *sinēha,* Sk. *snēha.*

2604. සනිටුහන **saniṭuhana,** s., st. f. °*han,* resolve. *saniṭuhan-karanavā* to resolve.—P. *sanniṭṭhāna.*

2605. සන්හිඳෙනවා **sanhiñdenavā,** සන්සිඳෙනවා **sansiñdenavā,** v., prt. *sanhiñdunā, sans*°, to be appeased, gratified. Caus. *sansiñduvanavā,* prt. *sansiñdevuvā,* to appease, gratify. — P. *sannisīdati,* Sk. *sam-ni-* + √*sad, saṃniṣīdati.*

2606. සන්හුන් **sanhun,** සන්සුන් **sansun,** a. pprt., calm, placid, quiet.— P. *sannisinna,* Sk. *saṃniṣaṇṇa.*

2607. සපත් **sapat,** සැපත් **säpat,** a. pprt., arrived, attained. — Pk. *saṃpatta,* P. *sampatta,* Sk. *saṃprāpta.*

2608. සපත **sapata,** සැපත **säpata,** s., st. ff. °*pat,* wealth, felicity. — Pk., Sk. *saṃpatti,* P. *sampatti.*

— සපන් **sapan**[1, 2]**,** see s.v. **hapan**[1, 2]**.**

2609. සපයනවා **sapayanavā,** v., prt. *säpayuvā, säpevuvā,* to procure, provide, supply. Intr. *säpayenavā,* prt. *säpayuṇā,* to become supplied.— Pk. *saṃpāēi,* P. *sampādēti,* Sk. *sam-* + √*pad, saṃpādayati.*

2610. සපයෝ **sapayō** (HJ), s., union. — P. *sampayōga,* Sk. *saṃprayōga.*

2611. **සපා sapā**[1], s., st. f. *sap*, snake. *sap-rada* king of serpents. — Pk., P. *sappa*, Sk. *sarpa* ; si. *sapu*, g. m. *sāp*, oṛ. *sāpa*, ass. *xāp*, bg. *sāp*, h. *sāṃp*, nep. *sāp*, pj. l. *sapp*.

2612. **සපා sapā**[2], s., st. ff. *sapu*, *hapu*, bee (Ruv 249).—Pk. *chappaa*, P. *chappada*, Sk. *ṣaṭ-pada*.

2613. **සපු sapu**[1], s., name of a tree, Michelia champaca. *sapu-mala* champac flower.—Pk. *campaa*, P., Sk. *campaka* ; si. *cambo*, g. *cāmpuṃ*, m. *cāṃpā*, oṛ. *campā*, bg. *cāṃpā*, h. nep. *cāṃp*, pj. *cambā*.

— **සපු sapu**[2], s., see s.v. **sapā**[2].

2614. **සපුව sapuva,** s., st. f. *sapu*, pleasure, happiness.—Pk. *saṃpaā*, P. *sampadā* (Sk. *saṃpad*, cf. *säpaya*).

2615. **සබඳ sabaňda,** a., connected with; s. °*ňdā* friend, companion. — Pk., Sk. *saṃbandha*, P. *sambandha*.

2616. **සබය sabaya,** s., council, tribunal, in *gam-s°* village council, village tribunal.—Pk. *sahā*, P., Sk. *sabhā*.

2617. **සබල sabala,** s., variegated colour. — P. *sabala*, Sk. *śabala*. Perhaps P. lw.

2618. **සම් sam,** a., dark coloured, in *sam-van* dark blue. — Pk., P. *sāma* (*sāmala*), Sk. *śyāma* (*śyāmala*) ; kśm. *hōmu*, si. *sāo* (, g. *sāmḷuṃ*, m. *sāvḷā*, oṛ. *sāuṃlā*), ass. *xāuṃ* (, h. *sāṃvlā*, *sāṃvrā*), nep. *sāuṃ* (*sāuṃlo*), pj. l. *sāvā* (, pj. *sāṃvalā*, *sāulā*).

2619. **සමග samaga,** °ඟ **°ňga,** postp., with, together with. *samagi*, °*ňgi* united, associated ; °*giya* agreement, concord ; *samagi-karanavā* to reconcile ; *s°-venavā* to become reconciled.—Pk. *samagga*, P. *samagga*, *sāmaggī*, Sk. *samagra*, *sāmagrī*, *sāmagrya*.

2620. **සමත් samat,** a., clever, skilful; s. *samatā* clever person. — Pk., P. *samattha*, Sk. *samartha*.

2621. **සමත samata,** a., all, the whole. — Pk. *samattha*, Sk. *samasta*.

2622. **සමන් saman,** s., jasmine. — P., Sk. *sumanā*. Cf. *dā-saman*, s.v. *dā*[2].

2623. **සමරනවා samaranavā,** v., prt. *samaḷā* or *sämäruvā*, to remember. — Pk. *sumaraï*, P. *sumarati* (*sarati*), Sk. $\sqrt{}$*smṛ*, *smarati*.

2624. **සමවත samavata,** s., mental concentration, deep meditation. — P., Sk. *samāpatti*.

2625. **සමවන් samavan,** a. pprt., attained, reached, arrived at. — Pk. *samāvanna*, P., Sk. *samāpanna*.

2626. **සමාම් samām,** s., company, assembly, HJ ; DhpAGp 31[21].— Pk., P., Sk. *samāgama*.

— **සමාව samāva,** s., see s.v. **kamāva.**

2627. සමු **samu,** s., l e a v e, p e r m i s s i o n. — *samu-gannavā* to take leave; *s°-denavā* to give permission (to go).— Pk. *saṃmaa*, P. *sammata*, *sammuti*, Sk. *sam-* + √*man*, *saṃmata*, *saṃmati*.

2628. සමුසු **samusu,** සු° **su°,** a., c o m m i n g l e d, b l e n d e d. — Pk. *saṃmissa*, P. *sammissa*, Sk. *saṃmiśra*.

2629. සය **saya,** සාය **sāya,** s., st. f. *sā*, h u n g e r, f a m i n e. — Pk. *chāa*, P. *chāta(ka)*, Sk. *psāta* (WICKREMASINGHE, EpZ I 51, n. 18).

— සයු **sayu,** see s.v. **yu.**

2630. සයුර **sayura,** s., st. f. °*ru*, o c e a n. — Pk. *sāara*, P., Sk. *sāgara*; m. *sāyar*.

2631. සර **-sara**[1], a., g o i n g, w a n d e r i n g. — P., Sk. *-cara*. Cf. *val-sara*, *dala-saraуā*.

2632. සර **sara**[2], s., st. f. *sara*, s a p, p i t h. — Pk., P., Sk. *sāra*.

2633. සර **sara**[3], s., st. f. *sara*, v o w e l. — Pk., P. *sara*, Sk. *svara*; si. *suru*, g. *sur*, m. *sūr*, h. nep. pj. l. *sur*.

2634. සරගා **saragā,** °ඞ්ගා **°ṅgā,** st. ff. °*ga*, °*ṅga*, a species of d e e r or g a z e l l e, Axis maculata. — Pk., P., Sk. *sāraṅga*.

2635. සරබයා **sarabayā,** s., st. f. °*ba*, 1) a f a b u l o u s a n i m a l; 2) g r a s s - h o p p e r. — Pk. *salaha* (2), P. *sarabha* (1), *salabha* (2). Sk. *śarabha* (1), *śalabha* (2); kśm. *hālav*, h. *sal*, nep. *salaha*, *salau*, pj. *salā* (2).

2636 සරසනවා **sarasanavā,** °හනවා **°hanavā,** v., prt. *särasuvā*, °*huvā*, t o a t t i r e, a d o r n, d e c o r a t e. Intr. *särasenavā*, °*h°*, prt. *särasuṇā*, °*h°*, to become adorned, adorn one's self. — Sk. √*rac*, caus. *racayati*, Pk. *raci*, P. **racēti*, *sam*+*racati*. It must, however, be noticed that the cpd. with *sam* does not exist in Sk., nor in P. and Pk.

2637. සරසුන **sarasuna,** s., st. f. °*sun*, b o w. — Lit. seat of the arrow (cf. s.v. *säraya*); P. *sarâsana*, Sk. *śarâsana*.

2638. සරා **sarā**[1], s., st. f. *sarā*, a u t u m n. — Pk. *saraya*, P. *sarada*, *sārada*, Sk. *śarad*, *śārada*.

2639. සරා **sarā**[2], s., st. f. *sarā*, l o t u s. — Sk. *sārasa*.

2640. සරාකල් **sarā-kal,** s., a u t u m n a l s e a s o n. — *s°*+*kala*; cf. Sk. *śarat-kāla*.

2641. සරි **sari,** a., s i m i l a r. — Pk. *sarisa*, Sk. *sadṛśa*; oṛ. *sarisā*, h. *saris*, nep. *sari*. Cf. *suruku*.

2642. සරු **saru**[1], a., p r o s p e r o u s, a g r e e a b l e, e a s y. — P., Sk. *cāru*.

2643. සරු **saru**[2], s., h i l t o f a s w o r d (Cl).—Pk. *charu*, Sk. *tsaru*; g. *charo*, *charī*, m. *sarū*.

2644. සරුප් **sarup,** a., f i t, s u i t a b l e, p r o p e r. — P. *sāruppa* id. (cf. Sk. s. *sārūpya*).

2645. සල **sala¹**, s., dart, spear; porcupine's quill.— Pk., P. *salla*, Sk. *śalya* ; si. *salu*, g. *sāl*, ass. *xāl*, bg. h. nep. *sāl*, pj. *sall*. Sinh. *sallaya* is P. lw.

2646. සල **sala²**, s., stone, rock.— Pk., P. *silā*, Sk. *śilā* ; si. *sira*, m. *śil*, oṛ. *siḷa*, ass. *xil*, bg. b. h. pj. l. *sil*, nep. *sili*. Cf. *hela*.

2647. සලකනවා **salakanavā**, v., prt. *sälakuvā*, to regard, notice; respect, esteem. — Pk. *saṃlakkhēi*, P. *sallakkhēti*, Sk. *sam-*+√*lakṣ*, *saṃlakṣayati* (T, s.v. *lākhinu*). Cf. *halakuṇa*.

2648. සලන්පත **salan-pata**, s., lit. shaking leaf, i.e. fan. — Sk. **calana-pattra*. Cf. *halanavā*.

2649. සලපත **sala-pata** or සලදල **sala-dala**, s., lit. having shaking leaves, name of the Bō tree, Ficus religiosa.—Sk. *cala-pattra*, *cala-dala*. See s.v. *halanavā*.

2650. සලල **salala**, a., (Ruv 240) porcupine; its quill.—lw. Sk. *śalala*.

2651. සවන **savana¹**, s., st. f. *savan*, hearing, ear. *savan-denavā* to give ear, listen to. — Pk. *savaṇa*, P. *savana*, Sk. *śravaṇa*.

2652. සවන **savana²**, s., the omniscient one, Buddha.—Pk. *savvannu*, P. *sabbaññu*, Sk. *sarvajña*.

2653. සවය **savaya**, සැවය **sāvaya**, s., st. ff. *sava*, *säva*, corpse. — P. *chava*, Sk. *śava*.

2654. සවුන **savuna**, s., preaching.— Sk. *śrāvaṇa*, BR. 3. *sr°*.

2655. සවුවා **savuvā**, s., st. f. *sav(u)*, disciple, pupil.—Pk. *sāvaga*, P. *sāvaka*, Sk. *śrāvaka*.

2656. සස් **sas**, s., st. f. *sas*, truth.— Pk., P. *sacca*, Sk. *satya* ; si. *sacu*, *saco*, g. *sāc*, *sācuṃ*, m. *sāṃc*, *sāṃcā*, oṛ. *sacā*, ass. *xaṃsā*, bg. *sāṃcā*, h. *sāṃc*, *sāṃcā*, *saccā*, nep. *sāṃco*, pj. l. *sacc*, *saccā*.

2657. සසක් **sasak**, s., moon. — P. *sasaṅka*, Sk. *śaśāṅka*.

2658. සසග **sasaga**, °ඟ **°ṅga**, s., union, association.— Pk., P. *saṃsagga*, Sk. *saṃsarga*.

— සසයා **sasayā**, see s.v. **hāvā.**

2659. සසර **sasara**, s., succession of re-births.—Pk., P., Sk. *saṃsāra* ; si. *saṃsāru*, g. m. h. nep. *saṃsār*.

2660. සසල **sasala**, s., moving, shaking; s. *sasalaya* shaking; thunder (Ruv 56) : eye (Ruv 289). — Pk., P., Sk. *cañcala* ; si. *caṃcalu*, m. g. bg. h. pj. *caṃcal*.

2661. සහය **sahaya**, s., st. f. *sahaya*, support, help.—Pk., P., Sk. *sahāya* friend.

2662. සහයුරු **sahayuru**, s., mango (Ruv 215).— Pk. *sahaāra*, P., Sk. *sahakāra*.

2663. සහසක් **sahas-ak** or සහසැස් **sahas-äs**, s., name of god Śakra (lit. having thousand eyes). — P. *sahassakkha*, Sk. *sahasrākṣa*.

2664. සහස්නෙත් **sahas-net,** s., name of the god Ś a k r a (lit. having thousand eyes). — P. *sahassa-netta*, Sk. *sahasra-nētra*.

2665. සළ **saḷa**[1] (? *sala*), s., d e c e p t i o n. — Pk., P., Sk. *chala* ; kśm. *chal*, g. *chaḷ*, m. *saḷ*, oṛ. *chaḷa*, ass. *sal*, bg. h. nep. pj. *chal*. — Cf. also P. *saṭha*, Sk. *śaṭha* (DE LANEROLLE).

2666. සළ **saḷa**[2], s., st. f. *saḷa*, name of a l u n a r m a n s i o n. *puva-s°*, *uturu-s°* 20th and 21st l. mm.—P. *pubbâsāḷha*, *uttarâsāḷha*, Sk. (*pūrvā*) *asāḍhāḥ*, (*uttarā*) *as°* ; KIRFEL, Kosmographie der Inder, p. 36. Cf. *ähäḷa*.

2667. සළාව **saḷāva,** s., st. f. *saḷā*, m u l t i t u d e. — Pk. *chaḍā*, Sk. *chaṭā*.

— සා **sā**[1], සාය **sāya,** s., see s.v. **saya.**

2668. සා **sā**[2], s., st. f. *sā*, b r a n c h of a tree. — Pk. *sāhā*, P. *sākhā*, Sk. *śākhā* ; cf. m. *sāvaḷ* large branch of a palm (Bl), nep. *syāulo* (T).

2669. සාමුවා **sā-muvā,** s., m o n k e y (lit. branch-animal). — *sā* (v. *sā*[2]) + *muvā* ; P. *sākhāmiga*, Sk. *śākhāmṛga*.

— සාර **sāra,** num., see s.v. **hatara.**

— සාලිස **sālisa,** num., see s.v. **hataliha.**

2670. සැඩ **säḍa**[1], °ඬ **°ňḍa** (Ruv 488), a., a s c e n d i n g. — Pk. *caḍaï* ; kśm. *carun*, si. *caṛhaṇu*, g. *caḍhvuṃ*, m. *caḍhneṃ*, oṛ. *caṛhibā*, ass. *sariba*, bg. *caṛā*, Eastern h. *carnā*, nep. *caṛnu*, *caṛhnu*, pj. *caṛhnā*, l. *caṛhaṇ*.

2671. සැඩ **säḍa**[2], සැඬ **säňḍa,** a., h a r d, s e v e r e, r o u g h ; s. *säḍayā* ruffian. — Pk., P., Sk. *caṇḍa*.

2672. සැඩොලා **säḍolā,** °ඬො° **°ňḍo°**, s., st. ff. *°ḍol*, R o ḍ i y ā. — Pk., P., Sk. *caṇḍāla* ; ass. *caṃrāl*. Gr. 50.4.

2673. සැතපෙනවා **sätapenavā,** v., prt. *sätapuṇā*, t o s l e e p, r e p o s e. Caus. *satappanavā*, *°pv°*, prt. *sätäppuvā* ; double caus. *satappavanavā*, prt. *sätäppevuvā*, to cause to sleep.— Base v. **satapanavā* = P. *santappēti*, Sk. *sam-* + $\sqrt{}$*tṛp*, caus. *saṃtarpayati* he satisfies, invigorates.

2674. සැද **säda,** s., a r m o u r, m a i l ; p a n n i e r for a horse.—Sk. *sajjā*. Cf. *sädi*.

2675. සැදැහැ **sädähä,** °දා **°dā,** s., f a i t h, p i e t y. *sädā-ḷen* with a pious heart, SälS 49.—Pk., P. *saddhā*, Sk. *śraddhā*. Probably Slw. P.

2676. සැදි **sädi,** සැදු **sädu,** a. pprt., a d o r n e d, o r n a m e n t e d.—Pk. *sajjia*, P., Sk. *sajjita*. Cf. *sadanavā*.

2677. සැදුලා **sädulā,** s., st. f. *sädul*, l e o p a r d, p a n t h e r —P. *saddūla*, Sk. *śārdūla*.

2678. සැපය **säpaya,** s., st. f. *säpa,* comfort, pleasure. *säpa-jīvikāva* comfortable life.—Sk. *sampad.* Cf. *sapuva.*

2679. සැබව **säbava,** සැබෑව **säbāva,** s., st. f. *säbā,* truth. — Generally derived from P. *sa-bhāva,* Sk. *sva-bhāva,* but I prefer to compare the word with Pk. *sabbhāva,* Sk. *sad-bhāva.*

2680. සැමිටිය **sämiṭiya,** s., whip. — Probably from *sam* (*ham*) leather+*miṭiya.*

2681. සැර **sära,** a., swift; s. *säraya* speed, velocity; *sära-yaṭiya* or *-miṭiya* walking stick.—P., Sk. *cārin*; Pk. cf. *cāra,* P. *cārikā.* Cf. T, s.v. *carnu.*

2682. සැරය **säraya,** s., st. f. *sära,* arrow. — Pk., P. *sara,* Sk. *śara*; si. *saru,* g. m. h. nep. pj. l. *sar.*

2683. සැරිසරනවා **särisaranavā,** v., prt. *särisäruvā,* to walk about. — Intens. st. **carīcar-* of Sk. √*car*; cf. P., Sk. *carācara.*

2684. සැව් **säv,** s., archer's bow. — Pk. *cāva,* P., Sk. *cāpa.*

2685. සැහැල්ලු **sähällu,** a., light (in weight), easy.— ? Metathesis of **sälāhu* = P. *sallahuka.*

2686. සෑ **sā-,** s., the Sākya tribe, in *sā-kula* id.; *sā-muni* the saint of the Sākyas, i.e. the Buddha.—P. *sākya, sākiya, sakka,* Sk. *śākya.*

2687. සෑය **sāya,** s., st. f. *sā,* funeral pile, monument, Thūpa. *sā-giri,* name of the Mihintale hill. — Pk. *cēiya,* P. *cētiya,* Sk. *caitya.*

2688. සිකල් **sikal,** s., mud, mire. — Pk., P. *cikkhalla,* but Sk. *cikhalla*; g. *cikkal,* m. *cikhal,* Eastern h. *cīkar,* pj. *cikkar.*

2689. සිකු **siku,** a., dry.—Pk. *sukka,* P. *sukkha,* Sk. *śuṣka*; kśm. *hokhu,* si. *suko,* g. *sūkuṃ.* m. *sukā,* ass. *xukān,* bg. *sukā,* h. *sūkhā,* nep. *suko,* pj. l. *sukkā.*

2690. සිකුරු **sikuru,** සුකුරු **sukuru,** a., white; s. *sikurā,* st. f. °*ru,* the planet Venus; *sikurā-dā* Friday.—Slw. Sk. *śukra* (, Pk., P. *sukka*; m. h. pj. *sūk* the pl. V., h. *suk* white).

— සිඟු **siṅgu,** s., see s.v. **aṅga**[2].

2691. සිතියම **sitiyama,** සිතු° **situ°,** s., st. ff. °*yam,* picture, painting, drawing. *sitiyarā, sittarā* painter. — Sk. *citrakarman, citrakāra.* cf. Pk. *cittaāra,* P. *cittakāra.* Sinh. also *sittama.*

2692. සිතුකුළු **situkuḷu,** in *s.-paruva,* s., name of a mountain. — P. *citta-kūṭa,* Sk. *citra-kūṭa.*

2693. සිතුමිණ **situ-miṇa,** s., st. f. *ṇa,* wishing gem said to bestow whatever its possessor desires.—Pk., Sk. *cintāmaṇi.*

2694. සිදත් **sidat,** s., settled doctrine, conclusion. *sidat-saṅgarāva* name of a Sinh. grammar. — P. *siddhanta,* Sk. *siddhânta.*

2695. සිදු **sidu,** a. pprt., effected, decided, proved.— Pk., P., Sk. *siddha* ; kśm. *syodu*, si. *sidho*, g. *sīdhuṃ*, oṛ. bg. *sidhā*, h. *sīdhā*, nep. *sidho* pj. l. *siddhā*.

2696. සිදුර **sidura,** s., st. f. *°ru*, perforation, hole.—Slw. Sk. *chidra*. Cf. *sikuru* (split *-kr-*) ; see s.v. *hida*[1].

2697. සිදුරා **sidurā** (Ca), s., st. f. *°ru*, elephant.— P., Sk. *sindhura*.

2698. සිදුහත් **siduhat,** s., white mustard; lay name of the Buddha. — Slw.—P. *sidhattha*, Sk. *siddhârtha*.

2699. සිඳු **siňdu,** s., sea, river.— Pk., P., Sk. *sindhu* ; kśm. *send*, si. *sindhu*, nep. *siṃdho*, l. *sinnh*.

2700. සිනිඳු **siniňdu,** a. pprt., oily, smooth, soft, gentle. *siniňdu-kama* smoothness.—Pk. *siṇiddha* P. *siniddha*, Sk. *snigdha*.

2701. සිප් **sip,** s., handicraft, art. *sipiyā*, s., st. f. *sipi*, artificer, artisan. —Pk. *sippa*, *sippiya*, P. *sippa*, *sippika*, *sippin*, Sk. *śilpa*. *śilpika*, *śilpin* ; m. *śīpī* tailor, ass. *xipini* a woman clever at spinning and weaving; nep. *sip* cleverness.

2702. සිපත **si-pata,** s., st. f. *sipat*, sword blade.—Sk. *asi-pattra*. Sinh. also *asi-pata*.

2703. සිය **siya**[1], s., roof.—P., Sk. *chada*. Cf. *siyana*.

2704. සිය **siya**[2], a., one's own; s. *siyā* kinsman; *nā-siyā* id. (v: *nāyā*) ; *s°-basa* native language. — Pk. *saa*, P. *saka*, Sk. *svaka* ; kśm. *sakh*, si. *sako*, g. *saguṃ*, *sagvuṃ*, m. *sagā*, h. *sagā*, *saggā*, nep. *sākh*, pj. *sagg*. l. *sakkā*.

2705. සියන **siyana,** s., st. f. *siyan*, roof. — P., Sk. *chadana*. Cf. *siya*[1].

2706. සියපත **siya-pata,** s., lotus, Nelumbium speciosum.—*siyaya* (q.v.) + *pata*, P. *satapatta*, Sk. *śata-pattra*.

2707. සියපා **siya-pā,** s., centipede.— P: *satapadī*, Sk. *śata-pad*.

2708. සියය **siyaya,** num., st. f. *siya*, hundred. *ek-siyaya* 100 ; *de-siyaya* 200 ; *tun-siyaya* 300 etc. : *siya-varak* a hundred times.— Pk. *saa*, P. *sata*, Sk. *śata* ; kśm. *hath*, si. *saü*, g. *so*, m. *śeṃ*, oṛ. *sa*, *sae*, ass. *xa*, bg. *saye*, h. *sai*, h. pj. *sau*, *sai*, nep. *sai*, l. *sô*.

2709. සියල් **siyal,** සියලු **siyalu,** a., all: s. *siyalla* all, the whole lot ; *siyallō*, pl., all (animates).—Pk. *saala*. Ap. Pk. *sagala*, P., Sk. *sakala* ; si. *saghḷuṃ*. m. *saglā*, h. *sagar*, *sagal*. *sagrā*, *saglā*, pj. *sagal*, *sagrā*. Gr. I. 2.

2709a. සියහ **siyaha,** a., continual, perpetual. — Pk. *saaa*, P., Sk. *satata*.

— සියුම් **siyum,** a., see s.v. **hin**.

2709*b*. සියුරා **siyurā,** සිවුරා **sivurā,** s., st. ff. °*ru*, Greek partridge, Perdrix rufa. — Pk. *caōra*, P., Sk. *cakōra* ; nep. *cākhuro*, *cyākhuro*. Cl also *sivru*.

2710. සියොතා **siyotā,** s., st. f. *siyot*, bird. — P. *sakunta*, Sk. *śakunta*.

2711. සියෝ **siyō,** s., union. — Pk. *saṃjōya*, *saṃjōga*, P., Sk. *saṃyōga*.

2712. සිර **sira,** s., head. — Pk., P. *sira*, Sk. *śiras* ; kśm. *hīrü*, si. *siru*, g. *sir*, m. *śīr*, oṛ. *sira*, ass. *xir*, bg. h. nep. pj. l. *sir*.

2713. සිරි **siri,** s., fortune, blessing, glory, in numerous cpds. as *siri-pā* blessed foot, *siri-yahana* blessed couch, etc. — Probably lw. Pk., P. *siri*, Sk. *śrī*.

2714. සිරිත **sirita,** s., st. f. *sirit*, habit, custom, traditional observance.— < MInd. **caritta* = Sk. *caritra*. Cf. P. *cāritta*, Sk. *cāritra*.

2715. සිරිය **siriya,** s., st. f. *siri*, small sword, dagger. — Pk. *churiā*, Sk. *churikā* ; si. g. *churī*, m. *surā*, *surī*, oṛ. *churi*, ass. *suri*, bg. *churi*, h. pj. *churā*, *churī*, nep. *churi*, l. *churī*. Cf. *karaya*. Gr. 50.4.

2716. සිරියා **siriyā,** සිරුවා **siruvā,** s., st. ff. *siri*, *siru*, locust, cricket.— P., Sk. *cīrī*, *cīrikā*.

2717. සිරුර **sirura,** s., st. f. *siruru*, body. *maḷa-sirura* corpse.— Pk., P. *sarīra*, Sk. *śarīra*.

2718. සිරුව **siruva,** s., st. f. *siru*, plough (Ruv 367).—Pk., P., Sk. *sīra*+suff. *-ka* ; h. pj. *sīr*, nep. *sir* land cultivated by the owner.

2719. සිල් **sil,** s. pl., religious observances. *sil-vatā* observer of religious duties ; *sil-gannavā*, *-rakinavā* to observe religious precepts. — Pk., P. *sīla*, *sīlavant*, Sk. *śīla*, *śīlavant* ; si. *sīluṃ*, *sīru*, g. m. *śīḷ*, h. pj. *sīl*.

2720. සිලිමුවා **silimuvā,** s., bee. — Sk. *śilīmukha*.

2721. සිලිල **silila,** s., st. f. *silil*, water. *silil-bemuva* (Ruv 139) whirlpool, eddy. — Pk., P., Sk. *salila*.

2722. සිලුටු **siluṭu,** a. pprt., smooth, soft, polished. *s°-kama* smoothness. — Pk., P. *siliṭṭha*, Sk. *śliṣṭa*. Cf. T, s.v. *lesnu*.

2723. සිලොව **silova,** s., st. f. *silō*, verse, stanza. — Pk. *silōga*, *silōa*, P. *silōka*, Sk. *ślōka*.

2724. සිව් **siv-,** සිවු **sivu-,** සූ **sū-,** num., four, in cpds. : *siv-at*, lit. having four arms, Vishn̆u ; *siv-vana*, a., of four kinds ; *sū-panas* 54 ; *sū-säṭa* 64; *suvāsū* 84. — Pk. *cau-*, P. *catu-*, Sk. *catuḥ-*, *catuṣ-*, *catur-* ; g. *co-*, m. oṛ. *cau-*, ass. *cau-*, bg. h. nep. pj. *cau-*. Cf. also *hatara*.

2725. සිවිය **siviya**[1], s., st. f. *sivi*, a species of pepper, Piper chavya; a creeper (Ruv 666). — Sk. *cavī*, *cavya*.

2726. සිවිය **siviya^2,** s., st. f. *sivi*, skin, bark. — Pk., P. *chavi*, Sk. *chavī*. Cf. *häva*.

2727. සිවිය **siviya^3,** s., st. f. *sivi*, palanquin, in *sivi-geya* litter, howdah. — Pk. *siviā*, P. *sivikā*, Sk. *śivikā*.

2728. සිවුමැලි **sivumäli,** a., soft, delicate, tender. — Pk. *suumāra*, P. *sukumāra*, *sukhumāla*, Sk. *sukumāra*.

2729. සිවුර **sivura,** s., st. f. *sivuru*, yellow robe (of a Buddhist monk). *sivuru-arinavā* to disrobe, retire from monastic life.—Pk., P., Sk. *cīvara*.

2730. සිවුරඟ සෙන් **sivurañga-sen,** s., army consisting of four parts.— Pk. *caüraṅga*, P. *caturaṅga*, Sk. *caturaṅga* + *sēnā*.

— සිවුරා **sivurā,** s., see s.v. **siyurā.**

2731. සිව්දෑ ගඳ **siv-dä-gañda,** s., the four kinds of perfumes. — P. *catu-jjāti-gandha*.

2732. සිව්දිග **siv-diga,** s., the four quarters of the compass.— Cf. Pk. *caü-ddisiṃ*, P. *catu-ddisa*, Sk. *catur-diśa*.

2733. සිව්දිව් **siv-div,** s. pl., the four continents. — Sk. *catur-dvīpa*.

2734. සිව්පස **siv-pasa,** s. pl., the four requisites of a Buddhist monk. — P. *catu-paccaya*.

2735. සිව්පාවා **siv-pāvā,** s., st. f. °*pā*, quadruped. — Pk. *caü-ppaa*, P. *catu-ppada*, Sk. *catuṣ-pāda* ; si. *caupāī*, g. *copāī*, m. *caupāyī*, oṛ. bg. *caupāyā*, h. *caupā*, *caupāyā*, nep. *caupāyo*, pj. *caupāiā*.

2736. සිව්රැස් **sivr-äs,** a., four-cornered, quadrangular.— P. *catur-assa*, Sk. *catur-aśra*. Sinh. also *satar-äs*. Cf. *asa^3*.

2737. සිව්සස් **siv-sas,** s. pl., the four truths. — P. *catu-sacca*.

2738. සිසි **sisi,** s., moon. — Pk. *sasi*, P. *sasin*, Sk. *śaśin*.

2739. සිසිපුත් **sisi-put,** s., the son of the moon, the planet Mercury. — Sk. *śaśi-putra*.

— සිසිර **sisira,** සිසිල් **sisil,** සිහිල් **sihil,** a., see s.v. **hil.**

2740. සිසු **sisu,** s., pupil, disciple. — Pk. *sīsa*, P. *sissa*, Sk. *śiṣya*.

2741. සිහ **siha,** s., st. ff. *siha*, *sī*, lion. *sī-giriya*, name of an ancient fortified rock in Ceylon. — Pk., P. *sīha*, Sk. *siṃha*.

2742. සිහස්න **sih'-asna,** සිහසුන **sih'-asuna,** s., lion seat, royal seat, throne. — Pk. *sīhâsaṇa*, P. *sīhâsana*, Sk. *siṃhâsana*.

— සිහින් **sihin,** a., see s.v. **hin.**

2743. **සිහිය sihiya,** s., st. f. *sihi,* wakefulness of mind, alertness; intellect, reason, mind. *sihi-näti* senseless, foolish ; *sihi-nuvaṇa* (dvandva compd.) intelligence and sagacity ; *sihi-karanavā* to remember. — Pk. *saï,* P. *sati,* Sk. *smṛti* ; m. *saī, say.*

2744. **සිළු siḷu,** s., hair on the top of the head, crest (of a cock), diadem. — Pk. *cūḍā, cūḷā,* P. *cūḷā,* Sk. *cūḍā* ; m. *cūḍ,* oṛ. *cuḷa,* ass. *suli,* bg. *culā,* h. *cūṛā,* l. *cūṃṛī* (T, s. vv. *cur*[2], *curi*[1] etc.). Cf. *tam̆ba-siḷuvā.*

2745. **සිළුමිණ siḷu-miṇa,** s., crest jewel in a diadem.—P. *cūḷā-maṇi,* Sk. *cūḍā-maṇi.*

2746. **සී sī,** s., laughing, laughter. — P. *sita,* Sk. *smita.*

2747. **සු su-,** pref., good, excellent, well, in many cpds. (see below). — Pk., P., Sk. *su-* ; MIAVs *su-.*

2748. **සුකු suku,** s., tax, toll, duty. — P. *suṅka,* Sk. *śulka.*

— **සුගඳ su-gaňda,** a., s., see s.v. **suvaňda.**

2749. **සුගිය sugiya,** s., st. ff. *sugi,* °*ī,* heaven. — P., Sk. *sugata.*

2750. **සුත suta,** s., st. f. *sut,* thread, string. — Pk., P. *sutta,* Sk. *sūtra*; kśm. *sathar.* si. *suṭru,* g. *sutar,* m. *sūt,* oṛ. *sutā,* ass. *xut,* bg. b. h. *sūt,* nep. *sut,* pj. *sūt, sūtar,* l. *sūtar.* Also Sinh. *suturu.* Cf. *huya.*

2751. **සුතු sutu,** s., any shell-fish. — Pk., P. *sutti,* Sk. *śukti.*

2752. **සුදත් sudat,** s., harem. — P. *suddhanta,* Sk. *śuddhânta.*

2753. **සුදනා su-danā,** s., st. f. °*na,* good person. — P., Sk. *su-jana.* Cf. *sadanā.*

2754. **සුදම් su-dam,** s., 1) excellent law or doctrine; 2) excellent council, council of the gods. — Pk. *su-hamma,* P. *su-dhamma* (1), ° *mmā* (2), Sk. *su-dharma*(1), °*mā*(2).

2755. **සුදවස sud'-avasa,** s., st. f. °*vas,* name of the Brahma-world. — P. *suddhâvāsa,* Sk. *śuddhâvāsa.*

2756. **සුදසුන් su-dasun**[1]**,** a., handsome, good-looking; s. °*suna* Krishna's discus, Indra's thunderbolt. — Pk. *su-daṃsana,* P. *su-dassana,* Sk. *su-darśana.*

2757. **සුදසුන් su-dasun**[2]**,** a., lit. having a good vision, pious. — *su-+dasun*=P. *dassana.*

2758. **සුදු sudu,** a., clean, pure; white. P. *suddha,* Sk. *śuddha.*

2759. **සුදුසු su-dusu,** a., fit; proper, suitable. — MInd. ***su-daccha** < Ved. *su-dakṣa.* Doubtful. — But cf. Sk. *sādṛśa* (De Lanerolle).

2760. සුන් **sun,** a. pprt., cut, broken. *sun-bun* crushed and broken, s. pl., broken things, lumber. — Pk., P., Sk. *chinna*. Cf. *hiňdinavā*.

2761. සුපිපි **su-pipi,** a. pprt., well-opened, full-blown (flower). — Sk. *su-puṣpita*. See *pipi*.

2762. සුපුව **supuva,** s., st. f. *supu*, sleep (Ruv 123). — P. *soppa*. See s.v. *hīnaya*.

2763. සුබ **suba,** a., fortunate, happy; s., good fortune. *a-suba* inauspicious. — Pk. *suha*, P. *subha*, Sk. *śubha*. Cf. *obina*.

2764. සුඹුළුව **suṁbuḷuva,** s., st. f. °*ḷu*, coil or roll of cloth, wreath. — P. *cumbaṭaka*.

2765. සුමඟුල් **su-magul** (°*ňgul*), a., very auspicious. — Sk. *sumaṅgala*.

2766. සුමු **su-mu** (Ca), a., having a lovely face, handsome. — Sk. *su-mukha*.

2767. සුමුග **sumuga,** s., st. f. °*gu*, casket. — Pk., P. *samugga*, Sk. *samudga*.

2768. සුමුව **sumuva,** s., st. f. *sumu*, multitude, assembly; army. —Pk., P., Sk. *samūha*.

2769. සුරඟ **surañga,** s., vermillion; orange.— Sk. *suraṅga*.

2770. සුරඟන **sur'-añgana,** s., celestial woman, nymph. — Sk. *surâṅganā*.

2771. සුරදෙටු **sura-deṭu,** s., st. f., chief of gods.— Sk. *sura-jyēṣṭha*, n. of god Brahma.

2772. සුරනා **sura-nā,** s., lord of the gods, name of god Śakra. — P. *sura-nātha*.

2773. සුරනී **sura-nī,** s., name of the celestial river. — P., Sk. *sura-nadī*. Cf. *niya*[2].

2774. සුරලොව **sura-lova,** s., st. f. *-lō*, the world of the gods, heaven. — Pk. *sura-lōya*, Sk. *sura-lōka*.

2775. සුරසෑව **sura-säv,** s., rainbow. — lit. devine bow, Sk. *sura-cāpa*.

2776. සුරැකි **su-räki,** a. pprt., well protected, safe. — P. *su-rakkhita*, Sk. *su-rakṣita*.

2777. සුරැදුරා **sur'-ädurā,** s., preceptor of the gods, n. of god Brihaspati. — Sk. *surâcārya*.

2778. සුරිඳු **sur'-iňdu,** s., chief of the gods, n. of god Indra or Śakra. — Sk. *surêndra*.

2779. සුරු **suru**[1], a., brave, manly. — Pk., P. *sūra*, Sk. *śūra*; si. g. *sūro*, h. pj. *sūrā*, nep. *suro*.

2780. **සුරු su-ru[2], °රූ °rū,** a., beautiful. — Pk. *su-rūva*, P., Sk. *su-rūpa*; si. *surū* (a boy) who is tall for his age.

2781. **සුරුකු suruku** (Ruv 407), a., similar, like.—P. *sarikkha-ka*, Sk. *sadṛkṣa*; si. *sarkho*, g. *sarkhuṃ*, m. *sārkhā*, *sārikhā*, h. *sārīkhā*, *sārkhā*, *sārkā*. Cf. *sari*.

2782. **සුරූප su-rūpa,** a., well-formed, handsome. — Sk. lw. *su-rūpa*.

2783. **සුලබ su-laba,** a., easily obtained, plentiful. — Pk. *su-laha*, P., Sk. *su-labha*.

2784. **සුවඳ suvaňda,** s., perfume, scent; n. of a plant, Kayea stylosa. — Pk. *suandha*, P., Sk. *sugandha*; Eastern h. *sōṃdhā* (H 54).

2785. **සුවන් suvan[1],** s., dog. — P. *suvāna*, *svāna*, *sōṇa*, *sūna*, *sāna*, Sk. *śvan*. Cf. Pk. *suṇaha*, Sk. *śunaka*; kśm. *hūnu*, m. *suṇeṃ*, h. *sūnā*.

2786. **සුවන් suvan[2],** s., st. f. *suvan*, name of the bird Garuḍa. — P. *su-paṇṇa*, Sk. *suparṇa*.

2787. **සුවන්කරුවා suvan-karuvā,** s., goldsmith. — Pk. *suvaṇṇaāra*, P. *su-vaṇṇakāra*, Sk. *suvarṇakāra*; kśm. *sŏnar*, si. *sonāro*, g. m. *sonār*, oṛ. *sunāri*, ass. *xonāri*, h. *sonār*, *sunār*, nep. *sunār*, pj. *suniārā*, l. *sunārā*. Cf. *suvaru*[1].

2788. **සුවන්න suvanna,** s., st. f. *suvan*, gold. — Pk., P. *suvaṇṇa*, Sk. *suvarṇa*; kśm. *sŏn*, si. *sonu*, g. *sonuṃ*, m. *soneṃ*, oṛ. *sunā*, ass. *xon*, *xonā*, bg. *sonā*, h. *sunā*, *sonā*, nep. *sun*, pj. l. *sonā*.

2789. **සුවන්වන suvan-vana,** s., gold colour, bright yellow. — P. *suvaṇṇa-vaṇṇa*, Sk. *suvarṇa-varṇa*.

2790. **සුවය suvaya,** s., st. f. *suva*, happiness, enjoyment, health. *suva-karanavā* to heal. — Pk. *suha*, P., Sk. *sukha*.

2791. **සුවයා suvayā,** s., st. f. *suva*, parrot. — Pk. *sua*, P. *suva*, *suka*, Sk. *śuka*; g. *śuḍo*, m. *suā*, *suvā*, h. pj. *sūā*.

2792. **සුවරු suvaru[1],** s., goldsmith. — See s.v. *suvan-karuvā*.

2793. **සුවරු suvaru[2],** s., cook. — P., Sk. *sūpa-kāra*; m. *suār*, h. *suārā*.

2794. **සුවස suvasa,** s., natron, alkali. *suvasa-luṇu* id. — Sk. *suvarcaka*.

2795. **සුවහස් suvahas,** num., hundred thousand, lakh. — P. *sata-sahassa*, Sk. *śata-sahasra*.

2796. **සුවාසූ suvāsū,** num., eighty four. — Cf. P. *caturāsīti*, Sk. *caturaśīti*.

2797. **සුසිර susira,** s., hole, perforation; something that is perforated, flute, elephant's trunk. — P. *susira*, Sk. *suṣira*.

— **සුහුනා suhunā,** s., see s.v. **hūnā**.

2798. **සුහුල් suhul,** s., mother-in-law (Ruv 266). — Pk., P. *sassū*, Sk. *śvaśrū*; kśm. *haś*, si. *sasu*, g. *sāsu*, m. *sāsū*, oṛ. *sāsu*, ass. *xāhu*, bg. *sāsuṛi*, h. *sās*, *sāsū*, nep. *sāsu*, pj. l. *sass*.

2799. **සුළු suḷu,** a., little, small, insignificant. — P. *cūḷa* (*culla*), Sk. *kṣulla*.

— **සූ sū[1],** num., see s.v. **siv-**.

2800. **සූ sū[2],** s., sauce, condiment (HJ). — Pk. *sūa*, P., Sk. *sūpa*.

2801. **සූදෙට sū-deṭa,** s., chief cook, chef. — *sū* = P., Sk. *sūda* cook + *d°*, q.v.

2802. **සෙට seṭa,** a., best, chief, eminent. — Pk., P. *seṭṭha*, Sk. *śrēṣṭha*; nep. *seṭh*. See *hiṭāṇō*, *heṭṭiyā*.

2803. **සෙත seta[1],** s., st. f. *set*, tranquillity, peace. — Pk., P. *santi*, Sk. *śānti*.

2804. **සෙත seta[2],** s., st. f. *set*, good fortune, happiness. — P. *sotthi*, Sk. *svasti*; cf. Pk. *sutthaṃ* (HSm).

2805. **සෙන් sen[1],** s., kite (the bird). — P. *sēna*, Sk. *śyēna*.

2806. **සෙන් sen[2],** s., multitude, army.— Pk. *sēṇā*, P., Sk. *sēnā*; kśm. *sīna*, h. nep. *sen*.

2807. **සෙනග senaga, °ඟ °ṅga,** s., multitude, army. — *sen[2]* + *aṅga*, Sk. *sēnāṅga*.

2808. **සෙනසුන් senasun,** s., lodging, abode. — P. *senâsana*=Sk. *śayana* + *āsana*.

2809. **සෙනසුරා senasurā,** s., the planet Saturn. — Sk. *śanaiścara*.

2810. **සෙනෙවිරද senevi-rada,** s., chief commander of an army. — *senevi* = Pk. *sēṇāvaï*, P., Sk. *sēnāpati* + *rada*, q.v.

2811. **සෙපත් se-pat,** s., swan. — Lit. having white feathers; *sē[2]* + *pata*, q.v. Sk. *śvēta-pattra*.

2812. **සෙබළා sebaḷā,** s., soldier, warrior. — < *se* = Sk. *sēvā* + *beḷē*, q.v.

2813. **සෙම sema[1],** s., st. f. *sem*, safety, peace, tranquillity. *semin*, *hemin*, adv., slowly, softly. — < MInd. **chēma* = Sk. *kṣēma*, but Pk., P. *khēma*. MIAVs see T, s.v. *jokhim*.

2814. **සෙම sema[2],** s., st. f. *sem*, mucus, phlegm. — Pk. *seppha*, *sēpha*, *ṣembhā*, *simbha*, *silimha*, P. *semha*, *silēsuma*, Sk. *ślēṣman*; m. *śem*, *śemb*, oṛ. *chepa*, ass. *xep*, bg. *chep*, h. *sembhā*, nep. *sep*.

2815. සෙමර **semara,** සෙමෙර **semera,** s., yak-tail used as fly-flap. — Pk., P., Sk. *cāmara* ; kśm. *cāmar*, si. *caṃvaru*, g. *cāmar*, m. *caṃvar*, oṛ. *caaṃra*, ass. *soṃvar*, bg. *camar*, h. *caṃvar*, nep. pj. *camar*, *caṃvar*. Cf. Pk., P., Sk. *camarī* ; g. *camrī*, m. *caṃvrī*, ass. *suṃvari*, bg. *camari*, h. *cauṃrī*, nep. *cauṃri*, *caṃvari*, *camari*, pj. *caṃvarī*. See the next word.

2816. සෙමරා **semarā** or සෙමෙරා **semerā,** s., yak, Bos gruniens. — Pk., P., Sk. *camara*. See the preceding word.

2817. සෙමිණ **se-miṇa,** සේ° **sē-°,** s. lit. white gem, crystal. — *sē*[2] + *miṇa*, q.v.

2818. සෙය **seya,** s., st. f. *sē*, shade, shadow; likeness, manner.— *-seyin* in (such and such) a manner ; *-sē* as, like, similarly ; *bohō-seyin* very much, exceedingly ; *e-sē* so.—Pk. *chāā*, P., Sk. *chāyā* ; kśm. *chāy*, si. *chāṃva*, g. *chāṃi*, m. *sāvlī*, oṛ. *chāi*, ass. *sāṃ*, h. *chāṃh*, nep. *chāhāri*, pj. l. *chūṃ*.

2819. සෙරැස් **se-räs** (also *sē-räs*), s., lit. having white rays, moon.— *sē*[2] + *räsa*[1]. Cf. Sk. *śvēta-rōcis* moon.

2820. සෙවටු **sevaṭu,** s., servant, attendant. — *seva*=Pk., P., Sk. *sēvā* + *ṭu*=Pk., P.*-ṭṭha*, Sk.*-stha*. Also *sēvaṭu*. See *hēvāyā*.

2821. සෙවෙල **sevela,** s., st. f. *sevel*, moss, n. of an aquatic plant, Blyxa zeylanica. — Pk. *sēvāḍa*, °*la*, P. *sēvāla*, Sk. *śaivāla* ; kśm. *hil*, si. *siṃaru*, *seṃvaru*, m. *śevāḷ*, *śevāḷī*, oṛ. *siuḷi*, bg. *seyālā*, h. *sivār*, nep. *siṃvāli*, *simāli*, *sēvāli*, *sāmali*, l. *sivāl*.

— සෙසු **sesu,** a., see s.v. **tesu.**

— සේ **sē**[1], s., shade, see s.v. **seya.**

2822. සේ **sē**[2], a., white, in cpds also *se-*: *se-pat*, *se-miṇa* ; s. *seya* white colour. — Pk. *sēa*, P. *sēta*, Sk. *śvēta* (; cf. oṛ. *setā*, ass. *xeṃtā*, nep. *seto* < Pk. *setta*). See *el*.

— සේවටු **sēvaṭu,** s., see s.v. **sevaṭu.**

2823. සේසත **sē-sata,** s., white umbrella (one of the insignia of royalty). — P. *sēta-cchatta*, Sk. *śvēta-cchattra*.

— සොඬ **soňḍa**[1], s., see s.v. **hoňḍa.**

2824. සොඬ **soňḍa**[2], a., addicted to drink, intoxicated. *surā-soňḍa* addicted to spirituous liquor ; *-soňḍā* drunkard. — Pk., P. *soṇḍa*, Sk. *śauṇḍa*.

2825. සොඳුරු **soňduru,** a., handsome, beautiful; s. *soňdura* wife. — Pk., P., Sk. *sundara*. Cf. *hoňda*.

2826. සොමි **somi,** a., soft, tender, smooth; s., moon.—Pk., P. *somma*, Sk. *saumya*.

2827. සොම්නස **somnasa,** s., joy, pleasure, delight. — P. *sōmanassa*, Sk. *saumanasya*.

2828. සොම්මරුවා **sommaruvā,** සොම්මරා **sommarā,** s., a man who, works in leather. Pk. *cammaāra*, P. *cammakāra*, Sk. *carmakāra* kśm. *camar*, si. *camāru*, g. *camār*, m. *cāmhār*, oṛ. *camāra*, ass. *samār*; bg. *cāmār*, b. h. nep. *camār*, pj. *camār*, *camiār*. Sinh. also *sam-karuvā*.

2829. සොයනවා **soyanavā,** v., prt. *sevuvā*, to seek, search for. — Pk. *sōhēi* cleans, searches, P. *sōdhēti*, Sk. √*śudh*, caus. *śōdhayati*; si. *sodhaṇu*, g. *sodhvuṃ*, m. *sodhṇeṃ*, ass. *xodhāiba*, bg. *sodhā*, *sudhā*, h. *sodhnā*, nep. *sodhnu*, pj. *sodhṇā*.

2830. සොව **sova,** s., st. f. *sō*, sorrow. — Pk. *sōa*, *sōga*, P. *sōka*, Sk. *śōka*.

— සොහොන **sohona,** s., see s.v. **hōna.**

2831. සොහොයුරා **sohoyurā,** °වුරා **°vurā,** s., brother; f. *°yurī* sister. — Pk. *sahōyara*, Sk. *sahōdara*.

2832. සොළොස **soḷosa,** සොළස **soḷasa,** num., st. f. *soḷos*, sixteen. *soḷos-veni*, *-väni* sixteenth. — Pk. *sōḷasa*, *°ha*, *sōḷā*, P. *sōḷasa*, Sk. *ṣōḍaśa*; kśm. *śurāh*, si. *soraṃhaṃ*, g. *soḷ*, m. *soḷā*, oṛ. *soḷa*, ass. *xola*, bg. *sola*, b. *solah*, h. *solah*, *sorah*, nep. *sora*, *sorah*, *sorha*, pj. *solāṃ*, l. *solaṃ*.

2833. සෝ **sō**[1], s., st. f., tumour. — P. *sōpha*, Sk. *śōpha*.

2834. සෝ **sō**[2], s., st. f., ear. — Pk. *sōa*, P. *sōta*, Sk. *śrōtas*.

2835. සෝවාන් **sōvān,** s., first of the four stages leading to Nirvāṇa. — P. *sōtāpanna*.

හ H

2836. හක **haka,** සක **saka,** s., st. ff. *hak*, *sak*, chank, conch shell.— Pk., P. *saṅkha*, Sk. *śaṅkha*.

2837. හකුරු **hakuru,** ස° **sa°,** සකර **sakara**[1] (Ruv 378), s., palm sugar, jaggery; gravel.— Pk. *sakkarā*, P. *sakkharā*, Sk. *śarkarā*; g. *sākar*, m. *sākar*, *sākhar*, h. pj. *sakkar*, nep. *sakkhar*. In the meaning "gravel" also Sinh. *akura*[3] (st. f. *°ru*) occurs.

2838. හක්ක **hakka,** s., st. *haku*, jaw. — I believe the word is a blending of Sk., P. *hanu* and Sk. *akṣaka*, P. *akkhaka* (v. *akuva*[1]).

2839. හක්මන **hakmana,** ස° **sa°,** s., walking, walk. — P. *caṅkamana*, Sk. *caṅkramaṇa*; cf. Pk. *cakkamaï*.

2840. හණ **haṇa,** s., hemp. — Pk., P. *saṇa*, Sk. *śaṇa*; si. *siṇu*, *siṇī*, g. m. *saṇ*, b. h. nep. *san*, pj. *saṇ*.

2841. හණගල **haṇa-gala, ස° sa°,** s., rub-stone, whet-stone.—*haṇa* = Pk. *sāṇa*, Sk. *śāṇa* ; m. *sāṇ*, g. bg. h. nep. *sān*, pj. *sāṇ* + *gala* stone.

2842. හත **hata,** සත **sata,** num., st. ff. *hat, sat,* seven. *hat-veni, -väni* seventh. — Pk., P. *satta*, Sk. *sapta* ; kśm. *sath*, si. *sata*, g. m. *sāt*, oṛ. *sāta*, ass. *xāt*, bg. h. nep. *sāt*, pj. l. *satt*.

2843. හතර **hatara,** ස° **sa°**, or හාර **hāra,** සා° **sā°**, num., four. *hataräs, s°* four-cornered. See also *siv-, sivu-*.—*hatara* =Pk. *cattāri*, P. *cattārō*, Sk. *catvāras* ; *hāra* = Ap. Pk. *cāri* ; si. *cāri*, g. *cār*, m. *cār*, *cyār*, ass. *sāri*, oṛ. bg. b. *cāri*, h. nep. pj. l. *cār*.

2844. හතලිහ **hataliha,** සතලිස **satalisa** or සාලිස **sālisa,** num., st. ff. *°lis,* forty.— Pk. *cattālīsaṃ*, *cāālīsaṃ*, Ap. Pk. *cālīsaṃ*, P. *cattārīsaṃ* (*°ḷīsaṃ*), Sk. *catvāriṃśat* ; si. *cālīha*, g. m. *cālīs*, oṛ. *cāḷisa*, ass. *sallih*, bg. *callis*, h. *cālīs*, nep. *cālis*, pj. *cālī*, l. *cālhī*. The spelling with *l* (not *ḷ*) in Sinh. is confirmed by EpZ I $33^{15\text{-}16}$: *sū-sālis* (10th c.).

2845. හතළොහ **hataḷoha,** සතළොස **sataḷosa,** num., st. ff. *°ḷos,* seventeen. — Pk. *sattarasa*, P. *sattadasa*, *°rasa*, Sk. *saptadaśa* ; kśm. *sadāh*, si. *satraha*, g. *sattar*, m. *satrā*, oṛ. *satara*, ass. *xatara*, bg. *satāra*, h. *satrah*, nep. *satra*, *satrah*, pj. *satārāṃ*, l. *satāraṃ*.

2846. හතුරා **haturā,** ස° **sa°**, s., st. ff. *°ru,* enemy, foe, opponent. — Sk. *śatru*.

2847. හත්ත **hatta,** s., st. f. *hatu*, fungus.— Sk. *chattraka, chattrikā*. Cf. *sata*[1].

2848. හද **hada,** හිද **hida,** s., st. ff. id., heart.— Pk. *hiaa*, *haḍakka*, P. *hadaya*, Sk. *hṛdaya*. Slw. Cf. *ḷaya*.

2849. හඳ **hañda,** ස° **sa°**, s., moon. *hañda-eḷiya, -pāna* moonlight. — Pk., P. *canda*, Sk. *candra* ; kśm. *candar*, si. *canḍru*, g. m. *cāṃd*, oṛ. *cānda*, ass. *sānd*, bg. h. nep. *cāṃd*, pj. *candar*, *cand*, l. *candr*.

2850. හඳුන් **hañdun,** ස° **sa°**, s., sandal, sandal wood.— Pk. *candaṇa*, P., Sk. *candana* ; h. etc. *candan*, bg. *sandal*.

2851. හපන් **hapan**[1], ස° **sa°**, a., clever, expert ; s. *hapanā* clever man ; *hapan-kama* cleverness. — P. *sappañña*, Sk. *sa-* + *prajñā*.

2852. හපන් **hapan**[2], ස° **sa°**, a. pprt., superior, wealthy, powerful, fortunate.—Pk. *saṃpaṇṇa*, P. *sampanna*, Sk. *saṃpanna*.

2853. හපනවා **hapanavā,** ස° **sa°**, v., prt. *häpuvā*, *s°*, to bite, gnaw, chew. *hapaya* what has been chewed, refuse. — P. *cappēti*, Stede, PTSPD ; kśm. *cāpun* to eat, nep. *capāunu* (T, s. v.). Cf. Sk. *carvati*.

— හපු **hapu,** s., see s.v. **sapā**[2].

2854. **හපුස් hapus,** s., H. Jayatilaka, Eḷu-akārādiya = *rōmôdgamaya* erection of the hair, horripilation. — Pk. *saṃphāsa*, P. *samphassa*, Sk. *saṃsparśa*.

2855. **හබරයා habarayā, ස° sa°,** s., archer, Väddā. — Sk. *śabara*.

2856. **හම hama, ස° sa°,** s., st. ff. *ham*, *sam*, skin, hide, leather.— Pk., P. *camma*, Sk. *carman* ; kśm. *cam*, si. *camu*, g. m. *cām*, oṛ. *cama*, bg. h. nep. *cām*, pj. l. *camm*.

2857. **හමනනවා hamananavā,** v., prt. *hämänuvā*, *häman°*, to equalise, make similar. — Denom. of *hamana* = Pk. *samāṇa*, P., Sk. *samāna*, *samānayati*.

2858. **හමාර hamāra,** s., st. f. id., conclusion, end. *hamāra-karanavā* to conclude, finish ; *h°-venavā* to come to a conclusion. — P., Sk. *samāhāra* accumulation, collection, multitude. Sinh. *hamāra* also means "half."

2859. **හමිය hamiya,** s., st. f. *hami*, temple, palace (H. Jayatilaka).— P. *hammiya*, Sk. *harmya*.

2860. **හමු hamu, හමුව hamuva, ස° sa°,** s., the presence of; adv., in front of, before. *hamu-venavā* to meet, encounter. — Pk. *saṃmuhaṃ*, P. *sammukhaṃ*, Sk. *saṃmukhaṃ* ; si. *samhoṃ*, g. *sāmuṃ* (, m. *samor*), h. *sāmuh*, nep. *sāmu*, pj. *sauheṃ*.

2861. **හඹ hamba, ස° sa°,** in *hamba-(s°-)karanavā* to procure, acquire ; *h°-(s-°)venavā* to meet, light upon.— *hamba* <**hambba* <**hambuva* = Pk., Sk. *saṃbhava*, P. *sambhava*.

2862. **හය haya, ස° sa°,** num., st. ff. *ha*, *sa*, *°ya*, six. *haya-veni*, *-väni* sixth ; *daha-saya* sixteen. — Pk., P. *cha*, Sk. *ṣaṣ*, *ṣaṭ* ; si. g. *cha*, m. *sahā*, oṛ. *chaa*, ass. *say*, bg. *chay*, b. *chau*, h. *cha*, *che*, nep. *cha*, pj. *che*, l. *che*, *chī*. Cf. *soḷosa*, *häṭa*.

2863. **හර hara,** s., string of pearls, pearl necklace. — Pk., P., Sk. *hāra* ; kśm. *hār*, si. *hāru*, g. m. *hār*, oṛ. *hāra*, ass. bg. h. pj. *hār*, nep. *hāri*.

2864. **හරකා harakā, ස° sa°,** s., st. ff. *°k*, ox, bullock. *harak-aṅga* bullock's horn. — Metathesis of **hakar* = Sk. *śakvara*, *śakkara*.

2865. **හරඟයා harañgayā,** s., st. f. *°ñga*, name of a bird, the Ceylon hornbill.—P., S. *sārañga*. Cf. *saragā*.

2866. **හරඹ haramba,** s., brandishing, fencing. *avi-saramba* id. (v.s.v. *aviya*) ; *haramba-karanavā* to brandish, fence.—P. *sārambha*, Sk. *saṃrambha* impetuosity, turbulence.

2867. හරය **haraya,** s., heart-wood, duramen.—Pk., P., Sk. *sāra*; kśm. *sār*, si. *sāru*, g. m. *sār*, oṛ. *sāra*, ass. *xār*, bg. h. nep. pj. *sār*. Cf. *sara*[2] (differentiation of meaning).

2868. හල් **hal,** සල් **sal,** s., name of a tree, Vateria acuminata. — Pk., P. *sāla*, Sk. *śāla*; m. *sāḷī*, oṛ. *sāḷa*, ass. *xāl*, bg. h. nep. pj. *sāl*.

2869. හල **hala**[1], ස° **sa°**, s., st. ff. *hal*, *s°*, hall, abode. *avan-hala* tavern; *ät-hala* (*ättala*) elephant-stable; *kam-hala* (*kamm°*) workshop, factory.—Pk., P. *sālā*, Sk. *śālā*; kśm. *hāl*, m. *sāḷ*, oṛ. *sāḷa*, bg. *sāl*, b. h. nep. *sār* cowshed, h. *sāl* hall.

2870. හල **hala**[2], s., st. f. *hal*, plough.—Pk. *hala*, *hālia*, P. *hala*, Sk. *hala*, *hālika*; kśm. *hal*, *hŏli*, si. *haru*, *hārī*, g. m. *haḷ*, oṛ. *haḷa*, *haḷiā*, ass. *haliyā* in couples, bg. *hal*, b. *har*, h. *hal*, *hālī*, nep. *hal*, *halī*, pj. l. *hal*, *hālī*.

2871. හලකුණ **halakuṇa,** ස° **sa°**, s., st. ff. *°ṇu*, mark, sign.— P. *sallakkhana*, Sk. *saṃlakṣaṇa*. Cf. *salakanavā*.

2872. හලදු **haladu,** s., turmeric.—Pk. *haliddā*, *haladdā*, *°ddī*, *hariddā*, P. *haliddā*, *°ddī*, Sk. *haridrā*; kśm. *lĕduru*, si. *haiḍra*, g. *haḷdar*, *haḷad*, *haḷadh*, m. *haḷad*, oṛ. *haḷadi*, ass. *hāldhi*, bg. *haldi*, b. *haldī*, *hardī*, h. *halad*, *haldī*, nep. *haledo*, pj. *haldī*, *haldhī*, *haldhar*, l. *haladr*, *hardal*. Gr. 49.401, 50. 14.

2873. හලනවා **halanavā,** ස° **sa°**, v., prt. *häluvā*, *s°*, to shake, move; to sieve. Intr. *hälenavā*, *s°*, prt. *häluṇā*, *s°*, to fall, drop.—Pk. *calaï*, caus. *cālēi*, P. *calati*, *cālēti*, Sk. *√cal*, *calati*, *cālayati*; kśm. *calun* to flee, g. *caḷvuṃ*, *cāḷvuṃ*, m. *caḷṇeṃ*, *cāḷṇeṃ*, oṛ. *caḷibā* (*cāḷuṇi* a sieve), ass. *saliba* (*sālnā* a sieve), bg. *calā*, *cālā*, h. *calnā*, *cālnā*, nep. *calnu* (*cālnu* a sieve), pj. *calṇā*. B 3.34, 78.

2874. හලු **halu,** a., like, similar (Ruv 407 has *°ḷu*).— Pk. *sarisa* (, P. *sadisa*, Sk. *sadṛśa*); oṛ. *sarisā*, h. *saris*, nep. *sari*. Cf. *sari*, *suruku*.

2875. හව් **hav,** සව් **sav,** a., all.—Pk. *savva*, P. *sabba*, Sk. *sarva*; si. *sabhu*, g. *sāv*, m. oṛ. *sabu*, bg. h. nep. *sab*, pj. *sabh*, l. *sabhā*. Gr. 50.17.

2876. හවුර **havura,** s., rampart.—Pk., P., Sk. *saṃvara*. Sinh. *mahavura* great rampart is haplology of **maha-havura*. Ruv 177 has *avuru-* id.

2877. හවුල **havula,** s., st. f. *°ul*, participation, partnership, common interest.—P. *sākhalya*, *sākhalla*.

2878. හස් **has**[1], s., goose, swan.—Pk., P., Sk. *haṃsa*; kśm. *ünzü*, si. *hañju*, g. m. *hāṃs*, ass. *hāṃh*, bg. h. nep. *hāṃs*, pj. *haṃs*. Cf. *as*[4].

2879. හස් **has**[2], s., laughter.—Pk., P., Sk. *hāsa*; kśm. *hās*, g. *hāṃsī*, m. *hās*, oṛ. *hāsa*, ass. *hāṃhi*, bg. *hāṃsā*, h. *hāṃsī*, nep. *hāṃso* (, pj. l. *hāssā*).

2880 හසර **hasara,** s., foot-path, way. — Pk., Sk. *saṃcāra*, P. *sañcāra*.

— හළ **haḷa,** a. pprt., see s.v. **aḷa.**

2881. හළුව **haḷuva,** ස° **sa°,** st. ff. *°ḷu*, shawl. — P. *sāṭaka*, Sk. *śāṭaka*; kśm. *sôḷu*, g. *sāḷu*, h. pj. *sālū*, nep. *sālu*.

2882. හා **hā,** cop. part., with, and. *hā-karanavā* to join, unite.—Pk., P., Sk. *saha*. In mediaeval inscs. also *isā*, as we also meet in older inscs. with *ica* (<*ca*). The initial *i* shows the enclitic character of both words. But *isā* cannot be derived from *ica* as Paranavitana, EpZ III 102, believes. In this case the length of the vowel in *isā* remains unexplained.

2883. හාත් **hāt,** in *hāt-pasa* or *-pasin*, adv., around; in every respect, entirely.—*hāt*<**havat* = Pk. *savvattha*, P. *sabbattha*, Sk. *sarvatra* + *pasa*, obl. c., or *pasin* instr. of *pasa* side.

2884. හාවා **hāvā,** සා° **sā°**, s., st. ff. *hā*, *sā*, hare.—Pk., P. *sasa*, Sk. *śaśa*; g. *saso*, m. h. pj. *sasā*.

2885. හැක **häka,** සැක **säka,** s., doubt. — Pk., P. *saṅkā*, Sk. *śaṅkā*.

2886. හැට **häṭa,** සැ° **sä°,** num., sixty. *häṭa-veni*, *-väni* sixtieth.— Pk. *saṭṭhī*, *°iṃ*, P. *saṭṭhi*, *°iṃ*, Sk. *ṣaṣṭi*; kśm. *śaiṭh*, *śeṭh*, si. *saṭhi*, g. m. *sāṭh*, oṛ. *sāṭhie*, ass. *xāṭhi*, bg. *sāiṭh*, h. *sāṭh*, nep. *sāṭhi*, pj. l. *saṭṭh*.

2887. හැටිය **häṭiya,** s., manner, means, mode.— MInd. **saṭṭhi*; Pk., *siṭṭhi*, Sk. *sṛṣṭi* (BR 1 b).

2888. හැත්තෑව **hättǟva,** num., st. f. *hättǟ*, seventy. *hättǟ-veni*, *-väni* seventieth.— Pk. *sattariṃ*, P. *sattati*, Sk. *saptati*; kśm. *satath*, si. *satari*, g. *siter*, m. *sattar*, oṛ. *satori*, ass. *xatari*, bg. h. pj. *sattar*, nep. *sattari*, l. *sattir*.

2889. හැව **häva,** සැ° **sä°,** s., snake's cast skin, slough. — See s.v. *siviya*[2] = Sk. *chavi*.

2890. හැළ **häḷa.** සැ° **sä°,** s., in *häḷa-lihiṇiyā*, name of a bird, Grocula religiosa (Maina bird). — Pk. *sārī*, P. *sāliyā*, *sālikā*, *sāḷikā*, Sk. *śāri*, *śārikā*; kśm. *hörü*, m. *sārī*, oṛ. *sāri*, h. *sār*, *sārī*, *sāro*, *sārū*, nep. *sāru*, *sārau*.

2891. හැළිය **häḷiya,** සැ° **sä°,** s., earthen pot. — P. *cāṭī*.

2892. හික් **hik,** s., learning, study, training (HJ). — Pk., P. *sikkhā*, Sk. *śikṣā* (cf. Bl, s.v. *śikṇem*, T, s.v. *siknu*). Sinh. *hikmenavā* to become trained, *hikmavanavā* to train, are, no doubt, connected with *hik*.

2893. හික්මීයා **hik-mīyā,** s., musk-rat. — *hik* = Sk. *cikka* + *mīyā*, q.v.

2894. හිගු **higu,** හිඟු **hiṅgu,** සි° **si°,** a., speedy, hasty; s. *hiṅguva* haste.— Pk. *siggha*, P. *sīgha*, Sk. *śīghra*.

2895. **හිට hiṭa, සි° si°**, postp., beginning from. — ger. of v. *hiṭinavā*, q.v.

2896. **හිටාණෝ hiṭāṇō, සි° si°**, s., st. ff. *hiṭu*, *s°*, nobleman, wealthy man, merchant. *hiṭu-dēvī* wife of a nobleman; *h°-duva* daughter of a nobleman.— Pk. *seṭṭhi*, P. *seṭṭhin*, Sk. *śrēṣṭhin*; si. *seṭhi*, g. *śeṭh*, *śeṭhiyo*, m. *śēṭh*, *śeṭhī*, *śeṭ*, oṛ. *seṭhi*, h. nep. pj. *seṭh*. Sinh. also *heṭṭiyā*, *s°*; *-āṇō* in *hiṭāṇō* is honor. suff. pl.

2897. **හිටිනවා hiṭinavā, සි° si°**, v., prt. *hiṭiyā*, *s°*, to stay, stand; to remain, be. Caus. *hiṭavanavā*, *hiṭuvanavā*, *s°*, prt. *hiṭevuvā*, *s°*, to cause to stand, place, set, stop. — Pk. *ciṭṭhaï* (, P. *tiṭṭhati*, Sk. √*sthā*, *tiṣṭhati*). Cf. Bl, s. v. *ṭheṇem*, T, s.v. *thiyo*.

2898. **හිත hita, සි° si°**, s., st. ff. *hit*, *sit*, mind, heart. *hit-dāḍi* hard-hearted. *hit-gannavā* to captivate the mind, please, satisfy. — Pk., P., Sk. *citta*; si. *citu*, g. m. *cit*, ass. *sit*, oṛ. bg. nep. *cit*, pj. *citt*.

2899. **හිතනවා hitanavā, සි° si°**, v., prt. *hituvā*, *s°*, to think. Intr. *hitenavā*, *hituṇā*, to occur to the mind.— Pk. *cintēi*, P. *cintēti*, Sk. √*cit*, *cintayati*; si. *citāiṇu*, g. *citvuṃ*, h. *cītnā*, *citānā*, nep. *cītāunu*.

— **හිතුල් hitul**, s., see s.v. **kitul**.

2900. **හිද hida[1]**, s., perforation.— Pk. *chiḍḍa*, P. *chidda*, Sk. *chidra*. Cf. lw. *sidura*.

— **හිද hida[2]**, s., see s.v. **hada**.

2901. **හිඳිනවා hiňdinavā, සි° si°**, v., prt. *hindā*, *s°*, to cut, cut off; to eradicate; to decoct, express (oil). Caus. *hiňduvanavā*, *s°*, *hindanavā*, *s°*, *hindāvanavā*, prt. *hinduvā*, *hindevuvā*, to boil down, extract. Intr. *hiňdenavā*, *s°*, prt. *hiňduṇā*, *s°*, to be cut off, dry up.—Pk. *chindaï*, P. *chindati*, Sk. √*chid*, *chind-*; g. *chidvuṃ* to pound, h. *chidnā* to be pierced, nep. *chidnu* to uproot. Semasiologically difficult.

— **හිඳුව hiňduva**, s., see s.v. **ida**.

2902. **හිම hima**, s., cold, frost, snow, dew.— Pk., P., Sk. *hima*; g. *him*, m. *himv*, nep. pj. *hiuṃ*. Perhaps lw.

2903. **හිමියා himiyā**, s., st. f. *himi*, owner, possessor. *himi-kama* ownership; *h°-karanavā* to make over to. — Pk. *sāmi*, P. *sāmin*, *sāmika*, Sk. *svāmin*, *svāmika*; kśm. *sāveñu*, si. *sāṃīṃ*, g. *sāṃī*, m. *sāī*, h. *sāṃī*, nep. *saiyāṃ*, pj. *sāīṃ*, l. *sāiṃ*.

2904. **හිරිය hiriya**, s., st. f. *hiri*, shame, timidity.— Pk., P. *hirī*, Sk. *hrī*.

2905. **හිරියල් hiriyal, සි° si°**, s., yellow orpiment. — Pk. *hariāla*, *haliāra*, P. *haritāla*; g. *hariyāḷuṃ*, m. *hariyaḷ* bg. h. *hariāl*, pj. *hariālā* green, green pigeon.

2906. **හිවලා hivalā,** s., jackal.— Pk. *siāla*, P. *sigāla*, Sk. *śṛgāla* ; kśm. *śāl*, g. *siyāḷ*, oṛ. *siaḷa*, ass. *xiyāl*, bg. nep. h. *siyāl.*

2907. **හිස් his, සිස් sis,** a., empty, useless. — Pk. *cuccha*, *chuccha* (Hem 1. 204, alternating with *tuccha* =P., Śk. *tuccha*).

2908. **හීන් hīn, සීන් sīn, සිහින් sihin, සියුම් siyum,** a., thin, fine. — Pk. *suhuma*, P. *sukhuma*, Sk. *śūkṣma*.

2909. **හීනය hīnaya, සී° sī°,** s., dream. — < **sivina* < **suvina* = Pk. *siviṇa*, P. *supina*. Cf. *supuva*.

2910. **හීය hīya,** s., furrow, ploughing.— Pk. *siā*, P., Sk. *sītā* ; oṛ. *siāi*, h. *sīyā*, nep. *siyo*, pj. *siyāṛ*, l. *sīyāṃ*.

2911. **හීල් hīl, සිහිල් sihil,** a., cold; s. *hīla*, *sihila*, coldness. Also *il* in *il-masa* the cold month, November-December. — Pk. *sīyala*, P. *sītala*, Sk. *śītala* ; g. *śiḷuṃ*, m. *śilā*, h. pj. *sīlā*. Sinh. *sisira* is lw. Pk., P. *sisira*, Sk. *śiśira*; and *sisil* seems to be a blending of *sisira* and *sihil.*

2912. **හුදු hudu, සු° su°,** a., pure, unmixed, white.— Pk., P. *suddha*, Sk. *śuddha* ; kśm. *hodu*, si. *sūdho*, g. *sūdhuṃ*, m. *sudhā*, ass. *xudh*, bg. *sudhu*, h. *sūdhā*, nep. *sudho*, pj. *suddhā*.

2913. **හුන් hun, සුන් sun,** a., empty (Ruv 664 = *his*).— Pk. *sunna*, *suṇṇa*, P. *suñña*, Sk. *śūnya* ; si. *suño*, g. *sūnuṃ*, m. *sunā*, h. *sūn*, *sūnā*, nep. *sun*, dj. *sunu*, *sunnā*, l. *sunj*, *sunjā*.

2914. **හුනු hunu,** s., lime, chunam.— Pk., P. *cuṇṇa*, Sk. *cūrṇa* ; kśm. *cūn*, si. *cunu*, g. *cuno*, m. *cūn*, oṛ. *cun*, *cunā*, ass. *sun*, bg. *cun*, *cunā*, h. pj. *cūn*, *cūnā*, nep. *cun*, l. *cūnā*. Often erroneously spelt *huṇu*.

2915. **හුය huya** s., st. ff. *hu*, *hū*, string, thread. *hū-vaṭa*, *-väṭiya*, *hu-v°* ball of thread. — < **sūta*, Pk. AMg. *sūya*. Cf. *suta*.

2916. **හුරු huru, සු° su°,** a., dexterous, apt. *huru-kama* dexterity ; *h°-ata* the dexterous or right hand. — <**hūru* < **hu.uru* = Pk. *caura*, P.. Sk. *catura*.

2917. **හූනා hūnā, සූ° sū°, සුහුනා suhunā,** s., house lizard, gecko. — P. *susu* infant+*nāga* snake ; Pk. AMg. *sisu-nāga*, Sk. *śiśu-nāga*.

2918. **හූනියම hūniyama, සූ° sū°,** s., st. ff. *°yam*, witchcraft causing evil, sorcery, black art. — Tam. *cūṉiyam* < Sk. *śūnya* (De Lanerolle). See W. Geiger, Hūniyam, ein Beitrag zur Volkskunde von Ceylon, Festschr. f. E. Kuhn, 1916, p. 185 sq.

2919. **හූරා hūrā,** s., brother-in-law. — Sk. *śvaśurya*. The word is in use among villagers in the interior parts of Ceylon. Cf. Pk., P. *sasura*, Sk. *śvaśura* father-in-law. T, s.v. *sasuro*.

2920. හෙට **heṭa,** adv., to-morrow.— Pk. *suvē*, P. *svē, suvē* (Sk. *śvas*) + dat. suffix. *-ṭa*.

— හෙට්ටියා **heṭṭiyā,** සෙ° **se°**, s., see s.v. **hiṭāṇō.**

2921. හෙණ **heṇa,** සෙ° **se°**, s., lightning, thunderbolt.— Pk. *asaṇi*, P. *asanī*, Sk. *aśani* ; nep. *asinu* hailstone, pj. *āhiṇ*.

2922. හෙද **heda,** සෙ° **se°**, adv., quickly, speedily, soon. — P. *sajju(-kaṃ)*, Sk. *sadyas*.

2923 — 2929 —

2930. හෙනවා **henavā,** සෙ° **se°**, v., prt. *huṇā*, to fall, drop.— Sk. √*śī*, *śīyatē* falls off.

2931. හෙබ **heba,** s., st. f. *hep*, brook, pond. — P. *sobbha*, Sk. *śvabhra*.

2932. හෙම **hema,** s., st. f. *hem*, gold.— Pk., P., Sk. *hēma*.

— හෙමින් **hemin,** adv., see s.v. **sema**[1].

2933. හෙම්කුළ **hem-kuḷa,** s., the golden mountain, name of the Mahāmēru mountain. — Sk. *hēma-kūṭa*.

2934. හෙය **heya**[1], සෙ° **se°**, s., st. ff. *hē, sē* (also *ē* in *ē-daṇḍa*, q.v.), foot-bridge.—Pk. *sēu*, P., Sk. *sētu*.

2935. හෙය **heya**[2], s., st. f. *hē*, reason, cause. *heyin*, postp., because of. — Pk. *hēu*, P., Sk. *hētu*.

2936. හෙරණ **heraṇa,** s., novice.— I derive the word from P. **saraññа* = Sk. *śaraṇya* needing (or asking for) protection.

2937. හෙල **hela,** සෙල **sela,** s., st. ff. *hel. sel*, hill, hillock. — Pk., P. *sēla*, Sk. *śaila* ; kśm. *śēl*, g. *sel*. T, s.v. *sili*.

2938. හෙවණ **hevaṇa,** සෙ° **se°**, s., shade, shadow; *hevaṇälla* id. ; *hevaṇa--karanavā*, *s°-k°* to shade. — *seya* (Sk. *chāyā*) enlarged by suff. *-ṇa*. Cf. *nuvaṇa*, *muhuṇa*.

— හෙවත් **hevat,** conj., see s.v. **hō**[1].

2939. හෙළනවා **heḷanavā,** v., prt. *heḷuvā*, to throw down, cast down. —MInd . **chāḍēti* =Pk. *chaḍḍēi*, P. *chaḍḍēti*, Sk. √*chard*, caus. *chardayati* ; kśm. *chaḍun*, si. *chaḍaṇu*, g. *chāṃḍvuṃ*, m. *sāṃḍṇeṃ*, oṛ. *chāṛibā*, bg. *chāṛā*, h. *chāṛnā*, *chāṃṛnā*, nep. *chāṛnu*, pj. *chaḍḍnā*, *chanḍnā*, l. *chaḍaṇ*.

2940. හේවායා **hēvāyā,** s., st. f. *hēvā*, soldier. — P., Sk. *sēvaka*. See *sevaṭu*.

2941. හොට **hoṭa,** s., beak, bill, snout, mouth. — kśm. *cômṭu* chin, si. *comṭa*, bg. *comṭ* ; but see also *hossa*.

2942. **හොටිය hoṭiya, සො° so°**, spear. — Turner. s. v. *soṃṭhā* cane : g. *soṭo* staff, m. *soṃṭā, soṭā*, oṛ. *soṭhā, soṇṭhā*, ass. *xoṭā*, bg. *soṃṭā*, b. *soṃṭh*, h. *soṃṭā*, pj. *soṭhā, soṭṭā*, l. *soṭā*.

2943. **හොඬ hoňḍa, සො° so°[1]**, s., st. ff. *hoňḍa*, s°, elephant's trunk, proboscis. — Pk., P. *soṇḍā*, Sk. *śuṇḍā* ; si. *sūṃḍhi*, g. *suṃḍ, suṃḍh*, m. *soṃḍ*, oṛ. *suṇḍa*, ass. *xuṃr*, bg. *suṃṛ*, b. h. *sūṃṛ*, nep. *suṃṛ*, pj. *suṇḍ*.

— **හොත් hot**, a. pprt., see s.v. **ot.**

2944. **හොඳ hoňda**, a., good, excellent, virtuous.— < MInd. **sunda*. Cf. *soňduru*.

2945. **හොරා horā**, s., st. f. *hora*, thief, robber, rogue; fem. *hera*. *hora-kama* theft, dishonesty ; *hora-karanavā* to act deceitfully. — Pk., P. *cōra*, Sk. *cōra, caura* (fem. *caurī*) ; si. *coru*, g. m. *cor*, oṛ. *cora*, ass. *sor*, bg. h. nep. pj. l. *cor*.

2946. **හොවිනවා hovinavā, හෝනවා hōnavā**, v., pprt. *ot, hot*, q. v., to lie down, repose, sleep. Caus. *hovanavā* (for **hōv°*) to cause to lie down. — Pk. *suvaï, sōvaï*, P. *supati*, Sk. √*svap, svapiti* ; kśm. *sāvun* to cause to sleep, g. *suvuṃ* to sleep, oṛ. *soibā*, h. *sonā*, pj. *soṇā*. T, s.v. *suinu*.

2947. **හොස්ස hossa**, s., snout, exterior mouth. — Pk. *cañcū*, Sk. *cañcu* ; si. *cūṃji*, m. *cūṃc, coṃc*, bg. h. *coṃc*, nep. *cuco, cucco*. See also *hoṭa*.

2948. **හෝ hō[1]**, conj., or, either. *hō...hō* either... or.—Pk. *ahavā*, P., Sk. *athavā*. Cf. Sinh. *hevat* or, or else.

2949. **හෝ hō[2]**, s., name of a tree, Fonesia asoca.— Pk. *asōa*, P. *asōka*, Sk. *aśōka* ; m. *osag*, nep. *asau*.

2950. **හෝන hōna, සෝන sōna, සොහොන sohona**, s., st. ff. *hōn, s°*, grave.— Pk. (*masāṇa*) *susāṇa*, P. *susāna*, Sk. *śmaśāna* (; g. *masāṇ*, m. *mhasaṇ, masaṇ*, oṛ. *masāṇi*, bg. h. nep. *masān*).

ළ Ḷ

— **ළඟ ḷaňga**, a., see s.v. **laňga.**

2951. **ළය ḷaya**, s., st. f. *ḷa*., heart, breast. *ḷa-kal* pleasing. — < **hàḷá*, Pk. *haḍakka*, P. *hadaya*, Sk. *hṛdaya* (; si. *hiṃo*, g. *haiyuṃ*, m. *hiyeṃ*, v. T, s.v. *hiyo*).

— **ළා ḷā, ළ ḷa**, see. s.vv. **lā, la.**

2952. ළැව් **ḷäv,** s., f o r e s t. *ḷäv-gini, ḷäv-aga* forest-fire ; *muva-ḷävuhi,* DhpAGp 31[24], trsl. of P. *migadāyē.*—Pk. *aḍavī,* P., Sk. *aṭavī* ; cf. P. *āḷavika* dwelling in forests = Sk. *āṭavika.*

— ළිහිණියා **ḷihiṇiyā,** s., see s.v. **lihiṇiyā.**

ADDENDA

2953. කරඳ **karaňda,** s., name of a t r e e, Pongamia glabra. — P., Sk. *karañja.*